Theoretical Empiricism

Theoretical Empiricism

A General Rationale for
Scientific Model-Building

Edited by
Herman Wold

An ICUS Book

Paragon House
New York

First edition, 1989

Published in the United States by
Paragon House
90 Fifth Avenue
New York, New York 10011

Copyright 1987 by Paragon House Publishers

An International Conference on the Unity of the Sciences Book.

Manufactured in the United States of America

Library of Congress Cataloging-in-Publication Data

Theoretical empiricism.

    "An ICUS book."
    Includes index.
    1. Science—Methodology. 2. Science—Philosophy.
3. Empiricism. I. Wold, Herman O. A., 1908–
Q175.T483 1987   502.8   86–22696
ISBN 0–89226–055–6
ISBN 0–89226-056-4 (pbk.)

The paper used in this publication meets the minimum requirements of
American National Standard for Information Sciences—Permanence of
paper for Printed Library Materials, ANSI Z39.48-1984

Contents

Introduction to the Second Generation of Multivariate Analysis

HERMAN WOLD

SUMMARY

This introductory chapter is a discourse at two levels, in line with the title of the present volume.

On the technical level: Methods of scientific model building, with special regard to path models with manifest and/or latent variables.

On the level of the philosophy of science: Theoretical empiricism—a generalization of Logical empiricism.

I. Technical Aspects of Model Building.

Scientific model building proceeds in four stages: (i) model specification, (ii) model estimation, (iii) model evaluation and (iv) model application.

Twelve stages or features of model building are discussed.

a. We start with the advent of model building in econometrics in the 1930s: Path models with manifest variables, PMV models.
b. Once the investigator has settled on a model, its properties under (i–iii) are explored with the full mathematical rigor, E.N. Lorenz (1984).
c. The advent of maximum likelihood (ML) methods under (i–iii) in the early 1940s. ML parameter estimates have optimal accuracy. Since 1950

statistical theory, econometrics and related sciences are dominated by ML methods (the ML mainstream).

d. Not content with the stringent, "hard" assumptions of ML methods, John Tukey (1958) broke away from the ML mainstream, introducing his jack-knife assessment of standard errors.

e. Sociology in the 1960s introduced path models with latent variables (PLV models), the LVs being indirectly observed by MVs. K.G. Jöreskog (1970) introduced LISREL for operational ML estimation of LVP models, a landmark achievement. LISREL inspired the PLS (Partial Least Squares) method for LS estimation of LVP models (H.Wold, 1973–1977).

f. The cross-validatory choice and selection method introduced by M. Stone (1974) and S. Geisser (1974) is a predictive device for hypothesis testing under model evaluation (iii).

g. C. Fornell in "A Second Generation of Multivariate Analysis" (1982) pays tribute to LISREL and PLS for being the most general and flexible methods of LVP modeling. LISREL is parameter-oriented, PLS is prediction-oriented. LISREL models the covariances of the observed MVs; PLS models the endogenous MVs as observed.

Four key features of PLS modeling will be noted.

h. Predictor specification gives the PLS approach to model building under (i–ii) broad scope relative to the LISREL approach, first in model specification (i), then in model estimation (ii) (H. Wold, 1958, 1961, 1963, 1985).

k. PLS uses Tukey's jackknife standard error and Stone-Geisser's hypothesis test. These methods for model evaluation (iii) have been generalized so as to work without assuming that the explanatory variables are mutually independent (R. Bergström and H. Wold, 1983).

m. FP-PLS modeling, an LS approach (i–iv), is easy in the statistical implementation, and easy and speedy on the computer.

n. Ever larger and more ambitious FP/PLS estimates are reported. In this volume seven substantive researchers in different scientific disciplines report on many pioneering, large systems estimated by FP/PLS. PLS has drastically reduced the distance between substantive research and statistical theory.

p. In view of the abundance of potential applications, PLS modeling is at an early stage of evolution.

II. Philosophy of science aspects of model building.

There are five points of view:

a. From antiquity onwards model building has its pedigree in the school of empiricism on the one side, and in the school of idealism on the other. The perseverant attempts at synthesis gradually led to the advent of the model building in the 1930s; cf C. Dagum. (Chapter 9 of this volume.)

b. Logical empiricism emerged in the Vienna school of the philosophy of science in the 1940s. Its main tenet is that empirical knowledge E, and pure theoretical knowledge T, are independent. Theoretical empiricism allows theory T to include substantive empiricist theory.

c. Predictor specification (cf. Ih) is instrumental as a pre-modeling device in the passage from logical empiricism to theoretical empiricism.

d. Scientific model building is a paradigm—the uniscience paradigm. This is a new twist of the paradigm concept introduced by T.S. Kuhn (1977).

e. Before a problem of theoretical empiricism is ripe for exploration by a model, it passes through several stages in the theoretical and empirical work (cf. J.-B. Lohmöller and C. Fornell in Chapters 1 and 11 of this volume).

In the first ten chapters of this volume the reader is at the research frontier, the territory where new human knowledge is produced. In Chapter 11 the reader sees the research frontier at a distance, from the perspective of the fund-dispensing bureaucrats of government or business science foundations. Chapter 11 shows that U.S. and European universities are far from uniform in the priority of quality versus quantity in the output of research.

Chapter 11 reveals a lacuna in the library of science: There exists no recent international overview of university conditions. Removing this lacuna is strongly recommended as the topic of a temporary or permanent task force of ICUS.

INTRODUCTION

I. The advent of model building.

Scientific model building as a synthesis of (i) model specification, (ii) model estimation, (iii) model evaluation and (iv) model application, emerged in Econometrics in the 1930s and 1940s, and was soon adopted in a great many sciences.

Edward N. Lorenz in his Crawford Prize lecture (1984)[1] salutes the advent of model building in the 1930s as a new era in science, and rightly praises *rigor* as the key advantage of the innovation: "Once the investigator has settled on a model, he can retain full mathematical rigor in studying its behavior." Disregarding the real-world aspects, the model is regarded as an *autonomous* construct.

The "flag table," in the form of a Scandinavian flag, is at the upper left in Figure 1, and marks (vertically) a general distinction between descriptive and explanatory theoretical knowledge, and (horizontally) between experimental and nonexperimental knowledge. The flag cross marks four intermediate domains of knowledge: descriptive, mixed experimental-nonexperimental; explanatory, mixed experimental-nonexperimental knowledge, and the other two possibilities.

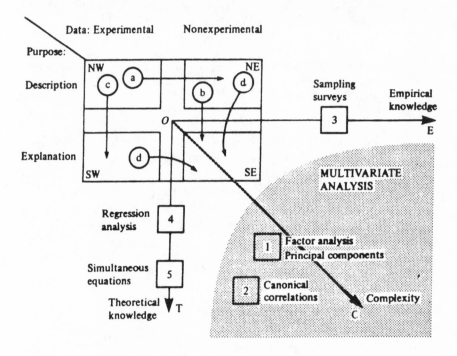

Figure I-1. Perspectives of statistical method: The flag table. (Wold 1982.)

Statistical method, like science in general, proceeds from simple problems to more complex and difficult problems. Arrow (a) in Figure I–1 marks the forceful evolution of public socio-economic statistics during the "era of enthusiasm," 1820–1860; this is an evolution along axis OE at the upper right. Arrow (b) marks the advent and breakthrough of the "English school of statistics" around 1900: the extension of statistical analysis to data in anthropology and the natural sciences revealed stable empirical regularities that incited novel statistical methods, including correlation and regression analysis. In the notation of Figure I–1 this evolution brought an expansion of statistics from axis OE to the upper part of axis OT.

Arrow (c) in Figure I–1 refers to R.A. Fisher's epoch-making work from 1915 to 1940.

Econometric model building in the 1930s and 40s developed along the middle and lower part of axis OT. The two arrows (d) mark the fact that developments in the explanatory-nonexperimental quadrant have origins both in the descriptive-nonexperimental quadrant and the explanatory-experimental quadrant. In the broad perspective OE-OT the shaded area denotes *multivariate analysis*. Multivariate analysis came of age with the advent of model building—the book by T.W. Anderson (1958) is the first with this title.

For brevity, this Introductory chapter will refer hereafter to the present volume as "Themp."

Path models. Figure I–2 highlights a scientific domain of central importance: path models. Chapters 1–11 of Themp report on the theory and application of path models.

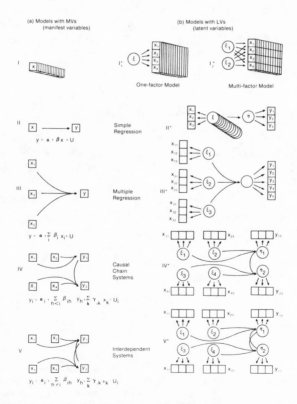

Figure I-2. Path Models with (a) Manifest Variables (PMVs) and with (b) Latent Variables (PLVs). (H. Wold 1985.)

To the left in Figure I–2 are path models with manifest (directly observed) variables (PMV models), including simple and multiple regressions, Causal chain systems, and Simultaneous equations systems. To the right are path models with latent (indirectly observed) variables, each LV being indirectly observed by multiple MVs, called *indicators*.

Path models were introduced by Sewall Wright (1918), a genealogist who analyzed the inheritance of human qualities from generation to generation in terms of MVP models. Pioneering in the path model design and in the causal interpretation of inheritance, Wright's innovations were developed as specific features in genealogy. With the advent of model-building in the 1930s, path models and their causal interpretation were recognized to be of universal scope in model building.[2]

Reading downwards in Figure I–2, each path model includes the previous model as a special case. Each PLV model includes its PMV counterpart as a special case.

Themp reports applications belonging under path models IV–V and I^*–IV^* in Figure I–2. The methodological developments of PMV and PLV models will now be briefly discussed, with due emphasis on ML v. LS approaches.

1. PMV Models: Path Models with
Manifest (directly observed) Variables.

C.F. Gauss (1777–1855), a pioneer in LS and ML methods, is an early example of the dominance of LS methods in the 19th century and well into the 20th.

Models II and III in Figure 2 are associated with the names of Karl Pearson and G.U.Yule. Karl Pearson (1900) introduced R^2 to measure "goodness of fit." R^2 is an early example of model evaluation. OLS (Ordinary Least Squares) estimation minimizes the residual variance in simple and multiple regression, and thereby maximizes R^2.

Table 1. PMV models II–IV: LS vs. ML methods in model-building stages i–iii.

Model operation	Method	LS	ML
(i)	Specification Purpose: What is modeled?	Prediction of endogenous MVs by exogenous MVs	The observed variances and covariances in terms of the parameters of the model
	Data	MVs, exogenous	Means and covariances

		and endogenous	
	Assumptions	Errors in equations	Errors in variables
			Distributional ML assumptions: The MVs are jointly ruled by a specified multivariate distribution, which is subject to independent observations.
(ii)	Estimation	OLS and other LS methods	ML methods
(iii)	Evaluation		Distributional ML assumptions
		Consistent para-meter estimates	Consistent and optimal parameter estimates

Models IV and V mark the advent of model building in Econometrics in the 1930s and 40s. Model IV includes the pioneering multi-relational systems of Jan Tinbergen (1939), who used OLS to estimate the system as defined by its structural form (SF). Tinbergen's models were discussed by H. Wold (1938) under the name "recursive systems."

Model V includes the Simultaneous Equations (SEQS) systems introduced by Trygve Haavelmo (1943). Most or all of the forecasting econometric systems launched since the 1950s are SEQS systems. Showing examples where OLS is biased when applied to the SF of an SEQS system, Haavelmo subjected OLS to wholesale dismissal, and recommended ML for the estimation of SEQS systems. R. Bentzel and H. Wold (1946) showed that SEQS systems are either recursive or non-recursive, and that OLS and ML are numerically equivalent when applied to the SF of recursive SEQS systems. Current names for recursive and non-recursive systems are Causal chain systems and Interdependent (ID) systems.

In the 1940s ML methods brought fundamental innovations to model evaluation, including confidence intervals and standard errors for the estimated parameters, the Cramér-Rao lower bound for standard errors, and the theorem stating that if the lower bound is reached, it can be reached by ML estimation. The ML innovations had tremendous impact; since 1950, statistical theory and wide domains of applied statistics are dominated by ML methods. Prediction was pushed aside in the ML mainstream, neglected or forgotten. In a widely-used textbook such as Ph.J. Dhrymes' *Econometrics* (1970, 2nd ed. 1974), the word prediction is not even mentioned.

Tables 1 through 3 serve to elucidate the contrast between LS and ML modeling methods. Table 1 compares the traditional LS methods of the 1940s with the new ML methods. Recent developments of LS and ML methods are summarized in Tables 2 and 3.

In Table 1 the brief statements on stages (i)–(ii) are in line with Harald Cramér's classical treatise (1945). In model estimation (ii) LS is a distinct parting of the ways from ML. As for model evaluation (iii), as it comes to the fore in Section 3 and Table 2, there is the distinction between point tests, which evaluate the accuracy of the estimated parameters, and holistic tests, which evaluate the entire model. The standard error is a point test used in both LS and ML modeling, whereas the holistic tests differ in LS and ML modeling.

2. Interdependent (ID) systems.

To repeat, Haavelmo's SEQS systems are either Causal chain systems of Tinbergen's type, or interdependent (ID) systems of non-Tinbergen type. How to estimate ID systems had been in my mind since the mid-1940s. In Causal chain systems the transformation from SF to RF (reduced form) can be performed by iterative substitutions, a feature that makes OLS applicable to both SF and RF. In ID systems the passage from SF to RF involves the reversion of at least one SF relation. In the early and mid-1950s I voiced concern on this trait of ID systems, since causal-predictive relations are nonreversible. (In fact, if E is a controlled experiment with stimulus S and response R, then there exists no controlled experiment with stimulus R and response S.) My concern had little or no impact, however. Hence I decided to leave causality aside, temporarily, and to focus on predictive relations designed in terms of conditional expectations. This device will now be reviewed.

2.1. PREDICTOR SPECIFICATION (PRESP) (H. Wold, 1963, 1961, 1959).

The Presp device belongs under model specification, the first stage of scientific model-building, and is an LS approach. To model a multivariate predictive relation in *structural* form (SF), for example

(1a) $y_{nt} = \beta_{ni} y_{ni} + \gamma_{1i} z_{n1} + \gamma_{2i} z_{n2} + \delta_{nt}$ or, in reduced form (RF),

(1b) $y_{nt} + \gamma_{1j} z_{n1} + \gamma_{2j} z_{n2} + \varepsilon_{nt}$, the Presp prediction is the conditional expectation of y, that is

(2) $y_{nt} = E(y_{nt} | y_{ni}, z_{n1}, z_{n2}) + \varepsilon_{nt}$.

In words: *Presp is imposed on relations that the investigator wants to use for prediction, and Presp provides the ensuing predictions.*

The Presp Equation 2 implies

(3) $E(y_{nt} | y_{ni}, z_{n1}, z_{n2}) = 0$, which gives:

(4 a-c) $E(\varepsilon_{nt}) = 0$; $r(z_{n1}, \varepsilon_{nt}) = r(z_{n2}, \varepsilon_{nt}) = 0$, that is, the familiar assumptions of OLS regression.

The evaluation test Q^2 of PMV models is:

$$(5) \qquad Q^2 = 1 - \sum_n \sum_t \frac{(\bar{z}_{nt} - \text{pred } y_{nt})^2}{(y_{nt} - \bar{y}_n)^2}$$

The model evaluation brings two possibilities:

(6a) $Q^2 \leq 0$. The model is not predictive. Try another model, for example, by changing one or more endogenous variables by exogenous variables from the same relation.

(6b) $Q^2 > 0$. The model does have predictive relevance.

Experienced cause-effect researchers often get (6b). Less experienced investigators often get (6a), and then try to improve the model.

Three points will be noted: a) Presp utilizes pre-model knowledge (substantive theoretical-empirical knowledge) to specify the direction of prediction, that is, z_{n1}, $z_{n2} \to y_{nt}$, thereby obtaining Equations 4 a–c as an implication, and not as an *ad hoc* assumption.

b) It is clear that Presp Equations 4 a–c extend to any number of variables $z_1, \ldots, z_M$ and $y_1, \ldots, y_N$. In econometric usage, part of the substantive pre-modeling knowledge is that z_m (m = 1, M) and y_n (n = 1, N) are exogenous and endogenous variables, respectively.

c) Except for Presp no distributional assumptions are made, and there is no stipulation of independent observations.

To elaborate point c): The predictors $z_1, \ldots z_m$ are distribution-free. The prediction error is distribution-free, except that $E(\varepsilon_{nt}) = 0$.

2.2. *The four stages (i)–(iv) of model building in ID systems.* The argument on ID systems is summarized in Table 2 with regard to the four stages of model building (cf. Table 1).

Table 2. ID systems: Methods and Stages i–iv of model building.

Model Method operation	ML	TSLS	FP (Fix-Point)	
(i) Specification	Classic ID		REID	GEID
(ii) Estimation	Parameter-oriented		Prediction-oriented	
		Prediction-oriented		
(iii) Evaluation				
a) Standard error, SE	Classical SEs SE often underestimated		Generalized jackknife More realistic SEs	
b) Holistic	Likelihood SF and RF ratio		R^2 in Stone-Geisser test Q^2 of predictive relevance	
(iv) Applications	Scarce	Many	Many	Many

Table 1 reports on ML methods of model-building versus traditional OLS methods. In Table 2 the perspective widens to the ML methods versus FP and Presp methods. Some specific comments are adduced:

Model specification.

The difference between the "hard" ML and the "soft" Presp assumptions has many implications. For one thing, Presp relaxes the *ceteris paribus* condition. For example, OLS estimation of a multiple regression model, Equation 1a, is consistent, and the impact on y of a change Δz_1 is $\Delta \beta_1 z_1$ with the *ceteris paribus* condition that z_2 remains constant. On Presp's FP assumption Equation 4 the impact of Δz_1 is $\Delta \beta_1 z_1$ with the *pari passu* condition that z_1 and z_2 vary in the same manner as in the analyzed data.

Model estimation.

Table 2 notes the parting of the ways between the parameter-oriented ML and the prediction-oriented FP and Presp. TSLS is interpreted as being ambiguous in this respect (cf. H. Wold, 1959).

The key advantages of model building based on FP and Presp carry over to model estimation. In addition, the statistical implementation is simple relative to ML estimation, and LS estimation is easy and speedy on the computer.

The statement in Section I that LS estimation is "inefficient" is typical in the ML mainstream. Well, ML focuses on parameters and LS on prediction. There is a choice between optimal parameter accuracy and optimal prediction accuracy; you cannot have both except in the special case of controlled experiments with nonrandom stimulus variables. As I have said before and gladly repeat, I could kick myself in the back for not having realized this dualism a long time ago. The analytic contrast between ML and LS estimation is well established in Cramér's treatise of 1945.

The choice between optimal parameters and optimal prediction is illustrated by simulation experiments in the context of FP estimation (R. Bergström and H. Wold 1983). Simulated on nonpathological conditions, the data give relatively small differences between the ML and LS parameters (and between the ML and LS predictions).

It is a paradox that such simulation experiments were never made before, to counteract the "inefficiency" of LS estimation. It is all the more surprising in view of the LS prediction efficiency of R.A. Fisher's (1935) orthogonal design of controlled experiments: The efficiency of his experiments increases by a quantum jump relative to that obtained with the method of varying only one factor at a time.

Model evaluation.

As to methods of point and holistic testing in model evaluation, the aims of standard errors and holistic test are complimentary, and not necessarily in tune: on ML assumptions the classical standard errors are the smallest possible; on LS assumptions the residual variance is the smallest possible. The same dualism between parameter- and prediction-orientation is here subject to measurement as in model estimation.

Applications.

For applications of ID systems using FP estimation, see H. Wold 1965 and 1981. As to further FP applications, B. Schips in Chapter 6 reports a large RE model on the exchange rates of the U.S. dollar, Swiss franc, and German Mark.

2.3. MVP MODELS: SPECIAL CASES OF PRESP, EQUATIONS 6–10.

Simple regression

Simple regression is the special case of Equations 1 a–b where $y_{ni} = z_2 = 0$. The empirical prediction based on N cases takes the form:

(7a) $\text{pred } y_{nt} = b_0 + b_1 z_{1t}, \qquad n = 1, N; t = 1, T$

with prediction error δ_{nt}. Thanks to Equations 4 a–c the OLS regression coefficients b_0, b_1 will on mild supplementary conditions be consistent estimates of β_0, β_1; in symbols

(7b) $\text{prob lim } b_m = \beta_m; \qquad m = 0, 1$
                    $N \to \infty$

The following condition is sufficient for consistency (Lyttkens, 1953):

(8) $\Sigma_k |r(\delta_{nt}, \delta_{(n+k)t})| < \infty; \qquad k = 1, 2, 3, \dots$

In what follows, without loss of generality, the observables are assumed to be measured as deviations from the mean, giving in Equation 7a

(9 a-c) $\bar{y} = \bar{z}_1 = 0, \qquad \bar{b}_0 = \bar{y} - b_1 \bar{z}_1;$

and all location parameters will be ignored. Throughout, it is an easy matter to carry over Equation 9c.

Multiple regression is the extension of Equations 3–4 to any number of predictor variables $y_1, \dots, y_N; z_1, \dots, z_M$.

The *parity principle*, a characteristic and fundamental property of model-building based on Presp, is illustrated by multiple regression: The prediction error δ_{nt} is uncorrelated with each predictor variable y_{ni}; z_{nt}, the unknown parameters thus being estimated in terms of the same number of zero correlations between the prediction error and the predictors (H. Wold 1982a). In this sense Presp is a full information method.

Causal chain systems.

Let us write
$$(10) \qquad y_{nt} = \beta_{ni} y_{it} + \gamma_{ni} z_{nt} + \delta_{nt}, \quad i, n = 1, N; t = 1, T$$
for the SF of a Causal chain system. After suitable reordering of the SF relations the matrix β_{nj} is subdiagonal. The reduced form (RF) is obtained by solving SF for the endogenous variables:
$$(11 \text{ a,b}) \qquad y_{nt} = \gamma_{nj} z_{nt} + \varepsilon_{nt} = y_{nt} + \varepsilon_{nj}$$
with matrix parameters $[\beta_{nj}]$ and vector residuals ε_{nj} (cf. Equations 1a and 3).

In Causal chain systems both SF and RF allow Presp. The OLS regression estimates of β_{ni}, γ_{ni} in SF and of γ_{nj} in RF, say B, G and W, are consistent. In practice, OLS regressions of SF give B and G, whereas W is obtained from G (cf. Equations 13 and 14).

2.4 ON THE RATIONALE OF THE JACKKNIFE POINT TEST AND THE STONE-GEISSER (SG) HOLISTIC TEST Q^2.

All real-world models are approximate; they are never exactly true. In the classical ML hypothesis testing, accordingly, the null hypothesis that the model is true is rejected sooner or later as the sample size increases indefinitely. That is, the null hypothesis of model evaluation is wrongly posed. In contrast, the SG test asks whether the model has predictive relevance. If the answer is in the affirmative, it is a matter of degree: the SG test then leaves the door open for improvement of the model.

ML modeling is an error-in-variables approach; LS is an error-in-equations approach.

ML model evaluation requires that the model assumptions be realistic, and that the estimation method be consistent. In contrast, the jackknife and the SG tests evaluate the computer output as a *fait accompli*, and work irrespective of whether Presp is realistic or whether the estimation is consistent. Inadequate modeling is expected to reduce the ensuing SG test criterion Q^2.

The jackknife test is CPU-time consuming: the model must be reestimated N times, where N is the number of observational units. The order of magnitude of a jackknife standard error is approximately constant for large or moderately large N. In Q^2, in contrast, the computer time can be reduced by a significant factor by grouping the cases in k groups of every kth case. Typically, k need not be larger than 6 or 7 (S. Wold 1977). As k increases, Q^2 soon becomes approximately constant.

ML point and holistic methods of model evaluation are valid asymptotically for an indefinitely large sample size N. In contrast, Tukey's jackknife and the SG test do not require the amount N of observed cases to be very large; the tests can be used for finite N, moderately large N, and even for quite small N (H. Wold 1986 and 1980).

Homogeneity.

As emphasized by A.A. Tschuprow in 1912, statistical data must be homogeneous, lest different groups of the sample give different results.

Speaking broadly, if a classical standard error differs from the corresponding jackknife, this reflects the fact that the data under analysis are not homogeneous.

Jackknife standard errors are sensitive to outliers. J.-B. Lohmöller reports a model which is highly influenced by the removal of one or two outliers (Chapter 1, Section 3B, Example 1).

2.5 MODELING OF ID SYSTEMS: A REVIEW. EQUATIONS 10–11 SUPPORT EACH OTHER FOR THE SF AND RF OF ID SYSTEMS.

Classical ID systems (H. Theil 1953, R.L. Basmann, 1957).

It is assumed that the residuals δ_{nt} of SF are (a) uncorrelated with the predetermined variables z_{nt}, and (b) multivariate observations uncorrelated over t. The SF and RF of classical ID systems do not permit joint Presp. For RF we adopt Presp, in accordance with its intended operative use, then OLS is inconsistent if applied to the SF on the classical ID assumptions (Haavelmo, 1943).

Since the SF cannot be estimated by OLS, the behavioral ID relations cannot be interpreted as conditional expectations. What is then their operative interpretation, if any? A positive answer is given by the following reformulation of SF.

REID (Reformulated ID) systems, and FP (Fix-Point) estimation (H. Wold 1961, 1966.)

The SF of ID systems can be rewritten as follows:

(12) $\qquad y^*_{nt} = \beta_{ni}\, y_{nt} + \gamma_{ni}\, z_{nt} + \varepsilon_{nt},$

with y^*_{nt} defined as in Equation 11 a–b. The reformulation does not change the parameters β_{ni}, γ_{ni} of SF, and the residual ε_{nt} remains the same as in Equation 11 a-b. The RF is the same before and after the reformulation (Equation 1b).

REID systems allow Presp in SF as well as in RF. The reformulation provides causal-predictive interpretation of the behavioral equations: each endogenous variable y^*_{nt} is explained by predetermined variables z_{nt} and expected values y_{ni} of other endogenous variables. At the same time, thanks to Equations 13 and 14, consistent estimates of the SF parameters are provided by the OLS regressions of Equation 12.

There is the snag that the predictors y^*_{nt} are not observed. The FP method solves this problem by an iterative procedure, say with steps $s = 1$, 2, 3,.... The FP algorithm is an iterative sequence of OLS regressions and linear operations. To be specific:

The proxies obtained in step s are denoted by superscripts (s). Each step has two substeps. In step s the first substep uses the proxy of y^*_{nt} obtained in substep s-1, and performs the OLS regression given by

$$(13) \qquad y_{nt} = \sum_i (B^{(s)}_{ni} \hat{y}^{(s\text{-}1)}_{nt}) + G^{(s)}_{nt} z_{nt} + \varepsilon^{(s)}_{nt}.$$

The second substep obtains $\hat{y}^{(S)}_{nt}$ by computing:

$$(14) \qquad \hat{y}^{(s)}_{nt} = \sum_i (B^{(s)}_{ni} \hat{y}^{(s\text{-}1)}_{nt}) + G^{(s)}_{nt} z_{nt}.$$

The model evaluation gives the two possibilities of Equations 6a and 6b. Trained cause-effect researchers often get Equation 6b. Less experienced investigators often get Equation 6a, and then try to improve the model.

A conventional convergence criterion closes the iterative procedure.

2.6. PMV MODELS II–V IN FIGURE 1–2: LS V. ML DEVELOPMENTS.

The ML methods referred to in Table 1, (i)–(iii), being based on stringent assumptions, are of narrow scope in theory and practice. As is only natural, LS countercurrents have emerged in the ML mainstream. In model specification (i) and model estimation (ii), Presp breaks radically away from the ML methods (i)–(ii) in being distribution free in the exogenous variables. As to model evaluation (iii), John Tukey's 1958 jack-knife assessment of standard errors is distribution free in the exogenous variables.

When initiating the FP and PLS algorithms for models IV–V and I*–IV* in Figure 1–2, my research was intensely preoccupied by model specification and model estimation using Presp, leaving little or no time for model evaluation. Then a fortunate junction of events pulled me into the realm of evaluation techniques.

Svante Wold, familiar with my LS algorithm for estimation of Principal Components (PC) models, used the PC algorithm as a classification method (H. Wold 1966, Section 4).

Then, when Svante visited the University of Wisconsin in 1974–75, he had the good luck to attend Merwyn Stone's first seminar outside London on Stone-Geisser's 1974 cross-validatory choice and assessment of predictive relevance. Adopting the Stone-Geisser (SG) method in his classification algorithm to choose the optimal number of Principal components, Svante thereby obtained his SIMCA classification algorithm (1977), where the SG device is given a new multivariate twist.

The SG adaptation in SIMCA is of general scope, and was very soon adopted in the FP and PLS algorithms (H. Wold 1977).

The ensuing SG test is formally related to R.G.D. Allen's "Press" (1957). Denoted Q^2 as in Equation 5, the SG test may be positive or negative (cf. Equations 6 a–b). Note that Tukey's jackknife standard errors are obtained as a by-product of the SG test Q^2. R.G. Miller (1974) uses the i.i.d. assumption. J.-B. Lohmöller in Chapter 1, Section 3 B gives several versions of pre-modeling information of Q^2.

2.7. RATIONAL EXPECTATIONS (RE) MODELS.

In RE models the rational expectations are conditional expectations formed in accordance with the model (J.F. Muth 1961 and B. Schips, Chapter 6 in this volume). General RE models may involve conditional expectations of the present, past, and future endogenous variables. Hence REID systems are the special case of RE models that involves expectations of the present, but not of the past or the future. Manfred Loesch (1984) has extended the FP method so as to estimate general RE models.

The classical ID assumptions are more stringent than necessary for the FP algorithm. What emerges here is the following generalization of REID systems.

GEID (General ID) systems (H. Wold 1966, 1981 and 1982).

Given the ID systems, the reformulated SF is defined by Equation 12. Instead of the classical ID assumptions, Equations 2–3, we now impose Presp only on SF, Equation 12. As to the RF, we suspend Presp, and obtain y^*_{nt} algebraically from y_{ni} and γ_{nt}. By Equation 11, Presp implies the *parity principle* of GEID systems: there are as many residual zero correlations of the type in Equations 4 b-c as there are explanatory variables. For corresponding classical ID systems the residual zero correlations are more numerous, as illustrated in Wold (1981).

Zero residual correlations, Equations 4 b-c, which are non-zero in GEID systems, are called *GEID correlations*. Clearly, non-zero GEID correlations reduce the SF residual variances, thereby improving the predictive performance of the GEID model. The FP algorithm is the only known operative method for consistent estimation of ID systems in the presence of GEID correlations.

3. PLV models: Path models with latent (indirectly observed) variables.

LVs, called factors, and the models I^*_1 and I^*_2 at the upper right in Figure 2, were introduced in Psychometrics, the birthplace of LVs.

3.1 FROM FACTOR AND PRINCIPAL COMPONENTS (PC) MODELS TO LISREL AND PLS.

Model I^*_1 is the famous One-Factor model of C.F. Spearman 1904, also known as the General Intelligence model:

$$(15) \qquad y_{kn} = \pi_k \, \zeta_n + \varepsilon_{kn}, \qquad\qquad k = 1, \ldots, K; \, n = 1, \ldots, N$$

In words, General Intelligence is the factor ζ. The mental traits y_{kn} (k = 1,...K) of the nth person are assumed to be fixed proportions (π_k) of the person's factor score ζ_n.

Spearman's General Intelligence model was saluted as the beginning of Psychometrics, quantitative analysis of the human mind. It was soon recognized that the One-Factor model is too simple—the human mind is not one-dimensional—but the road to more realistic models was uphill and thorny.

The avenue of Multiple Factor models was opened up and explored by Louis L. Thurstone (1927, 1947). Before the computer era, however, only a minority of psychologists had Factor Analysis as a principal line of research. Under the impact of R.A. Fisher's "Statistical Methods for Research Workers" (1925, 13th ed. 1958) the scene of quantitative psychology was dominated by OLS regression and analysis of variance.[3] So much the more devoted to Factor Analysis were its leading names, among those Joy P. Guilford (1936, 1967), Raymond B. Cattell (1962, 1968) and John L. Horn (1988, 1988).

Psychometrics was, for a long time (up to the 1950s), an isolated field in the broad domain of statistical methods. The pioneering "Multivariate Statistical Analysis" of T.W. Anderson (1958) marks the integration of psychometrics with general statistical analysis, with scientific model-building.

Table 3. LISREL vs. PLS: Methods and Stages of Model Building

Model operation	Method	LISREL	PLS
(i)	Specification	Arrow scheme	Arrow scheme
(ii)	Estimation	Covariance structure Parameter-oriented	Endogenous MVs and LVs Prediction-oriented
(iii)	Evaluation		
	a) Standard error, SE	Classical SEs SE is often under-estimated	Generalized jackknife More realistic SEs
	b) Holistic	Likelihood ratio	Generalized Stone-Geisser test Q2 of predictive relevance
(iv)	Applications	Many	Many

3.2 LVP MODELS ENTER AS A MERGER OF ECONOMETRICS AND PSYCHOMETRICS.

Sociology in the mid-1960s introduced PLV models of types III^*-V^* in Figure 2; cf. O.T. Duncan, 1966. Models III^*-V^* posed entirely novel estimation problems, which at the outset were handled by *ad hoc* methods. For estimation of general PLVs, Karl G. Jöreskog (1970) launched his ML algorithm LISREL (Linear Structural Relations), a landmark achievement.

LISREL includes as a special case, Jöreskog's algorithm ACOVS (1967) for ML estimation of factor models. Factor models and Principal Components (PC) models take the same form, for example, Equation 12. The difference is that the factor models assume the residuals ε_{kn} to be "white noise," giving

(16) $r(\varepsilon_{kn}, \varepsilon_{kn'}) = 0$ for each k and any $n, n' = 1, \ldots N$

whereas the zero correlations are not imposed on the PC model. In the context of the FP algorithm, Equations 2–3, I had found an iterative LS algorithm for estimation of PC (Principal Components) models (H. Wold 1965).

LISREL gave me the clue that the iterative algorithm for LS estimation of Principal Components might be extended so as to cover general PLV models. After preliminary reports from 1973 to 1977 the ensuing algorithm was completed in late 1977, first called NIPALS (Nonlinear Iterative Partial Least Squares) and later, PLS. The first comprehensive exposition of PLS was preceded by precursory reports (H. Wold 1980a, 1980b).

3.3. ANOTHER FORTUNATE JUNCTURE.

In 1980 at the Fourth World Congress of the Econometric Society the paper by J. Romański and W. Welfe (1980) brought the exciting news that using their macroeconomic SEQS systems for Poland the FP estimation gave higher R^2 than the FIMLD (Full Information Maximum Likelihood with Diagonal Disturbance Matrix) method. Well, it was known from Reinhold Bergström's doctoral thesis (1974) that the estimation of real-world SEQS models and data sometimes gives higher R^2 for FP than for FIMLD, as is only natural because of the stringent FILMD assumptions. The Romański/Welfe report inspired a joint project in which Bergström and I explored the performance of FP relative to PLS.

In the first stage of the project we made extensive experiments on data simulated on the FIMLD assumptions. We found that the larger the sample size, the more accurate are the FIMLD parameter estimates relative to FP, and the more accurate are the FP predictions relative to FIMLD. At first surprised, we soon realized that this result was to be expected: the ML equations for parameter estimation are analytically different from the LS equations of prediction. Hence there is a choice between parameter accuracy and prediction accuracy: you cannot have both, except in the very special case of controlled experiments with non-random stimulus variables.

The second stage of the Bergström/Wold project brings out in full relief the extension from FP to PLS, and thereby the extension of SG tests and John Tukey's "jackknife" against traditional methods of model evaluation. We used data from the first stage of the project, from Bergström's earlier applications of FP estimation, and from a medium-large macroeconomic ID system 1949–59 for Greece, published by P. Pavlopolous (1966). For the 34 parameters of the Greek model the jackknife standard errors of the FP parameter estimates are on the average 10.3% higher than the classical ML standard errors. The classical ML formula for standard errors assumes that the observations are mutually independent: if this assumption is unrealistic the classical formula may be biased. As shown by the Greek model the bias of the classical standard error may be quite considerable.

Tables 2 and 3 show that our FP and PLS results have come at two levels. In Table 2 the models are PMV models; in Table 3 they are PLV models. At the second level the OLS estimates gives results that are 10.3%

higher than the classical standard error. It seems perfectly all right that the FP and PLS results should be quite different.

In the context of the ASA-Census-NBER conference in October 1981, it is explained that Tukey's jackknife and the SG test Q^2 are distribution- and independence-free (H. Wold 1983, p. 370). The sharp contrast with the stringency of ML model evaluation will be noted.

3.4 SIMILARITIES AND DIFFERENCES BETWEEN LISREL AND PLS.

Introductory comments: LISREL is fine in small or smallish models where emphasis is placed on each separate parameter. In large models the interest shifts to prediction in terms of packages of variables. LISREL modeling with more than 30 or 50 MVs is beyond current technical resources.[4] For PLS the size of the model is no problem.

Model specification.

The conceptual-theoretical design of the model is specified by its arrow scheme (Figure 2). The arrow scheme is much the same for PLS and LISREL.

Purpose of the model. PLS serves to predict endogenous MVs and LVs in terms of exogenous MVs and/or LVs. LISREL models the covariances of the MVs, briefly called the *structure,* as well as the structure of the LVs.

Specification of data. The data are measurements on observational units, which in PLS are called *cases,* in LISREL *the sample.* Both in PLS and in LISREL it is essential to specify which set of data is being used in the model.

Specification of assumptions. PLS modeling subjects the predictive relations of the model to Presp (Predictor specification) (Section 2). Apart from Presp, PLS is distribution-free, and there is no stipulation that the cases under analysis are mutually independent or uncorrelated.

LISREL assumes that the MVs involve measurement errors. The MVs are assumed to be jointly ruled by a specified multivariate distribution (often normal), where the measurement errors are mutually independent.

Due to their stringent, "hard" assumptions, LISREL models are valid in a range which is very narrow relative to the broad PLS assumptions. As regards the assumption of a specified multivariate distribution LISREL modeling is rather robust, whereas it is far from robust with respect to the assumption of independent observations; see Table 3 (iii)a for evidence on this important point.

Presp predicts an endogenous variable in terms of one or more exogenous or endogenous variables. That is, Presp involves an element of substantive/empiricist theory, inasmuch as the exogenous-endogenous distinction is substantive and empirical. In this context an essential feature of Presp is the direction of the inner arrows in the arrow scheme: Presp specifies the direction to an LV from one or more LVs. In LISREL the direction of the inner arrows is not predictive in the PLS sense.

Model estimation.

PLS estimation involves for each LV an optimal choice of two alternatives, called PLS Mode A and PLS Mode B. Once the choice is made, the PLS algorithm can be written from the arrow scheme. PLS estimation is automatic, an iterative sequence of the OLS regressions, linear operations, and square root extractions. In the usage of P.M. Hauser (1966) the indicators of the LVs are *reflective* in Mode A, *formative* in Mode B.

The LVs may form hierarchic structures in the arrow scheme; see R. Noonan and N. Sellin in Chapters 3 and 4. In the PLS algorithm the MVs at the bottom level of a hierarchic structure are duplicated at each higher level of the structure.

LISREL estimation is a search procedure for the parameters that maximize the Likelihood Function of the model. The estimated parameters include the variances and covariances of the LVs of the model. LISREL provides no estimates of the case values of the LVs.

Consistency. PLS estimation of the parameters and of the LV case values is *inconsistent.* PLS is *consistent at large* in the sense that the estimation is consistent in the limit as the number of indicators of each LV increases indefinitely.

As usual in ML estimation, LISREL parameter estimates are asymptotically consistent in the limit as the sample size increases indefinitely.

Model evaluation.

In the specification and estimation stages of scientific model-building we have seen that PLS brings great advantages with its broad scope, simplicity and flexibility. Further, we have seen that the advantages are very much due to the key feature of Preps to be distribution- and independence-free in the explanatory variables. These advantages remain an asset when it comes to model evaluation. Here PLS exploits the generalized jackknife and SG tests referred to in Table 2, methods which fit PLS hand-in-glove in being distribution- as well as independence-free.

To repeat the above, PLS is inconsistent and consistent at large. Further we know that the qualified consistency does not hamper the model evaluation, which automatically takes the lack of consistency into account.

As noted in Section 3 the jackknife and the SG tests work for any size N of the data set, and even for quite small N. The PLS model in H. Wold (1986, 1980, 1978) is an extreme case with 1 endogenous and 27 exogenous variables and N = 10 cases; there are two LVs. $Q^2 = 0.42$ shows that the model has predictive relevance. J.-B. Lohmöller in Chapter 1, Section 3.2, analyzes the same data set, and shows that the Q^2 verdict varies greatly as the blindfolding shifts from the N cases to the 27 indicators, or is applied to different versions of the model.

Model application.

K.F. Fox (1980) rightly notes that there is a long distance and even some hostility between substantive research and statistical theory. The broad scope, simplicity, and flexibility of PLS models are being reported. R. Noonan in Chapter 3 shows the largest PLS model thus far published. The model has 59 LVs, 14 inner relations, 18 hierarchic LV structures, and 451 MVs, of which there are 191 different MVs at the lowest hierarchic level. 1,300,000 cells (1.3 megabyte) are required in the memory space. The PLS estimation converges in 4 iterations, using a total of 25.4 seconds on an IBM 360 computer.

Diversity in substance and uniformity in statistical method are characteristic features of the present volume. Substantive researchers report pioneering applications in seven scientific disciplines: education (R. Noonan, Chapter 3), economics (R. Schips, Chapter 6), management science (C. Fornell, Chapter 11), political science (J.W. Falter, Chapter 13), psychology (J. Horn, Chapter 14), morphology (F.L. Bookstein, Chapter 15), social science applications of contingency tables (J.-L. Bertholet, Chapter 16). The statistical methods are uniform and of broad scope in model saprification and model estimation by the FP and PLS methods, model evaluation by the generalizations of Tukey's jackknife and the Stone-Geisser test for predictive relevance.

In these applications there is no distance between substantive research and statistical method; instead there is collaboration. The substantive researcher is in charge of the model design and the data work; on the statistician's side is the statistical implementation and the computer work.

Since 1978, under a grant from the Stiftung Volkswagenwerk, J.-B. Lohmöller and I have developed a program for a three-day Course on PLS modeling. The two first days we lecture on OLS, FP and PLS model-building and model evaluation, and provide training on the computer in the afternoon. On the third day the participants bring their own data and model projects, and take their first steps on the PLS avenue. A desirable size of a three-day course is 30 to 40 participants. The course is announced several months in advance, and the participants book for the course one month in advance. After giving some ten courses, we have found that the more substantive researchers there are among the participants, the more active is the computer work on the third day, and the more successful the course. After the first few courses we now select participants who are active in substantive research and/or statistical applications.

A concluding comment on Section 3 and Table 3: LISREL is fine in small or smallish models where emphasis is placed on each separate parameter. In large models the interest shifts to prediction in terms of packages of variables. LISREL modeling with more than 30 or 50 MVs is beyond the current technical resources.[4] For PLS, the size of the model is no problem.

PLS is gaining momentum, but within the broad scope of potential applications its use is limited, for the double reason that PLS modeling breaks away markedly from the ML mainstream, and its methods of model evaluation are of recent origin.

Within its broad scope of potential applications PLS is at an early stage of evolution.

3.5. SCIENTIFIC MODEL-BUILDING AS A PARADIGM: THE UNISCIENCE PARADIGM.

The notions of paradigm and shift of paradigm introduced by T.S. Kuhn (1976) have in a short time become greatly appreciated in the scientific literature. Whether and to what extent Kuhn's paradigms are related to the term paradigm in the title of this section will now be discussed.

C. Dagum (Chapter 9) in a historical overview from antiquity onwards refers to the chasm between theory-oriented and empiricism-oriented schools, and he refers to the perseverant attempts at synthesis: Aristotle, St. Thomas Aquinas, Malthus, and so on, leading up to theoretical empiricism, with Auguste Comte and Ernst Mach in the mid- and late 19th century as important—but largely misunderstood—forerunners.

The antagonism between empiricism and idealism again emerged in the late 19th century with the fight between Harald Schmoller of the historical school of socioeconomics and Karl Menger of the mathematical school, but the antagonism gradually faded away without resolution. The requisite instrument for the resolving synthesis did not arrive until the advent of econometrics in the 1930s (W. Meissner and H. Wold, 1974).

The introduction and chapters 1-22 emphasize that scientific model building is an instrument of general scope. The two theoretical chapters (1 and 9) show how scientific model building expands human knowledge by combined use of theoretical knowledge and empirical knowledge. The seven applied chapters give examples of striking advances at the research frontier.

Section 3.6 of this introductory chapter will focus on a philosophical theme: scientific model-building constitutes a *paradigm* in the formation of fresh human knowledge. This paradigm is an innovation; there was no shift from an earlier paradigm, inasmuch as a number of major schools contributed to the previous formation of fresh knowledge.

3.6. FROM LOGICAL EMPIRICISM TO THEORETICAL EMPIRICISM.

The foundation of human knowledge was the central concern of many eminent names in the philosophy of science in the 20th century, among those Rudolf Carnap (1925), Carl G. Hempel (1952), Karl Popper (1962) and Thomas S. Kuhn (1972). Initiated by the Vienna school of philosophers, the circle soon expanded into an international movement: Logical empiricism.

R. Carnap in "Der logische Aufbau der Welt" (1950) describes how the body of human knowledge expands as scientific research brings fresh knowledge. Way back when first reading "Aufbau" I had a picture of human knowledge as a massive, solid body. I do not claim that this picture is a correct understanding of Carnap's message. What I do claim is that when the knowledge established by a scientific model is called a body of human knowledge, the total of human knowledge is not a solid, massive body, but a loosely connected set of bodies.

"Evolution of the Solar System" by H. Alfvén and G. Arrhenius (1976) lends support to my claim. This massive treatise (599 pages) is a comprehensive review of established knowledge concerning limited parts of the solar system, and, furthermore, the authors refer to investigations concerning the areas between these limited parts, studies with more or less plausible hypotheses which have not (as yet) been established.

C.G. Hempel (1952) is a prominent name in Logical empiricism. The characteristic claim of Logical empiricism is that theoretical knowledge is always pure, nonempiricist knowledge. Equivalently, the claim is that theoretical knowledge and empiricist knowledge are mutually independent. In contrast, Theoretical empiricism allows theoretical knowledge to draw from substantive, empiricist knowledge.

K. Popper widens the perspective of statistical methods by placing emphasis on the philosophy of science aspects. His famous "Conjectures and Refutations: The Construction of Scientific Knowledge" (1962) is a program for the ML method of hypothesis testing under the null hypothesis that the model is true. The ensuing model evaluation is valid in situations where the stringent ML assumptions are valid. In contrast, for model evaluation in Theoretical empiricism the present volume sets forth generalizations of Tukey's jackknife and the Stone-Geisser test for predictive relevance, methods which are subject to virtually no restrictions in applicability.

The scientific community has found that the concepts of paradigm and paradigm shift introduced by T.S. Kuhn (1977) are practical and eminently useful. In the context of the present volume Georg Süssmann in Chapter 2 pays tribute to the importance of Kuhn's concept of paradigm as a consolidating and unifying world-view. The Alfvén-Arrhenius just referred to is an excellent example of research conducted in the paradigm spirit. Incidentally, their discourse on the solar system provides material from the Newton paradigm as well as the Einstein paradigm shift.

Ralph B. Medawar in "Advice to a Young Scientist" (1979) pays tribute to the toilsome and exciting life devoted to research, and describes research as *imaginative guesswork*. I have referred to this description before, and, full of admiration, I do so again. In line with his characterization of research activity, Medawar's "Advice" contains some disapproving comments on Kuhn's evolution from "The Structure of Scientific Revolutions" (1962) to his paradigm articles (1977). In the course of this evolution T.S. Kuhn modifies the "normal science" stage of a scientific revolution. In the paradigm articles Kuhn instead argues that "research is riddle solving with answers given by the paradigm." This argument has no support in Medawar's "Advice." At the research frontier, research poses problems, the answers to which are not given by the paradigm; solving the problems requires imaginative guesswork.

The problem posed at the research frontier aims at an expansion of established knowledge by a specific, more advanced hypothesis (see Carnap's "Aufbau"). Typically, the hypothesis combines pure theory and substantive-empiricist argument: the hypothesis poses an open problem that requires fresh research beyond established knowledge, research that requires imaginative guesswork, imagination how to solve the problem by some new element in the theory combined with some fresh turn in the data work.

Note how well Medawar's imaginative guesswork agrees with what E.N. Lorenz writes about models as answers to scientific problems (Section 1): sometimes the models "are based on ...intelligent guesses."

The above references to Medawar are not intended as an appraisal of Kuhnian paradigms relative to the uniscience paradigm. It is just a comment on similarities and differences between Kuhn's concept of paradigm and the theme of the present volume, the uniscience paradigm of scientific model building.

J.-B. Lohmöller has kindly allowed me to respond to Georg Süssmann's discussion paper in Chapter 2. Süssmann argues that "the unity of the sciences should be more than the common denominator of the scientific method," that is, more than the uniscience paradigm of scientific model building. More specifically: "Most physicists, including myself [G.S.] feel they have good reason to accept the physical universe not only as an imaginative idea (a formally connecting notion), but as a realistic entity (a substantially comprehending concept)."

Yes, the universe around us is the source of a paradigm that is indispensable in scientific and practical endeavors. However, the universe as we see it occupies just one quantum level. At the next lower level of the atom, or the next higher level of the galaxies, human knowledge has no guidance from the universe as we see it: at each level research is nothing other than scientific model-building.

3.7. THEORETICAL EMPIRICISM: A BROADER PARADIGM THAN SCIENTIFIC MODEL BUILDING.

The evolution from Logical empiricism to Theoretical empiricism is not a shift of paradigm: Logical empiricism is included in Theoretical empiricism as a variant of limited scope.

The key feature of Theoretical empiricism is that theoretical knowledge flows from two sources, namely, pure theory and substantive-empiricist theory.

The statement on Theoretical empiricism in the previous paragraph is true also for scientific model-building. Accordingly, Theoretical empiricism is a broader paradigm than scientific model building.

As to the origin of the terms at issue, the 13th ICUS, 2-5 Sept. 1984, approved for Committee Two, a theme with "The general rationale of scientific model-building" as sub-title. The term "Theoretical empiricism" was proposed by Juergen W. Falter at the pre-ICUS at Paris, 7-8 April 1985.

3.8. SCIENTIFIC MODEL-BUILDING CONSTITUTES A PARADIGM.

In E.N. Lorenz' (1984) brilliant review of the advent of models to the scientific community two points will be noted: 1) in contrast to earlier usage in scientific research the model is adopted as an autonomous unit, which is explored and developed with full mathematical rigor; 2) in the earlier usage the theoretical model served as an approximation to (the laws governing) the real world.

In the light of Lorenz' paper it seems appropriate to define the paradigm of scientific model-building as the rigorous construction of models in four stages: (i) model specification, (ii) model estimation, (iii) model evaluation and (iv) model application.

The question arises as to whether the uniscience paradigm of scientific model building brought a paradigm shift. Again with reference to E.N. Lorenz, the earlier scientific research might be called "Theory as an approximation to the laws governing the real world." Lorenz notes that the change in approach represents a change in attitude rather than a change in substance. It seems to me that the change in attitude is important enough to be called a paradigm shift.

3.9. SCIENTIFIC AREAS OUTSIDE THE UNISCIENCE PARADIGM.

Large areas of science work without models that combine theoretical and empirical knowledge in the sense of model-building. To repeat from Section 2, a research problem passes several stages in the theoretical and empirical work before it is ripe to be explored by a model. The intermediate area between Theoretical empiricism and scientific model-building is very wide. The Faculty of Law and the Faculty of Divinity—two of four faculties of the classic university—are examples of science that bring contributions which typically belong to Theoretical empiricism.

This last comment raises the question as to whether "Science" and "Theoretical empiricism" are synonyms. This high-level topic of the philosophy of science is outside the scope of this introductory chapter.

3.10. HINDSIGHTS, PROSPECTS, AND CURRENT ISSUES IN THE UNISCIENCE PARADIGM.

To the Logical empiricist, theoretical knowledge is pure non-empirical knowledge (Section 3.8). Concepts such as causality and utility are not permitted in the scientific vocabulary, since they break the strict distinction between pure theoretical knowledge and empirical knowledge. Theoretical empiricism resolves the dilemma by allowing theoretical knowledge to be combined theoretical-empirical knowledge. Typically, such combined knowledge enters into model-building by way of pre-modeling knowledge. The concept at issue is part of the theoretical specification of the model, and the validation of the model constitutes an empirical test of the concept.

For causality and utility the question of appropriate definition of the concept is of old standing, and remained a controversial question until the advent of model building. To paraphrase the dilemma: it is impossible to give a theoretical definition that is exactly confirmed by empirical observation (H. Wold, 1983).

Model II* in Figure 2 is the special case of Model III* where the LVs ζ_1 and ζ_2 are absent. Canonical correlation as defined by H. Hotelling (1965, 1966) maximizes the correlation of two weighted sets of variables, say x_j ($j = 1, J$) and y_k ($k = 1, K$). However, to call Model II* canonical correlation is inadequate since there are no LVs in Hotelling's models, and, further, because a directed arrow is inadequate to illustrate the maximum intercorrelation between the two blocks of MVs.

Multivariate scaling

Multivariate scaling, associated with J.B. Kruskal (1964), is a multi-block extension of canonical correlation. There are no LVs, and no specified directions for the lines between selected pairs of MV blocks for which the intercorrelations of weighted MV aggregates are maximized.

PLS is a "soft" approach to modeling, using LVs estimated as weighted aggregates of indicator MVs. Canonical correlation and multivariate scaling are approaches that are less soft than PLS in using MVs but no LVs, and more soft than PLS in not using directed arrows between the intercorrelated blocks of MVs.

The Rational Expectations (RE) models of J.F. Muth (1961), another soft approach, is comparable to FP modeling, rather than PLS. RE joins FP modeling in being predictive, thereby breaking away from the ML mainstream. Until recently the RE literature was largely ML-oriented, and the operative results were of limited scope. C. Dagum's discussion in Chapter 8 of Muth's RE models criticizes the ambiguity of the basic RE concepts, and salutes B. Schips's adaptation of RE modeling, with estimation of the ensuing models by M. Loesch's (1984) extension of the FP algorithm.

The *fuzzy sets* of L.A. Zadeh (1975) is a soft approach which is more soft than PLS inasmuch as the scope of the reported operations with fuzzy sets is very limited.

3.11. THE UNISCIENCE PARADIGM IS AT AN EARLY STAGE OF EVOLUTION.

Reference is made to C. Dagum's summary in Chapter 9, Section IV of six stages in the advent of a paradigm. The fourth stage is the period of confusion. The sixth stage is the period of innovation and opposition.

The paradigm introduces novel concepts and terms. Earlier concepts and terms become obsolete or change their meaning. To consolidate the uniscience paradigm it is important to clarify and fix the terminology.

An example at the philosophy of science level: *Positivism* is given many meanings in the schools of philosophy of science. Positivism as introduced by Auguste Comte in 1850 is an important forerunner of Theoretical empiricism (Section 3.7). Hence it seems adequate to use Positivism as a synonym for Theoretical empiricism.

Terminology is a source of confusion in the realm of statistics since the same term does not always have the same meaning in different sciences in which statistics is applied. A case in point is reduction and reductionism. G. Süssmann (Chapter 2, discussion) and W.R. Gruner (Chapter 18) use these terms in the sense well-known in physics and related sciences: Two (or more) fields of science develop theories that at first are conceived as different or related, and are later found to be equivalent. That is, the different theories have been *reduced* to one. To put it otherwise, each of the different fields *expands* to comprise the aggregate field. Note the imminant dualism or ambiguity of reduction/expansion.

The term reductionism has another meaning in statistical method and its fields of application: reductionist versus holistic approaches. In reductionism the problem at issue is split up into parts which are modeled separately, and then combined as a synthesis, in patchwork-quilt style. In the holistic approach the problem at issue is modeled as an intact entity. PLS modeling is holistic: the system defined by the inner and outer relations that make the formal model is estimated simultaneously by the PLS algorithm. The model reported by R. Noonan is holistic, a synthesis of six models which other authors had analyzed and reported separately (Chapter 3, Section IV, 3).

To conclude: the reduction usage involves the conceptual ambiguity of reduction/expansion. In the reductionist/holistic usage there is no such ambiguity.

Large complex models are the forte of PLS, and in large models the data terminology is of special importance. A case in point is R. Noonan's PLS model in Chapter 3, where the observational units are subject to a highly commendable terminology: The term *frame* indicates a grouping of the observational units, such as the social frame or the interpersonal frame. The *intrapersonal* frame is the observational unit itself. Noonan's attributes of the observational units are of two types, *characteristics* and *behavioral.* This terminology replaces the current usage in which attributes and characteristics are synonyms.

Ambiguities also occur in the terminology of variables. An example which we give without comment is *intervening variable.*

Innovations in statistical methods sometimes bring operational shifts in the terminology. A case in point is the shift from *ceteris paribus* to *pari passu* (Section 2.2).

In the construction of large complex models—the forte of PLS (and FP)—it is essential to have access to rich and reliable data. (As in statistics in general, PLS is subject to the GIGO principle: garbage in, garbage out.) The reliable educational and econometric models reported by R. Noonan (Chapter 3) and B. Schips (Chapter 6) are in line with this truism.

Sociological data are typically surveys of limited size and scope. This is not so in the large sociological/politometric model of J.W. Falter (Chapter 13), who uses the rich and reliable voting data of pre-War Germany 1930-1933. Psychometrics is the birthplace of latent variables because direct measurements have been virtually impossible in the problem area of mind/brain relations. J. Horn and J. Risberg (Chapter 14) exploit the rich source of data opened up by the technology of isotope-inhalation methods for direct measurement of the blood flow in the brain.

PLS modeling is of broad scope thanks to the generality of the underlying assumptions. The basic PLS algorithm (1982) was primarily designed for scalar observables. J.-L. Bertholet (Chapter 16) shows that since PLS modeling is distribution-free except for Presp, the PLS estimation algorithm requires little or no modification when extending it to categorical variables. As noted by B. Muthen (Chapter 17, discussion), the contrast between PLS and ML approaches to categorical variables is an important field for comparable studies.

The basic PLS algorithm is designed with emphasis on simplicity; hence in the wide field of potential applications problems arise that call for more elaborate designs.

J. Rogowski (Chapter 5, discussion) generalizes the PLS estimation algorithm by merging PLS Mode A and PLS Mode B.

In the basic PLS design the MVs are observed either over time or a cross-section. History and many other sciences use MVs observed over both time and a cross-section. J.-B. Lohmöller in Chapter 1 refers to his generalized PLS algorithm for estimation of linear models with two-way observation of the data, i.e., over time and a cross-section, or over two cross-sections.

The basic PLS design is linear. For extension to some models that involve non-linearities, see H. Wold (1982), and G. Mensch, R. Kaasch and H. Wold (1986).

The device of "adjacent" or "adjoint" variables is a deliberate simplification in the basic PLS design. The rationale of the device is questioned in J.-B Lohmöller's and S. Wold's research centers of PLS modeling. A relaxed version of the PLS algorithm is on the agenda of S. Wold and H. Wold; the revised design involves LVs in two or more dimensions.

4. The importance of interdisciplinary research in the evolution of Theoretical empiricism and Scientific model-building.

An established scientific model can be described as a kernel of knowledge around which there is a gray zone where theoretical and empirical knowledge is being gathered with the purpose of expanding the kernel. J.-B. Lohmöller and C. Fornell in Chapters 1 and 11 describe consecutive stages that can be interpreted as levels in the gray zone around the kernel.

The gray zone around an established model is an area where the model-builder can receive insights and impulses from outside, by engaging in discourses and exchanges of thought with researchers in related sciences, and with other non-specialists.

Substantive researchers are often model-builders, whereas philosophers and philosophers of science, not being engaged in a specific science, usually have no personal experience in the substantive research and data work of model-building.

It is often said that there is some friction and even hostility between scientists on the one side, and philosophers and philosophers of science on the other. Where such friction or hostility exists, it is very unfortunate. Science has much to gain by turning the friction into an exchange, where philosophers and philosophers of science collaborate with scientists; collaboration is in the mutual interest of the participants.

Any scientific model is approximate, and can be improved and expanded. The gray zone around the model is an area where the model-builder can receive valuable impulses from non-specialists, be it interdisciplinary ideas, exchanges of thought with philosophers of science and philosophers, or insights of non-science laymen.

ICUS is unique as an open forum for interdisciplinary discussion of important problems. Until recently ICUS has been philosophy oriented. By the reorganization with task forces for study of specific problems, ICUS has become science oriented. I voice the hope that the ICUS reorganization will bring philosophers and philosophers of science together with scientists in fruitful collaboration on the expansion of human knowledge.

The present volume is one of the first ICUS products after the reform when the comprehensive double volumes of yearly ICUS proceedings were substituted for separate volumes on the results of the task forces. The ostensible purpose of the reform is to strengthen the impact of ICUS on the scientific community.

The authors, the discussants, and the editor join in expressing gratitude for the opportunity to prepare this volume under the sponsorship of ICUS.

NOTES

1. E.N. Lorenz presented his prize lecture in 1983.
2. For this information I am indebted to Professor J.J. McArdle, University of Virginia, Charlottesville.
3. Here, I am indebted to Professor John Horn, University of Southern California, Los Angeles.
4. Here, I am indebted to Professor Karl Jöreskog and Dr. Dag Sörbom.
5. ibid.

REFERENCES

Alfvén, H., and G. Arrhenius. 1976. *Evolution of the solar system.* Washington, D.C.: National Aeronautics and Space Administration.

Allen, R.G.D. 1957. *Mathematical economics.* London: Macmillan. 2d ed. 1963, New York: St. Martins.

Anderson, T.W. 1958. *An Introduction to multivariate statistical analysis.* New York: Wiley.

Basmann, R.L. 1957. *Econometrica* 25:27–83.

Bergström, R. 1974. *Studies in the estimation of interdependent systems: Especially the Fix–Point and Iterative Instrumental Variables Methods.* Uppsala University: Institute of Statistics.

Bergström, R., and H. Wold. 1983. *Fix-Point estimation in theory and practice.* Göttingen: Vandenhoeck & Ruprecht.

Carnap, R. 1925. *Der logische Aufbau der Welt.* Berlin.

Catell, R.B. 1971. *Abilities: Their structure, growth, and action.* Boston: Houghton Mifflin.

Cramér, H. 1945. *Mathematical methods of statistics.* Stockholm: Almqvist & Wiksell. 2d ed. 1946, Princeton, N.J.: University Press.

Dhrymes, Ph.J. 1970. *Econometrics: Statistical foundations and applications.* 2d ed. 1974, New York: Harper & Row.

Duncan, O.T. 1966. Path analysis: Sociological examples. *American Journal of Sociology* 72:1-16.

Fisher, R.A. 1935. *The design of experiments.* 6th ed. 1953, Edinburg: Oliver and Boyd.

Fornell, C. 1982. *A second generation of multivariate analysis, I–II.* New York: Praeger.

Fox, K.A. 1980. *Philosophics* 25:33–54.

Geisser, S. 1974. Contribution, p. 141f, to the written discussion of M. Stone 1974.

Guilford, J.P. 1956. The Structure of intellect. Psychological Bulletin 53: 276-293.

Guttman, L. 1941. An outline of the statistical theory of prediction. In *Social Science Research Council, Bulletin* No. 48, 253–311. New York: Social Science Research Council.

Haavelmo, T. 1943. *Econometrica* 11:1–12.

Hauser, R.M. 1966. *Family, school and neighborhood factors in educational performances in a metropolitan school system.* Ph.D diss., University of Michigan, Ann Arbor.

Hempel, C.G. 1952. *Fundamentals of concept formation in empirical science.* 10th ed. 1969, Chicago: University Press.

Horn, J. 1988. Thinking about home abilities.

Horn, J. 1988. Models for intelligence in Lynn: Intelligence theory and public policy.

The essential tension: Selected studies in scientific tradition and change. Chicago, Ill.: Univ. of Chicago.

Hotelling, H. 1936. *Biometrika* 28:321–377.

ICUS 13, 1984, The J.W. Marriott Hotel, Washington, D.C., September 2–5. Pre-ICUS, 1985, Paris, April 7–8.

Jöreskog, K.G. 1970. *Psychometrika* 36:408–426.

Kruskal, J.B. 1964. *Psychometrika* 29:1–27.

Kuhn, T.S. 1972. *The Structure of scientific revolutions.* Paperback. ed. 1964, Chicago: University Press.

Kuhn, T.S. 1977.

Loesch, M. 1984. *Fixpunkt-Schätzverfahren für Modelle mit rationalen Erwartungen.* Köningstein/Ts.: Athenäum.

Lorenz, E.N. 1984. Crawford Prize Lecture, 1983. *Tellus* 36A:98–110.

Lyttkens, E. 1953. *Journal of the Royal Statistical Society* A 136:353–394.

May, S. 1981. In *The fix-point approach to interdependent systems,* ed. H. Wold, 303–318. Amsterdam: North-Holland.

Medawar, R.B. 1979. *Advice to a young scientist.* New York: Harper & Row.

Meissner, W., and H. Wold. 1974. The foundations of science on cognitive mini-models, with application to the German methodenstreit and the advent of econometrics. In *Developments in the methodology of social science*, vol. 6, eds. Leinfellner and Köhler, 111–146. Doordrecht: Reidel Publ.

Mensch, G., K. Kaasch, and H. Wold. 1986. Transfers between industrial branches in the course of a Schumpeter-Mensch long wave. In *Proceedings of IIASA Conference 1–14 June 1985 at Weimar, DDR*. Berlin: Springer.

Miller, R.G. 1974. The jackknife - a review. *Biometrika* 61:1–15.

Muth, J.R. 1961. *Econometrica* 29:315–335.

Pavlopolous, P. 1966. *A statistical model for the Greek economy 1949–59*. Amsterdam: North-Holland.

Popper, K. 1962. *Conjectures and refutations: The construction of scientific knowledge.* 4th ed. 1972. New York: Harper & Row.

Romański, J., and W. Welfe. 1980. Paper at the Fourth World Congress of Econometric Society. France: Aix-en-Provence.

Stone, M. 1974. *Journal of the Royal Statistical Society* B 36:111–147, with discussion.

Theil, H. 1953. Mimeo paper. The Hague: Central Planning Bureau.

Thurstone, L.L. 1947. *Multiple-factor analysis: A development and expansion of the vectors of mind*. Chicago: University Press.

Tinbergen J. 1939. Statistical testing of business cycle theories. II. *Business cycles in the United States of America 1919–32*. Geneva: League of Nations.

Tukey, J.W. 1958. *Annals of Mathematical Statistics* 29:614.

Wold, H. 1986. Factors influencing the Outcome of Economic sanctions. Sixto Rios Honorary Volume, ed. P.Ibarrda,325-338, Madrid Conejo Superior de Investigacienes Cientificas.

Wold, H. 1985. Systems analysis by Partial Least Squares. In *Measuring the unmeasurable*, eds., Nijkamp et al., 221–251. Doordrecht: M. Nijhoff.

Wold, H. 1983. Comments on four papers integrated with a briefing of PLS (Partial Least Squares) soft modeling. In *Applied time series analysis of economic data*, ed. A. Zellner, 363–371. Washington D.C.: Bureau of the Census.

Wold, H. 1983. Utility analysis from the point of view of model-building. In *Foundations of utility and risk theory with applications*, eds. B.P. Stigum and F. Wenstøp, 87–93. Doordrecht: Reidel Publ.

Wold, H. 1982. Models for Knowledge. In *The making of statisticians*, ed. J. Gani, 190–212. New York, etc.: Springer.

Wold, H. 1982b. Soft modeling: The basic design and some extensions. In *Systems under indirect observation: Structure, prediction, causality*, Vol. 2, eds. K.G. Jöreskog and H. Wold, 1–54.

Wold, H. ed. 1981. *The Fix-Point approach to interdependent systems*. Amsterdam: North-Holland.

Wold, H. 1980. Earlier version of H. Wold, 1986. Paper presented at the Fourth

World Congress of Econometric Society. France: Aix-en-Provence.

Wold, H. 1980. Model construction and evaluation when theoretical knowledge is scarce: Theory and application of Partial Least Squares. In *Evaluation of Econometric Models*, eds. J. Kmenta and J.B. Ramsey, 47–74. New York: Academic Press.

Wold, H. 1980. Soft modeling: Intermediate between traditional model-building and data analysis. Warsaw: Banach Center Publications 6:333–346.

Wold, H. 1978. First version of H. Wold, 1966 and 1977. Presented at the International Workshop for Conflict Resolution, June 19–24, 1978, University of Haifa.

Wold, H. 1977. On the transition from pattern recognition to model-building. In *Mathematical economics and game theory: Essays in honor of Oscar Morgenstern*, eds. R. Henn and O. Moeschlin, 536–549. Berlin: Springer.

Wold, H. ed. 1975. Group report: Modeling in complex situations with soft information. 8 chapters in paper at the Third World Congress of Econometric Society, Aug. 21-26 at Toronto. Also Research Report 75:4, Uppsala University, Institute of Statistics.

Wold, H. 1969. Nonexperimental statistical analysis from the general point of view of scientific method. *Bulletin of the International Statistical Institute* 42 (1): 391–424.

Wold, H. 1966. Nonlinear estimation by iterative least squares procedures. In *Research papers in statistics: Festschrift for J. Neyman*, ed. F.N. David, 411–444. New York: Wiley.

Wold, H. 1965. A fix-point theorem with econometric background, I-II. *Arkiv för Matematik* 6:209–240.

Wold, H. 1963. On the consistency of least-squares regression. *Sankhyā A* 25:211–215.

Wold, H. 1961. Unbiased predictors. In *Proceedings of the Fourth Berkeley Symposium on Mathematical Statistics and Probability*, Vol. 1, ed. J. Neyman, 719–761. Berkeley: University of California Press.

Wold, H. 1959. Ends and means in econometric model-building. Basic considerations reviewed. In *Probability and Statistics. The Harald Cramér Volume*, ed. U. Grenander, 355–434. Stockholm: Almqvist & Wiksell. 2nd ed. 1960, New York: Wiley.

Wold, H. 1938. *A study in the analysis of stationary time series*. Stockholm: Almqvist & Wiksell.

Wold, S. 1977. Cross-validatory estimation of the number of components in factor and principal components models. *Technometrics* 20:397–405.

Wright, S. 1918. *Genetics* 3:367–374.

Zadeh, L.A. et al. 1975. *Fuzzy sets and their application to cognitive and decision processes*. New York: Academic Press.

Theoretical Empiricism

1

Basic Principles of Model Building: Specification, Estimation, Evaluation

JAN-BERND LOHMÖLLER

SUMMARY

Scientific knowledge of reality comes in form of models. Wold's conception of scientific knowledge introduces a clear separation of the theoretical (T) and empirical (E) content of the model, within a frame of reference which helps to keep T and E apart. The important class of causal models is discussed, with emphasis on the question of whether latent variables can be causes.

Model building is outlined as a procedure with the three steps: specification, estimation, and evaluation. With respect to specification, it is stressed that before any theoretical formulation, the phenomena under exploration and explication (i.e., the data) have to be defined carefully. It is shown that the distinction between applied and general science corresponds to the distinction between cases and replications as observational units, and in particular to the distinction between principal components and factor models.

It is argued that the assumption leading to the estimation of the model parameters should not be relaxed in order to facilitate the evaluation of the model. Four distribution-free, robust evaluation methods are presented, and some recent developments in predictive testing with latent variables are presented.

1

I. WOLD'S MODEL FOR KNOWLEDGE

Scientific knowledge, as distinguished from everyday knowledge, is characterized by the clear distinction between theoretical and empirical aspects.

Because the distinction between the two cannot be part of the theoretical or the empirical, the frame of reference has to be introduced as a third element of the model for scientific knowledge. The frame of reference, formulated (more or less) in everyday language, contains a mixture of theoretical ("T") and empirical ("E") components, and is shown as a rectangle in the small graph that is taken from Wold (1969):

$$T \Leftrightarrow E$$

Within the frame of reference, T and E are kept apart in order to prove that they match. Matching (denoted by the double-headed arrow) means that conclusions can be drawn from T about E (deduction) and from E about T (induction). The process of matching E and T is the model validation and can be understood as a general description of the job of science (Cronbach & Meehl 1955, Wold 1969, Bentler 1978). Matching E and T may involve a reduction of the range of observations E explained by the theory, which is adverse to the basic esthetical qualities of theories: a theory should be as simple, elegant, consistent and general as possible.

1.1. Levels of theory and data

The process of matching becomes more transparent and controllable when the rigid distinction between E, T, and the frame of reference is relaxed in favor of more levels. Five levels, T1, T2, E3, E2, E1, may be distinguished, with a matching process between each pair of neighboring levels, as shown in Table 1. Each level has its own language, with its own primitive elements, syntax and semantics.

T1 is the level of substantive theory. The elements of the theory are concepts (constructs). The syntax, which determines which elements are put together to form a correct statement, is the syntax of a natural language like German or English. The semantics of a statement is determined within the frame of reference of the whole model, in which the concepts are also defined and limited to a meaning which may be different from everyday meaning. What is depicted in the upper part of Table 1–1 is the theoretical statement that the socioeconomic status (SES) of the parents has a direct influence on the intellectual abilities (IQ) of the children, as well as an indirect influence which is mediated by the learning environment at home.

Table 1–1.

Matching between different levels of theoretical and empirical knowledge.

	Diagram	Level	Elements	Statements
T1	SES ⟶ IQ / Environment	substantive theory	concepts, hypotheses	causal, functional, correlational
T2	ξ ⟶ ζ / η	mathematical model	random variables	functional, correlational
E3	X, Y, Z	aggregated data	compound variables, (numbers)	correlational (functional)
E2	x1 x2 x3 y1 y2 z1 z2	data	numbers	correlational
E1		observations	observational units	verbal

T2 is the level of a mathematical-statistical model. The elements are random variables, here denoted by ξ, η, ζ. The syntax is the algebra of expectations and linear algebra. The meaning of model T2 is given by the correspondence to the substantive theory T1. When limited to path models with latent variables, the elements can be inner and outer variables, inner and outer residuals, and the syntax determines how to formulate correct equations.

E1 is the level of observations. The elements are observational units like individuals, or countries, or points in time. The statements on this level are natural-language statements about the characteristics and attributes of the units. E2 is the level of data. The elements are real numbers. The mapping of attributes onto numbers is called measurement. E3 is the level of functions of the data. The elements are real numbers, again, but they are formed as functions of the numbered data. This can include compound variables, or estimation functions for parameters.

The five levels (the number five has some arbitrariness) form a chain, and each member has to link up with and to adjust to its neighbor. The mathematical model T2 must represent as completely as possible the substantive theory T1. The statistical function on the level E3 must be determined from the data on E2 so as to best estimate the model variables on T2. The data E2 must be gathered from the level E1 so as to be informative for a comprehensive estimation (on E3) of the latent variables (on T2) which stand for the constructs (on level T1).

Residuals. The matching of E and T is never perfect, and there remain unexplained parts on both sides. The deductive specialization of Equation 1–1 shows the empirical content to be partly a function of the theoretical content and partly unexplainable by the theory. The formal notation is:

(1–2a) $E = E(T) + \varepsilon$,

and, in plain words:

(1–2b) data = systematic part + residual part

(1–2c) data = fit + rest

The systematic part of Equation 1–2 is often called the model, in a narrower sense. The residual ε may be interpreted as measurement error, prediction error, sample fluctuation, or "systematic" variation which is left out from the systematic part because it related only to small and specific parts of the observation (unique variation, specification error).

The inductive specialization of Equation 1–1 shows the theoretical content to be partly a function of the observation and partly unobserved:

(1–3) $T = T(E) + \delta$

The residual δ may be interpreted to be the theoretical supplement or the empirical deficiency of the model. If, for example, T is the theoretical concept of intelligence, and E is an intelligence test, then $T(E)$ is the IQ and δ is that which the test fails to measure, which can be understood as the lack of validity of the test.

In the process of model building the researcher tries to minimize ε and δ, to extend E, and to simplify T.

The notion of the model has different meanings for different scientists. Some scientists use a concept of the model identical to what is here called T, or E(T); some call the right-hand side of Equation 1–2 the model, which is then contrasted with the data; some call Equation 1–2 together with Equation 1–3 the model. Wold's notion of the model goes beyond this, in that he includes the frame of reference in the notion of a model.

1.2. Causality and latent variables

Time, space, and causality are the basic categories of our understanding of the world. The development of science in the past centuries has not undercut the use of the concepts of time, space and causality in everyday language, and even scientists use these concepts. Geographers use a continuous and three-dimensional concept of space, even if physicists talk of bent space. Historians would not change their notion of time if theoretical physicists told them that time runs unsteadily, jerkily, or even backwards. Empirical observations have led physicists to extend the concepts of time and space.

CAUSALITY

The notion of causality has a different history. Assaults on the concept of causality came from philosophical considerations, not from empirical findings, and it came in the form of an anathema and a prohibition sign. Basically, the rejection of the concept of causality (Hume, Russell) can be seen as a delayed consequence of William of Occam's principle of parsimony: *Pluralitas non est ponenda sine necessicate.* Taking the philosophical objections into consideration, the usage of causal notion was reestablished in the fifties by Lazarsfeld, Wold and Simon (Bernert, 1983); it was mainly for practical reasons that they introduced causal terminology. The theoretical content of a relation $X=f(Y)$ does not become better or richer or more powerful if a causal interpretation is added; the difference lies in the practical implications. Whether the notion of cause-effect relationships can be applied to the relation of latent (LVs) and manifest variables (MVs), will be considered in this chapter.

Cause and effect are two different things. No thing can be the cause of itself. When I "compel myself" to write a paper, I have introduced the distinction between my willing mind and my weak flesh, two different things. Whether mind and body really are different entities in an ontological sense, is a question left to philosophers.

By having more than just the two levels of latent and manifest variables, the problems to be addressed in this chapter become more clear. A model with several hierarchical levels of LVs is presented by Noonan (this volume). He distinguishes two types of relationships between LVs, the hierarchical and the causal-predictive relationships. Are the hierarchical relations causal or not? Are the variables involved in a hierarchical relationship "different things", i.e., "things" at all?

Theoretical Constructs Versus Intervening Variables.

Variables, whether latent or manifest, are creatures of the human mind, constructions which are found helpful in ordering the chaos of sensory impressions. Some of these constructions, which are called intervening (or supplementary) variables, are merely mathematical constructions and can be removed from a model without loss of predictive power. Others cannot be removed in this sense, and these variables are called theoretical constructs (Maccorquodale and Meehl, 1948; Falter, 1977; Falter and Lohmöller,1982). As an example, consider a canonical correlation model for ten manifest predictors x and ten manifest predictands y, which are transformed into a ten-dimensional latent predictor ξ and a ten-dimensional latent predictand η. For the sake of argument, assume that in the sequence of ten decreasing canonical correlations, the first two are of remarkable size, and the other eight correlations are negligible. Then the eight last dimensions of ξ and η can be retained to ease the algebraic treatment of the model, but they can also be removed without loss of predictive power. The first two dimensions, however, cannot be removed, and these two dimensions are empirical constructs, or even theoretical constructs if they can be interpreted and named in the framework of a substantive theory. Latent variables, which, according to this criterion, are not theoretical constructs, are not different from their indicators in the sense that they are "different things", hence they cannot enter a cause-effect relationship between LVs and MVs.

Dispositional Terms

The researcher has to decide which one is the "real thing," the MV or the LV, or, the LV in which level of a hierarchy. In the social sciences the latent variables often denote dispositions. Examples for dispositions of individuals are intelligence, extroversion, party identification, anomia. The manifest behavior can then be understood as being caused—*inter alia*—by the disposition; e.g., solving a cognitive task requires intelligence, addressing unknown people requires some sort of extroversion, etc. In case the LVs are theoretical constructs as well as dispositional terms it seems appropriate to apply the realistic (not ontological) interpretation to the LVs and to understand the LVs as causes of the MVs, the MVs being "reflections" of the LVs.

There is no question that if the LVs can be understood as causes of the MVs, they can also be understood as causes of each other, and a causal interpretation can then be applied to the inner part of an LV path model. This, however, becomes more difficult if an LV is not a theoretical construct, but merely an intervening variable, a transformation or collection of MVs, a basket full of candidates for a cause-effect relationship or a mixed bag of MVs with suspected explanatory power. Note that typically this is so when the indicators are understood to be "formative" and PLS mode B weight estimation is advised (Noonan, Fornell in this volume).

2. STEPS IN MODEL BUILDING

Model building can be described as a three-step procedure, consisting of (i) model specification, (ii) estimation of unknowns, and (iii) model evaluation.

MODEL SPECIFICATION

Model specification includes at least two decisions, the first about the empirical phenomena to be explained, and the second about the theoretical form of the explanation. The specification of the theoretical content of the model may be more or less rigorous. We will focus on models which require a statistical treatment, i.e., which on the one hand are sufficiently specified so that a formal treatment is possible, but on the other hand are non-deterministic. The elements of a model of this type may in the theoretical part include manifest and latent variables, which are specified with respect to either the total distribution, or only the conditional expectations.

MODEL ESTIMATION

Model estimation may require additional assumptions which have no counterpart in the first, substantive-oriented level of the theoretical model part. Estimation methods like least squares and maximum likelihood can be characterized in terms of availability, precision and robustness of the resulting estimates.

MODEL EVALUATION

Model evaluation, in its classical form, requires a sample of independent observations on a completely specified distribution. The evaluation may involve the model as a whole, or single parameters (by means of standard errors). In Section 3 less demanding evaluation methods will be discussed.

2.1 Specification of the data

OBSERVATIONAL UNITS

The phenomena to be explained by the model can be the data as observed, say, x_{kn} for k=1 to K attributes of n=1 to N observational units, or an aggregation of the data, say, the covariances s_{kl}, k,l=1 to K. This choice involves a decision about the character of the observational units: If the observational units are considered to be genuinely different, with interpretable individual differences, like the children in a classroom (one child is known to be the *primus* and the other the clown) and the years in an economic time series (one year is known to be the oil crisis and the other the "1968 cultural revolution"), then the observational units must be specified to be part of the phenomenon under exploration. If, however, the observational units are considered to be replications of one and the same experiment, without any individual differences, all being identically distributed, like the repeated throws of a die or the different fish in a shoal, then one can sum over the observational units without losing any information of substantive interest.

CASES VERSUS REPLICATIONS

In the first type of data, the observational units are called cases; they are specified by the model builder, and the model must provide certain unknowns, or incidental parameters, or "factor scores," accounting for the individual differences. In the second type the units are mere replications, anonymous sample points, unspecified. The distinction between "cases" and "replications" introduced in this way points, of course, to the extremes of a series with several intermediate steps of more or less specified, more or less randomly chosen observational units.

INDIVIDUAL VERSUS POPULATION INFERENCE

The distinction between cases and replications corresponds to two types of inference, which are called here individual (specific, applied) and populational (general, aggregate), and which can lead to a distinction between two types of science, applied and general science. A problem of general psychology, for example, is the dependence of school success on intelligence, which is stated with respect to a specified population and not to a specific individual. The corresponding problem of applied psychology is the prediction of school success of the *primus* and the classroom clown when their IQs are known to be 120 and 100 respectively. The individual psychology problem presumes that—on the level of general psychology, valid for a specified population—it has been established that a relation between intelligence and school success exists. Hence, the individual psychology problem includes as a subproblem the general psychology problem, and not the other way around; the applied science includes general science.

EXAMPLE. In order to demonstrate the implications of the distinction between cases and replications, and between individual and population inference, the statistical methods of principal component analysis and factor analysis will serve as examples. The not-completely-specified form of the linear model which is common to both methods is:

$$(2\text{--}1) \quad x_k = \Sigma_j \pi_{jk} \xi_j + \varepsilon_k, \qquad j=1 \text{ to } J, \ k=1 \text{ to } K$$

where the ξ_j denote latent variables, the ε_k residual variables, and the coefficients π_{jk} are the so-called loadings. Further specifications on the first and second moments of the right-hand variables in Equation 2–1 lead to the common factor model. The index n for observational units does not occur in Equation 2–1, demonstrating that it represents a general, a populational, but not an individual, specific, applied model. The model Equation 2–1 is re-stated on the individual level:

$$(2\text{--}2) \quad x_{kn} = \Sigma_j \pi_{jk} \xi_{jn} + \varepsilon_{kn} \qquad n=1 \text{ to } N.$$

Now there are two sorts of unknowns on the right-hand side of Equation 2–2: the parameters π_{jk}, which, as before, account for the structural relations among the latent variables, and the unknowns, which carry the index n, the LV scores ξ_{kn} and the residual scores ε_{kn}. Knowing only the distribution and the moments of these variables, instead of the scores, one would be unable to reconstruct the observed values x_{kn}.

The comparison of Equation 2–1 with Equation 2–2 demonstrates that prior to the specification of the model comes the specification of the data, the left-hand side of both equations. Indices which happen to appear on the data-side of the equation also have to show up on the right-hand side, the model side. If the observational units are considered to be more than replications, the researcher has to specify them by including the index n on the left-hand side, and consequently he has to put up a systematic model part on the right-hand side which also includes the case index.

The problem of specifying the data becomes more complex—and perhaps even more clear—when there are three sets of indices, e.g., for units, time points, and attributes. Then two of the sets of indices may be considered to be specified and known, and one set to be random and unspecified. For more details see Section 4.

3. MODEL EVALUATION

Model evaluation should make use of no more than what has been assumed when specifying the model and the data. The most critical assumption that leads to a parting of the ways is related to the distribution of the variables. If the distribution has been fully specified, maximum likelihood estimates of the model parameters can be obtained, and likelihood ratio tests can be performed, at least for some simple models. If no distributional assumptions are made for the estimation of the model, introducing these for the model evaluation is like a rope trick. From an array of distribution-free methods we name blindfolding, bootstrapping, jackknifing and perturbation. The methods are different with respect to their assumptions and their sensibility. Assumptions which may or may not be adopted are independence of observations, identical but unspecified distributions, and known zero points in the scales of variables.

3.1 Distribution-free evaluation methods

PERTURBATION

Suppose a set of parameters P has been estimated from a data set X, and the aim is to explore to what degree small changes in X influence the consequent changes in P. Let $s(X)$ and $s(P)$ denote the Euclidean lengths, $s(X) = \sqrt{\Sigma_i x_i^2}$. A new "perturbated" data set x* is created by adding a random error, $x_i^* = x_i + \alpha e_i$, where α is a small number (say one percent), and $e_i \sim N(0, s(X))$. The new data set has the variation $s(X^*) = (1+\alpha)s(X)$. Then a new set of parameters P* is estimated from X*. If the ratio $s(P-P^*)/s(P)$ is close to α, this is an indication of stable results. Belsley (1984) reports a small artificial data set where a 1 percent change in the data produced a 40 percent change in the parameters, clearly a demonstration of unreliable results. As Belsley points out, the critical assumption is whether the data are treated as raw values or as deviations from their means. If the means are removed, results become smooth. For further examples concerning the importance of the mean see, Table 1.2.

BOOTSTRAPPING

Bootstrapping implies the assumption that the residuals are independent. If they are independent, they can be exchanged without disturbing the estimates. Let a time series y_t, t = 1950...1980 be given, and the model $y_t = \beta y_{t-1} + \varepsilon_t$. Now a new time series x_t^* is created: by exchanging residuals, e.g., $y_{1961}^* = by_{1960} + e_{1971}$ and $y_{1971}^* = by_{1970} + e_{1961}$, or by a random exchange of residuals. Then the model is reestimated on the new time series y_t^* giving a new estimate b^* and new residuals e_t^*. The redistribution of residuals and reestimation of the model is continued until a stable estimate of β is established. Clearly, the bootstrapping method requires the assumption of independence of residuals.

BLINDFOLDING

Blindfolding means omitting one part of the data matrix while estimating the parameters from the remaining data, and then reconstructing the omitted part by the estimated parameters. The procedure of omitting and reconstructing is repeated, until each data point is omitted and reconstructed once. The blindfolding technique provides two types of results, (a) the generalized cross-validation criterion for evaluation of the model as a whole, and (b) the jackknife standard errors for individual parameter estimates. Both types of results are helpful in deciding on the quality and relevance of a model. The blindfolding technique requires neither distributional assumptions nor independence, so it fits the PLS technique "hand-in-glove" (Wold 1981, Wold and Apel 1982).

THE JACKKNIFE TECHNIQUE

The jackknife technique was developed in order to construct the distribution of parameter estimates without assumptions about the distribution of the variables involved (Quenouille, Tukey). This is done by estimating the parameters N times in a data set with N observations, each time omitting just one observation. Assuming independent observations, the N estimates for the same parameter are then used to compute the mean, the standard deviation, and other distributional characteristics of the parameters.

THE GENERALIZED CROSS-VALIDATION

The generalized cross-validation criterion indicates how well the observed values can be reconstructed by the model and its parameters. Standard cross-validation uses one data set to estimate the parameters, and another data set to test the validity of the estimates. For example, regression coefficients and R_1^2 are estimated in the first data set; then the regression coefficients are applied to the second data set, and the squared correlation R_2^2 (y; ŷ) is computed, and usually the shrinkage phenomenon $R_2^2 < R_1^2$ is observed (see Stone, 1974; and, for a counterexample, Winteler, 1983). In generalized cross-validation, however, the blindfolding technique is used to split the data set at hand repeatedly into an estimation set and a test set which may contain a single data point only.

PRE – THE PROPORTIONAL REDUCTION OF ERROR

PRE - The proportional reduction of error is the basis for a general principle for constructing measures of predictive power (Guttman, 1941; Goodman and Kruskal 1954). This principle implies the comparison of errors made under two prediction rules. The RuleOne prediction (often called the trivial prediction) is based on the distribution of the predictand y alone, without any knowledge of the predictors x. The RuleOne prediction for continuous variables is, for example, the mean ȳ or the jackknifed mean $\bar{y}_{(-i)}$. The RuleTwo prediction is based on the joint distribution of x and y. The definition of the error depends on the scale quality of the variables. If y is a categorical variable, the error is simply the number of misclassifications. If y is continuous, the summed squares of the differences between observed and predicted values is an appropriate error measure, $\Sigma_n (y_n - \hat{y}_n)^2$. The standard formula for PRE measures is:

(3–1) PRE = 1 – (RuleTwo error) / (RuleOne error)

For the (descriptive) multiple regression model, the RuleOne prediction is the mean of y, and the RuleOne error is the variance of y; the RuleTwo prediction is ŷ, and the RuleTwo error is the variance of the residual variable e; the PRE measure is identical to the squared multiple correlation.

(3–2) PRE = 1 $s_e^2/s_y^2 = (s_y^2 - s_e^2)/s_y^2 = \text{var}(\hat{y})/\text{var}(y) = R^2$

THE SG TEST

If both prediction rules involve the blindfolding device, the PRE measures belong to the realm of methods proposed by Stone (1974) and Geisser (1974). To rephrase the title of Stone's article: Cross-validatory (= using blindfolding) choice (= estimation) and assessment (= testing) of statistical predictions. (The content of the article itself justifies why Professor Stone has chosen this title, and why he does not agree with my free rephrasing.) Stone proposes to use the deletion procedure for both the estimation of the unknowns of a model and the test of the predictive validity of that model. Geisser applies his "Predictive Sample Re-use Method" only for the estimation, and does it by deleting more than one case at a time.

If 0<PRE<1 the model has predictive relevance. The relevance is then a matter of degree, and the door is left open for improvement of the model. If with RuleTwo all of the errors made under RuleOne can be eliminated, then PRE = 1, and the prediction rule (prediction model) is exactly valid. PRE = 0 indicates that RuleTwo has no relevance for the data at hand and that RuleTwo is no improvement over RuleOne. If PRE is negative, the non-blindfolded parts of the data matrix are misleading when guessing the blindfolded parts, and then, in general, RuleTwo is misleading for the prediction of the data. This can happen when the model is unrealistic, or when the parameter estimates for RuleTwo are unstable or when the data set is not homogeneous (i.e., influenced by outliers) with respect to the hypothesized model.

3.2 Predictive testing

The blindfolding device can be designed in very different ways and can be used for different sorts of inference. This will be demonstrated—omitting technical fine points which will be reported elsewhere—on a very common model, a multiple regression model. The predictors are at the beginning considered to be directly observed, and later as weighted aggregates (estimated LVs) of observed variables (MVs). Three aspects of prediction will be distinguished here—description, forecasting, and generalization—and corresponding PRE measures will be presented. The three models generate RuleTwo predictions, and the respective residual sums of squares will be called DRESS, FRESS and GRESS. Two different RuleOne residual sums of squares will be considered, called RESS0 and RESS1. Then FRESS, GRESS and RESS1 are based on different designs of blindfolding, whereas DRESS and RESS0 are the usual OLS residuals such that R^2 = 1-DRESS/RESS0.

THE MULTIPLE REGRESSION MODEL

The multiple regression model to be investigated relates the predictor values $\mathbf{X}$ = $[x_{jn}]$ (j=1...J predictor variables, n=1...N cases) to the predictand values $\mathbf{y}$ = $[y_n]$, in symbols:

(3–3) $y_n.= \Sigma_j\beta_j x_{jn}+\epsilon_n$, $\mathbf{y} = \mathbf{bX}+\epsilon$,

where ϵ = $[\epsilon_n]$ is the residual variable and β = $[\beta_j]$ is the vector of regression coefficients. If the variables are not centered to zero mean, the first variable has to be taken as unity, x_{1n} = 1 for all n, and consequently β will be the regression constant. The well-known LS estimator for the regression coefficients is $\hat{\beta} \equiv \mathbf{b}$ = $\mathbf{m}_{yx}\mathbf{M}_{xx}^{-1}$, where $\mathbf{m}_{yx}$ = $(\mathbf{yX'})/N$ and $\mathbf{M}_{xx}$ = $(\mathbf{XX'})/N$.

The different designs of the blindfolding vary along the dimensions "Which model parameters and which data points do we take as known, and what must be reestimated for each blindfolding sample?" With respect to the data points which are blindfolded or not blindfolded we distinguish three cases:

(D) Description: Nothing is blindfolded.
(F) Forecasting: The predictand value y_i is blindfolded.
(G) Generalization: Both x_{ji} and y_i are blindfolded.

What is called generalization here, amounts, in fact, to Allen's PRESS, $\underline{P}$rediction $\underline{RE}$siduals $\underline{S}$um of $\underline{S}$quares. However, prediction is understood here to be a broader concept, covering description (or reconstruction), forecasting and generalization, with manifest or latent variables. Crossvalidated prediction is a narrower concept, covering forecasting and generalization. As the forecasting approach is an innovative application of generalized crossvalidation, the terms D, F and G are newly coined and chosen so as to reflect the typical (not the only) interpretation of the prediction approach.

With respect to the model parameters and the moments of the variables we distinguish the following cases:

(P0) Only the regression parameters are unknown.
(P1) The mean $\bar{y}$ is known.
(P2) The means $\bar{x}_j$ are known.
(P3) The weights for forming the predictor LVs are known.

Taking a parameter as known means, technically, to estimate it in a premodeling phase, and to use the remaining information for the modeling and model testing.

Whether a case is omitted totally or only partly from the data matrix depends on the intended conclusions. We shall consider the description, the forecasting, and the generalization approaches. With respect to Figure 1-1, in forecasting only the double-shaded data point y_i is blindfolded, whereas in the generalization approach all shaded data points x_{ji} and y_i are omitted. (Index i indicates the blindfolded case; index n runs over the non-blindfolded cases.)

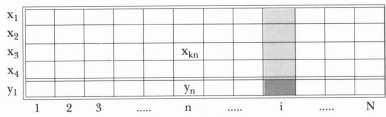

Figure 1-1. Blindfolding for a multiple regression model

RESS0 AND RESS1—TRIVIAL PREDICTION RESIDUAL.

As RuleOne error terms, two residual sums of squares will be defined. RESS0 is the residual sum of squares when the mean $\bar{y}$ of y is taken as a prediction of y_i. The residual is:

$$(3\text{-}4) \qquad e_i = y_i - \bar{y}, \qquad i = 1 \text{ to N},$$

and the residual sum of squares, called RESS0, is identical to the variance of y:

$$(3\text{-}5) \qquad RESS0 = \frac{1}{N} \Sigma_i e_i^2 .$$

RESS1 is the residual sum of squares when the mean $\bar{y}_{\text{-}i}$ of y is taken as prediction of y_i, but when this mean is computed, y_i is omitted. It can be demonstrated that

$$(3\text{-}6) \qquad e_{J,i} = y_i - \frac{N}{N\text{-}1}\, \bar{y} ,$$

and that RESS0 and RESS1 are related by

$$(3\text{-}7) \qquad RESS1 = (\frac{N}{N\text{-}1})^2\, RESS0 .$$

Hence RESS0<RESS1. Note that RESS0 requires a pre-modeling assumption, namely P1, and this pays off in a smaller error term.

DRESS—DESCRIPTION RESIDUAL

The descriptive regression model makes use of the total data sample (**X,y**) when estimating the parameters. The residuals are denoted by e_D; the residual sum of squares associated with this model is:

$$(3\text{-}8) \qquad DRESS = \frac{1}{N} \Sigma_i e_{D,i}^2 ,$$

where for Equations 3–8, 3–9 and 3–11, $e_i = y_i - \hat{y}_i$, and where the prediction $\hat{y}_i$ takes a different form, depending on the model.

FRESS—FORECASTING RESIDUAL

In the forecasting approach it is assumed that N-1 cases are known completely, and that for the remaining case, say the ith, only the predictor values are known, but not the predictand value. In order to make the most efficient use of the information at hand when estimating the regression parameters, $\mathbf{b'} = \mathbf{m'}_{yx}\, \mathbf{M}_{xx}^{-1}$, the inverse of $\mathbf{M}_{xx} = (\mathbf{XX'})/N$ is based on the total sample; on the other hand the predictor-predictand relation can be based only on N-1 cases, $\mathbf{m}_{yx,\text{-}i}$, where the subscript-i indicates that the ith case is omitted. When the actual value of y_i becomes known, the residuals $e_{F,i}$ are calculated. Note that the value y_i was not used when the parameters $b_{\text{-}i}$ were estimated and the prediction $\hat{y}_{F,i}$ was derived. The real-world forecasting situation can be simulated N times, by blindfolding each value y_i once and estimating the parameters and the prediction. The residual sum of squares is:

(3-9) $FRESS = \dfrac{1}{N} \Sigma_i e_{F,i}^2 .$

GRESS—GENERALIZATION RESIDUAL

In the generalization approach it is stipulated that N-1 cases are known and the estimates are to be generalized on an Nth case. In order to test this stipulation, each case is omitted once from the data, and both the predictor and the predictand values are blindfolded. With case i blindfolded, the regression parameters are estimated by $b'_{G,i} = m'_{-i} M_{-i}^{-1}$. It can be shown that the DRESS-residuals and the GRESS-residuals are related by

(3-10) $e_{G,i} = (1/(1-q_i)) \, e_{D,i} ,$

where q_i is the normed Mahalanobis distance (also called the leverage value), a function of the predictor values of i. The residual sum of squares for the generalization approach is:

(3-11) $GRESS = \Sigma_i e_{G,-i}^2 .$

PRE-COEFFICIENTS

Five PRE-coefficients $\dfrac{1}{N}$ based on the error sums defined above, are defined as follows:

(3–12) $Q_{D0}^2 = 1 - DRESS/RESS0 \; (= R^2)$
             $Q_{F0}^2 = 1 - FRESS/RESS0$
             $Q_{G0}^2 = 1 - GRESS/RESS0$
             $Q_{F1}^2 = 1 - FRESS/RESS1$
             $Q_{G1}^2 = 1 - GRESS/RESS1$

The first coefficient Q_{D0}^2 is identical to the squared multiple correlation coefficient in case the variables are centered to zero mean. The ordering of the five coefficients is roughly according to the diminishing information used for their estimation, and hence according to the expected decreasing order of magnitude.

EXAMPLES

The behavior of Q^2 in three different data sets, with different model specifications, and with different blindfolding designs, is demonstrated in Table 1–2. The first data set (Table 2, row 10) is artificial, and analyzed by classical methods, the regression is significant. Here the data are analyzed under two models, first as raw data under a model with a location parameter (row 11), and then, centered to zero mean in a premodeling phase, under a model without a location parameter (row 12). If the average of y is considered as *a priori* known and exempted from estimation (row 12), then the model has predictive relevance, whereas the model of row 11 is not predictive. A close inspection of the data reveals that the all-cases results are strongly influenced by two single cases. If the tenth case is omitted, R^2 jumps from 0.77 to 0.99, and if the ninth case is omitted, the regression parameters change completely.

Table 1–2

How predictive validity Q2 is influenced by data, model, and blindfolding design

Data set, model, and testing design	D0	F0	G0	F1	G1
10 Gaensslen & Schubö (1973), N=10					
11 Raw data	.77	-.04	-.44	.16	-.16
12 Centered data, no regression constant	.77	.30	.41	.43	.53
20 Economic sanctions (Wold 1986), N=10					
21 Four MV predictors	.78	.07	-.70	.24	-.04
22 Two MV predictors	.66	.22	.30	.37	.44
Two LV predictors, all-cases weights:					
23 – no regression constant	.80	.51	.69	.61	.75
24 – with regression constant	.80	.38	.60	.50	.67
Two LV predictors, without-one weights:					
25 – no regression constant	-	-.40	-.41	.24	.23
26 – with regression constant	-	-.40	-.41	.23	.23
30 Forging force (Gerd Lohmöller), N=24					
31 Three predictors	.41	-.44	.26	-.32	.20

The second data set (row 20) is analyzed with four (in 21) and with two predictors (22). With two predictors the model is predictive, and with four it is not: R^2 increases with increasing numbers of predictors, but Q^2 drops in this case, because the additional parameters cannot be estimated reliably. In rows 11 and 21 the rank order of the five coefficients is as expected, G0 < F0 and G1 < F1, whereas the other models show lower validity measures for the forecasting than for the generalization approach. This is especially so for the third data set (row 31); although the generalization approach uses less information from the data than the forecasting approach, the prediction is better.

LV PREDICTORS

The two predictors of the successful model 22 in Table 2 are, in fact, sign-weighted sums of 27 observed predictors; so one can understand this model as one with 2 LV predictors and 27 MV predictors, where the weights w_k were chosen as either -1 or +1, depending on the sign of the correlation of x_j with y, and

$$(3–13) \qquad X_j = \Sigma_{kj} w_k x_{kj}, \qquad j=1,2.$$

(As always, X_j is no more than an estimate of a latent variable.) The weights were exempted from estimation and blindfolding. Now, in the next two steps on the way from a multiple regression to an LV path model, the weights are no longer treated as known.

ALL-CASES LV WEIGHTS

Following the PLS Mode A technique, the LV weights are taken to be proportional to the correlation of MV predictors x_k with predictand variable y,

$$(3–14) \qquad w_k \propto corr(x_k;y) ,$$

and the LVs are scaled to zero mean and unit variance. In this step, we use all cases for the estimation of the LV weights and the scaling of the LVs, and execute the blindfolding procedure only on the regression parameters. As the LVs have zero mean, the constant in the regression model must come out as zero, and can be omitted. However, even if the LVs are standardized over all N cases, they are not standardized in the blindfolded N-1 data set, and results are different for models with and without a regression constant—see Table 1-2, rows 23 and 24. As compared to the MV predictor model (row 22), R^2 is higher because the weights from Equation 3–14 are more predictive than the sign weights. The PRE measures for this model vary between 0.38 and 0.75, depending on the choice of forecasting or generalization approach, RESS0 or RESS1, constant included or not. But under all these variations the PRE is positive, indicating that the model has predictive validity.

WITHOUT-ONE LV WEIGHTS

Now the LV weights are also subject to blindfolding, and the correlation in Equation 3–14 is computed with one case omitted. As the predictor LVs change their values due to the different weights, there is no unique R^2, but N different R^2s, as indicated by a dash in Table 1–2. Also, the scaling of the LVs becomes ambiguous, and one has to decide whether the LVs are to be standardized over N or over N-1 cases, whether only the predictand, or the predictors as well, are to be rescaled, and whether the regression model should have a constant or not, which gives a total of 16 models. For all the variations of the data and the model, the PRE measures Q^2_{F1} and Q^2_{G1} vary from 0.08 to 0.36, and only the results for the two most reasonable models are reported in rows 25 and 26 of Table 1–2. As compared to the all-cases weights, there is a sharp drop in the PRE, but, nevertheless, it is positive, indicating that the additional 27 parameters (the weights) can in fact be estimated reliably from the data. Compared, however, to row 21, the two superfluous predictors do harm to the model, and the two additional regression parameters disturb the prediction more than the 27 weights do.

EXAMPLE: RESIDENTIAL MOBILITY

A novel and remarkable application of the SG test is reported by van Donkelaar and van der Knaap (1982) in a study on residential mobility in the city of Rotterdam. Their Figure 3, reproduced here as Figure-2a, displays the first indicator of residential mobility, the mobility ratio, as varying over the different city districts. In the central districts more than 20 percent of the households change their residence within a year, but in the suburbs less than 10 percent do.

The second indicator of mobility is duration of residence. Residential mobility is high where the percentages of old houses, of apartment houses, of non-private housing property and of unmarried, young, and non-Netherlands inhabitants are high. By these variables the residential mobility can be predicted well ($R^2 = 0.85$, $Q^2 = 0.69$), but the predictability is different for the different districts. To demonstrate this, the summation in Equations 3–5 and 3–9 is executed over the two indicators but not over the observational units. This gives a separate Q^2 for each district, which is displayed in Figure 1–2b. The validity of the prediction model is low "for the districts where much new construction has been realized and where city reconstruction takes place" (van Donkelaar & van der Knaap, 1982: 29).

VERHUISRATIO's PER WIJK IN 1978

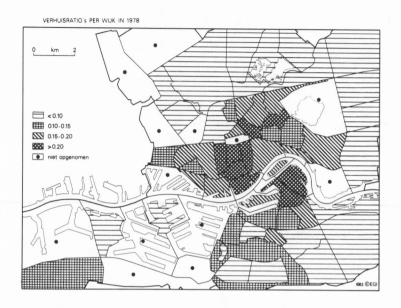

RESULTATEN VAN DE STONE-GEISSERTEST VOOR DE WIJKEN

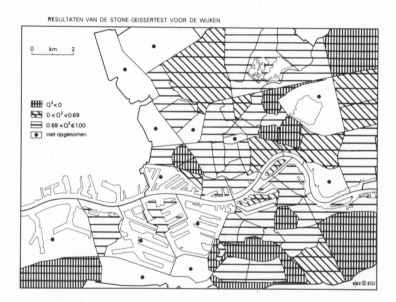

Figure 1–2. Residential mobility in Rotterdam.
    a) Mobility ratio in districts
    b) Validity of prediction model in districts

CONCLUSION

It has been demonstrated that the predictive testing by the blind-folding device is a flexible tool for the evaluation of the predictive models. The model to be tested is not presumed to be true, but to have predictive power. Consequently a negative test result does not imply that the model is wrong, but that the model is useless. Unlike perturbation analysis, the stability of the results is not tested by adding something to the data (it has to be specified what form and distribution the added error should have), but by omitting given data. For more technical and detailed information on predictive modeling with blindfolding, the reader is referred to Chapter 1, Sections 2 and 3, of this volume, and to Wold (1985).

The blindfolding device requires no assumption about independent observations. The assumption that the data set is homogenous with respect to the hypothesized model can turn out to be violated in two ways: The total data set comes from different subpopulations, or it contains outliers. Individual outliers can be detected by their individual Q^2 (see Figure 1–2b).

The blindfolding procedure is sensitive to scaling, in two respects: In very small data sets, it makes a difference whether the LVs are standardized over N or over N-1 cases. (In this respect, the three stages of the PLS Basic Design may need some refinement.) And it may well happen that the regression constant is the most volatile and susceptible parameter.

Obviously, the differences between DRESS, FRESS and GRESS, and between all-cases and without-one LV weights do not matter much in big samples, and as $N \to \infty$, they vanish asymptotically. However, the smaller the sample size, the more impact they have.

4. THREE-WAY DATA MODELS

Three-way data are ordered by three indices; for example, y_{ptr} may denote the election outcome of a party p at election time point t in a region r, and x_{gtr}, the number of employed, and of unemployed, workers at time t in region r. If theory is concerned only with the influence of unemployment categories (x_g) on voting outcome (y_p), time points or regions or both may be used as observational units, and we have a two-way ordering of observations. In this case, the indices p and g refer to "specified" (individualized—see Section 1.3) coordinates of the data array, and t and r refer to "unspecified" (populational) coordinates or replications.

It may, however, turn out that the time dimension taps a causal influ-

ence of its own (see Falter, in this volume). Then the time must be specified theoretically; the model considers the variables x_{gt} and y_{pt} with
regions as the only observational units, and we have a two-way ordering of
variables. As a general method for modeling variables ordered in two ways
and observed in one way (three-way or three-mode data), the three-mode
path analysis with latent variables can be used (Lohmöller and Wold 1980,
Lohmöller 1983).

5. SOME POINTS AND RESPONSES FROM THE DISCUSSION

Theoretical versus empirical knowledge

Professor Njock firmly expressed his view that "making a clear distinction between theoretical and empirical aspects is quite inadequate."
Other discussants doubted that the two-language model inherent in this
distinction is tenable. To rephrase my Section 1: Wold's model for knowledge, Equation 1–1, subscribes to both the two-language and the one language model. The frame of reference is cast in only one language, which
contains both sorts of terms—theoretical and empirical. The description
of a controlled experiment or of an observation belongs to the frame of
reference, and the description has to include the definition of what a theoretical concept is and what an empirical result is. Only with a frame of
reference is it possible to keep apart what is a theoretical concept and
what is an empirical result, i.e., what belongs to which one of the two languages.

Werner Heisenberg, in his endeavor to understand the philosophical implications of his physical theories ("Der Teil und das Ganze"),
points out that quantum mechanical experiments which are designed to
disprove classical, Newtonian mechanics inevitably have to be described
in terms of Newtonian mechanics: The frame of reference is Newtonian,
the theoretical content transcends, and the empirical result even invalidates the language of the frame of reference.

Mathematical model building

Professor Njock rightly states "that the Scientific method...is the
basis for the unity of the sciences, since such a unity can hardly be found
in the content." The very concept of a model, and a theory, however,
varies from one discipline to another. I am delighted to summarize his
outline on mathematics: Mathematical theory is the postulational form of

thinking. To establish a model (or discourse, or theory), one starts with a finite body of statements, without formal proof. These statements are the postulates or axioms, and all other statements of the discourse must be logically implied by them. Axiomatic theory is concerned with the problem of the consistency of the postulated set of axioms. Professor Njock's characterization fits completely into what is called level T2 in Figure 1-1. Mathematical model building can be seen as a very special case of model building as defined in Equation 1-1, as it has no empirical content.

Experimentum vs. empiria

Professor Njock characterizes the scientific method by: "Instead of relying on chance happenings of occasional experiences, one systematically invokes certain types of experiences. This conscious use of experience is experimentation." Judging from this statement, it is not clear to me whether he shares my view of the narrow concept of experimental and the broad concept of empirical knowledge. From the etymological roots of the concepts "experimental" and "empirical," there is no reason to assign different meanings to the words, as the Latin "experimentum" and the Greek "empiria" both mean experience. It is useful to distinguish the occasional experience from the systematically evoked, planned and controlled experience, briefly called experiment. What type of experience is available, and what sort of evidence it presents, depends on the different sciences and on the different hypotheses. The hypothesis that there exist no black swans cannot be proved by systematic, carefully planned and controlled scrutiny of all available swans, but an unplanned single encounter with a black swan disproves the hypothesis. If one admits only experience from controlled experiments as scientific experience, one rejects a compelling refutation of a well-formulated hypothesis.

The concept of scientific model building is intended to cover both forms of empirical knowledge: the controlled experiment on the one hand, and the carefully planned, rigorously executed, and accurately recorded observation of occasional, accidental events on the other hand.

REFERENCES

Allen, R.G.D. 1938. *Mathematical analysis for economists*. 2d ed. 1962. London: Macmillan.

Apel, H., and H. Wold. 1982. Soft modeling with latent variables in two or more dimensions: PLS estimation and testing for predictive relevance. In *Systems under indirect observation: Causality, structure, prediction,* vol. 2, eds. K.G. Jöreskog and H. Wold, 209–248. Amsterdam: North Holland.

Belsley, D.A. 1984. Demeaning conditioning diagnostics trough centering. *American Statistician* 38:73–77, 90–93.

Bentler, P.M. 1980. Multivariate analysis with latent variables: Causal modeling. *Annual Review of Psychology* 31:419–456.

Bernert, C. 1983. The career of causal analysis in American sociology. *British Journal of Sociology* 34:230–254.

Cronbach, L.J., and P.E. Meehl. 1955. Construct validity in psychological testing. *Psychological Bulletin* 52:281–302.

Falter, J.W. 1977. Zur Validierung theoretischer Konstrukte: Wissenschaftstheoretische Aspekte des Validierungskonzepts. *Zeitschrift für Soziologie* 6:349-385.

Falter, J.W., and J.B. Lohmöller. 1982. Manifeste Schwächen im Umgang mit latenten Variablen: Ein Kommentar zu Hans-Hermann Hoppes Theologie der LV-Pfadmodell in ZfS Juli 1981. *Zeitschrift für Soziologie* 11:69-77.

Gaensslen, H., and W. Schubö. 1973. *Einfache und komplexe statistische Analyse.* München: Ernst Reinhardt Verlag.

Geisser, S. 1974. A predictive approach to the random effect model. *Biometrika* 61:101–107.

Goodman, L.A., and W.H. Kruskal. 1954. Measures of association for cross classifications. *Journal of the American Statistical Association* 49:732–764.

Guttman, L. 1941. An outline of the statistical theory of prediction. In *The prediction of personal adjustment; supplementary study B-I,* SSRC Bulletin No. 48, ed. P. Horst, 253–311. New York: Social Science Research Council.

Lohmöller, J.B. 1985a. *Path models with latent variables and partial least squares (PLS) estimation.* Würzburg: Physica Verlag.

Lohmöller, J.B., and H. Wold. 1980. *Three-mode path models with latent variables and Partial Least Squares (PLS) parameter estimation.* Paper presented at the European Meeting of the Psychometric Society; University of Groningen, The Netherlands, June 18–21, 1980. Forschungsbericht 80.03 Fachbereich Pädagogik. München: Hochschule der Bundeswehr.

MacCorquodale, K., and P.E. Meehl. 1948. On a distinction between hypothetical constructs and intervening variables. *Psychological Review* 55:95-107.

Mueller, J.H., and K.F. Schuessler. 1969. *Statistical reasoning in sociology.* 2d ed. 1970 New York: Houghton Mifflin.

Stone, M. 1974. Cross-validatory choice and assessment of statistical predictions. *Journal of the Royal Statistical Society* B 36:111–147.

van Donkelaar, J.H., and G.A. van der Knaap. 1982. *Kausale relaties in multivariate analyse: de PLS-methode.* (Working paper series A, nos. 82–2). Rotterdam: Erasmus Universiteit Rotterdam, Economisch Geographisch Instituut.

Wold, H. 1966. Estimation of principal components and related models by iterative least squares. In *Multivariate analysis,* ed. P.R. Krishnaiah, 391–420. New York: Academic Press.

Wold, H. 1969. Mergers of economics and philosophy of science: A cruise in shallow waters and deep seas. *Synthese* 20:427–482.

Wold, H. 1981. *Systems under indirect observations using soft modeling.* (Working paper no. 48). Cleveland, Ohio: Case Western Reserve University, Economics Department.

Wold, H. 1985. Systems analysis by Partial Least Squares. In *Measuring the unmeasurable,* eds. P. Nijkamp, H. Leitner, and N. Wrigley, 221–251. Dordrecht, Boston, Lancaster: Martinus Nijhoff.

Wold, H. 1986. *Factors influencing the outcome of economic sanctions.* In Sixto Rios Honorary Volume, ed. P. Ibarrola, 325-338 Madrid: Cosejo Superior de Investigacienes Cientificas.

2

Comment on Lohmöller's Paper

GEORG SÜSSMANN

Last year in Chicago, in a conversation with Professor Wold, I said to him that to my mind the unity of the sciences should be more than the common denominator of the scientific method. His answer was that he would like to see the background of my contention, and he invited me, a physicist, to his planned committee on Scientific Model-Building. I readily accepted this honorable invitation, and, later on, Professor Wold allocated my comments to one of the two theoretical papers in this volume.

Concentrating on a few observations arising from my perspective and experience as a physicist, my remarks will be mainly concerned with the idea of an ontologically based unity of science. Most physicists, including myself, feel they have good reasons to accept the physical universe not only as an imaginative idea (a formally collecting notion), but as a realistic entity (a substantially comprehending concept). There is, we think, this one world, inherently whole, and thus a genuine cosmos, all its differentiation notwithstanding. Therefore, there should be a unity of the sciences.

Here the term *unity* is not to be taken too literally, of course. It need not mean that we will be able to establish one and only one ultimate principle like the water of Thales or the nous of Heraclitus, or the abstract One of Parmenides. What "unity" does mean here is an integrity and solidarity which does not allow for definitive separations like that between the mind and the matter of Descartes. It is not necessary to define life in opposition to physics nor humanity in opposition to biology. None of these distinctions can be denied, and they all are important enough, but they do not exclude a connecting continuum. To derive biological physiology from physics and chemistry or human sociology from biology and psychology need not be a category mistake. The reasoning may be teleological as well, as is exemplified by the anthropic principle of recent years. According to this postulate, the astrophysical structures are chosen so as to allow for organic life, and the biological structures are chosen so as to allow for the human spirit.

These considerations are supported, I think, by the history of the natural sciences, and especially well by the manifestly unifying trends in physics. To mention only a few examples: Acoustics has been genuinely reduced to hydrodynamics, thermodynamics to statistical mechanics and cosmology, electricity, magnetism and optics to the unified electrodynamics, and chemistry to physics via quantum theory. The remaining problems of the initial conditions versus the laws of motion, which are sometimes raised in this context, are not at all alien to our present concept of physics, so they do not involve any new or irreducible feature which could separate chemistry from physics or physiology from chemistry. I admit an interesting polarity here—the dichotomy of the contingent versus the necessary aspects of the universe. These are evidently related to the empirical versus the rational elements of a sound methodology. (You see now a main reason for my endorsement of Theoretical Empiricism.) But this polarity does not imply any fundamental split between the physical and mental nature of the universe. It only means that we have to deal with both: with accidental existence as well as with symmetric essence. Their close interconnections became even stronger in the last decade through our studies of the so called broken symmetries, where the contingent and necessary features of the fundamental fields and particles are intertwined in a very interesting manner.

An important contingency besides that of the initial (or final) conditions is the indeterministic or stochastic aspect of quantum theory. Its equations of motion are deterministic, but in a formal sense only, as they do not predict (or postdict) the factual events but merely the probabilities of these events. This structure is much more open than Pythagorean or Eleatean philosophy would have it. It allows for a plurality much richer than rigid rationalism permits.

On the other hand, we have found a surprisingly simple set of fundamental laws which are identical all over this huge universe. This fundamental simplicity is not a result of our will only. There were often surprising, sometimes even unwelcome accomplishments. In some cases they came about in an entirely unexpected way. Let me remind you of Einstein, who disliked the quantum theory even though he had made crucial contributions to its evolution. The kind of simplicity which we have encountered in quantum theory did not satisfy the epistemological or ontological tastes of Einstein, but we cannot deny its physical validity. To be sure, we have not yet arrived at the foreseen unified fundamental theory but we have come, I think, a good deal closer to this goal during the last few years.

When speaking about the essential unity of science and the wholeness of this world, or creation, I am calling it neither fundamentally material nor fundamentally mental. Neither the so-called objective nor the so-called subjective pole can claim, I think, metaphysical priority. Quite the contrary: The substantial coherence of the physico-mental universe implies, among other things, the impossibility of disentangling its material from its mental aspect. This is one of the important lessons we have learned from the quantum theory of particles and fields. The idea of a physical object is an approximation only; and its representation by physical concepts would not make any sense without its fundamental relation to a conscious subject. The world is not a system of localized objects; it consists of phenomena. (Remarkably enough, Whitehead came close to such insights rather independently of the quantum theory in the very years when Bohr and Heisenberg coined the quantum theoretical concepts of complementarity and indeterminacy, and shortly before von Neumann provided his rigorous formulation of quantum theory.) This remarkable inseparability of physical reality has been clearly explained in non-technical terms by d'Espaquat in his most recent book. For example, because of Pauli's anti-symmetry principle we cannot sharply distinguish between two electrons even if they are miles apart from each other.

Much less can we separate a body in motion showing up from the conscious eye seeing it. This is not simply an epistemological relation of the Kantian type: according to von Neumann's thorough interpretation of quantum theory, a much more dynamic physico-mental correlation is taking place. This is not Berkeleyan nor Platonic idealism—much less solipsism—in the sense of a metaphysical priority of mind over and above matter; and it is not realism—or materialism—either. What it really means is the impossibility of a Cartesian separation of mind from matter. Von Neumann's position is, I feel, close in spirit to that of Leibniz.

Let me close by drawing your attention to the most recent book of Morton A. Kaplan (1984) , especially its first part, which consists of four chapters dealing with science. One of Kaplan's basic notions is that of a *correlative concept pair*. With this he expounds the fundamentals of meaning and reality in a way which can be, I feel, of great help in our endeavors toward a better understanding of the nature and scope of science, its internal unity, and its relations to other ways of understanding.

REFERENCE

Kaplan, M. 1984. *Science, language, and the human condition.* New York: Paragon House Publishers.

Jan-Bernd Lohmöller has kindly asked me to report on Georg Süssmann's comment. For my response, see pp. xxxi by Herman Wold in his introduction to this volume.

3

Evaluation of School Systems Using Partial Least Squares (PLS): An Application in the Analysis of Open Social Systems

---

RICHARD NOONAN

SUMMARY

Aims

This paper describes an application of Partial Least Squares (PLS) to the analysis of open social systems. School systems are highly complex open social systems, and no single approach to evaluation can possibly provide all the kinds of information needed for policy making. PLS is well suited to the analysis of complex open systems, however, and is superior in many applications because it does not require the user to impose hard assumptions on the model. In the present paper we restrict our view to the evaluation of the impact of school variables on the measured cognitive and affective outcomes in students. We shall try to avoid the use of technical jargon as much as possible, but it cannot be altogether eliminated.

Organization of the Paper

The present study places evaluation of school systems within a systems-analytic perspective. This puts extremely high demands on the statistical analysis methods used. Section 1 describes some of the essential requirements for the statistical methods.

Evaluation research must be based on theory. Theory is required at all stages of research, from sampling design, to instrument construction, to data analysis, to interpretation and reporting. Section 2 provides an overview of the theoretical model used in the present study. Section 3 describes the population and the sample investigated. Section 4 describes the data set and the PLS hierarchically structured path model used in the analysis. Section 5 reports some of the main results and discusses their implications. The main aim of Section 5, however, is not to draw substantive conclusions but to illustrate the potential of PLS for the analysis of social systems.

1. REQUIREMENTS FOR THE STATISTICAL METHODS

1.1. Causal Modeling as Systems Analysis

The term "systems analysis" is widely used to cover a number of different approaches to the study of phenomena. Common to these approaches is a holistic view of the phenomena. Studies in the field of education falling under the heading of systems analysis have typically examined one of three areas: (1) flows of students through the various stages and types of schooling; (2) flows of resources, such as financial resources; and (3) flows of information, for example in decision making. In line with the pioneering work of Wright (1934; 1954), H. Wold (1952; 1954), Simon (1957), and Blalock (1964) and Duncan (1971), we wish to include a fourth category, namely (4) flows of causal effects through the system, such as effects on student learning outcomes.

The present paper treats school system evaluation as a kind of systems analysis which focuses on the flow of causal influences through the school system. Such analysis must of course rely heavily on statistical material derived from nonexperimental research. The size and complexity of school systems has several implications concerning (1) the relationship between the measures and the underlying phenomena, (2) the dimensionality of the school system, and (3) the multiplicity of goals of the school system and of conflict among these goals. These areas are taken up below.

1.2. Manifest Variables and Latent Variables

Many of the theoretical constructs of greatest interest in educational evaluation cannot be measured by single observations, such as questionnaire items. Constructs such as Achievement and Attitudes are examples:

they are typically measured by batteries of instruments involving tens or hundreds of items. The underlying dimensions are often inferred only with the help of factor analysis. *These theoretical constructs are referred to as latent variables, and their measures are referred to as manifest variables.* In studying school learning, the school variables cannot be studied in isolation from variables describing the students and their environments. Measurement of these constructs or latent variables can only be done indirectly through multiple indicators or manifest variables. Thus statistical estimation methods for the analysis of school systems must be capable of handling manifest variables as estimators of latent variables.

1.3. Dimensionality of the School System

School systems are highly complex. To illustrate the dimensionality of the schooling experience, it may be noted that the IEA studies of national school systems and student outcomes involve thousands of distinct measures (Husén, ed., 1967; Comber and Keeves, 1973; Purves, 1973; Thorndike, 1973; Carroll, 1975; Lewis and Massad, 1975; Peaker, 1975; Walker, 1976). A structuring of these variables into conceptually homogeneous groups is a hopelessly large task unless a hierarchical taxonomic system is used. Otherwise either the number of groups becomes so large that it is impossible to obtain an overview, or else the more limited number of groups are so large and heterogeneous that they are uninterpretable. Thus statistical estimation methods for the analysis of school system evaluation data must be capable of handling large numbers of dimensions, preferably within a hierarchical conceptual framework, and must at the same time enable the exploration of the interrelationships among them.

1.4. Multiplicity of Outcomes of the School System

The school system is a matter of importance to the whole society. Many different interest groups influence educational decision making. The system itself is made up of many levels of participation—from the top administration to the classroom, the teacher, and the student. Thus the school system has multiple goals, and there is inevitably tension and conflict between goals. For example, there are both quantitative and qualitative goals of schooling. Trade-offs are inevitable where resources are scarce, and all resources are more or less scarce. Multiplicity of goals and conflict among the goals is a common characteristic of social systems in the real world. Thus statistical estimation methods for school system evaluation must be capable of handling multiplicity of goals and conflict among the goals.

1.5. Partial Least Squares (PLS) as a Tool for the Study of Open Social Systems

Partial Least Squares (PLS) path analysis with latent variables (Wold, 1982; 1985) is a family of methods that fills well the requirements referred to above. The definitive work on PLS is given by Wold (1982), and the largest collection of studies involving PLS is given in Jöreskog and Wold (eds. 1982, Vol. 2). Educational applications are found there and in Noonan and Wold (1980; 1983; 1984) and Noonan (1978; 1982).

2. SCHOOL LEARNING: MODEL OF AN OPEN SOCIAL SYSTEM

2.1. Introduction

2.1.1. SCHOOL LEARNING

To learn is to change. School learning is distinct from other kinds of learning by virtue of the central formalized role that schools play in the transmission of culture and the preparation of young people for work. It involves the learning of some particular task or set of tasks which take place within a formal instructional setting, involving a teacher, a group of students, and a formal (more or less explicit) curriculum. The archetypical example of school learning is the development of literacy and numeracy in school children.

2.1.2. TOWARDS A GENERAL MODEL OF SCHOOL LEARNING

The purpose of the present model is to explain variation in school learning. We pose several requirements on our model. First, it must be general or holistic, i.e., comprehensive, involving a wide range of variables, from the most proximal to the most distal in relation to school learning. Second, it must explain a wide range of empirical observations, indicating not only which variables are most relevant but also the relative strengths of the effects. Third, it must embrace a causal mechanism sufficient to explain the observed phenomena. Fourth, it must provide a parsimonious conceptual structure. The model described below is illustrated in Figure 3–1.

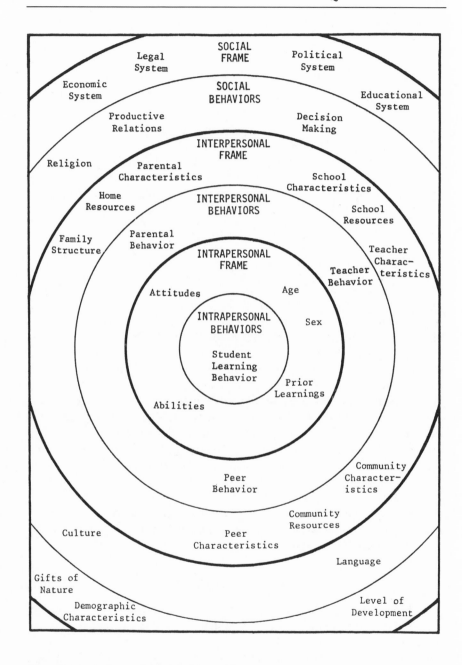

Figure 3–1. A Gerneral Model of School Learning

2.2. School Learning: The Orderly Combination of Structures and Processes to Achieve Learning Goals

2.2.1. A Student-Centered Model

Schooling is an enormous undertaking involving coordination of massive amounts of financial and human resources in order that students may achieve selected kinds of cognitive, affective, and conative outcomes. Ultimately, however, the outcomes of this massive undertaking are crucially dependent on the student. It is not the classrooms or the schools which learn, it is the student. Thus the first essential feature of the model of school learning is that *the primary actor is the student*. Moreover, the student is not an object but a subject — a thinking, feeling, active human being who has a will of his or her own.

2.2.2. Student Learning Activities and the Restless Neuron

In its most covert forms, learning involves mainly the neurological processing of information—perceiving new information, remembering stored information, analyzing, synthesizing. In its most overt forms, learning involves overt practice and the gradual establishment of new behaviors. The minimal requirement for learning to occur is neurological activity. Students learn through a complex of activities referred to here as learning activities. School learning is largely an overtly active process. To be sure, sometimes learning occurs without conscious effort on the part of either the student or the teacher. School learning, however, is formalized, institutionalized, and officially sanctioned in such a way as to minimize the chance element in learning. Curricula are written so as to guide the teaching-learning process. Teaching is structured so as to guide student learning activities. The ceaseless activity of the restless neuron is to be carefully guided and directed, for without it no quality or quantity of teaching can lead to learning in the student. Thus the second essential feature of the model is that *it is student learning activities which are the creative factor in student learning*.

2.2.3. Student Characteristics

Knowledge of student learning activities alone is not sufficient to explain variation in student outcomes. The effectiveness of a given learning activity varies among students, and this variation is a function of such characteristics of the student as prior learnings, aptitudes and ability, and affective characteristics, including motivation. The student is, to be sure, to some extent plastic and can "learn to learn." While the teaching-learning process is going on, however, the student's ability to understand instruction and his capacity to respond is restricted. Thus the third essential feature of the model is that *the outcomes of the learning activity are constrained and enabled by characteristics of the student.*

2.2.4. Significant Others in the Near Environment

The student does not operate in isolation from his or her environment. At school, the teacher strives to guide the student's overt and covert learning activities by the teaching process. At home, the parents and other family members strive to guide these activities by encouraging and helping and by expressing attitudes and opinions. Outside the home and the classroom, peers exert a guiding influence (positive or negative) by providing encouragement and by expressing attitudes and opinions. Thus the fourth essential feature of the model is that *student characteristics and behaviors are influenced by interactions with significant others in the near environment.* Moreover, it is *only* through influencing student characteristics and behavior that others in the environment can influence student learning.

2.2.5. Characteristics of Significant Others

What students derive from others is largely a function of the interaction process itself. It is not what people *are* but what they *do* which influences students. What people do is, of course, partly a function of their characteristics, such as their cognitive structures—knowledge, understanding, beliefs, attitudes and options. For example, teacher training itself does not directly influence student outcomes, but it does influence teacher doings, which in turn influences student learning behavior. Similarly, parental socioeconomic status or educational level does not in itself influence student learning, but it does influence their interaction with their children. Thus the fifth essential feature of the model is that *the interaction processes in the near environment of the student is influenced by the characteristics of the actors and of the objects in the environment.*

2.2.6. Objects in the Near Environment

The student interacts not only with persons but also with objects in the near environment, such as textbooks, laboratory equipment, magazines, television sets, chemistry sets and so on. Student learning behavior is both enabled and constrained by the availability and nature of the objects in the near environment. Thus the sixth essential point about the model is that *student behavior is influenced by interaction with objects in the environment.* Note that the point concerns *interaction* with the objects, not the mere *existence* of the objects. Availability of textbooks and laboratory equipment is in itself not a condition which directly promotes school learning, but the student's interaction with them does.

2.2.7. THE FAR ENVIRONMENT

School learning takes place not only in the near environment of the student but also in a more remote or global environment. This far environment includes the society at large, the economy, the legal system, the polity, the culture, the physical environment and so on. In the far environment, as in the near environment, there are both people and objects. The people are all actors—thinking, feeling, active human beings who have wills of their own. The environment both enables and constrains social behavior. Human beings also construct the environment, within the realms of the possible. The global social processes influence students, but their influence on school learning is much less direct than the influence of the interactions which take place in the near environment. Thus the seventh essential feature of the model is that *the far environment of school learning indirectly influences school learning, partly by influencing students directly and partly by influencing the near environment of school learning—the parents, teachers, and peers.*

2.3. A Conceptual Framework

2.3.1. FACTORS

In the above description of school learning can be found many elements and relations among elements. This complexity can be greatly reduced by a hierarchical structuring of the elements. First, two categories of factors are conceived of: (1) *Processes,* which include learning activities and social interaction, and (2) *Structures,* which include the availability and nature of objects as well as characteristics of individuals, groups, or societies. Structures and Processes are the productive factors which combine to influence, both directly and indirectly, student outcomes of school learning. Second, these two categories are further divided into three levels: (1) *Individual* or *Intra-personal,* referring to the student; (2) *Social* or *Inter-personal,* referring to the near environment of

school learning and the persons with whom the student has direct interaction; and (3) *Societal,* referring to the global environment of school
learning and persons who indirectly influence the student but with whom
the student has no direct interaction. At the Individual level, the student
combines Structure with Process to directly produce learning outcomes.
At the Social level, Structure and Process are combined to influence
learning outcomes indirectly by influencing the characteristics and behaviors of the student. At the Societal level, Structure and Process are combined to influence learning outcomes both through direct influences on
the student and through indirect influences through others in the near
environment of school learning.

2.3.2. GOALS

Learning behavior is neither random nor completely determined by
external factors. Explanation of learning behavior requires reference to
the goals of the learner. Goals are multiple and complex and can involve
internal contradiction. In addition, the actors at the Individual, Social,
and Societal levels combine Structures and Processes in order to attain
their own goals or their own perception and understanding of the goals
of others. Thus according to the model, *Structures and Processes are combined in order to attain Goals.*

2.3.3. RULES

The actors do not combine Structures and Processes in complete
freedom. They are guided by laws, regulations, their understanding of the
way things work, culture, conventions, technology and so on. These are
referred to as Rules. Thus according to the model, Structures and
Processes are combined in accordance with Rules in order to attain Goals.

2.4. Seven Governing Empirical Observations

The taxonomy presented above for Elements (Structures, Processes,
Goals, and Rules) and Levels (Individual, Social, and Societal) provides a
framework for the collection of empirical data, but there is nothing in the
model yet presented to indicate the relative strengths of the influences
predicted by the model. There are seven principles which enable prediction of the empirical strength of influences.

2.4.1. THE PROXIMITY PRINCIPLE

Only student characteristics and behaviors influence learning outcomes directly. Other factors operate only *indirectly* through influences on learning behavior or characteristics. It is thus appropriate to think in terms of *causal chains,* leading from more distal through more proximal variables, to student characteristics and behaviors, and finally to student learning. Through each link in the chain, however, the influences of the *causally prior* variables are progressively weakened by the influence of the *causally subsequent* variables. Teacher training, for example, can promote effective teaching behavior, but there are many other influences on teacher behavior. Effective teaching behavior can lead to effective learning behaviors by students, but teaching behavior is only one of many influences on student learning behavior. At each link the influence of teacher training becomes progressively modified by the influence of other factors. This may be expressed in terms of the *Proximity Principle: For each successive link in a causal chain model, the influence of a given predictor on a given predictand is progressively weakened by the influence of other variables.* In other words, in general the closer a predictor is, causally, to a predictand the greater the influence will tend to be, *ceteris paribus;* the more remote a predictor is, the less its influence will tend to be. It follows from the Proximity Principle that the effects of student characteristics and behaviors on student learning will be powerful, teacher-student interactions less powerful, teacher behavior still less powerful, teacher training still less powerful, and expenditure on teacher training still less powerful.

2.4.2. THE MULTIPLICITY PRINCIPLE

Some factors influence learning via simple causal chains while others exert influence via more complex causal chains. For example, the influence of teaching behavior operates primarily via student learning behaviors. The influences of parental behaviors, however, are much more complex and operate through a great multiplicity of paths—through verbal ability, attitudes, help with homework, encouragement, etc. This confluence of forces on student learning behavior may be more powerful than the simpler influence of teacher behavior, even though the influence of teacher behavior on student learning behavior is more direct. If all the effects via all the paths operate in the same direction (i.e., all positive or all negative) the multiplicity of effects may be said to be "coordinated." If there are many paths and the effects are coordinated, then the total effects can be much larger than if there is a smaller number of paths or the effects are uncoordinated. This may be expressed as the *Multiplicity Principle: In general, the greater the number of paths by which the influence of a given cause variable operates on a given effect variable, the greater the total effect that is possible, ceteris paribus* (see Note). It follows from the Multiplicity Principle that the effect of the home Structure and Process variables on student outcomes are likely to be stronger than the effects of the school and classroom Structure and Process variables, unless the latter are extraordinarily effective.

2.4.3. THE CONTINUITY PRINCIPLE

Some links in a causal chain are more powerful than others because of the continuity of the influence. For example, student attitudes are more powerfully influenced by the attitudes of parents than by the attitudes of teachers. This is because children are typically subject to the influence of their parents over much longer periods of time, more continually or permanently, and more frequently than to the influence of their teachers. Children enter the school at the age of five or six or seven, by which time the characteristic features and behaviors of the child are already well established. The child attends school typically fewer than half the days of a calender year. The typical school day represents about half or less of the waking hours of the child. The child typically constitutes a major focal point in the the activities and interactions in the home. By contrast the same child at school typically claims one-twentieth or less of the attention of the teacher's time. The child typically changes teachers often. In primary school the child typically changes teacher yearly. In secondary school the student typically meets a given teacher a few hours per week during a single school year. Even in broken homes, the child typically lives with one parent and has contact with the other. Even other adults with whom the child has contact within the framework of the family tend to exert an influence similar to that of the parents. Thus the observed effects of parental variables actually represent the cumulative effects of frequent and continuous interactions over a long period of time, while the observed effects of teacher variables actually represent the cumulative effects of infrequent and discontinuous contacts over relatively short periods of time.

In other words, because of the sustained and stable nature of the parental influence, the observed effects of parental variables on outcomes would tend to be higher than the observed effects of the teacher variables even if the influence of any given single isolated interaction were the same for both parents and teachers. This may be expressed as the

Continuity Principle: In general, the more frequent, continuous, permanent and sustained the influence of a factor is on learning, the greater the effect of that factor, ceteris paribus.

2.4.4. The Effectivity Principle

Some links in causal chains are stronger than others. Some parental behaviors, for example, have stronger effects on student outcomes than others because they leave stronger and more impressions. Similarly some teacher behaviors have stronger effects because they more powerfully stimulate thought, provide insights, raise interests, lead to more effective practice, etc. This may be expressed as the *Effectivity Principle: In general, the stronger the direct causal effects of the links making up the causal chain segments, the stronger is the total effect, ceteris paribus.* It should be noted, however, that the strength of the effect of a given cause variable, operating through a causal chain, on a given effect variable is determined not as a sum but as a product. Thus if any one of the links in the causal chain has a null effect, the resulting effect is null (see Note).

2.4.5. The Specificity-Generality Principle

Some phenomena are relatively general, in the sense that they appear in a wide variety of contexts. They are responses to a wide range of stimuli. Others are relatively specific, in the sense that they appear in only a few contexts. They are responses to a narrow range of stimuli. For example student attitudes toward education (i.e., attitudes toward school education in general) are more general than student attitudes toward science (i.e., attitudes toward school education in science). Following the same reasoning, parental attitudes toward education are more general than parental attitudes toward science. According to the model, parental attitudes should influence student attitudes. The influences are varying and complex.

More *general* phenomena tend to constitute more *general stimuli* and to elicit more *general responses* in turn. More *specific* phenomena tend to constitute more *specific stimuli* and to elicit more *specific responses* in turn. This relationship may be expressed as the *Specificity-Generality Principle: In general, more specific cause variables tend to be more strongly related to more specific effect variables, and more general cause variables tend to be more strongly related to more general effect variables.*

2.4.6. The Rules Principle

The principles discussed above concern the magnitude of causal effects, where the notion of "causal effect" is understood in the same sense as the outcome of a controlled experiment. In the present section we shall discuss non-causal association. Non-causal association is one of the characteristics of open social systems, and can have a profound influence on the observed relationships in social settings. They are also among the most difficult to understand and to deal with.

Factors directly involved in schooling can usually be more or less readily manipulated by school authorities, such as the length of the school year, the availability of instructional material and equipment, class size and level and type of staffing. Three classes of manipulation are possible: (1) changing the overall level or volume of resources available; (2) changing the mix between different factors; and (3) changing the pattern of allocation of resources among schools or students.

Consider, for example, the allocation of financial resources among schools. Three cases can be identified. First, in some countries, resources are allocated in such a way that school mean expenditure per student is in practice positively correlated with the socioeconomic status of students, for example where financing is based to a high degree on local taxation, and residential patterns reflect social segregation. Second, in other countries resources are allocated more equally, for example, where financing is largely centralized (Noonan, 1976). Third, in some school systems school resources may be allocated in such a way that school mean expenditure per student is in practice *negatively* correlated with the socioeconomic status of the students, for example where low achieving students receive remedial instruction. Causal effects of expenditure are not identical for all students. Thus in a school system, the *observed* effect of expenditure, i.e., the association the researcher observed between expenditure per student and the level of student outcomes, is confounded with the way in which financial resources are allocated. In other words, the way in which school systems allocate their resources has a profound influence on the observed correlations between expenditure per student and student outcomes. Although the discussion here has concerned the effects of school financial resources, the same problem appears in all areas of research in which allocation of *treatments* can be steered by human will. In such situations, correlation and even regression coefficients can be capricious—they can change from sample to sample, and they can change over time as the rules of the game change. The problems discussed here can be expressed as the *Rules Principle: The relationships observed in open social systems are subject to influence by the socially established rules prevailing in the system.*

2.4.7. THE MEASUREMENT ERROR PRINCIPLE

The principles given above in Sections 1 to 5 concern the magnitudes of the causal effects, and the principle discussed in Section 6 concerns the impact of non-causal association on the observability of causal effects in non-experimental settings. The present section concerns the impact of measurement error on empirical estimates of causal effects. Complex social phenomena are difficult to measure. Multiple indicators, or manifest variables, are used in order to estimate the underlying latent variables. Although this approach improves measurement, the survey researcher is often faced nevertheless with measures containing a great deal of error. Usually very little is known about the error. In the area of educational evaluation, measures of school achievement are relatively well developed after decades of work in educational testing. Measurement of affective outcomes of schooling is more difficult, and measurement of student learning behaviors is still more difficult. Measurement of teacher, class, and school variables suffers from severe definitional problems. School measures available to researchers often originate in the routine data collected by the school administration.

In a multivariate analysis, the effects of measurement error can be exceedingly complex even for the simplest kinds of errors. In school evaluation research the measurement problem concerns primarily variables used as predictors of achievement, and above all, teacher, class, and school variables. Despite the complexity, two rules of thumb can be given for aiding in the interpretation of empirical results in the face of severe measurement problems. Suppose X1 and X2 are both causes of Y, that the causal effects are of the same magnitude, and that X1 and X2 correlate with each other. First, random error in X1 and X2 tends to attenuate the respective parameter estimates, and the greater the error, the greater the attenuating effect. Second, random error in X1 tends to reduce the value of X1 as a "control variable" and thus tends to inflate the parameter estimate for X2.

3. CASE STUDY: THE TEACHING AND LEARNING OF SCIENCE IN SWEDEN

3.1. The School System in Sweden

Compulsory schooling in Sweden is made up of nine years of comprehensive education, beginning at age 7 and ending at age 16. It is divided into six years of primary and three years of lower secondary schooling. Compulsory schooling is followed by voluntary upper secondary schooling including a wide range of academic and vocational programs, generally ranging in duration from two to three years. The present study investigated students at the lower secondary level. At this level virtually all children attend regular public schools. At the time of the data collection (spring 1970), the school system was highly centralized in most essential respects, including curriculum, financing, and teacher training. Compared with many other countries, Sweden is relatively homogeneous culturally and socially, and variation between schools is lower in Sweden than in most other countries.

3.2. The Data Set

The data used in the present study were collected in Sweden in 1970 as part of the Six Subject Study of the International Association for the Evaluation of Educational Achievement (IEA), carried out in 22 countries (Peaker, 1975; Walker, 1976). That study included science, reading comprehension, literature, English and French as foreign languages, and civics. The present study concerns science education (Comber and Keeves, 1973).

The population investigated here included all students of age 14.0 to 14.11 at the time of testing who are enrolled in regular schooling. These students were in grades seven and eight. The sample included 2360 students, 622 teachers, and 95 schools. The response rate was approximately 95 percent.

3.3. The Analysis

The Swedish data file from the IEA archive set M2002 was used. In this file the student data were linked to the school and teacher data. Thus analyses concerning school and teacher effects on student learning, with the student as the unit of analysis, could be carried out.

In the selection of variables for entry into the analysis, two main sources of guidance were employed. The first was the model presented in Section 2 above. This model provides a hierarchical conceptual framework in which virtually all variables in the IEA study can be classified. The second source of guidance was previous studies involving the same data set (e.g., Noonan, 1978; Noonan and Wold, 1980; Noonan, 1982; Noonan and Wold, 1983). Altogether a great deal of exploratory analysis was carried out. Variables were chosen for both conceptual and empirical qualities.

In all, 191 manifest variables were finally selected for entry into the analysis. These variables were distributed over 41 basic blocks, representing basic latent variables, each block containing between 1 and 17 manifest variables. This alone represents a great reduction in complexity, but even 41 blocks is far too much to handle conceptually.

Table 3–1

Latent Variables in the Model:
Name, Label, Number of Manifest Variables

Var. No.	Name	Label	Manifest Variables
1	PARENSTA	PARENTAL SOCIOECONOMIC STATUS	3
2	SIBLINGS	HOME SIBLINGS	3
3	HOMERESC	HOME READING RESOURCES	3
4	*HOMESTR	HOME STRUCTURE	6
5	PARENBEH	PARENTAL BEHAVIOR	7
6	PEERSTA	PEER SOCIOECONOMIC STATUS	1
7	PEERACH	PEER EDUCATIONAL ACHIEVEMENT	2
8	PEERATT	PEER EDUCATIONAL ATTITUDES	2
9	*PRSTME	PEER STRUCTURE: MEAN	5
10	PEERSESD	PEER SOCIOECONOMIC VARIATION	1
11	PEERACSD	PEER ACHIEVEMENT VARIATION	2
12	PEERATSD	PEER ATTITUDE VARIATION	2
13	*PRSTRVA	PEER STRUCTURE: VARIATION	5
14	**PRSTR	PEER STRUCTURE	10
15	PEERBEHV	PEER BEHAVIOR	3
16	PEERBESD	PEER BEHAVIORAL VARIATION	3
17	*PEERBEH	PEER BEHAVIOR	6
18	SCHLSIZE	SCHOOL SIZE	1
19	PRINCPL	SCHOOL PRINCIPAL'S QUALIFICATION	4
20	SCHLRESC	SCHOOL PERSONNEL RESOURCES	10
21	*SCHLSTR	SCHOOL STRUCTURE	15
22	CLASSIZE	CLASS SIZE	4
23	CLASTIME	CLASS CLASS TIME	8

24	CURRICLM	CURRICULUM OPPORTUNITY TO LEARN	4
25	TEACHSEX	TEACHER SEX	1
26	TEACHEXP	TEACHER EXPERIENCE	3
27	TEATRAIN	TEACHER TRAINING	17
28	TEAATCRI	TEACHER TEACHING CRITERIA	5
29	TEAATSCI	TEACHER ATTITUDES ON PRACTICAL	10
30	*TEAATTS	TEACHER ATTITUDES	15
31	**TEASTR	TEACHER STRUCTURE	36
32	TEAMETHD	TEACHER BEHAVIOR: TEACHING METHODS	10
33	EVLMETHD	TEACHER BEHAVIOR: EVALUATION METHODS	5
34	ENCOURAG	TEACHER BEHAVIOR: ENCOURAGES STUDENTS	2
35	GROUPING	TEACHER BEHAVIOR: WITHIN CLASS GROUPING	1
36	*TEABEH	TEACHER BEHAVIOR	18
37	STUDNSEX	STUDENT SEX	1
38	STUDMATR	STUDENT MATURITY	2
39	*STUDSTR	STUDENT PERSONAL CHARACTERISTICS	3
40	STUDVERB	STUDENT VERBAL ABILITY	3
41	REASONL	STUDENT LOGICAL THINKING STAGE	1
42	*STSTRCG	STUDENT STRUCTURE: COGNITIVE	4
43	ATTEDUC	STUDENT: ATTITUDES TOWARD EDUCATION	10
44	ATTSCIEN	STUDENT: ATTITUDES TOWARD SCIENCE	7
45	*STSTRAF	STUDENT STRUCTURE: AFFECTIVE	17
46	**STSTR	STUDENT STRUCTURE	24
47	LEISACTV	STUDENT BEHAVIOR: LEISURE ACTIVITIES	7
48	LEISREAD	STUDENT BEHAVIOR: LEISURE READING	5
49	*STBEHHN	STUDENT BEHAVIOR: HOME NONSCHOLASTIC	12
50	HWPRACT	STUDENT BEHAVIOR: HOMEWORK PRACTICES	6
51	TIMEONHW	STUDENT BEHAVIOR: TIME ON HOMEWORK	5
52	STUDYHAB	STUDENT BEHAVIOR: STUDY HABITS	6
53	*STBEHHS	STUDENT BEHAVIOR: HOME SCHOLASTIC	17
54	**STBEHH	STUDENT BEHAVIOR: HOME	29
55	TEXTBOOK	STUDENT BEHAVIOR: USE OF TEXTBOOKS	4
56	LABWORK	STUDENT BEHAVIOR: LABORATORY WORK	12
57	*STBEHS	STUDENT BEHAVIOR: SCHOOL	16
58	***STBEH	STUDENT BEHAVIOR	45
59	SCIENACH	SCIENCE ACHIEVEMENT	5

Hierarchical structuring of the blocks reduced the complexity still further. Thus although the total number of blocks was increased from 41 to 59 (including 18 blocks representing "higher order" concepts in the latent variable hierarchy), the total number of predictors of science achievement was reduced from 40 to 13. Table 3–1 shows the number of manifest variables used to measure each latent variable. Conceptually higher order variables are denoted with one or more asterisks (*, ** or ***), each additional asterisk representing a higher conceptual level. There are eight hierarchically structured latent variables, taxonomically arranged below:

1.	HOME STRUCTURE
1.1	Siblings
1.2	Reading resources
2.	PEER STRUCTURE
2.1	Mean Level
2.1.1	*Socioeconomic status*
2.1.2	*Educational Achievement*
2.1.3	*Educational Attitudes*
2.2	Variation in Level
2.2.1	*Socioeconomic Status*
2.2.2	*Educational Achievement*
2.2.3	*Educational Attitudes*
3.	PEER BEHAVIOR
3.1	Behavioral Mean
3.2	Behavioral Variation
4.	SCHOOL STRUCTURE
4.1	School Size
4.2	Principal's Qualifications
4.3	Personnel Resources
5.	TEACHER STRUCTURE
5.1	Sex
5.2	Experience
5.3	Training
5.4	Attitudes
5.4.1	*Teaching Criteria*
5.4.2	*Attitudes toward Practical Work*
6.	TEACHER BEHAVIOR
6.1	Teaching Methods
6.2	Evaluation Methods
6.3	Student Encouragement
6.4	Within Class Grouping
7.	STUDENT STRUCTURE
7.1	Personal Characteristics
7.1.1	*Sex*
7.1.2	*Maturity*
7.2	Cognitive Characteristics
7.2.1	*Verbal Ability*
7.2.2	*Logical Thinking Stage*
7.3	Affective Characteristics
7.3.1	*Attitudes toward Education*
7.3.2	*Attitudes toward Science*
8.	STUDENT BEHAVIOR
8.1	Home
8.1.1	*Nonscholastic*
8.1.1.1	Leisure activities

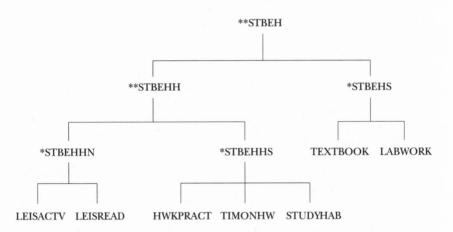

Hierarchical Latent Variables:

***STBEH	STUDENT BEHAVIOR
**STBEHH	STUDENT BEHAVIOR :HOME
*STBEHS	STUDENT BEHAVIOR : SCHOOL
*STBEHN	STUDENT BEHAVIOR : HOME NONSCHOLASTIC
*STBEHHS	STUDENT BEHAVIOR : HOME SCHOLASTIC

Figure 3–2. Student Behavior Latent Variable Hierarchy

Thus ***STBEH, STUDENT BEHAVIOR represents the highest level of the hierarchy, **STBEHH, STUDENT BEHAVIOR: HOME and **STBEHS, STUDENT BEHAVIOR: SCHOOL represent intermediate levels, and *STBEHHN, STUDENT BEHAVIOR: HOME NONSCHOLAS-TIC and *STBEHHS, STUDENT BEHAVIOR: HOME SCHOLASTIC rep-resent lower levels. The prediction equations for the statistical model may use all the relevant latent variables or only the highest level of a latent variable hierarchy, depending on the interest of the user. If the user is interested in a macro-model, covering the whole system, then it is impera-tive for the sake of interpretability to restrict the model to the highest hierarchical level. If the user is interested in a micro-model, covering some subsystem, then the model may involve some disaggregation of the latent variable hierarchies. Thus in the initial analysis for the present study, the regression equation for predicting Science Achievement contained only 13 predictors, including 8 hierarchical latent variables which represent altogether 35 basic latent variables.

3.4. Hypothetical Relations

On the basis of the model discussed in Section 2 above, 14 causal relations were hypothesized. They were specified as predictor relations in the usual way:

H01: TEAMETHD = F1(**PFSTR, *PEERBEH, *SCHSTR, CLASSIZE, ** TEASTR)

H02: EVLMETHD = F2(**PFSTR, *PEERBEH, *SCHSTR, CLASSIZE, **TEASTR)

H03: ENCOURAG = F3(**PFSTR, *PEERBEH, *SCHSTR, CLASSIZE, **TEASTR)

H04: GROUPING = F4(**PFSTR, *PEERBEH, *SCHSTR, CLASSIZE, **TEASTR)

H05: STUDVERB = F5(PARENSTA, *HOMESTR, PARENBEH, *STSTR-PR)

H06: REASONL = F6(PARENSTA, *HOMESTR, PARENBEH, *STSTRPR)

H07: ATTEDUC = F7(PARENSTA, *HOMESTR, PARENBEH, **PRSTR, *PEERBEH, *TEABEH, *STSTRPR, *STSTRCG)

H08: ATTSCIEN = F8(PARENSTA, *HOMESTR, PARENBEH, **PRSTR, *PEERBEH, *TEABEH, *STSTRPR, *STSTRCG)

H09: LEISACTV = F9(PARENSTA, *HOMESTR, PARENBEH, **PRSTR, *PEERBEH, **STSTRPR)

H10: LEISREAD = F10(PARENSTA, *HOMESTR, PARENBEH, **PRSTR, *PEERBEH, **STSTRPR)

H11: HWKPRACT = F11(PARENSTA, *HOMESTR, PARENBEH, **PRSTR, *PEERBEH, **STSTRPR)

H12: TIMEONHW = F12(PARENSTA, *HOMESTR, PARENBEH, **PRSTR, *PEERBEH, **STSTRPR)

H13: STUDYHAB = F13(PARENSTA, *HOMESTR, PARENBEH, **PRSTR, *PEERBEH, **STSTRPR)

H14: SCIENACH = F14(PARENSTA, *HOMESTR, PARENBEH, **PRSTR, *PEERBEH, *SCHSTR, CLASSIZE, CLASTIME, CURRICLM, **TEASTR, *TEABEH, *STSTR, ***STBEH)

The hierarchical relations were expressed with a similar set of equations.

4. RESULTS

4.1. Purpose of the Present Report

The analysis described in Section 3 yields a rich variety of results. Because of space limitations, only a small portion of these results can be reported. The purpose of this report is not primarily to draw substantive conclusions but to demonstrate the use of PLS path analysis using hierarchically structured latent variables as a tool for the analysis of open social systems.

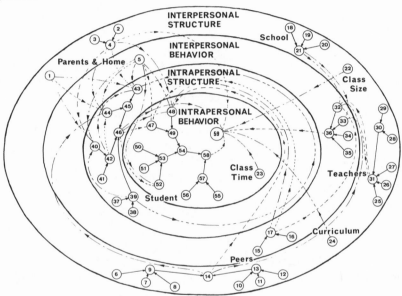

Figure 3–3. A General Model of School Learning: An Empirical Analysis

4.2. Path Coefficients; Total Effect Coefficients

The complete analysis is illustrated in Figure 3–3. In this report, path coefficients and total effect coefficients (the sum of direct and indirect effects) are reported for selected relations. The following dependent variables are considered: (1) Verbal Ability; (2) Attitudes toward Education; (3) Attitudes toward Science; and (4) Science Achievement.

Table 3–2

Effect Coefficients for Factors Influencing Student Verbal Ability

| | | Effect Coefficient | |
Factor	Correlation	Path	Total
PARENSTA	0.277	0.195	0.195
*HOMESTR	0.339	0.282	0.282
PARENBEH	0.136	0.066	0.066
*STSTRPR	0.122	0.112	0.112

R = 0.415, R(2) = 0.172

Verbal Ability, STUDVERB. The effects of factors influencing verbal ability were estimated in accordance with hypothesis H05 above. Three effect coefficients are reported in Table 3–2: (1) simple correlations; (2) path coefficients; and (3) total effect coefficients. In the present case only one multiple regression is involved, so there are no indirect effects, and the total effect coefficients are equal to the path coefficients. Home Structure has by far the strongest influence on Verbal Ability, followed by Parental Status. The next strongest effect is shown by Student Personal Characteristics, and the weakest effect is shown by Parental Behavior. Only 17 percent of the variance in STUDVERB is explained, however, suggesting that the most important sources of variation are not tapped by the model.

A more variegated picture of causal influence is shown for the latent variables representing attitudes toward education and science. Hypotheses H07 and H08 reflect the greater volatility of affective characteristics, as compared with cognitive characteristics. Thus while peer characteristics and behaviors and teacher behaviors cannot be expected to have effects on such basic characteristics of the student as verbal ability, the origin of which is in the home during the early years of the child's development, these variables can be expected to influence affective characteristics.

Table 3–3

Effect Coefficients for Factors Influencing Student Attitudes toward Education

Factor	Correlation	Effect Coefficient Path	Total
PARENSTA	0.330	0.171	0.231
*HOMESTR	0.320	0.149	0.230
PARENBEH	0.310	0.216	0.235
**PRSTR	0.156	0.036	0.026
*PEERBEH	0.137	0.050	0.055
*TEABEH	0.041	-0.026	-0.027
*STSTRPR	-0.087	-0.139	-0.103
*STSTRCG	0.409	0.293	0.293

R = 0.560, R(2) = 0.314

Table 3–4

Effect Coefficients for Factors Influencing Student Attitudes toward Science

Factor	Correlation	Effect Coefficient Path	Total
PARENSTA	0.185	0.068	0.108
*HOMESTR	0.186	0.072	0.126
PARENBEH	0.228	0.167	0.180
**PRSTR	0.181	0.106	0.087
*PEERBEH	0.153	0.049	0.060
*TEABEH	0.024	-0.051	-0.051
*STSTRPR	0.026	-0.013	0.012
*STSTRCG	0.276	0.196	0.196

R = 0.378, R(2) = 0.143

The estimated effects of factors influencing attitudes toward education and science are shown in Tables 3–3 and 3–4 respectively. It is seen that the strongest influence on both Attitudes toward Education and Attitudes toward Science are exerted by the home variables, especially Parental Behavior. We shall investigate further below the effects of Student Personal Characteristics. Peer influences are weaker for Attitudes toward Education than for Attitudes toward Science. The general impression emerging from Tables 3–3 and 3–4 is that attitudes toward both education and science are more powerfully influenced by the home than by forces outside the home, but this distinction appears to be more pronounced in the case of attitudes toward education. In general, variation in Attitude toward Science is less strongly related to the variables in the model than is Attitude toward Education, as indicated by the fact that the squared multiple correlation for ATTEDUC is 0.31, while the squared multiple correlation for ATTSCIEN is only 0.14.

Table 3–5

Effect Coefficients for Factors Influencing Science Achievement

Factor	Correlation	Effect Coefficient Path	Total
PARENSTA	0.250	0.017	0.177
*HOMESTR	0.249	-0.045	0.157
PARENBEH	0.147	-0.031	0.086
**PRSTR	0.177	-0.021	0.017
*PEERBEH	0.089	-0.038	-0.002
*SCHSTR	0.037	-0.021	-0.023
CLASSIZE	-0.092	-0.040	-0.043
CLASTIME	-0.278	-0.059	-0.059
CURRICLM	-0.136	-0.059	-0.059
*TEASTR	0.093	-0.007	0.011
*TEABEH	0.182	0.079	0.062
**STSTR	0.715	0.571	0.664
***STBEH	0.585	0.240	0.241

R = 0.756,   R(2) = 0.572

The influences on Science Achievement are the subject of Hypothesis H14. The estimated effects are shown in Table 3–5. Of the 13 predictors, only 7 show statistically significant effects ($p < 0.05$ based on the classical distributional assumptions applied): *HOMESTR, CLASSIZE, CLASTIME, CURRICLM, *TEABEH, **STSTR, and ***STBEH. That the two strongest effects are shown by **STSTR and ***STBEH is completely consistent with the model presented in Section 2 above. The third strongest effects are shown by *TEABEH. The remaining variables show weak and inconsistent results, which may be attributed to sampling error and measurement error. Two variables which show unexpected negative effects are Class Time and Curriculum. The fact that *all* effect coefficients for these variables are negative suggests compensatory allocation of instructional time and possibly severe measurement problems for the measurement of students' opportunity to learn the material tested. It should be noted that in Sweden, because of a tradition of a highly central-ized school system, the variation in instructional time and curriculum is low by international comparison.

The overall impression given by the results is one of general consis-tency with the model given in Section 2. The model predicts that *only* student characteristics and behaviors will remain as predictors of Achievement, and that all other variables will operate through these. It follows that other predictors which show independent effects are capturing some variance in student characteristics and behaviors which is not captured by the latter measures. This provides an interpretation of the effect shown by *TEABEH.

There are altogether 18 manifest variables measuring teacher behavior, summarized by *TEABEH, and 16 measuring student classroom behavior, summarized by *STBEHS. Only two aspects of student behavior are measured by *STBEHS, namely use of textbooks and use of laboratory equipment. Nothing concerning teacher-student interaction or other learning behaviors appears. A comparison of the manifest variables making up *TEABEH and *STBEH reveals that there is very little overlap between the two sets of measures. Thus *TEABEH appears to measure teacher behaviors which *influence* some aspects of student learning behavior which are not measured by *STUBEH but which more directly influence science achievement. Since these behaviors are not measured by *STBEHS, there is inadequate statistical control on the influence of *TEABEH. Thus the indirect effect of teacher behavior *appears* as a direct effect.

4.3. Micro-Modeling

By hierarchically structuring the latent variables in the macroanalysis presented in Section 4.2, it was possible to obtain a comprehensible overview of the essential causal interrelations in a large and complex system. Such an analysis does not eliminate the need for more intensive analyses focusing more sharply on specific parts of the system. Instead it aids in identifying those parts of the system (i.e., those subsystems) for which more intensive analyses are of special interest.

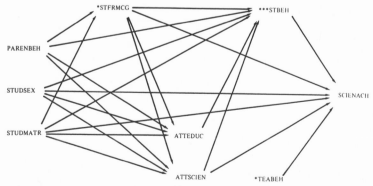

Figure 3-4. A Micro-Model of Influences on Science Achievement

We may identify two types of models: (1) macro- or global models, which cover systems as a whole, and (2) micro- or local models, which cover subsystems selected for more intensive investigation. Such a macro-model is identifiable from the results seen in Tables 3–2 to 3–5. The associated micro-model is shown in Figure 3–4. In the micro-model, the set of latent variables representing student characteristics in the macro-model, **STSTR, is disaggregated into its component parts: STUDSEX, STUDMATR, *STSTRCG, ATTEDUC, and ATTSCIEN. It could be still further broken down by disaggregating *STSTRCG into its component parts, STUDVERB and REASOML. Likewise, ***STBEH and *TEABEH could be disaggregated. Complete disaggregation of all these variables simultaneously, however, would increase the total number of variables in the model from the present nine to nineteen. This would render the model exceedingly difficult to overview and interpret. A more suitable approach for the researcher interested in examining these variables in greater detail might be to first disaggregate ***STBEH but use the aggregated form of **STSTR and *TEABEH, and then disaggregate *TEABEH and use the aggregated forms of **STSTR and ***STBEH. Of course many other choices are available.

Once the model to be analyzed is specified, as in the equation in Section 3.6 above, the analysis is carried out in the usual way. The model here was simplified by removing paths with coefficients less than 0.04, (corresponding closely to the p<0.05 level of significance) and re-estimating. The path coefficients are shown in Table 3–6 and the total effect coefficients are shown in Table 3–7.

Table 3–6

Path Coefficients for the Micro-Analysis

Predictand	(1)	(2)	(3)	(4)	(5)	(6)	(7)	(8)	R²	e
*STSTRCG	13	.	16	.	.	.	.	.	04	98
ATTEDUC	26	05	-14	39	.	.	.	.	25	86
ATTSCIEN	20	-19	-09	27	.	.	.	.	16	92
***STBEH	04	-24	24	36	10	21	.	.	42	76
SCIENACH	.	-17	14	57	.	11	18	06	64	60

NOTE: Coefficients are multiplied by 100.

Three striking features emerge from the micro-analysis, as seen in Table 3–6. First is the absence of a direct influence of Parental Behaviors on Science Achievement. The Parental Behavior variable was entered into this analysis as the single variable most likely to capture the largest portion of the total home influence. It shows a direct influence on student cognitive and affective characteristics and thus has a powerful *indirect* effect on achievement, as seen in Table 3–7. It has no direct influence on achievement, however. This is completely consistent with the model presented in Section 2.

Table 3–7

Total Effect Coefficients for the Micro-Analysis

Predictand	(1)	(2)	(3)	(4)	(5)	(6)	(7)	(8)
				Predictors				
*STSTRCG	13	.	16	.	.	.	.	.
ATTEDUC	31	05	-07	39	.	.	.	.
ATTSCIEN	24	-19	-05	27	.	.	.	.
***STBEH	17	-27	28	46	10	21	.	.
SCIENACH	13	-24	27	68	02	15	18	06

NOTES: 1. Coefficients are multiplied by 100.
   2. Predictors: (1) PARENBEH
            (2) STUDSEX
            (3) STUDMATR
            (4) *STSTRCG
            (5) ATTEDUC
            (6) ATTSCIEN
            (7) ***STBEH
            (8) *TEABEH

The second striking feature in Table 3–6 is the the absence of a direct effect of Attitudes toward Education on Science Achievement. There appears to be a stronger influence of Student Cognitive Characteristics on Attitudes toward Education than on Attitudes toward Science. The influence of Attitudes toward Science on Student Learning Behavior and Science Achievement, however, appears to be greater than the influence of Attitudes toward Education. It may be noted that ATTSCIEN, ***STBEH, and SCIENACH are related specifically to science, whereas *STSTRCG and ATTEDUC are more general. Thus, in accordance with the Specificity-Generality Principle, the more specific stimuli are more strongly related to the more specific responses, and the more general stimuli are more strongly related to the more general responses.

The third striking feature of Table 3–6 is the high proportion of variance explained, with R^2-0.64. This value may be compared with 0.57 achieved in the macro-analysis (Table 3–5), or 0.53 reported in earlier analyses using the same data set (Noonan and Wold, 1980), or 0.36 given for the same data set in the international report of the IEA study (Comber and Keeves, 1973). This increase from 0.57 to 0.64 is due to the disaggregation of the hierarchical latent variable **STSTR and the use of its component parts as distinct predictors in the micro-analysis. This illustrates an important principle: the use of hierarchically structured latent variables in macro-analysis renders large and complex systems sufficiently simple to enable a comprehensive overview and at the same time sufficiently structured to preserve meaningfulness. However, it does not lead to the highest possible R^2. The use of micro-analysis with some degree of disaggregation of the hierarchical structure leads to a higher R^2, but it cannot yield a comprehensive overview of a large and complex system. The use of macro- and micro-analysis together can be very fruitful in systems analysis. Thus macro-analysis is a first stage in the extraction of information from a data set covering a large and complex system, revealing the structure of the system as a whole. This information can then be used in a second stage, involving micro-analysis, to reveal the structure of subsystems.

4.4. Model Evaluation

Three kinds of tests are available for the evaluation of PLS models: (1) Classical estimation of standard errors; (2) Stone-Geisser test of predictive relevance; and (3) Tukey's Jackknife. These methods and their application to PLS models are discussed elsewhere (Wold, 1982; Wold, 1984; Noonan and Wold,1983). It may be noted that model evaluation using Least Squares methods is not disturbed by measurement errors, as it is using Maximum Likelihood methods. Instead, measurement errors and other inaccuracies are embedded in the inference to be evaluated.

5. CONCLUSIONS

5.1. PLS as a Tool for Systems Analysis

A rational society requires the analysis and evaluation of social systems. Such systems are typically large, complex and open. Theoretical information about the structure and process of social systems is generally scarce. PLS represents a middle way between pure data analysis and classical model building. It is Least Squares oriented and thus offers wide scope, great flexibility and optimal accuracy in predictive relations. These features make it a superior tool for the analysis of large and complex open social systems. It is relatively easy to use and is fast on the computer. For example, the computer run for the present study required only 26.4 seconds of CPU time on an IBM 370.

5.2. PLS as a General Tool for Scientific Development Work

PLS is not only a tool for systems analysis, but also a general tool for scientific development work. Three areas can be mentioned: (1) exploratory data analysis, (2) instrument development and (3) theory development.

5.2.1. EXPLORATORY DATA ANALYSIS

In many cases the investigator is faced with massive quantities of data and very little theoretical information. The ease of using PLS and the rapid computation enable the user to have a close dialogue with the data, exploring a variety of models, moving manifest variables from one block to another, breaking up blocks, etc. Even when the user intends to report only simple descriptive results, such as frequency distributions and descriptive statistics for the total sample and selected groups, PLS is a valuable tool for identifying key variables and suggesting ways of examining the data.

5.2.2. INSTRUMENT CONSTRUCTION

In the study of large and complex social systems, instruments (e.g., questionnaires) are often of questionable quality because of the lack of theoretical information. The ordering of variables into blocks and the examination of the results of the analyses provide a great deal of information about the way the instruments work. From the computer output it is possible to identify individual items or groups of items which do not function as expected. In some cases the problem can be traced to the incorrect use of a variable, e.g., the user discovers that the variable should be placed in another block. In other cases the problem can be traced to poor instrument construction, e.g., ambiguous phrasing of an item, inadequate conceptualization, etc. Such information is valuable in the construction of new instruments.

5.2.3. THEORY DEVELOPMENT

Because of its ease of use, scope and flexibility, PLS enables the user to obtain an overview—a holistic perspective—that promotes the development of systemic models. It encourages broad and comprehensive theory, rather than narrow and restricted theory. It can be seen in Noonan and Wold (1984), for example, how the use of PLS encouraged the development of a much wider range of variables than previous models of school learning. This model, developed further in the present paper, extends the range of explanation far beyond psychological and curricular factors to school resources and structure, home and parental factors and societal factors.

NOTE

I am indebted to Norbert Sellin for pointing out to me the implication of contradictory influences among the multiplicity of indirect causal paths and the implication of null links in a causal chain. These points were made in his original discussion paper (Sellin, 1984).

REFERENCES

Blalock, H.J. 1964. *Causal inferences in non-experimental research.* Chapel Hill: University of North Carolina Press.

Carroll, J.B. 1975. *The teaching of French as a foreign language in eight countries.* Stockholm: Almqvist & Wiksell International.

Comber, L.C., and J.P. Keeves. 1973. *Science education in nineteen countries.* Stockholm: Almqvist & Wiksell.

Duncan, O.D. 1971. *Introduction to structural education models.* New York: Academic Press.

Husén, T., ed. 1967. *International study of achievement in mathematics: A comparison of twelve countries.* Stockholm: Almqvist & Wiksell.

Jöreskog, K.G., and H. Wold, eds. 1982. *Systems under indirect observation: Structure, prediction, causality.* 2 vols. Amsterdam: North-Holland.

Lewis, E.G., and C.E. Massad. 1975. *The teaching of English as a foreign language in ten countries.* Stockholm: Almqvist & Wiksell International.

Noonan, R. 1976. *School resources, social class, and student achievement.* Stockholm: Almqvist & Wiksell.

Noonan, R. 1978. An empirical study of two countries: Chile and India. In *Teacher training and student achievement in less developed countries*, Part II, T. Husén, L. Saha and R. Noonan, *Teacher training and student achievenment in less developed countries*. Staff Working Paper, No. 310. Washington, D.C.: The World Bank.

Noonan, R. 1982. School environments and school outcomes: An empirical study using the IEA data. In *Comparative research in education 1975–1980*, eds. M. Niessen and J. Reschar, 169–202. Oxford: Pergamon.

Noonan, R., and H. Wold. 1980. PLS path modelling with latent variables: Analysing school survey data using Partial Least Squares - Part II. *Scandinavian Journal of Educational Research* 24 (1):1–24.

Noonan, R., and H. Wold. 1983. Evaluating school systems using Partial Least Squares. *Evaluation in Education: An International Review Series* 7(3): 219–364. Oxford: Pergamon.

Noonan, R., and H. Wold. 1985. Partial Least Squares. In *International encyclopedia of education*, vol. 7, ed. T. Husén and T.N. Postlethwaite, 3769–3775. Oxford: Pergamon.

Peaker, G.F. 1975. *An empirical study of education in twenty-one countries: A technical report*. Stockholm: Almqvist & Wiksell International.

Purves, A.G. 1973. *Literature education in ten countries: An empirical study*. Stockholm: Almqvist & Wiksell.

Sellin, N. 1986. On path models in educational research. Presented at the Thirteenth International Conference on the Unity of the Sciences, Washington, D.C., September 2-5, 1984.

Simon, H.A. 1957. *Models of man*. New York: Wiley.

Thorndike, R.L. 1973. *Reading comprehension education in fifteen countries: An empirical study*. Stockholm: Almqvist & Wiksell.

Walker, D.A. 1976. *The IEA six subject survey: An empirical study of education in twenty-one countries*. Stockholm: Almqvist & Wiksell International.

Wold, H. 1952. *Demand analysis*. Stockholm: Almqvist & Wiksell. 3rd reprint ed. 1983 Westport, Conn.: Greenwood Press.

Wold, H. 1954. Causality and econometrics. *Econometrics* 22:162–177.

Wold, H. 1982. Soft modelling: The basic design and some extensions. In *Systems under indirect observation: Structure, prediction, causality*, vol. 2, eds. K.G. Jöreskog and H. Wold, 1–59. Amsterdam: North-Holland.

Wold, H. 1985. Partial Least Squares. In *Encyclopedia of statistical sciences*, vol. 6, eds. S. Kotz and N.L. Johnson, 481–491. New York: Wiley.

Wright, S. 1934. The method of path coefficients. *Annals of Mathematical Statistics* 5:161-215.

Wright, S. 1954. The interpretation of multivariate systems. In *Statistics and mathematics in biology*, eds. D. Kempthorne *et al.*,11–33. Ames, Iowa: The Iowa State College Press.

4

Comment on Noonan's Paper

NORBERT SELLIN

1. INTRODUCTION

Richard Noonan's paper gives a comprehensive presentation which captures a general theoretical model for school system evaluation, a set of propositions about factors and processes influencing observed relations, and the empirical test of a complex model. The paper also demonstrates the use of hierarchically structured PLS models, which constitutes a newly developed methodology for the analysis of large and complex path models. It is an impressive piece of work. As it is impossible to cover all parts of Noonan's paper, my comments will concentrate on the estimation of hierarchical structures.

The statistical implementation seems to be the most problematic aspect of the concept of hierarchical structures. Section 2 presents a critique of Noonan's algorithm for estimating hierarchically structured latent variables. Section 3 briefly describes two alternative algorithms.

2. CRITIQUE OF NOONAN'S ALGORITHM

2.1. Estimation of Hierarchical Structures

This section examines some conceptual and statistical aspects of

Noonan's algorithm for estimating hierarchically structured PLS models.
The introduction of hierarchically structured latent variables (LVs)
requires some special terminology in order to distinguish between models
that involve hierarchical latent variables and analogous models that do
not involve hierarchical latent variables. In the present paper the terms
macro-model and *aggregated model* are used to refer to models that involve
hierarchical latent variables. The terms *micro-model* and *disaggregated model*
are used to refer to models that do not involve hierarchical latent variables.

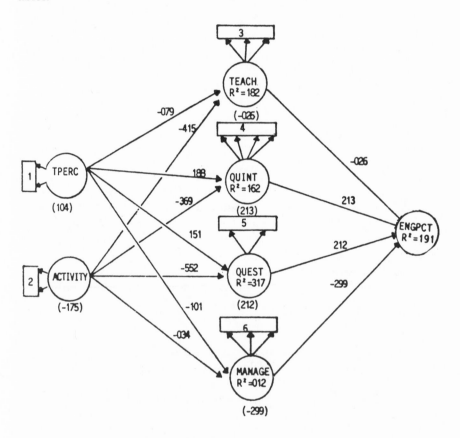

*Figure 4–1: Micro Model, with Total Effects on ENGPCT in Parentheses. (All
Coefficients multiplied by 1000; All Blocks Specified as "Outward")*

The introduction of hierarchically structured latent variables (LVs)
requires some modification of the basic PLS procedure, and it is there-

fore not to be expected that macro-models and corresponding micro-models yield numerically equivalent results. It is desirable, however, that macro-models and corresponding micro-models generally imply similar conclusions in terms of the relative importance of lower level LVs and in terms of the relative importance of manifest variables used to estimate the LVs. The following discussion deals with peculiarities of Noonan's procedure which may lead to a lack of substantive correspondence between macro- and micro-model results.

Table 4–1

Basic Block Structure for Figure 4–1

LV/LV-label	MV/MV-label
TPERC: Teacher perception of class ability	RNEED: Majority of class needs remedial work (1=yes, 0=no)
	ABIL: Low average class ability (1=yes, 0=no)
ACTIVITY: Major class activity	LECTURE: Lecture, explanation, demonstration
	SEATWRK: Seatwork on written assignments
TEACH: Teach students	LE: Verbal lecture
	LEM: Lecture with materials
	EX: Use of examples
QUINT: Questioning, evaluation, feedback	PB: Probes
	RD: Redirect questions
	EF: Effectiveness questions
	AC: Acknowledge correct answer
QUEST: Questions	QTGP: Questions—teacher to group
	QTST: Questions—teacher to student
MANAGE: Classroom management	DI: Discipline
	PR: Procedural interactions
	DR: Directives
ENGPCT: Percent academically engaged students	ENGPCT: Observer rating of percentage of academically engaged students in class

To illustrate possible differences between (hierarchical) macro-models and corresponding (non-hierarchical) micro-models, the PLS model presented in Figure 4–1 will be used as an empirical example. The model is based on data from the Classroom Environment Study conducted by the International Association for the Evaluation of Educational Achievement (IEA). A major aim of this study is to examine relations among observed teacher behaviors, student behaviors and student achievement (cf. Ryan, 1981). The model shown in Figure 4–1 was used in the analysis of data from 65 fifth-grade mathematics classes observed in an Asian country.

A short description of the included constructs and the associated manifest variables is given in Table 4–1. The model relates an observer rating of the percentage of academically engaged students in class (ENGPCT) to four intervening constructs (TEACH, QUINT, QUEST, and MANAGE) comprising indicators of different types of teacher-student interactions. These intervening LVs are related to two exogenous blocks labeled TPERC ACTIVITY. The block TPERC involves two questionnaire items reflecting the teacher's perception of the average class ability. Note that the scaling of the manifest variables implies a *high* value of TPERC if the teacher perceived the class as of comparatively *low* ability. The block ACTIVITY involves two observational indicators reflecting general activities (seatwork and lecture). ACTIVITY is scaled in such a way that a high value indicates a comparatively large amount of seatwork and a small amount of lecture activity.

The recorded teacher-student interactions were aggregated to the teacher or class level by transforming the total frequencies with which each interaction was observed to percentages of all coded interactions. Hence the manifest variable LE, for example, indicates the percentage of all interactions classified as "verbal lecture." A similar procedure was used to aggregate the variable ENGPCT and the activity categories included in the block ACTIVITY.

Figure 4–2 displays a hierarchical model that corresponds to the PLS model shown in Figure 4–1. The intervening blocks from TEACH to MANAGE are summarized by a higher level LV labeled ACTIVE. This higher level LV can be interpreted as reflecting the extent to which the teacher was actively involved in different types of classroom instruction. The hierarchical model depicted in Figure 4–2 has been specified in accordance with two basic principles noted by Noonan and Wold (1983, p. 284): (1) all influences on a given hierarchy operate via lower level LVs, and (2) all influences of lower level LVs are summarized by the top level LVs.

Figures 4–1 and 4–2 display the estimated path coefficients, the R^2 values, and the total effects on ENGPCT. The coefficients displayed in Figure 4–1 were estimated by the basic PLS procedure (non-hierarchical),

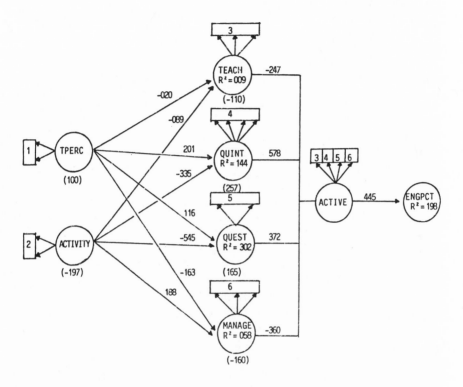

Figure 4-2. Macro-model, with Total Effects on ENGPCT in Parentheses. (All Coefficients Multiplied by 1000; All Blocks Specified as "Outward")

and the coefficients shown in Figure 4–2 were estimated by Noonan's algorithm (hierarchical), with ACTIVE specified as an "outward" block. It can be seen that the model results differ in several respects. The most striking difference concerns the R^2 value of ENGPCT. The R^2 value determined in the hierarchical model is larger than the R^2 values obtained from the micro-model. Noonan states that R^2 values of hierarchical PLS models are generally smaller than the R^2 values for the corresponding micro-models. The above example demonstrates that this assertion is not generally true. A loss of predictive power occurs with regard to the *overall* model results, however, since the mean R^2 value of the hierarchical model is 0.142, while the mean R^2 value of the micro-model is 0.173. This is because the hierarchical model yields smaller R^2 values for the intervening LVs TEACH, QUEST and QUINT. In terms of the estimated effect coefficients, a comparatively large difference is observed for the total effect of TEACH on ENGPCT, for example. The micro-model effect is close to zero (-0.026) while the macro-model yields a relatively strong negative effect (-0.110).

The differences alluded to above occur because Noonan's algorithm departs from the key features of the basic PLS design. To show this it is necessary to present some aspects of both estimation procedures in greater detail. A thorough exposition of the basic PLS procedure and Noonan's procedure for estimating hierarchical structures is to be found in Noonan and Wold (1983).

Noonan's algorithm for estimating hierarchically structured models departs from the basic PLS design with respect to the determination of adjacent constructs (see Wold, 1981 and Noonan and Wold, 1981 for a discussion of the determination of adjacent constructs according to the PLS basic design; see Noonan and Wold, 1983, for a discussion of the determination of adjacent constructs when employing hierarchically structured latent variables). As indicated in Figure 4–2, the manifest variables associated with the blocks from TEACH to MANAGE are summarized in the higher level LV ACTIVE. Noonan's estimation procedure works, intuitively speaking, "downward" from the top level of a given hierarchy to the lowest level. The PLS iteration is performed at the top level using *subsequent* LV's only for determining the corresponding adjacent construct (cf. Noonan and Wold, 1983, p. 284). That is, in Figure 4–2 the weights of the manifest variables belonging to the blocks TEACH to MANAGE are determined with regard to ENGPCT only. These weights are then inserted into the lower level blocks and are transformed so as to give the lower level LVs unit variance. The difference between adjacent constructs used to estimate the intervening blocks is the source of the deviations between the micro-model and the macro-model results described before.

Three further aspects of Noonan's procedure should be noted: First, causal chains consisting of hierarchically structured LVs are estimated by moving from the last endogenous part of the model, over intervening parts, to the exogenous part. For example, the model shown in Figure 4–4 could be estimated by completing, first, an iteration sequence using the blocks ACTIVE and ENGPCT only, and then by continuing with a second iteration sequence for estimating the blocks TPERC and ACTIVITY. Above all, this implies that information coming from exogenous blocks is not used for estimating intervening and endogenous LVs.

Second, Noonan's procedure allows specification of causal relations among lower level LVs, but these relations are not incorporated into the iteration process. This feature may constitute an additional source of deviations between micro- and macro-modelling results.

Third, the same estimation mode is applied to all LVs in a given hierarchy. That is, the estimation mode used to determine the top level LV is also applied to all lower level LVs.

The critical point of Noonan's algorithm is not the mere occurrence of numerical differences between macro-models and corresponding micro-models. Rather, it is the departure from fundamental principles of the basic PLS design which ought to be questioned. While it is true that the introduction of hierarchically structured LVs helps to test large and complex path models, the option chosen by Noonan to modify the original PLS estimation procedure seems to be somewhat less than optional. My main objection is that the algorithm introduces a reductionist component into the estimation of hierarchical PLS models. During iteration, causal chains are divided into separate parts which are consecutively estimated by moving from the last endogenous segment to the exogenous segment of a given model. This is because the estimation of hierarchical blocks is exclusively directed toward subsequent LVs, while information from causally prior LVs is discarded. That is, Noonan's procedure treats each hierarchy as if it were an exogenous LV, irrespective of whether a given hierarchy is specified as exogenous or as intervening. It is primarily this feature which seems to be questionable.

The basic PLS design, on the other hand, can be expected to approximate intervening blocks as "best mediating factors," since these blocks are explicitly estimated as predictors and predictands. This property appears to be jeopardized in Noonan's approach. Another critical point in Noonan's procedure concerns primarily practical aspects. As noted by Noonan, hierarchical models are primarily intended to aid in identifying micro-models for more intensive investigations. Due to the differences between estimation procedures, however, macro- and micro-modeling results are not necessarily consistent in the sense that macro-models and corresponding micro-models generally imply similar conclusions in terms of the relevance of lower level LVs and manifest variables. Hence, PLS analyses on the basis of hierarchical models may occasionally suggest model modifications or interpretations of results which differ substantially from conclusions based on the analysis of corresponding micro-models.

3. ALTERNATIVE ALGORITHMS

This section briefly describes two algorithms which constitute possible alternatives to Noonan's algorithm. For convenience, Noonan's algorithm will be labeled Algorithm I, and the two alternative algorithms will be labeled Algorithms II and III. An obvious alternative to Algorithm I is to estimate the lowest level LVs directly and to construct hierarchies by moving "upwards" from lower level LVs to higher level LVs. This is the basic idea of Algorithms II and III.

Algorithm II assumes the same basic model structure as illustrated in Figure 4–2. That is, influences on the hierarchy are assumed to operate via the lowest level LVs, and influences on variables outside the hierarchy are assumed to operate through the top level constructs. For estimating the lowest level LVs it is necessary to create appropriate adjacent constructs. This is done by considering the predictors of a given lower level LV and the predictands of the top level LV as adjacent LVs. For the model in Figure 4–2 this results in exactly the same adjacent constructs of the blocks TEACH to MANAGE as used in the corresponding micro-model. Note that the above rule allows for the use of different estimation modes for lower level LVs in the same hierarchy, and that causal relations among lower level LVs would be incorporated into the iteration process.

In a second step, lower level LVs need to be combined into higher level LVs. This is accomplished by treating lower level LVs in exactly the same way as manifest variables and by applying the normal PLS estimation procedure. That is, higher level LVs may be specified as "outward" or "inward" blocks, and the associated lower level LVs are simply treated as indicators. The predictands of the top level LV are considered as adjacent LVs, i.e., the estimation of higher level LVs is directed toward subsequent blocks only. Note that the estimation mode applied to higher level LVs may be different from the estimation mode applied to lower level LVs. In short, Algorithm II simply applies the basic PLS procedure to all blocks involved in a given hierarchy and determines adjacent composites in accordance with the assumed flow of information.

Figure 4–3 illustrates the hierarchical model that corresponds to Algorithm III. This algorithm works in much the same way as Algorithm II, but allows for the specification of direct effects on the top level LV. Accordingly, predictors and predictands of the top level LVs are defined as adjacent to the lower level LVs as well as adjacent to the top level LVs.

For comparative purposes, Tables 4–2 and 4–3 present selected results (total effects on ENGPCT and R^2 values) obtained on the basis of the example used before. It is not possible to discuss the estimation procedures and the respective results in detail, but the following brief comments should suffice: (1) The largest R^2 value of ENGPCT is obtained by Noonan's algorithm, with ACTIVE specified as an "inward" block. Since

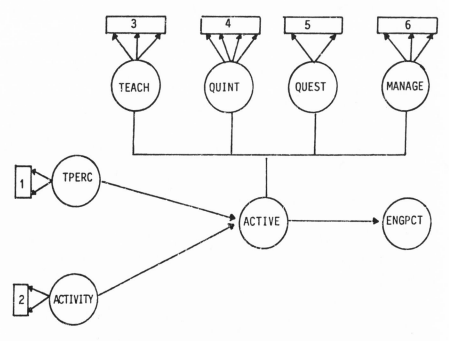

Figure 4-3. Hierarchical Model Corresponding to Algorithm III.

Noonan's algorithm involves a multiple regression on ENGPCT on all manifest variables belonging to the intervening LVs, this value is, in fact, the maximum R^2 that can be achieved on the basis of the blocks TEACH to MANAGE. It will be noted, however, that a loss of predictive power occurs with respect to the overall model results (compare Table 4–3). (2) Due to the use and definition of adjacent constructs, Algorithm II results in a very close correspondence between macro-model and micro-model coefficients. If ACTIVE is specified as an "inward" block, the macro-model is, in fact, equivalent to the underlying micro-model. This is a direct consequence of the way in which Algorithm II has been designed. It must be noted, however, that the numerical equivalence is due to the fact that ENGPCT involves just one manifest variable. Differences will normally occur if a given endogenous LV involves multiple manifest variables. In general, however, Algorithm II can be expected to produce macro-model results which are fairly close to the results obtained from corresponding micro-models. (3) The outcomes of Algorithm III appear to be rather unsatisfactory. The procedure results in the largest loss of information, and therefore some further modifications seem to be necessary. The

examples and the results presented here are, of course, by no means sufficient to allow definitive conclusions, and further research on the estimation of hierarchical structures will therefore be necessary.

Table 4–2

Total Effects on ENGPCT: Disaggregated Model and Hierarchical Model.
(Coefficients multiplied by 1000)

		Algorithm					
		I		II		III	
	Disaggr.	Mode		Mode		Mode	
LV	Model	A	B	A	B	A	B
TPERC	104	100	117	097	104	070	075
ACTIVITY	-175	-197	-155	-214	-175	-227	-238
TEACH	-026	-110	-145	021	-026	084	099
QUINT	213	257	225	238	213	195	167
QUEST	212	165	167	225	212	224	258
MANAGE	-299	-160	-330	-198	-299	-074	-144
ACTIVE	-	445	490	423	437	371	394

Note: Mode A: hierarchical block ACTIVE outward
Mode B: hierarchical block ACTIVE inward

Table 4–3

R2 Values: Disaggregated Model and Hierarchical Models.
(Coefficients multiplied by 1000)

		Algorithm					
		I		II		III	
	Disaggr.	Mode		Mode		Mode	
LV	Model	A	B	A	B	A	B
TEACH	182	009	095	182	182	060	074
QUINT	162	144	116	162	162	197	170
QUEST	317	302	284	317	317	294	272
MANAGE	012	058	037	012	012	001	000
ENGPCT	191	198	240	178	191	138	155
Mean	173	142	154	170	173	138	134

Note: R^2 values for Algorithm III were determined by substitutive prediction.

REFERENCES

Noonan, R., and H. Wold. 1982. PLS path modeling with indirectly observed variables: A comparison of alternative estimates for the latent variable. In *Systems under indirect observation: Structure, prediction, causality*, vol. 2, eds. K.G. Jöreskog and H. Wold, 75–94. Amsterdam: North-Holland.

Noonan, R., and H. Wold. 1983. Evaluating school systems using partial least squares. *Evaluation in Education: An International Review Series* 7(3): 219–304. Oxford: Pergamon.

Ryan, D.W. 1981. An organizing framework for the IEA classroom environment study: Teaching for learning. Toronto: The Ontario Institute for Studies in Education.

Wold, H. 1982. Soft modeling: The basic design and some extensions. In *Systems under indirect observation: Structure, prediction, causality*, vol. 2, eds. K.G. Jöreskog and H. Wold, 1–54. Amsterdam: North-Holland.

5

Discussion of Noonan's Paper

JOSEF ROGOWSKI

Richard Noonan wrote in his paper: "Evaluation research must be based on theory. Theory is required at all stages of research, from sampling design, to instrument construction, to data analysis, to interpretation and reporting." Each theory contains theoretical concepts (for example, in economic science, the level of development of industry is talked about) which have no direct interpretation in the real world. We can specify such concepts in terms of empirical knowledge by means of indicators (manifest variables), using deductive or inductive inference. The PLS soft-modeling of Herman Wold (1979, 1982) uses two types of inference, called Mode A and Mode B. So for any latent variable all indicators are assumed to provide the same type of inference: either Mode A (outward directed) or Mode B (inward directed). The decision to apply Mode A or Mode B is facilitated by the following rules (cf. J.-B. Lohmöller, 1981):

– If all indicators for the given LV are formative, then Mode B is chosen and, in the case of reflective indicators, Mode A.

– If the given LV is exogenous, then Mode B is chosen, and in the case of endogenous LV, the choice is Mode A.

In this paper Mode K is introduced. In this Mode, we can specify theoretical concepts in deductive and inductive ways at the same time. In other words, we can obtain an LV where one group of indicators is formative (Mode B) and the other one is reflective (Mode A); this hybrid mode is called Mode K. An example of an arrow scheme for an LV with the new mode is exhibited in Figure 5–1.

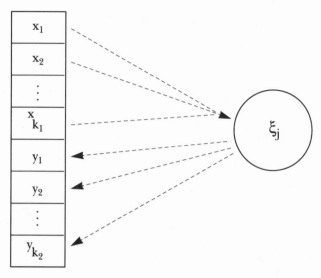

Figure 5-1. Arrow Scheme Mode K for an LV in a PLS model

The estimation of a model with LVs having Mode K combines PLS Mode A and Mode B. Assume that Figure 5–1 shows part of a soft model. We shall now describe how the model is estimated by PLS Mode K.

The difference between this method and Wold's PLS is that in one and the same block some weights are computed using Mode A, other weights are computed using Mode B (cf. Wold, 1979).

Assume that we have obtained the new weights w_{ij}^s, v_{ij}^s and the new proxy values of the estimated LVs: KSI_{jt}^s at the sth cycle. At iteration s+1 the inside estimates A_j^{s+1} of the LVs are calculated. Then we can estimate the new weights 'w_{ij}^{s+1} and 'v_{ij}^{s+1} in the following way:

(i) for i=1, ..., k_1 the weights w_{ij}^{s+1} are the OLS estimators of parameters of the following equation:

$$(s\text{-}1)\ A_{jt}^{s+1} = \sum_{i=1}^{k_1} {}'w_{ij}^{s+1}\, x_{it} + error\ (t=1,...,T)$$

(ii) for i=1, ..., k_2 the weights 'v_{ij}^{s+1} are the OLS estimators of parameters of the following equations:

$$(2)\ y_{it} = {}'v_{ij}^{s+1}\, A_{jt}^{s+1} + error\ (t=1,...,T).$$

Subsequently we standardize the new weights to give w_{ij}^{s+1} and v_{ij}^{s+1} as is done in Wold's basic PLS design, and we calculate the new proxy values of the LVs by applying the following formula:

$$(\text{s-3}) \quad kSI_{jt}^{s+1} = \sum_{i=1}^{k_1} w_{ij}^{s+1} x_{it} + \sum_{i=1}^{k_2} v_{ij}^{s+1} y_{it}.$$

The remaining part of the estimation process is the same as in the basic PLS design.

Note that formula (s-1) is the way of obtaining the new weights in PLS Mode B, and formula (s-2) in PLS Mode A.

Mode K has been applied to a socio-economic PLS soft model for Poland with 75 MVs and 9 LVs. It has been assumed that all endogenous MVs (for example, production per capita in an industrial sector) are reflective (Mode A) and obtain the LVs in the deductive way, and the remaining MVs are formative (Mode B) and obtain the LVs in the inductive way. This model has been estimated on real data from 1950 to 1982. The resulting SG test criterion Q^2 is equal to 0.707.

REFERENCES

Lohmöller, J.-B. 1981. LVPLS 1.6 program manual: Latent variables path analysis with Partial Least Squares estimation. (Forschungsbericht 81.04 Fachbereich Pädagogik.) München: Hochschule der Bundeswehr. 1983; Köln Universität, Zentralarchiv für empirische Sozialforschung.

Noonan, R. 1989. Chap. 3 in the present volume, especially the beginning.

Wold, H. 1983. Fix-Point method. In *Encyclopedia of statistical sciences*, vol. 3, eds. S. Kotz and N.L. Johnson, 148–156. New York: Wiley.

Wold, H. 1985. Partial Least Squares. In *Encyclopedia of statistical sciences*, vol. 6, eds. S. Kotz and N.L. Johnson, 481–491. New York: Wiley.

6

Estimation of RE-models and Some Remarks on Model Specification in Econometrics

---

BERND SCHIPS

1. RE-MODELS IN ECONOMIC THEORY AND ECONOMETRICS

In the scientific explanation of economic phenomena in the real world expectations play an essential part (see for example Drazen, 1980). Therefore, different hypotheses on the formation of expectations have been discussed. The rational expectations (RE) hypothesis was first formulated by Muth (1961). The term 'rational expectations' is used here in accordance with the classical definition given by Muth which usually is summarized in the statement that predictions of economic units are as correct as those of the economic model applied. This idea now has been recognized as an important step towards understanding how expectations are formed. The full impact of this hypothesis has been appreciated in economic theory and its policy implications have been assessed.

Parallel to these research efforts on a more theoretical level, an increasing number of econometricians have turned their attention to the problem of estimating RE-models and testing the RE-hypothesis.

The existing econometric literature on RE-models draws on known estimating techniques. In most cases the maximum estimation principle has been used to solve the estimation problem for the unknown structural form coefficients of the RE-models. The theoretical superiority of the maximum-likelihood approach, as far as the estimation of the structural parameters is concerned, is well known. A fully developed asymptotic theory is available and it is possible to assess the properties of the estimators in terms of consistency and efficiency. Furthermore, the asymptotic theory also provides the basis for hypotheses testing and for statistical inference.

However, the maximum-likelihood procedure leads to serious practical difficulties. It necessitates the identification of the structural parameters and the full specification of the form of the distribution of the errors; it leads to highly complicated non-linear systems whose solutions may not easily converge numerically; it is not readily applicable to the case of models of even moderate size (Wallis, 1980).

Another estimation principle in the case of RE-models is given by the minimum-distance estimation. Similar to the maximum-likelihood procedure, this estimation technique has to solve a system of equations which is non-linear in the unknown structural form coefficients. Furthermore, the instrumental variable principle is used by substituting suitable variables that were obtained from outside the considered model for the unobservable RE. This approach, moreover, seems to be unsatisfactory from a theoretical point of view since it is not compatible with the RE-hypothesis which assumes that RE are predictions of the model considered.

2. CLASSICAL AND PREDICTION ORIENTED ESTIMATION METHODS

The proper identification of dynamic macroeconomic models is difficult. The reason for this is that the identifying restrictions are pragmatically adjusted so as to avoid obvious conflicts with the data, so that these restrictions can only be regarded as simplifications, not as *a priori* knowledge imposed on the data (Sims, 1980). Though this is a critical point in econometric model building, it does not lead to the conclusion that macroeconomic models are of no value in the preparation of economic policy decisions. The well known rational expectations critique (Lucas and Sargent, 1978)is only a special case of the fact that statistical models are likely to become unreliable for conditions far outside the historically normal range experienced in the sample data.

But the traditional econometric methods for estimating simultaneous equation models require the identification of the structural parameters. Only if the identification problem is really solved can asymptotically justified estimation methods be used. However, the identification problem cannot be solved by the more or less pragmatic use of exclusion restrictions. The basic hypothesis that the considered model is correct (at least the non-stochastic part of the model specification) is the critical and important point. Econometric models are approximations only; they are never correct. Identification is a necessary condition for the existence of estimators with the desired asymptotic properties like consistency. Therefore, the identification problem gives a further argument supporting the choice of a prediction oriented method estimating simultaneous equation models, instead of a parametric asymptotically justified estimation procedure. Examples of this class of estimation techniques are the fix-point method suggested by Wold (1965), the estimation principle which minimizes simultaneously the residuals of a dynamic prediction simulation (Lange and Schips, 1983) and the prediction oriented estimators for disequilibrium models recently developed by Frei (1984).

Alternative methods proposed for the necessary exploratory data analysis—methods for analyzing the direction of causality and methods which involve the estimation of general unrestricted vector autoregressive systems—do not eliminate the identification problem mentioned above; however, with these time series approaches the problem will not be 'solved' by simple use of arbitrary exclusion restrictions (Sims,1980).

The main point is that only careful statistical model building of the historical structure can be used to make conditional forecasts which will be appropriate for economic policy analysis. Statistical models and estimation methods should be used which do not insist on identifying parameters of behavior which are invariant to unprecedented changes.

The concepts of objectivity, consistency and efficiency—in fact, all the concepts of traditional estimation theory—utterly lose their meaning by the time an applied econometrician starts to work (Leamer, 1983). Often the relevant economic theory does not yield precise information regarding functional forms of relationships, lag structures, and other elements involved in a stochastic specification of a model. Therefore, a trial-and-error process is necessary. The usual specification search invalidates the supposed theories of inference. Good formal sequential testing procedures for model specification have only recently been developed.

The model building activities in econometrics should be concentrating on prediction-oriented estimation procedures, like the fix-point method, in combination with data-oriented approaches for measuring the accuracy of the model and the parameter estimates. Predictions are in general more relevant for inference than parameter estimation, since predictions can often be adequately assessed in real situations. The prediction-oriented estimation methods are not focused on asymptotic properties of the estimators and therefore they need only weak assumptions on the model, especially on the distribution of the error terms. Since the fix-point method belongs to the least-squares oriented estimation procedures, tests like Stone-Geisser's Q^2 and Tukey's jackknife can be used, because these tests and the fix-point estimation principle are distribution-free in the exogenous variables (Stone, 1974; Geisser, 1974; Tukey, 1958; Bergström and Wold, 1983). All these methods are in line with the fact that econometric model building is a trial-and-error process, and in line with one of the main questions in applied economics: can a chosen model be used to predict an interesting economic phenomenon in the real world, or not?

Now the fix-point method is well known, but widespread use is still restrained. The maximum-likelihood mainstream constitutes a substantial resistance to the acceptance of these new ideas and methods by scientists.

3. FIX-POINT ESTIMATION OF RE-MODELS

The conditional expectation interpretation of the explanatory endogenous variables in a simultaneous equations model by Wold is intimately related to the concept of RE. As a consequence, the application of the fix-point principle to RE-models is a natural step.

It has been shown that the fix-point principle of Wold (1980) can be easily extended to static linear models which do not contain future rational expectations, and still produce consistent estimators for the unknown structural form coefficients (Loesch 1981). The fix-point principle can be extended even to linear dynamic models which do include future expectations models (Loesch, 1983). The fix-point principle turns out to be essentially less restrictive than the maximum-likelihood procedure with regard to the size of those models, and beyond this the fix-point method can be extended to nonlinear models which are linear in the unknown coefficients.

For example, a linear rational expectations model with future rational expectations has the form:

$$y(t) = \sum_{h=0}^{H} B_h\, y(t-h) + \sum_{k=0}^{K} A_k y^* \,(t+k \mid t-1) + \sum_{r=0}^{R} D_r x(t-r) + u(t),\ t=1,\ldots,T$$

The endogenous variables $y(t-h)$ and the exogenous variables $x(t-r)$ are observables. In accordance with the rational expectations hypothesis, the $y^*(t+k|t-1)$ are defined as the expectations of $y(t+k)$. These expectations are generated by the model depending on information I_{t-1} available at time t-1 (conditional expectations):

$y^*(t+k \mid t-1) := E[y(t+k) \mid I_{t-1}]$

A detailed analysis of the system of equations shows that there is a feedback not only from the past to the present, but also from the future to the present. In the case of K>0 and $A_k \neq 0$, it is well known that the model is not completely specified, since a unique expectation mechanism does not exist. "Thus, the solution is not determined by initial conditions determined by past actual values of variables, but by terminal conditions in people's minds relating to what people will expect in the future" (Shiller, 1978). To overcome the indeterminacy of the solution of future expectation variables, "an advocate of rational expectations needs to supply an additional condition" (Chow, 1980). Such an additional condition is given by the fact that the expectations $y^*(t+k \mid t-1)$, k=0,...,K, as they are explicitly contained in the model, are determined by the mechanism provided by the model and the assumption that the expectations $y^*(t+K+k \mid t-1)$, k=1,...,K are determined outside of the model and are observable. If the ARMA(p,q) model for the exogenous variables x(t) is known, the expectations $\hat{x}(t+k \mid t-1) = E[x(t+k) \mid I_{t-1}]$, k=0,1...,K can also be considered observable. These predictions and the considered model successively allow the determination of values for the $y^*(t+k \mid t-1)$, k=0,...,K in accordance with the rational expectations hypothesis.

The expectations of the exogenous variables in the RE-models are described by ARMA-models in accordance with the rational expectations hypothesis.

4. EXAMPLE: AN ECONOMETRIC EXCHANGE RATE MODEL WITH RE

Many studies deal with the results of empirical exchange rate models. Recently Meese and Rogoff (1983) found that a random walk model performs as well as any estimated model. The two authors compare the out-of-sample forecasting accuracy of various structural and time series models. Even the exchange rate in the forward market does not predict any better than the random walk model. Meese and Rogoff try to analyze possible reasons for the poor out-of-sample fit of the structural models. They argue that difficulties in modeling expectations of the explanatory variables are a source of these troubles. Accordingly, the role of expectations is an important element of the following econometric exchange rate model (for details see Abrahamsen and Schips, 1983). Primarily, the model was chosen as an example of the possibility of estimating an econometric RE-model with the extended fix-point method. Furthermore, to our own surprise, the model worked quite well.

In explaining the spot rates between the German Mark, the Swiss Franc and the U.S. Dollar, an attempt is made to describe the structure of the relevant economic system. Since 1973, exchange rates have been managed in three different ways: by official interventions in the foreign exchange market, by monetary policy and by capital controls. These possibilities are taken into account as arguments in the specification process of the model.

The following abbreviations are used:

B	: Monetary Base	
D	: Governmental Debt (nominal)	
e	: Exchange Rate	
f^i	: Forward Premium i Months	
i_1	: Interest Rate 1 Month Euromarket	
i_6	: Interest Rate 6 Months Euromarket	
I	: Imports (deflated)	
M_1	: Monetary Aggregate M1	
M_3	: Monetary Aggregate M3	
Pc	: Consumer Price	
Pw	: Wholesale Price	
r	: Inflation Rate	
T	: Retail Sales (deflated)	

dummy: Dummy Variable: 0   : until 1980

1/k   : 1981, k = 1,...,12

1   : from 1982

Suffixes:

g	: Germany / DM
s	: Switzerland / frs
u	: U.S.A. / U.S.$
n	: Nominal Values
*	: Expected Values
Q^2	: Stone-Geisser Test on predictive relevance

The coefficients in the following equations are results of the fix-point estimation and the jackknifed fix-point estimation. (The figures in the first line of the equations are the RE fix-point parameter estimates; those in the second line, the jackknifed RE fix-point estimates. The figures in brackets are the standard errors of the jackknifed RE fix-point estimates (Bergström and Wold, 1983).

The model is primarily based upon the monetary approach, which in our specification implies the validity of the purchasing power parity model. In measuring purchasing power, the consumer price indices are used, and both the current price levels and the expected future levels appear directly as explanatory variables. Furthermore, the effect of international capital movements are taken into account by comparing the interest rates for the expectation horizons in the Euromarket:

$$(1) \quad e_t^{s/g} = \quad 182.98 + \quad 0.050 \ Pc_t^{*,g} - \quad 0.21 \ Pc_t^{*,s} + 1.23 \ Pc_{t+6}^{*,g}$$
$$\phantom{(1) \quad e_t^{s/g} = } 179.03 \quad -0.14 \qquad\quad -1.97 \qquad\quad 1.36$$
$$\phantom{(1) \quad e_t^{s/g} = } (16.87) \quad (1.17) \qquad\quad (0.53) \qquad\quad (1.06)$$

$$ - 1.87 \ Pc_{t+6}^{*,s} - 4.35 \ i_{6t}^g + 5.07 \ i_{6t}^s$$
$$ - 1.97 \qquad\quad - 4.28 \qquad 4.95$$
$$ (0.53) \qquad\quad (1.20) \qquad (1.04)$$
$$ Q^2 = 0.7857$$

$$(2) \quad e_t^{s/u} = \quad 0.37 + \ 0.46 \ Pc_{t+6}^{*,s} - 0.024 \ Pc_{t+6}^{*,u} + \ 0.12 \ i_{6t}^s - 0.11 \ i_{6t}^u$$
$$\phantom{(2) \quad e_t^{s/u} = } 0.38 \quad 0.046 \qquad\quad - 0.024 \qquad\quad 0.12 \quad - 0.11$$
$$\phantom{(2) \quad e_t^{s/u} = } (0.59) \ (0.011) \qquad (0.0071) \qquad (0.0097) \ (0.017)$$
$$ Q^2 = 0.8998$$

The influences of the expected price levels and the interest rates partly differ from the usual *a priori* knowledge. These results may be a consequence of currency substitution (Boehm, 1984).

The price levels are assumed to be determined by economic processes theoretically close to the quantity theory, that is to say, the wholesale price level is explained by the lagged quantity of money and the level of economic activity in the countries analyzed. Economic activity is described by retail sales which are deflated by consumer prices. For Switzerland, a typical small, open economy, the foreign exchange rate is assumed to be an important by way of influencing import prices, and for the U.S.A., the interest rate is taken into account:

$$(3) \quad Pw_t^g = \quad 141.70 + \ 0.22 \ M_{1, \ t-16} + 0.12 \ M_{1, \ t-31} - 0.85 \ T_{t-2}^g$$
$$ 141.59 \quad 0.22 \qquad\quad 0.12 \qquad\quad - 0.85$$
$$ (1.46) \ (0.0060) \qquad (0.0050) \qquad (0.014)$$
$$ Q^2 = 0.9992$$

$$(4) \quad Pw_t^s = \quad 133.72 + 0.50 \ M_{1t-22}^s + 0.95 \ M_{1t-37}^s - 0.59 \ T_{t-2}^s + 7.00 \ e_{t-2}^{s/u}$$
$$ 134.18 \quad 0.50 \qquad\quad 0.95 \qquad\quad - 0.60 \qquad 6.97$$
$$ (11.74) \ (0.038) \qquad (0.020) \qquad (0.12) \qquad (0.36)$$
$$ Q^2 = 0.9901$$

$$(5) \quad Pw_t^u = \quad 77.92 + 0.036 \ M_{3t-4}^u - 0.0016 \ M_{3t-16}^u - 0.79 \ T_{t-2}^u + 1.29 \ i_{1t}^u$$
$$ 77.14 \quad 0.036 \qquad\quad - 0.0016 \qquad\quad - 0.78 \qquad 1.29$$
$$ (5.87) \ (0.0068) \qquad (0.0072) \qquad (0.063) \qquad (0.045)$$
$$ Q^2 = 0.9960$$

The consumer price levels are determined by the current or the past wholesale price levels, which are adjusted by the money aggregates and the deflated retail sales, respectively:

$$(6\text{-}6)\, Pc_t^g = 19.08 + 0.68\, Pw_{t-6}^g + 0.092\, M_{1,t-11}^g - 0.043\, T_{t-1}^g$$

$$\quad\quad\quad 19.07 \quad\quad 0.68 \quad\quad\quad 0.092 \quad\quad\quad -0.043$$

$$\quad\quad\quad (2.22)\ (0.011) \quad\quad (0.0039) \quad\quad (0.015)$$

$$Q^2 = 0.9995$$

$$(6\text{-}7)\quad Pc_t^s = -88.27 + 0.92\, Pw_{t-6}^s + 0.40\, M_{1,t-5}^s + 0.22\, T_{t-1}^s$$

$$\quad\quad\quad -88.40 \quad\quad 0.92 \quad\quad\quad 0.40 \quad\quad\quad 0.22$$

$$\quad\quad\quad (2.54)\ (0.0041) \quad\quad (0.011) \quad\quad (0.024)$$

$$Q^2 = 0.9969$$

$$(6\text{-}8)\quad Pc_t^u = 28.68 + 0.59\, Pw_t^u + 0.020\, M_{3,t-7}^u - 0.27\, T_{t-2}^u$$

$$\quad\quad\quad 28.72 \quad\quad 0.59 \quad\quad\quad 0.020 \quad\quad\quad -0.27$$

$$\quad\quad\quad (0.64)\ (0.0056) \quad\quad (0.0003) \quad\quad (0.0072)$$

$$Q^2 = 0.9990$$

According to several publications on interest rates, the real rate of return is not postulated to be constant (for example, Granziol and Schelbert, 1983). The interest rates in the Euromarket—at least in the short run—are considered to vary with changes in money variables such as the money base, the money aggregates M_1 resp. M_3, and foreign interest rates. The dollar interest rate is also considered to vary with governmental debt. However, the effects of changes in money base and M_1 are, in both cases, of an ambiguous nature. First, these variables have a liquidity effect on the money market and tend to decrease the interest rate. But, at the same time, these changes may be interpreted as a change in monetary and possibly fiscal policy. In this way, the change in the quantity of money has a crucial effect on the expected rate of inflation, and the change indirectly influences the interest rate in a way opposite from that indicated by the liquidity effect. That is to say, a money expansion leads to a rise or fall of the interest rates, depending on the inflation experiences of an economy. As a matter of fact, the empirical results show a different influence of the money aggregate on interest rates in the U.S.A. as compared to the other two countries. An attempt to explain these results by way of the redundance of the monetary policy is described by Buettler and Schiltknecht (1982).

$$(6\text{-}9)\, i_{1,t}^g = 1.97 - 0.015\, B_t^g + 0.62\, i_{1,t}^s + 0.44\, i_{1,t-1}^u$$

$$\quad\quad\quad 1.88 \quad -0.014 \quad\quad 0.62 \quad\quad 0.43$$

$$\quad\quad\quad (0.47)\ (0.0059) \quad (0.051)\ (0.050)$$

$$Q^2 = 0.9745$$

(6-10) $i_{1,t}^s = 4.00 + 0.74\, i_{1,t-1}^s - 0.20\, B_t^s + 0.22\, i_{1t}^u$
          3.97   0.74 -0.19 0.12
          (0.33)   (0.021)   (0.016)   (0.016)
    $Q^2 = 0.9974$

(6-11) $i_{1t}^u = 1.00\, i_{1,t-1}^u + 0.047\, M_{3,t-3}^u - 0.046\, M_{3,t-4}^u + 0.25\, Pc_{t-12}^u$
          1.00   0.047 -0.046 0.26
        (0.023)   (0.023)   (0.024)   (0.42)

          $-0.28\, Pc_{t-2}^u - 0.0007\, \text{dummy}*D_{t-1}^u$
          $-0.29 - 0.0007$
          (0.41) (0.0003)
    $Q^2 = 0.9986$

(6-12) $i_{6,t}^g = 0.47 + 0.90\, i_{1,t}^g + 0.035\, i_{6,t-1}^u$
          0.47   0.90   0.035
        (0.093)(0.021)   (0.018)
    $Q^2 = 0.9639$

(6-13) $i_{6t}^s = 2.05 + 0.35\, i_{1,t}^s - 0.073\, M_{1,t}^s - 0.15\, Pw_{t-2}^s + 0.15\, Pw_{t-8}^s + 0.72\, i_{6,t-1}^g$
          2.36   0.35 -0.074 -0.17 0.17   0.74
        (1.78) (0.10)   (0.016)   (0.11)   (0.11)   (0.15)
    $Q^2 = 0.9591$

(6-14) $i_{6,t}^u = 0.21 + 0.84\, i_{1,t}^u + 0.0012\, M_{3,t-1}^u$
          0.22   0.84   0.0012
        (0.17) (0.014)   (0.0002)
    $Q^2 = 0.9936$

In addition to the money base, further important factors in the equation for the money aggregate (M_1 resp. M_3) are the price level and retail sales which take the nominal level of economic activity into consideration. Finally, the opportunity costs of money holding are taken into account by interest rates:

(6-15) $M_{1,t}^g = 51.24 + 1.28\, B_t^g - 1.04\, Pc_t^g + 0.73\, T_t^{n,g} - 0.86\, i_{1,t-1}^g$
          50.93   1.29 -1.03 0.73 -0.88
                (4.05) (0.031)   (0.064)   (0.065)   (0.094)
    $Q^2 = 0.9986$

(6-16) $M_{1,t}^s = -79.88 + 1.82\, B_{t-1}^s + 0.057\, Pc_t^s \quad + 0.73\, T_t^s - 0.71\, i_{1,t-1}^s$
          -79.30 1.81   0.062   0.72 -0.72
        (10.63) (0.055)   (0.035)   (0.094)   (0.11)
    $Q^2 = 0.9764$

(6-17) $M_{3,t}^u = -163.14 + 0.91\, M_{3,t-1}^u + 2.26\, Pc_{t-2}^u + 1.68\, T_{t-1}^u - 1.17\, i_{1t-1}^u$
          -158.03 0.92   2.20   1.63 -1.14
        (23.11) (0.012)   (0.30)   (0.23)   (0.17)
    $Q^2 = 1.000$

Retail sales at constant prices are, on the one hand, described by a first order autoregressive process. On the other hand, it is assumed that changes in the level of sales are caused by price movements, monetary policy, and current imports (supplied on the home market):

$(6\text{-}18)$ $T_t^g = 7.49 + 0.96\ T_{t-1}^g + 0.012\ M_{1,t-3}^g - 0.055\ Pw_t^g$
$\qquad\quad\ 7.69\quad\ 0.96\qquad\ 0.012\qquad\ -0.056$
$\qquad\quad (4.05)\,(0.032)\quad (0.0097)\qquad (0.021)$
$\quad Q^2 = 0.9939$

$(6\text{-}19)$ $T_t^s = 17.93 + 0.83\ T_{t-1}^s - 0.027\ Pc_t^s + 0.88\ I_{t-1}^s$
$\qquad\quad 17.85\quad 0.84\qquad -0.027\qquad\ 0.88$
$\qquad\quad\ (4.10)\,(0.041)\quad (0.0055)\qquad (0.15)$
$\quad Q^2 = 0.9758$

$(6\text{-}20)$ $T_t^u = 4.58 + 0.96\ T_{t-1}^u - 0.013\ Pc_t^u$
$\qquad\quad\ 4.56\quad\ 0.96\qquad -0.013$
$\qquad\quad (0.70)\ (0.0085)\ (0.0011)$
$\quad Q^2 = 0.9945$

In addition, the complete model contains the following identities (The Q^2–test measures indicate the discrepancies between observed and predicted variables):

$(6\text{-}21)$ $e_t^{g/u} = 100\ e_t^{s/u} / e_t^{s/g}$
$\qquad\quad Q^2 = 0.9047$

$(6\text{-}22)$ $I_t^s = 100\ I_t^{g,s} / Pc_t^s$
$\qquad\quad Q^2 = 0.9993$

$(6\text{-}23)$ $r_t^g = 100\ (Pc_t^g / Pc_{t-12}^g - 1)$
$\qquad\quad Q^2 = 0.9629$

$(6\text{-}24)$ $r_t^s = 100\ (Pc_t^s / Pc_{t-12}^s - 1)$
$\qquad\quad Q^2 = 0.9503$

$(6\text{-}25)$ $r_t^u = 100\ (Pc_t^u / Pc_{t-12}^u - 1)$
$\qquad\quad Q^2 = 0.9249$

$(6\text{-}26)$ $T_t^{n,g} = 0.01\ T_t^g\, Pc_t^g$
$\qquad\quad Q^2 = 0.9993$

$(6\text{-}27)$ $T_t^{ns} = 0.01\ T_t^s\, Pc_t^s$
$\qquad\quad Q^2 = 0.9962$

$(6\text{-}28)$ $T_t^{nu} = 0.01\ T_t^u\, Pc_t^u$
$\qquad\quad Q^2 = 0.9986$

The parameters of the Arma(p,q) models for the four exogenous variables—B^g, B^s, D^u, $I^{n,s}$—in the present econometric model can be estimated with the well–known Kalman technique. This approach takes into account the possibility of certain forms of stochastic parameter variations. The structural model contains 28 equations only, but the explicit estimation model has 224 equations, because of the expectation variables.

The model is specified and estimated on the basis of monthly data. Monthly data have been used in order to have as many observations as possible. The first period of observation was November 1975 to July 1981. Later on, the series were updated until September 1982 and the estimation procedure was repeated. For the comparison of the predictive power of the model the data until March 1983 were used. According to the hypothesis of rational expectations the assumption seems to be reasonable that economic units know the seasonal pattern of the variables. Therefore, the time series—except for the exchange rates—were seasonally adjusted. A possible seasonal pattern in the series of the exchange rates would be used by speculators. However, the differences between the seasonally adjusted and unadjusted series of the exchange rates were one of the criteria for the choice of the seasonal adjustment procedure. For the results presented in this paper, a filter design approach suggested by Stier (1983) was used.

Many studies deal with the predictive power of forward markets. The general results are as follows: The forward market may be a poor predictor but still the best available (see, for example, Levich, 1978). The theoretical possibility for making forecasts which are systematically better than the forward market will exist only for a limited period of time. It is exactly that time which the market requires to accept the forecasts. Afterwards, the formerly superior forecasts lose that quality because they are integrated into the forward market. The predictive power of any exchange rate model is limited in the long run by the predictive power of the forward market. However, such a model provides some basic insights into structural relationships which seem to be at work in the real world. The overall impression given by these results is that the model is predictive in the sense of the criteria discussed. Only in equations (6-1) and (6-2) are the Q^2's below 0.9. But more important are the hints for further improvements of the model given by the application of the jackknife–technique and the Stone–Geisser test.

Furthermore, the predictive performance of the present econometric model can be demonstrated by a forecasting simulation over the entire estimation period (Figure 6–1, Table 6–1). For numerical comparison, the prediction errors of the forward markets and simple random–walk models are listed in Table 6–1. These comparing hypotheses are specified as follows:

$$(6\text{-}29) \quad e_t = e_{t-i} + f_{t-1} + u_t \qquad i = 1, 3, 6 ; \qquad u_t: \text{white noise},$$

$$(6\text{-}30) \quad e_t = e_{t-i} + u_t \quad i = 1, 3, 6 ; \qquad u_t: \text{white noise}.$$

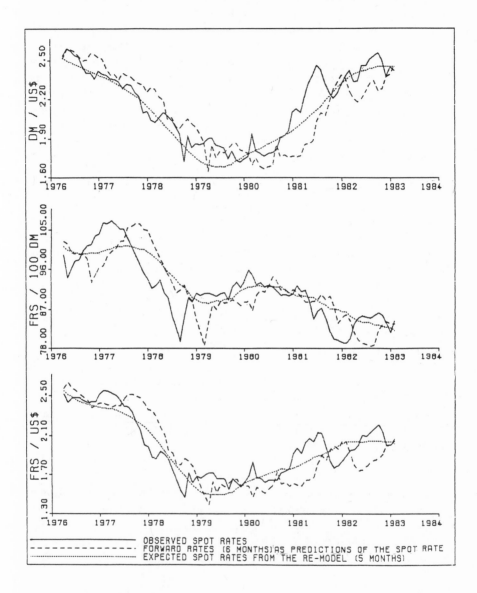

Figure 6–1. U.S.$, Frs and DM Currency Rates: Observed Spot Rates vs. Observed Forward Rates (6 Months) vs. Expected Forward Rates (5 Months) as given by the RE-model.

The expectations in the Figures and Tables are k–step–ahead forecasts, which are in a way similar to ex ante forecasts. Calculating the
k–step expectations, only estimated values for the endogenous and exogenous variables (Arma–models) are used. With respect to the information
base, the six–month forward rates are to be compared with the expected
exchange rates five months ahead. Compared with the forward market,
the forecasts of the model are quite good. The prediction errors of the
model are in the longer prediction periods smaller than those of the forward market. The turning–point errors in some cases are a consequence
of the Arma–modeled exogenous variables. The Arma–models are of the
following form:

$$(6\text{-}31) \quad x_{t+k} = a + bx_{t-1} + cx_{t-2} + dx_{t-3} + ex_{t-4} + u_t \quad k = 0,\ldots,6 \quad u_t : \text{white noise}$$

The coefficients are time–variable and estimated with a Kalman–filter approach (cf. G.C. Chow, 1983). As a matter of fact, the results also
provide an insight into other parts of the monetary sectors in the three
economies, which are described by the model. This can be shown with
regard to the descriptive and predictive capacity for the other endogenous variables of the model, for example, the American inflation rate and
the six month interest rate for the U.S. Dollar at the Euromarket (Figures
6–2 and 6–3).

The author is grateful to Professor Camilo Dagum and Professor
Herman Wold for their comments on the first draft of this paper.

Table 6–1

	random walk	forward market	$E[e(t+k) \mid I(t-1)]$ $k = 0,2,5$
1 month DM/U.S.$ (November 1975–September 1982):			
mean square error :	0.0043	0.0045	0.0061
average error in % :	2.35	2.35	3.00
maximum error in % :	12.37	11.76	9.31
3 months DM/U.S.$ (January 1976–November 1982):			
mean square error :	0.013	0.014	0.011
average error in % :	4.39	4.36	3.70
maximum error in % :	18.40	16.94	13.60
6 months DM/U.S.$ (April 1976–February 1983):			
mean square error :	0.028	0.031	0.011
average error in % :	6.34	6.23	3.67
maximum error in % :	19.87	21.14	13.67
1 month frs/100DM (November 1975–September 1982):			
mean square error :	3.37	3.47	17.45
average error in % :	1.53	1.55	3.77
maximum error in % :	6.81	7.05	15.94
3 months frs/100DM (January 1976–November 1982):			
mean square error :	13.43	13.82	16.69
average error in % :	3.10	3.23	3.47
maximum error in % :	12.38	11.89	15.98
6 months frs/100DM (April 1976–February 1983):			
mean square error :	30.34	30.80	16.39
average error in % :	4.97	5.04	3.44
maximum error in % :	15.99	14.52	16.21
1 month frs/U.S.$ (November 1975–September 1982):			
mean square error :	0.0051	0.0053	0.013
average error in % :	2.86	2.92	4.90
maximum error in % :	14.33	15.09	16.31
3 months frs/U.S.$ (January 1976–November 1982):			
mean square error :	0.019	0.019	0.016
average error in % :	5.63	5.83	5.47
maximum error in 5 :	20.43	18.31	13.98
6 months frs/U.S.$ (April 1976–February 1983):			
mean square error :	0.044	0.045	0.016
average error in % :	8.77	8.89	5.43
maximum error in % :	31.18	26.74	14.91

The prediction errors of the exchange rate by random–walk models, by the forward market and by the expected exchange rates of the model. The estimation period of the model is November 1975 to September 1982.

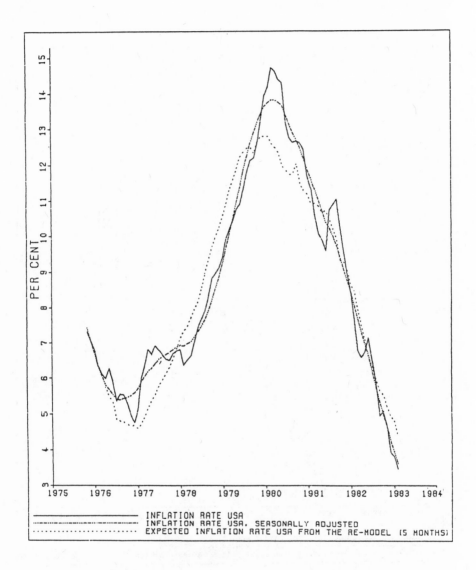

Figure 6–2. Inflation Rate USA: Observed vs. Seasonally Adjusted vs. Expected from the RE-model (five months).

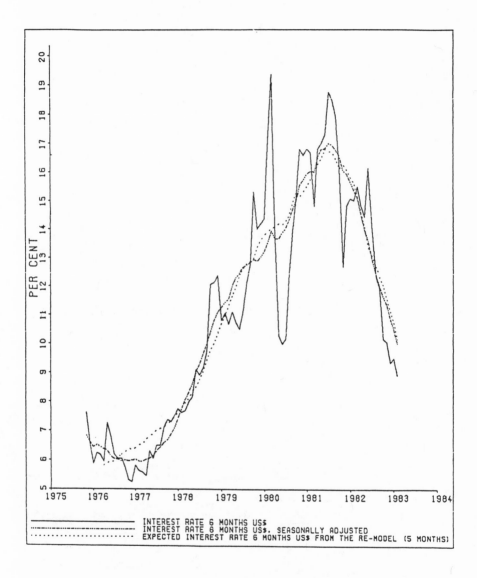

Figure 6–3. Interest Rate, six months, USA: Observed vs. Seasonally Adjusted vs. Expected from the RE-model.

REFERENCES

Abrahamsen, Y., and B. Schips. 1983. An econometric model with rational expectations for the exchange rates between the Deutsche mark, the Swiss franc and the U.S. dollar. Hochschule St. Gallen: Diskussionsbeitrag 29, Volkswirtschaftliche Abteilung.

Bergström, R., and H. Wold. 1983. *Fix-point estimation in theory and practice.* Göttingen: Vandenhoeck & Ruprecht.

Boehm, P. 1984. *Zur Theorie der Währungssubstitution.* Diessenhofen

Buettler, H.J.: Ruegger, and K. Schiltknecht. 1982. Transitory changes in monetary policy and their implications on money-stock control. Paper presented at the Carnegie-Rochester conference on public policy, Pittsburg.

Chow, G.C. 1980. Econometric policy evaluation and optimization under rational expectation. *Journal of Economic Dynamics and Control* 2:47–59.

Chow, G.C. 1983. *Econometrics.* New York: McGraw-Hill.

Drazen, A. 1980. Recent developments in macroeconomic disequilibrium theory. *Econometrica* 48:238–306.

Frei, G. 1984. Methoden zur Schätzung des kanonischen Ungleichgewichtsmodelles. St. Gallen: Econometric Department. Mimeopaper.

Geisser, S. 1974. A predictive approach to the random effect model. *Biometrika* 61:101–107.

Granziol, M., and H. Schelbert. 1983. Ex ante Real-Zinssätze am Euromarkt. *Zeitschrift für Wirtschafts- und Sozialwissenschaften* 103:437–459.

Lange, W., and B. Schips. 1984. Zur Frage der Verwendung unvollständiger Modelle bei der Vorbereitung wirtschaftspolitischer Entscheidungen. Hochschule St. Gallen: Diskussionsbeitrag 30, Volkswirtschaftliche Abteilung.

Leamer, E.E. 1983. Let's take the con out of econometrics. *American Economic Review* 73:31–43.

Levich, R.M. 1978. Test of forecasting models and market efficiency in the international money market. In *The economics of exchange rates: Selected Studies,* eds. J.A. Frenkel and H.G. Johnson, 129–158.

Loesch, M. 1981. Estimation of econometric models containing rational expectations variables. Paper presented at the European meeting of the Econometric Society, Amsterdam.

Loesch, M. 1983. Estimation of future rational expectation models. Hochschule St. Gallen: Diskussionsbeitrag 27, Volkswirtschaftliche Abteilung.

Loesch, M. 1984. *Fixpunkt-Schätzverfahren für Modelle mit rationellen Erwartungen.* Königstein/Ts: Athenäum.

Lucas, R.E., and T.J. Sargent. 1978. After Keynesian macroeconomics. In *After the Phillips curval persistence of high inflation and high unemployment*, ed. Federal Reserve Bank of Boston. Conference Series 19, 295–319.

Meese, R.A. and K. Rogoff. 1983. Empirical exchange rate models of the seventies. Do they fit out of sample? *Journal of International Economics* 14:3–24.

Muth, J.F. 1981. Rational Expectations and the theory of price movements. *Econometrica* 29:315–335.

Shiller, R.J. 1978. Rational expectations and the dynamic structure of macroeconometric models. *Journal of Monetary Economics* 4:1–44.

Sims, C.A. 1980. Macroeconomics and reality. *Econometrica* 48:1–48.

Stier, W. 1983. On new procedures in the analysis and seasonal adjustment of time series. Paper prepared for the Third International Symposium on Forecasting, Philadelphia.

Stone, M. 1974. Cross-validatory choice and assessment of statistical predictions. *Journal of the Royal Statistical Society* B 36:11–133.

Tukey, J.W. 1958. Bias and confidence in not-quite large samples (abstract). *Annals of Mathematical Statistics* 29:614.

Wallis, K.F. 1980. Econometric implications of the rational expectation hypothesis. *Econometrica* 48:49–73.

Wold, H. 1965. A fix-point theorem with econometric background, I-II. *Arkiv for Matematik* 6:209–240.

Wold, H. 1980. *The fix-point approach to interdependent systems*. Amsterdam: North-Holland.

7

Discussion of Schips' Paper

JOHN F. MUTH

I have been asked to discuss Professor Schips' paper, emphasizing the relation between rational expectations and fix-point estimation. The application of rational expectations primarily to macro-economics has been a source of amusement to me because I do not now, and never have, understood macro-economics. It has always seemed to be "half obvious, half un-understandable." The work in expectations has taken a customarily doctrinaire stance: comparing naive or exponentially weighted moving averages with rational expectations. There has been little work on developing other hypotheses, particularly those which recognize known cognitive biases in human decision making (Hogarth and Makridakis, 1972).

EXCHANGE RATE MODEL

Professor Schips describes an exchange rate model involving, for three countries, monetary aggregates, government debt, prices, retail sales, and short- and medium-run Euromarket rates in the period from 1976 to 1983. Expectations are included for consumer prices expected to prevail six months ahead in the three countries, and in 2 of the 28 equations.

His comparison of the exchange rate predictions of the model with those of the random walk and with those of the forward market shows that the model is slightly inferior to the other two for the rates one month ahead (which could probably be corrected by recognizing the serial correlation of the residuals of the equations). The model appears to be markedly superior to the other two for rates three and six months ahead. The predictive performance of the model should be emphasized.

Two observations should be made about the comparison. First, there are certain other forecasting techniques, such as the Box-Jenkins method or exponentially weighted moving averages, which are more serious contenders, perhaps, than the naive forecasts implied by the random walk model. Second, there is no comparison of the accuracy of the structural coefficients of the model, a comparison which is possible only with simulations where the true structure is known or the predictions of the model take place under unusual conditions (one of the main claims for the FRB-MIT-Penn model is the prediction of inflation and unemployment after the 1973 oil boycott).

ESTIMATION AND RATIONAL EXPECTATIONS

Schips first discusses rational expectations models in economics and econometrics, particularly the effect of this modeling technique on estimation according to the maximum-likelihood and minimum-distance criteria. He then examines the difficulty of achieving the over-identification necessary for maximum-likelihood to have its nice properties. This is taken as an argument for considering other estimation techniques, especially a prediction-oriented method, and particularly the fix-point method of Professor Wold.

Schips then discusses the fix-point method applied to models containing expectations formed in accordance with the rational expectations hypothesis. He refers to work of Loesch showing how consistent estimators can be obtained in static linear models when concurrent expectations (1981) and future expectations (1983) variables appear in the system.

RATIONAL EXPECTATIONS MODELS

Like all other models, rational expectations (RE) simplifies reality. One way the RE model does this is to assume that all structural coefficients are perfectly well-known. Only the realizations of certain variables are not. Consequently, the model (in its simplest form) assumes away the very problem that fix-point estimation (FPE) and, indeed, econometrics address.

PARAMETER ESTIMATION UNDER RATIONAL EXPECTATIONS

Estimation of coefficients under rational expectations is not, therefore, inconsistent with any technique, including maximum-likelihood. As early as 1960, I discussed the problem and estimation methods (only recently published, in 1981). The presence of rational expectations merely imposes some restraints that the maximum-likelihood method must satisfy.

The most natural estimation method with rational expectations is Bayesian because the economic actor and the econometrician have the same decision problem. There has been considerable interest in Bayesian techniques and the conditions under which they are approximated by other, simpler methods. It appears that the main problem otherwise with Bayesian methods is the extensive amount of integration required and the specification of priors. It may be that other informationally symmetric forms of the problem may be possible.

IS OVER-IDENTIFICATION POSSIBLE?

The most telling problem is the need for just- and over-identification. I don't see how it can ever be found, even without rational expectations. Two recent papers illustrate the point. In one, Simon (1979) contends that fits to data of the Cobb-Douglas and ACMS (SMAC) production functions are artifactual in concluding constant returns to scale because the data reflect the accounting identity between the values of outputs and inputs.

More recently, Hall (1984) argued that the observed positive correlation between income and consumption cannot be the consumption function. Since income is a variable chosen by the household, choosing to work more, and therefore to consume less time away from work, is a sign of diminished well-being. The structural equation between income and consumption should have a negative slope. The explanation of the positive correlation of consumption and income must rest on shifts on the consumption-income relation, not movements along it.

If production functions and consumption functions are statistical artifacts, what functions are not?

Sims (1980) proposed a way based on time-series analysis for circumventing the identification problem, but it comes dangerously close to committing the *post hoc, ergo propter hoc* fallacy.

PREDICTION ORIENTATION

There are two distinct issues in the matter of prediction orientation: (1) reduced-form versus structural estimation and (2) the necessity of any estimation at all. Comparisons by Cooper and Nelson (1975) and Sims (1967) do not lend much confidence that forecasts with structural models are better than time-series or other techniques.

A standard approach in statistics is to forecast on the basis of some model whose parameters have been estimated from historical data. Least-squares or Box-Jenkins require some estimate of the underlying structure of the time-series process. The resulting model is then used to make forecasts conditional on the information currently available.

However, the intermediate step of identifying the underlying structure is unnecessary. Several well-known, and effective, forecasting techniques impose no such requirement: naive forecasts, regressions with seasonal and trend factors and exponentially-weighted moving averages. Past data are used to determine the values of the free parameters leading to the most accurate forecasts, but there is no presumption that the resulting formulas resemble the underlying structure in any way. Studies by Chatfield and Prothero (1973), Groff (1973), and Makridakis and Hibon (1972) certainly indicate that simple time-series models often predict as well as or better than more sophisticated techniques. But such simple techniques are demonstrably better than unaided intuition (Hogarth and Makridakis, 1972).

CONCLUSIONS

The forecasting performance of Schips' model is significant because, relative to some alternatives, it improves with the length of the forecast span. I don't quite agree that rational expectations and fix-point estimation are highly complementary. However, I certainly agree with his evaluation of the ills of econometrics. Prediction orientation may be desirable because the lack of identification of econometric models cannot really be solved, either with or without rational expectations. The problem is not entirely with estimation techniques. As Wold (1983) indicated, estimates according to different methods are not wildly different. Perhaps the answer, as Leamer (1983) suggested, lies more in the use of experimental evidence (laboratory or the Seattle/Denver income maintenance experiment) or special historical events. Another partial answer is to reduce the reliance on forecasts for policy purposes through explicit attention to the decision-making problem under conditions of uncertainty.

REFERENCES

Chatfield, C., and D.L. Prothero. 1973. Box-Jenkins seasonal forecasting problems in a case study. *J. Roy. Stat. Soc.* 136A:295–315.

Cooper, J.P., and C.R. Nelson. 1975. The ex-ante prediction performance of the St. Louis and FRB-MIT-PENN econometric models and some results on composite predictors. *J. Money, Credit & Banking* 7:1–32.

Cooper, R. 19.... The predictive performance of quarterly econometric models of the United States. In *Econometric models of cyclical behavior*, vol. 2, *Studies in income and wealth*, ed. Bert G. Hickman, 813–926. New York: Columbia University Press.

Groff, Gene K. 1973. Empirical Comparison of Models for Short-Range Forecasting. *Management Science* 20:22-31.

Hall, Robert E. 1984. The role of consumption in economic fluctuations. National Bureau of Economic Research, Working Paper No. 1391, June, 1984.

Hogarth, Robin., and Spyros. Makridakis. 1981. Forecasting and planning: An evaluation. *Management Science* 27:115–138.

Leamer, Edward. E. 1983. Let's take the con out of econometrics. *Amer. Econ. Rev.* 73:31–43.

Makridakis, S., and M. Hibon. 1972. Accuracy of forecasting: An empirical investigation. *J. Roy. Stat. Soc.* (A) 142:97–125.

Muth, John F. 1981. Estimation of economic relationships containing latent expectations variables. In *Rational expectations and econometric practice*, vol. 1, eds. R.E. Lucas and T.J. Sargent, 321–328. Minneapolis: University of Minnesota Press.

Schips, Bernd. 1986. Estimation of RE-models and some remarks on model specification in econometrics. Paper read at this conference, Chap. 4.

Simon, Herbert. A. 1979. On parsimonious explanations of production relations. *Scand. J. Econ.* 459–474.

Sims, C.A. 1967. Evaluating short-term macroeconomic forecasts: The Dutch performance. *Rev. Econ. & Stat.* 49:225–236.

Sims, C.A. 1980. Macroeconomics and reality. *Econometrica* 48:1–48.

Wold, H. 1983. Fix-point method. In of *Encyclopedia of Statistical Sciences*, vol. 3, eds. S. Kotz and N.L. Johnson, 148–156. New York: Wiley.

8

Comment on Schips' Paper

CAMILO DAGUM

This study is organized in two sections. Section 1 discusses B. Schips' paper, "Estimation of Rational Expectations Models and Some Remarks on Model Specification in Econometrics." Section 2 deals with the foundation, relevance and realism of rational expectations (RE) model specifications, and the method of parameter estimation frequently used by their practitioners.

1. ON B. SCHIPS' "ESTIMATION OF RATIONAL EXPECTATIONS MODELS AND SOME REMARKS ON MODEL SPECIFICATION IN ECONOMETRICS"

Bernd Schips' research paper deals with the spot rates of exchange between the German mark, the Swiss franc and the U.S. dollar. The model is a sound and appropriate specification of some of the most relevant explanatory variables accounting for the variations of the spot rates of exchange of the Swiss franc with the German mark and the U.S. dollar respectively. It includes a careful selection of memory (lagged endogenous and exogenous) and expected variables.

B. Schips presents a cogent discussion of the choice among methods of parameter estimation. Drawing from Wold's seminal contributions

(Wold, 1981, 1982, 1985), Schips addresses the issue of parameter-oriented vs. prediction-oriented methods of estimation. It leads to the choice of a prediction-oriented method, and for simultaneous equation models with non-latent variables, Wold's (1965, 1981) fix-point (FP) method of estimation is selected.

The main features of the econometric analysis of the specified model are:

i) A sound application of the FP method as a prediction-oriented method of estimation;

ii) The estimation of the model applying the FP and the jackknifed FP method;

iii) The jackknifed FP standard errors of the estimated parameters; and

iv) Obtaining the Stone-Geisser's Q^2 to test the predictability power of the estimated model.

Although the model specification and the parameter estimation are supported by a thorough theoretical economic and econometric analysis, some minor observations are in order.

a) Economic theory and the econometric estimates (jackknifed FP and jackknifed FP standard errors) suggest the combination of some variables to arrive at a more rigorous model specification and parameter estimates that are expected to be significantly different from zero and, at the same time, to reduce the risk of high colinearity among these variables. Some cases in point are:

1) In equation (6-1), which purports to explain the Swiss-German exchange rate variation, there is no need to specify two separate terms, one for the expected consumer price index of Switzerland and another for Germany. An improved specification that would produce significantly non-zero regressor coefficients could be obtained after replacing the additive specification of the expected consumer price indexes by their corresponding ratios, i.e., by $Pc_t^{*,g}/Pc_t^{*,s}$ and $Pc_{t+6}^{*,g}/Pc_{t+6}^{*,s}$ or their inverses. Similar comment applies to the Swiss-U.S. exchange rate equation.

2) The econometric estimate of equation (6-11) clearly indicates that the U.S. interest rate (one month Euromarket) as a function of the U.S. monetary aggregate M3, with lags of three and four months, i.e., $M3_{t-3}^u - M3_{t-4}^u$. The author's estimate of $0.047M3_{t-3}^u - 0.046M3_{t-4}^u$ is a clear specification for these two variables, and that an estimate of about 0.047 for the coefficient of this new variable could be obtained. Besides, a smaller variance for the estimate of the regressor coefficient of ΔM_{t-3}^u should be expected, eliminating at the same time a possible high degree of colinearity between M_{t-3}^u and M_{t-4}^u.

b) An explicit discussion should be presented of the economic reasons leading to the choice of future expected variables, such as Pc^*_{t+6} (six months forward) in equations (6-1) and (6-2), and the choice of lags, such as those for the monetary aggregates Ml, in equations (6-3), (6-4), (6-6) and (6-7), and M3, in equations (6-5) and (6-8).

c) The Stone–Geisser Q^2 test on predictability performance of the estimated model is exceptionally good and the jackknifed FP estimates are informative and, in general, show very good agreement with the non-jackknifed FP estimates.

d) A more explicit discussion of the structure of the specified model, including an explicit analysis of its endogenous, exogenous and expected variables would enhance the accessibility of this important applied econometric contribution to a wider audience of economists.

B. Schips' contribution is an excellent applied econometric analysis of the Swiss spot exchange rate with respect to the German mark and the U.S. dollar. The specified variables capture two of the essential dimensions of economics as a science: The history of the phenomenon under inquiry, and its future, brought out by the lagged explanatory variables and the expected variables, respectively. They substantiate the basic decision-maker attributes *qua* human being who are supposed to be *homo sapiens, homo faber* and *homo ludens* (Dagum, 1983, 1984).

An innovative approach that departs from mainstream econometrics is the application of the FP method of estimation and its theoretical justification as a predictor-oriented and distribution-free method. It contrasts with the much too restrictive and unrealistic required conditions for the application of the maximum likelihood (ML) method, which is a parameter-oriented and parametric method of estimation.

The quality of the paper, its economic interpretation and its conclusion could be enhanced if the author would ignore the RE hypothesis and frame his contribution in terms of history (lagged variables) and expectations. This leads us to Section 2.

2. THE RE HYPOTHESIS IN THEORETIC AND APPLIED ECONOMIC RESEARCH

In the seventies, mainstream economists discovered Muth's (1961) contribution on rational expectations and monopolized and colonized it for strictly ideological reasons. The challenge was provided by the stubborn observed facts of inflation and unemployment, which stand against the neoclassical mode of theorizing. Preoccupied with *status quo* preservation, the RE hypothesis justified the *laissez-faire* as the most efficient economic policy to deal with the twin problems of inflation and unemployment. It was afterward extended to deal with other economic phenomena such as investment and the business cycle.

Although the RE hypothesis is placed in historical time, it is neutralized by the arbitrary RE definition which operates in logical time, similar to the Walrasian tâtonnement process that is outside history, or more precisely, *sub specie aeternitatis.*

Expectations and time play a prominent role in economic theorizing since they incorporate both the future and the past in accounting for the present. They belong to the core of Keynes' *General Theory* (1936). Chapter 5 of the *General Theory* has the revealing title "Expectations as Determining Output and Employment." It presents a very rational analysis of expectations and of time, without implying the false pretense of unbiased rational expectations. Keynes (1936, p. 46) states that the "entrepreneur has *to form the best expectations he can* as to what the consumers will be prepared to pay when he is ready to supply them (directly or indirectly) after the elapse of what may be *a lengthy period*; and he has no choice but to be guided by these expectations, if he is to produce at all by processes which occupy time" (italics added). On the method of arriving at an *equivalent* to these expectations, Keynes observed that the entrepreneur entertains several hypothetical expectations held with varying degrees of probability. In this context, Keynes (1936, p. 24, n. 3) observed that, "by his [the entrepreneur's] expectation of proceeds I mean, therefore, that expectation of proceeds which, *if it were held with certainty*, would lead to the same behavior as does the bundle of vague and more various possibilities which actually makes up his state of expectation when he reaches his decision" (italics added). Should we add the *a priori* probability distribution of the possible states of "nature," we would have a complete Bayesian framework of analysis.

In contrast to Keynes, Muth (1961, p. 316) stated that "expectations, since they are informed predictions of future events, *are essentially the same* as the predictions of *the relevant economic theory*" (italics added). Without loss of continuity, Muth (1961, p. 316) added that "Reported expectations generally underestimate the extent of changes that actually take place." This contradicts his definition of RE given on the same page, i.e., that "expectations of firms (or, more generally, the subjective probability of outcomes) tend to be distributed, for the same information set, about the prediction of the theory (or the 'objective' probability distribution of outcomes)."

In his analysis of expectations, Muth (1961, p. 317) assumes that,
i) random disturbances are normally distributed;

ii) certainty equivalents exist for the variables to be
predicted; and

iii) the equations of the system, including the expectations formulas, are linear.

That expectations are informed predictions of future events no one denies. Any prediction leads to an expectation and, in science, predictions are deduced from a scientific model or theory, hence they are obtained by application of reason. But Muth's assertion that they are the same as the prediction of "the relevant economic theory" is an *ad hoc* hypothesis, advanced for the sole purpose of deriving the RE results. Which is *the* relevant economic theory? The Keynesian? the neoclassical? the Marxian? or the structuralist? Let us assume that there exists a consensus on which is *the* relevant economic theory. Since quantitative "informed predictions" have to be done via a model, we may pose the question of what is *the* relevant economic model for *the* relevant economic theory. Then which one of the thousand possible model specifications is *the* relevant economic model? Each model, with a different number of equations and hence vector of endogenous variables, different number of predetermined variables, different mathematical law of correspondence among the specified variables and different observed length of time, will yield different predictions. How can these predictions be considered "the objective probability distribution of outcomes," and about what mathematical expectation? Besides, the subjective probability distribution of outcomes of each firm's expectation is not invariant with respect to the organization, resources and the information set available to it. The latter is not the same among firms and households as Muth claims, since information is costly. It has to be gathered, processed and used as an input of *a*, not *the*, model. It stands to reason (it is *rational*) that the best organized firm, endowed with the largest resources and most superior information set will predict best the "objective expected outcome." This predictive accuracy will unfold, for a minority of firms, a dynamic process of faster capital accumulation, higher rates of profit and output growth, and a larger market share. The remaining, generally small, firms will cluster the predictive outcomes at the two tails of the "subjective probability distribution," suffering the costs and consequences of systematically larger prediction errors.

Muth's assumptions of normally distributed random disturbances and linear models are purely convenient *a priori* assumptions used to justify the use of the ML method of parameter estimation and to exploit the nice properties of mathematical expectation as a linear operator.

Wold's groundbreaking contributions on the comparative properties of ML and least squares (LS), and FP and partial least squares (PLS) have not yet been absorbed by a majority of the RE hypothesis practitioners (Wold, 1965, 1981, 1982, 1985). However, Wold's path models with latent variables and the PLS method of parameter estimation are the only sound approach to formalize and estimate models with latent variables and, *a fortiori*, the so-called RE models.

Muth (1961, p. 318) stated that "if *the* prediction of the theory *were substantially better* than the expectations of the firms, then there would be opportunities for the 'insider' to profit from the knowledge—by inventory speculation if possible, by operating a firm, or *by selling a price forecasting service to the firms*" (italics added). However, since the Sixties, some econometricians, being good Schumpeterian entrepreneurs, do not operate firms to produce goods; rather *they operate firms to sell forecasting services and econometric models*, thus contradicting Muth's rational expectations. Indeed, consulting services and, in particular, forecasting services have been one of the most dynamic economic sectors in the last twenty years. The International Institute of Forecasting was created in 1980 and, since 1981, has held annual meetings.

Under the title of "Deviations from Rationality," Muth stressed that certain imperfections and biases in the expectations may also be analyzed with the methods he introduced. He then stated (1961, p. 321) that "allowing for cross-sectional differences in expectations is a simpler matter, because their aggregate effect is negligible as long as the deviation from the rational forecast for an individual firm *is not strongly correlated* with those of the others" (italics added). This *a priori* assumption is unsubstantiated and, in fact, refuted by everyday observation, because of the psychological and sociological phenomena that support the existence of strong forecasting correlations. The very existence of leader and follower firms is a case in point. There exist contagious and demonstration effects; when run out of control, they evolve into panics such as the well known 1929 stock exchange crash which started the Great Depression.

Several pages of revealing statements by RE practitioners can be quoted. For the sake of brevity, let me conclude this section with some quotations which need no further comment:

After stressing the hypothesis that the expectations of the public are rational in the sense of Muth and "*are equivalent with the optimal predictions* of economic and statistical theory" (italics added), Sargent (1973, p. 167) adds: "For purposes of the analysis here, this hypothesis would involve assuming that *the public* (a) *knows the true reduced form* for the price level, (b) *knows the probability distributions or rules governing the evolution* of the exogenous variables, and (c) *combines this information to form optimal (least-squares) forecasts* of the price level" (italics added).

Certainly, *the public* that Sargent had in mind is either formed by

Laplacian or ET (extra terrestrial) genii. No econometrician in the world can claim the knowledge of either the *true reduced form* or the *rules governing the evolution of the exogenous variables*, let alone to combine his (the public's) information *to form optimal (least-squares!) forecasts.* Besides, neither the government nor its advisors *know* the probability distribution or rules governing the evolution of the exogenous variables.

As if this set of assumptions did not reveal enough scientism, Sargent (1973, p. 168) stresses that "the public is assumed to know, or at least to have estimated, the parameters" of a system of autoregressive processes involving the money supply, the "normal" productive capacity, "such as the logarithm of the stock of labor or of capital or some linear combination of the two" (p. 163), the vector of exogenous variables explaining the money supply, and the vector of random terms. Then he adds (1973, p. 172) that "in essence, two features of the model must hold to validate these propositions. First, expectations must be rational. Second, the model must possess *super-neutrality.*"

The best and most compact way to assess this string of counter-factual assumptions is with a quotation from B. Russell (1919, p. 71): "The method of postulating what we want has many advantages; they are the same as the advantages of theft over honest toil."

3. CONCLUSION

Since expectational variables are nonobservables, we need to state how expectations are formed. The adaptive expectations (AE) and RE hypotheses are among the most preferred modes of specification.

A standard simultaneous equations model with both endogenous (y_t^*) and exogenous (x_t^*) vectors of expectations takes the form

$$(8\text{-}1) \quad A_o y_t + A_1 y_{t-1} + B_o y_t^* + C_o x_t^* + \Gamma_o x_t + \Gamma_1 x_{t-1} = u_t$$

where the coefficients are conformable matrices and u_t is a random noise vector. Provided that A_o, B_o, and C_o are non–singular matrices, it can be proved that the solution to (1) under AE hypotheses is

$$(8\text{-}2) \quad \sum_{i=0}^{3} G_i y_{t-i} + \sum_{i=0}^{3} H_i x_{t-i} = \sum_{i=0}^{2} N_i u_{t-i}$$

and under RE hypotheses,

$$(8\text{-}3) \quad A_o y_t + A_1 y_{t-1} + E_o x_t + E_1 x_{t-1} = u_t + N \upsilon_t$$

where υ_t is also a random noise vector.

Hence, comparing the AE and RE solutions, i.e., the system of equations (8-2) and (8-3), respectively, we conclude that the AE model outperforms the RE as far as the power to retain and use longer memory is concerned. Indeed, the former is a VARIMA (3,3,2), i.e., an integrated third-order autoregressive process in the vectors of endogenous and exogenous variables and a second-order moving average process, whereas the latter (RE model) is a VAR (1,1), i.e., a first-order autoregressive process with respect to both y and x. Moreover, it follows from equations (8-2) and (8-3) that the solved RE model is a particular case of the solved AE model. This should come as no surprise to anyone making a comparative analysis of the AE and RE hypotheses. The former can rigorously account for both (behavioral, technological and institutional) rigidities and uncertainties affecting the modes of action and interaction of the decision-makers, as well as the mode of production and the social relations of production (Dagum and Dagum, 1974, chapter 9). The latter, however, is only a set of *a priori* assumptions contradicted by actual performance of the economic system.[1] Therefore, the AE model is an ontological, epistemological and methodological realist, whereas the RE model is not.

At the very base of the distributed lag rationale supporting the AE specification are the facts that it takes time to make a decision, it takes time to monitor a non-optimal decision and it takes time to correct it. Moreover, decision-makers have different powers, information sets, economic and technological resources, and different amounts of time to process the gathered information.

Wold's fix-point (1965, 1981) and partial least squares (1982) contributions provide efficient and consistent methods of parameter estimations in models with expectations (nonobservable variables). In particular, the partial least squares methods have the potential to redirect the whole RE model specification free of its build-in circularity.

NOTE

[1]Those entertaining some doubts about this statement are invited to perform a statistical test on the difference between the forecasts of the most prestigious and best informed (having the best information set) econometric and forecasting research firms in the U.S. and the observed outcomes, in particular for the quarterly reports of 1981 and 1982.

REFERENCES

Dagum, C. 1983. On structural stability and structural change in economics. *Proceedings of the American Statistical Association, Business and Economics Section*, 143rd meeting, 654–659.

Dagum, C. 1984. Stabilita strutturale, mutamento strutturale e previsione economica. *Rassegna Economica* 48:7–8.

Dagum, C., and E. Dagum. 1974. Construction de modeles et analyse econometrique. *Collection Economies et Societes, ISMEA*, Serie EM Number 5, Paris.

Joreskog, K., and H. Wold, eds. 1982. *Systems under indirect observation, I-II*. Amsterdam: North-Holland.

Keynes, J. 1936. *The general theory of employment, interest and money*. London: Macmillan.

Lucas, R.E. Jr., and Sargent, T.J., eds. 1981. *Rational expectations and econometric practice*, vols. 1 and 2. Minneapolis: The University of Minnesota Press.

Muth, J. 1961. Rational expectations and the theory of price movements. *Econometrica* 29:315-335.

Russell, B. 1919. *Introduction to mathematical philosophy*. London: George Allen and Unwin.

Sargent, T. 1973. Rational expectations, the real rate of interest, and the natural rate of unemployment. In *Bookings papers on economic activity*, eds. R. Lucas and T. Sargent, 159–198.

Wold, H. 1965. A fix-point theorem with econometric background, 1–2. *Arkiv for Matematik* 6:209–240.

Wold, H., ed. 1981. The fix-point approach to interdependent systems. In *Review and Current Outlook*,1–36. Amsterdam: North-Holland.

Wold, H., ed. 1981. *The fix-point approach to interdependent systems*. Amsterdam: North-Holland.

Wold, H. 1982. Soft Modeling: The basic design and some extensions. In *Systems under indirect observation: Structure, prediction, causality*, vol. 2, eds. K.G. Jöreskog and H. Wold, 1–54. Amsterdam: North-Holland.

Wold, H. 1987. Specification, predictor. *Encyclopedia of statistical sciences*, eds. S. Kotz and L.N. Johnson. New York: Wiley.

9

Scientific Model Building:
Principles, Methods, and History

CAMILO DAGUM

SUMMARY

Two of the most important purposes of scientific model building can be synthesized by the statements "model for a theory" and "model as a theory." The former specifies a model within the framework of an established theory, whereas the latter embodies a theory, and thus, model and theory comprise the same scientific knowledge.

Strongly related to the tenet "model as a theory" is the theoretical empiricism approach to scientific model building. It purports to find a new theory, a new scientific explanation, as the outcome of a process of interaction among observations, ideas and reason, which distinguishes theoretical empiricism from both empiricism and idealism. To this philosophy of science approach belongs Wold's model for knowledge.

Since economics is a science for action, an economic model embodies its policy implication. In economics as a science, the historical (memory), the teleological (project) and the expectational variables underline the economic units' modes of action and interaction.

Following the main tenets of mathematical spaces and dynamic systems, a general definition of *model* in science, and a specific definition of *economic model* are given, motivated and explained. These definitions incorporate the essential features of structure, function and evolution within a given environment, and belong to the model specification within the six steps of a proposed program for a methodology of economic research.

Within the context of economics, and bearing a specific relation to the proposed definition of economic model, Wold's model for knowledge is interpreted and used, and Lakatos' categories, introduced in his methodology of scientific research programs, are reinterpreted. This reinterpretation allows for the criticism and refutation of the hard core, which is and will continue to be observed among practitioners of rival research programs. It reveals a conflict or controversy *between* school of thoughts, such as that between the neoclassical and Marxian research programs, whereas a controversy *within* a given school of thought recognizes that the same hard core and their practitioners differ in the content of the protective belt. It is characterized by the specification of alternative models within a shared hard core. The controversies within either the neoclassical or the Keynesian research programs illustrate this.

1. INTRODUCTION

In the history of the philosophy of science we can identify three main streams of thought in the quest to provide a foundation for scientific knowledge. They can be recognized by the names empiricism, idealism and theoretical empiricism. The corresponding approaches to model-building are already suggested by their respective names. The latter, i.e., theoretical empiricism, is the only sound philosophy of science capable of accounting for a given aspect of reality and providing a meaningful explanation of it, and which leads to the specification of scientific models with increasing explanatory power and having the potential for relevant applied work. As a consequence, under appropriate structural constraints, scientific models are powerful constructions to be used for predictions and decision-making.

The theoretical empiricism philosophy of science can be cogently illustrated using Wold's (1969) model for knowledge. It subsumes into a unified and coherent structure the three main inputs to the process of scientific model-building as a relevant scientific enterprise, i.e., factual observations, ideas, and the use of reason to elaborate upon the ideas germane to and evolving from initial observations. Therefore, the empiricist and rationalist (idealist) philosophies of science have their places as parts in a coherent whole.

The purpose of this study is to discuss the philosophy of science approaches to scientific model building and Wold's models for knowledge, illustrating them with some historical examples from several domains of the factual and methodological sciences, and to present a program of scientific research in economics. This program is integrated with one essential characteristic of economics as a science for action, i.e., the policy implication of economic knowledge.

The content of this paper is organized as follows: Section 2 presents a classification of scientific knowledge; Section 3 deals with three main philosophy of science approaches to scientific model building; Section 4 presents Wold's models for knowledge; Sections 5 and 6 deal with economics as a science, discussing its properties and a program of scientific research, and its relationship to Lakatos' methodology of scientific research programs; Section 7 presents some historical cases of theoretical empiricism in science; and Section 8 concludes this study.

2. PHILOSOPHY AND SCIENTIFIC KNOWLEDGE

Wold (1984) observed that up until the time of "the early medieval universities, philosophy was a catch-all science."[1] Thereafter, specialized knowledge, such as physics and astronomy, started to acquire scientific autonomy. Each disciplines' secession from philosophy occurred as soon as a new autonomous scientific knowledge was built. Such are the cases of chemistry, biology, economics and sociology. This sequence of secessions prompted some philosophers to specify their field as a residual. In this context, Munz (1982, p. 1235) states: "Plato and Aristotle wrote about morals and physics, about mathematics and politics, about literature, cosmology and psychology. In our century, every one of these topics has become the subject matter of a special discipline. People who call themselves philosophers in the 20th century are mostly people who deal with the residual problems—that is, with those problems with which Plato and Aristotle also dealt, minus all the important fields of knowledge which have since become the subject of special sciences."

Without completely subscribing to Munz's comment, we should observe that the main problem of philosophy seems to be its own object of knowledge, which is much too ambitious to be successfully dealt with by the human intellect. It is concerned with first causes and ultimate foundation, and its aspiration is to deal with reality as a whole. The following essential properties of philosophy emerge:

i) totality of theme (pantonomia);
ii) autonomy of mode (autonomia).

From these properties becomes apparent the reason for the success of the specialized disciplines stemming from philosophy, and the failure of the human intellect to successfully deal with philosophy's subject matter. However, among the "residual problems" remain specialized fields of knowledge such as epistemology, philosophy of science and logic which are the subject matter of intensive inquiry and systematic development.

At the risk of raising an unnecessary polemic, let us present in Table 9–1 a classification of knowledge, including an incomplete presentation of the "residual problems," i.e., the third group in Table 9–1.

Table 9–1

Classification of Scientific Knowledge

1.	Factual sciences	Natural sciences:	matter as object of knowledge
	(substance of	Biological sciences:	life as object of knowledge
	knowledge)	Social sciences:	society as object of knowledge
2.	Methodological sciences (form of knowledge)	Mathematics Logic Statistics	
3.	Metaform of knowledge	Methodology Epistemology Philosophy of science	

The factual or empirical sciences deal with an aspect of reality. The material reality (nature), life and society are the object of knowledge for the natural, biological and social sciences, respectively. To the latter belong economics and sociology. Economics seceded from philosophy in the later 18th and early 19th centuries, the result of contributions by F. Quesnay, A. Smith, T. Malthus and A. Cournot. Sociology seceded in the 19th century, mainly due to A. Comte's contributions.

The factual sciences are concerned with the *substance* of knowledge, whereas the methodological sciences are concerned with the *form* of knowledge; the metaform of knowledge deals with the procedures by which new *substantive* knowledge is acquired by a knower, and with the validation and assessment of the body of scientific knowledge. In synthesis, the metaform of knowledge deals with the methodology leading to the specification, validation and evaluation of scientific research projects.

3. TYPES OF APPROACHES TO MODEL BUILDING

Three main approaches can be identified as the sources of ideas leading to a theoretical construction, and they owe their origins to the contributions of the Greek philosophers. They are,

i) empiricism (Democritus);
ii) idealism (Plato);
iii) theoretical empiricism (Aristotle).

i) The empirical approach can be traced to Democritus, a follower of Thales, who maintained that the senses allow the mind to comprehend the truth by means of the factual observation of the corresponding aspect of reality. For him, ideas and knowledge recognize the senses as their unique source.

With Bacon, Locke and Condillac, Democritus' approach is revived. They maintained an empiricism based on the principle that observations made by sense perception are the foundation for human knowledge. Condillac criticized Locke's tenet that the senses provide intuitive knowledge and contributed to a further polarization of this one-sided approach by asserting that all human knowledge is transformed sensation. This philosophical approach also includes the 19th century German historical school of economics. Because of its very narrow empirical foundation and its rejection of the appropriate use of a sound mathematical methodology, this school missed a historic opportunity to be the founder of the modern and powerful econometric methods in economic inquiry, which belong to the theoretical empirical approach. Instead, it became the forerunner of a descriptive mode of quantitative inquiry, which characterizes the content of economic statistics; cf. Meissner, W. and H. Wold (1974) in the introduction of this volume.

ii) The idealist approach can be traced to Plato, followed by Descartes, Kant, Hegel and von Schelling, and in economics, by Leon Walras, the founder of the Lausanne school of mathematical economics, and one of the founders of the neoclassical school of economics. This approach neglects the role of experience and maintains that knowledge is an *a priori* intellectual construction aimed at providing a logical structure capable of describing the observed events. For the philosophers embracing this philosophy of science approach, the mind perceives the truth through reason, i.e., the intelligence in action, without the control of factual events. The most elaborate development of idealism is found in Hegel. He asserted that what is rational is real and what is real is rational. In economics, Walras adopted a similar doctrine, which seems also to be the tenet of today's neoclassical economists in their interpretation and use of Muth's (1961) seminal contribution on rational expectation.

iii) Theoretical empiricism adopts the positive and one-sided contributions of both empiricists and idealists, to advance a relevant and conclusive approach to scientific discoveries. This approach is associated with Aristotle and, in the Middle Ages, with Saint Thomas Aquinas. In the first half of the 20th century, Ortega y Gasset went beyond the pure reason dominant philosophy and developed his principle of the historical reason, which rigorously belongs to the theoretical empirical approach. Among the most distinguished economists and econometricians adopting this philosophy of science approach, we should include Adam Smith, Malthus, Ricardo, Marx, Pareto, Keynes, Schumpeter, Frisch, Tinbergen and Wold. Herman Wold's models for knowledge are testimony to the meaning and relevance of the theoretical empirical approach to scientific model-building.

In the context of the philosophy of science approaches to model-building, two types of intellects can be distinguished: the passive one, which receives the facts from the senses without further elaboration, and the active intellect, which goes beyond the factual observations to elaborate on them with the help of a set of initial and imaginative (working) hypotheses. The senses receive the information (signals) about an aspect of reality and stimulate in the mind the generation of ideas; information and ideas are elaborated by reason, as the intelligence in action, which provides a general, rational theoretic explanation. That is, the intellect has the power to generalize, going beyond the narrow bounds of sensations. In this context, St.Thomas Aquinas wrote (Part 1, Question 1, Art. 9), "we are of the kind to reach the world of intelligence through the world of sense, since all our knowledge takes its rise from sensation." Then he illustrated his viewpoint with an interesting example. He observed that a triangle is first perceived by the senses which stimulate in the observer ideas, and the intellect will be able to pass from the observed triangle to the theoretical concept of triangularity. *Mutatis mutandis*, we can imagine the earliest time of civilization, when a man counted his possessions and thus got the idea of a set of numbers, generalizing afterward to the theoretical concept of the set of positive integers. Following this empirical theoretical process we achieved a logical construction of the set of real numbers, complex numbers and vector space. It was the necessity of accounting for the existence of $\sqrt{2}$ in the directed straight line as the point of length equal to the hypothenuse of the isosceles triangle OAB (Figure 9–1) that led to the bijective relation between the set of real numbers and the set of points in the directed straight line. It was the observation of birds' flying that stimulated the idea of a device allowing human beings to fly, and from there to the theoretical development of the flying machine mechanics initiated by Leonardo da Vinci and Jean Bernouilli. These are instances of the intellect's capacity to generalize.

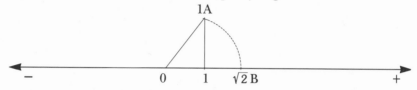

Figure 9–1.

Theoretical empiricism represents a harmonic integration between observation-sensation and reason, within a given frame of reference, leading to model specifications possessing properties of rigor, relevance and realism. Thus, it integrates both empiricism and idealism within a coherent whole as a rigorous, relevant and realistic approach to scientific model building.

Although Kant's contributions belong mainly to the idealist philosophical school, he wrote a revealing paragraph, which clearly describes the sequence sensations-ideas-reason. He stated (Kant, 1787, p. 14) "that all our knowledge begins with experience there can be no doubt.... In respect of time, therefore, no knowledge of ours is antecedent to experience, but begins with it. But, though all our knowledge begins with experience it by no means follows that all arises out of experience." Consequently, if we start from scratch, *seeing* things in the light whose source is not to be found in the observations, methods and results of the preexisting state of the science, our knowledge begins with experience. When we start our own research from the work of our predecessors, that is, from the scientific heritage of civilization, our knowledge is the joint outcome of ideas and reason, whereby reason elaborates and develops the new ideas into a more ambitious and powerful abstract knowledge.

Hence, theoretical empiricism is a cogent synthesis of the following age-old and vitally important three worlds (Lakatos, Vol. 1, 1978, p. 119): "the first world is that of matter, the second the world of feeling, beliefs, consciousness, the third the world of objective knowledge, articulated in propositions." This trichotomy is clearly part of the Aristotle-Saint Thomas Aquinas approach. Leading contemporary proponents are Popper (1972, Chapters 3 and 4) and Wold (1969).

It follows from Table 9–1 and the theoretical empirical philosophy of science that the first world is that of matter, life and society, according to the scientist's object of inquiry; the second, the world of intuitions, ideas, consciousness and working hypotheses; the third, the world of reason leading to objective knowledge, articulated in propositions. It is the synthesis of a dialectical process between the first two worlds, within a given frame of reference (circumstance, purpose, verisimilitude and standards).

Therefore, theoretical empiricism possesses the property of being ontologically and epistemologically realist. By asserting that there exists an external world—whose objects of knowledge are matter, life and society—even if we were not able to make observations, it is ontologically realist. It is epistemologically realist because it maintains that the function of scientific methodology is to find out the properties of this external world. Nikolaas Tinbergen (1974) stressed the importance of open-minded observation, of "watching and wondering," which is in perfect harmony with Saint Thomas Aquinas' sequence, observations-ideas-reason, and as such belongs to the theoretical empirical approach.

Idealism is ontologically realist and epistemologically idealist since it does not deny the existence of an external world, but asserts that the model representing this external world is the scientist's mental construction, constructed with the purpose of providing the scientist with a convenient instrument to be used in accomplishing objectives such as the description and prediction of events.

Vollmer (1984) cogently objected the coexistence of ontological realism and epistemological idealism. He stated that "ontology is prior to epistemology, and both ontology and epistemology are prior to methodology. That is, ontological statements have epistemological consequences, and both ontology and epistemology have methodological consequences.... Holding a realistic ontology, we must—in order to avoid inconsistencies-transfer our realism to epistemology and methodology. The converse is not true. From a successful methodology, we may not cogently infer that our underlying ontology and epistemology are correct."

Several independently formulated philosophical and methodological comments and discussions can be conceived as implicit criticisms of the instrumentalist philosophy of science, such as Aristotle's "transition to another kind" (μεταβασισ εισ αλλο γενοσ), Yule's spurious correlations, and some econometricians' criticisms of regression without theory, i.e., according to Yule's terminology, spurious regression. Gilbert Ryles, a mid-20th century English analytical philosopher, introduced the concept of category mistakes, which is indeed Aristotle's transition to another kind. Its meaning is that, if a form or entity belonging to one category is substituted into a statement in place of one belonging to another, a nonsensical assertion must result.

An extreme form of idealism is solipsism, which could be characterized as being both ontologically and epistemologically idealist, since it maintains that, for any scientist, only his mind and his sensations exist.

To the idealistic, and *a fortiori* to the solipsistic approach to scientific model building could be rightly applied Kierkegaard's assessment of Hegel's system—a luxurious palace of ideas, wonderfully built, endowed with great aesthetic and logical values, but without the least existential value.

4. WOLD'S MODELS FOR KNOWLEDGE

The factual sciences build their theories and models from the observation of reality. The unknown theoretical structure object of inquiry provides incomplete information (signals) about its essential nature which define a sample realization of its functioning. The signals (the empirical domain E) and the unknown structure (the theoretical domain T) give rise to a matching process (Wold, 1969) between theory and observation, which leads to a model specification M as a formal theoretical representation of T. In the Aristotle-Saint Thomas Aquinas approach, M is the outcome of the observations-ideas-reason sequence, whereby observation and ideas correspond to Tinbergen's watching and wondering. Wold (1969, p. 431) formalized it (Figure 9–2) as a model for knowledge. It is a representation of a dialectical process between E and T, within a specified frame of reference, whereby each synthesis is a model specification of T (Dagum, 1977, 1979).

$$E \Leftrightarrow T$$

Figure 9–2

Kuhn's (1962) structure of scientific revolutions leading to paradigm constructions and paradigm changes can also be seen as a dialectical process. It can be summarized in the following six steps (Dagum, 1977, 1979):

1) "Normal" science evolving from an accepted paradigm;
2) Small unexplained phenomena which orthodox researchers are confident can be fitted in;
3) Stretching the theory in an effort to fit unexplained phenomena;
4) A period of confusion and opposition;
5) A period of innovation and paradigm shift;
6) "Normal" science again, *qua* synthesis of the former five steps.

In Wold's models for knowledge (Figure 9–2), the dialectical process between E and T and the frame of reference enrich the first three steps in Kuhn's structure of scientific revolutions. They lead to a sequence M_1, M_2, ..., M_h of model specifications, within a common frame of reference, whereby each M_i satisfies a higher level of aspiration, i.e., a higher level of rigor, relevance and realism than the formerly specified models. This is the situation when "stretching" the theory achieves the purpose of fitting unexplained phenomena. A case in point could be a sequence of Keynesian's models of income determination, such that all of them recognize Keynes' (1936, p. 246–7) frame of reference, and hence Keynes' paradigm, which includes (i) his fundamental analytic categories, such as the propensity to consume, the attitude towards liquidity and the expectation of future yield from capital-assets; (ii) the wage-unit as determined by the bargains reached between the employers and the employed, and (iii) the quantity of money as determined by the action of the central bank. A more elementary example is given by the alternative Keynesian consumption function specifications, such as the absolute, relative, permanent and life cycle hypothesis.[1]

Wold's frame of reference, illustrated by the rectangle in figure 9–2, is a mixture of T and E, theoretical and empirical knowledge, and serves to keep T and E strictly apart *within* the frame. Wold introduced the frame to counter the philosophical argument that T and E are always intertwined, and can never be kept apart. For background purposes it should include references to earlier relevant work. The frame represents the primitive ideas, the design and purpose of the model to be specified, which determine the researcher's level of aspiration, verisimilitude and standards, and the environment or circumstance[2] that conditions T and the signals E generated by T. In economics, the "national structures," and, in an open economy, we should add the "international structures relevant to a given national economy" contribute to spell out the circumstance. By national structures we mean the economic, social and political structures, and the socio-economic infrastructure. The economic structures are mainly integrated by the structures of production (technology), distribution (institutions) and exchange (the economic units' target functionals, and the institutions regulating the market structure, which determine the economic units' modes of action and interaction). The double arrow denotes the "matching" of the dialectical process between T and E, and thereby serves as a symbol for model evaluation in general.

In the context of the spirit of the institutional laws, Montesquieu (1748) advanced an illuminating statement which is relevant to both Wold's frame of reference and the concept of national structures. He wrote (T. II, p. 238) that the laws "must be relative to the physiognomy of the country; to its climate, i.e., burning or temperate; ... to the religions of its inhabitants, to their inclinations, to their wealth, to their number, to their trade, to their customs, to their manners. Finally, they are related to each other .... I shall examine these relationships: together they constitute what one calls the spirit of the laws."

Taking into account the substance of Montesquieu's statement, we could replace the last sentence by saying that "together they constitute what one calls the national structures," since Montesquieu's *esprit des lois* is a structural concept.

Wold (1984a) observed that A. Comte, in the second quarter of the 19th century, and E. Mach, in the fourth quarter of the same century, introduced the systematic coordination of T and E as a methodology for scientific inquiry.[3] The former used the term "positivism" and the latter the German term "Bild" (i.e., picture), and both were misunderstood. Karl Pearson, at the turn of the 19th century, introduced the goodness-of-fit statistical test to assess the closeness of model M to T by means of M and E, whereby E is treated as a sample realization of T.

5. PROPERTIES OF ECONOMICS AS A SCIENCE

Economics belongs to the social sciences. Hence, according to Table 9–1 it is a factual science. As a social science, its aspect of reality is defined by the economic units' specific activities of production, distribution and exchange within an organized society (circumstance) and conditioned by it. The markets are the immediate institutional structures within which the economic units' activities take place and evolve. However, it should be stressed that there are no markets without society, and there is no society without power. This fundamental statement underlines the basic interdisciplinary relationship of economics with both sociology and political science, and brings to the fore the role of power in the functioning of an economic system.

Some of the most relevant properties of economics as a science are:

i)   factual or empirical;
ii)   non-experimental;
iii) ontological;
iv)   evolutionary;
v)   historical;
vi)   teleological;
vii) ideological.

Thom (1975, p. 1) stated that "whatever is the ultimate nature of reality (assuming that this expression has meaning), it is indisputable that our universe is not chaos. We perceive beings, objects, things to which we give names. These beings or things are forms or structures endowed with a degree of stability; they take up some part of space and last for some period of time."

This paragraph underscores several of the properties listed above. The very name of science attached to economics is a statement of the existence of stable regularities whose coherent representation takes the form of models. Since our economic universe is not chaotic, it is a well-defined object of knowledge, hence there is a place for and a role to be played by economics as a science.

The economic reality object of inquiry could be thought of as an unknown stochastic structure to be identified. This unknown stochastic structure corresponds to the theoretical domain T (Figure 9–2), and the economic agents' performance and interaction within T induce the generation of a set of signals, factual information, which belong to the empirical domain E. These signals are the raw material to be elaborated by an appropriate use of the methodology of science for arriving at the specification of a model M *qua* inference of the unknown stochastic structure T. For this, we have to follow the theoretical empirical path, i.e., observations-ideas-reason, the scientific model. In this context, 25 centuries ago, Heraclitus advanced the cogent statement that the lord whose oracle is at Delphi neither speaks nor conceals, but gives signs. That is, by means of Delphi's oracle, Heraclitus' lord provides the empirical domain *qua* sample realization of an unknown theoretical structure T. This sample realization stimulates ideas in the scientist, and the ensuing application of reason leads to the identification or inference of T. In economics, the signals are in the form of prices, output, income, consumption, investment, employment and other quantities.

Economics, and, in general, the social sciences, are factual and non-experimental sciences, for social sciences phenomena can not be replicated.

Researchers in the experimental sciences can replicate the outcome of the phenomena which is the object of their inquiry, as is the case in the important domains of physics, chemistry and biology; they can recreate the physical, chemical and biological morphology. Therefore, these are factual and experimental sciences. Other disciplines are factual and non-experimental because of spatial distance (astronomy), temporal distance (history, geology, paleontology), or behavioral and institutional non-replicability (economics, sociology). For the latter, it should be observed that the *object* is also the *subject* of knowledge, and thus the subject is able to assimilate theories and experience to justify a change of decision when faced with the same set of circumstances. That is, the subject can absorb a theory or rationalize the circumstance of an experiment, or an empirical outcome, leading to the re-assessment of the responses. Morgenstern (1972) dealt with this characteristic in the field of economics and called it absorption theory.

An "experiment' in the social sciences certainly is not a constant replication of the circumstances under which a controlled variable is steered (entering as an input), where a specified effect is observed as an output. The so called "experiments" in the social sciences are nothing more than simulations, where very often a teacher makes the "social experimental design" and his students play the roles corresponding to the specific social agents, performances. The students' circumstances, psychology, motivation and risks, when playing in a classroom stock market simulation for example, cannot be construed as a replication of real stock market investors. If we accept Borel's (1937) theorem stating that the human mind cannot imitate chance, which is universally accepted and is at the very base of the construction of random number tables, then we should *a fortiori* accept that a human mind cannot replicate other human minds' rationality.

As a factual science, economics searches for a coherent explanation of an aspect of reality. It is achieved when a meaningful economic structure is identified as the generator of signals and offered as an answer to the question "what is?" This property characterizes the ontological dimension of economics, and is also common to all the factual sciences.

The properties of evolution and historicity overlap to some degree. Thom's (above) statement that the "beings or things are forms or structures endowed with a degree of stability; they take up some part of space and last for some period of time," clearly stresses the evolution of the forms or structures; hence they are historically parameterized. In economics, the acceptance of this property implies that it has no structural stability. What is its time horizon? Unlike important domains of the natural sciences which present a structural stability for millions of years, and the biological sciences with a structural stability lasting for thousands of years, in the second half of the 20th century an economic structure takes up some part of space and lasts for some period of time which is often shorter than the life span of a generation of human beings.

Historicity underlines the economic agents' memory variables which are inputs for the decision-makers, and are specific to the social sciences' active units.

Unlike the natural and biological sciences, the dominant dimension of the economic units is not "nature" it is history. As Ortega y Gasset (1947, T. VI, p. 182) cogently wrote, "history is not only seeing; it is thinking what has been seen. And in one sense or another, thinking is always contruction." This statement contains the important sequence by which we characterize theoretical empiricism, i.e., observations-ideas-reason, scientific model.

The economic units have not only memory variables (historicity), but also project variables, purposeful aims or final causes, revealed by means of implicitly or explicitly specified objective functionals to be optimized. This underscores the teleological dimension of economics, which is not a property of the natural sciences, but was the subject of a heated polemic in the biological sciences

The explanation of an aspect of the economic reality, incorporating the memory and project (planned and expected) variables, was the subject of important models such as partial adjustment, adaptive expectations, and rational expectations. These models contain expected and/or planned variables which are non-observable and to which Wold's (1980, 1982, and with Jöreskog eds., 1982) soft modeling methodology can be fruitfully applied.

Palomba (1981, 1984) provides a rigorous and stimulating analysis of time and economics, motivating it by means of several illuminating quotations. They underline the role of history and expectations in economic theorizing. One of them is by Saint Augustine who wrote (Palomba, 1984, p. 32): "three are the times, the past, the present and the future; however, it could be said: three are the times, the present of the past, the present of the present, and the present of the future. Although they are already in our mind, we can see them from another perspective: the present of the past is the memory, the present of the present is the direct representation of a given reality, and the present of the future is the expectation."

Ideology has a dual role in the social sciences, and, therefore, in economics. There are circumstances in which ideology and social philosophy enter, by their own nature, as inherent realities in a program of economic research. In other cases, they are sources of bias, impairing and damaging the whole content of a research program. 0. Lange (1964, p. 524) stated, "all social sciences are in some way connected with the major ideological trends which form social consciousness in modern societies." Then he added (p. 525), "ideological influences do not always lead to the apologetic degeneration of social science. Under certain conditions, they may be a stimulus of true objective research. The aspiration for social justice, progress and welfare generally stimulate scientific research because true knowledge is needed in order to successfully control social processes," i.e., true knowledge is needed to make the best decisions.

6. A PROGRAM FOR A METHODOLOGY OF ECONOMIC RESEARCH

The teleological property of economics and the roles of the project variables emphasize that economics is a science for action. These specific aspects are integrated in the following six steps of a program for a methodology of economic research (Dagum, 1977, 1979):

1) specification of a field of research;
2) model specification of the observed structure;
3) estimation of the theoretical structure;
4) specification of a target structure;
5) testing the null hypothesis about the difference between the estimated theoretical structure and the specified target structure;
6) specification of a decision model.

We now present a brief discussion of the meaning and content of each one of these steps in economic research. Figure 9–3 illustrates their structure.

6.1. Specification of a Field of Research

This first step refers to that aspect of reality which is the object of inquiry, and as such is a statement of existence. It commands an unequivocal definition of the committed field of inquiry. H. Poincaré stressed its essential role for the successful explanation or solution of a research project when he stated that a well-defined problem is already 50 percent solved.

Ortega y Gasset (1946) stated it with both philosophical rigor and poetic beauty, when he wrote that (p. 144), "before a thing becomes an

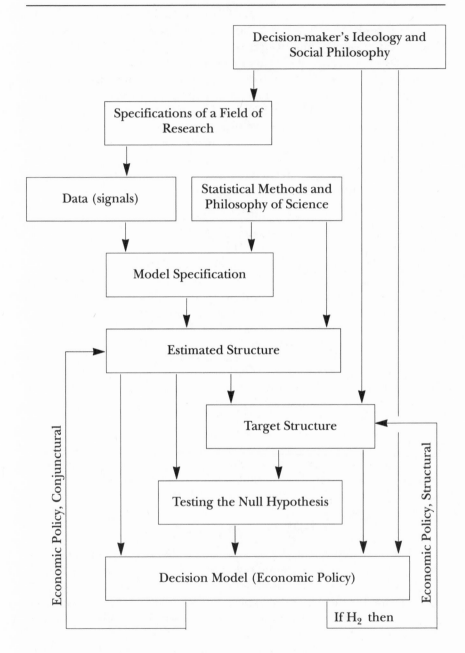

Figure 9-3. The Sturcture of Economics as a Science for Action

object of cognition it must have been a problem, and before it becomes a problem we must have found it strange." This statement emphasizes the role of observations and ideas, i.e., watching and wondering, in motivating the specification of a research project. It clearly embraces the theoretical empirical philosophy of science.

The specification of a field of research is either the aftermath of a preanalytic knowledge, which Schumpeter calls vision, or the pursuit of the research so far accomplished. Schumpeter (1954, p. 41) states that "in order to be able to posit to ourselves any problem at all, we should first have to visualize a distinct set of coherent phenomena as a worthwhile object of our analytic efforts. In other words, analytic effort is of necessity preceded by a preanalytic cognitive act that supplies the raw material for the analytic effort. In this book, this preanalytic cognitive act will be called vision." Schumpeter's *vision* is thus another form with which to approach the rationalization of the interface between observations and ideas as a powerful force leading to scientific inquiry and scientific model building.

Schumpeter's *vision* takes the form of an intuitive and preliminary structure, where the empirical domain in Wold's models for knowledge plays a relevant role. This is apparent when Schumpeter states (p. 561) that "in every scientific venture, the thing that comes first is Vision. That is to say, before embarking upon analytic work of any kind we must first single out the set of phenomena we wish to investigate, and acquire intuitively a preliminary notion of how they hang together or, in other words, of what appears from our standpoint to be their fundamental properties."

6.2. Model Specification of the Observed Structure

The specification of a field of inquiry demands a coherent explanation by means of a theoretical construction. It usually takes the form of a scientific model. Whether we start from scratch, or *see* things in a different light not to be found in the facts, methods and results of the preexisting state of the science (which is the case that would lead to a paradigm change, or the formulation of a new scientific research program), or follow up the research from the state left by our predecessors (which is the case when we work within an established paradigm, i.e., the practicing of "normal" science, or within a given scientific research program, with the expectation of keeping it as a progressive research program), we have to interrogate "nature," i.e., monitor the information it provides in relation to our specified field of inquiry. In this context, we can elaborate Heisenberg's (1958) statement[4], saying that although the object of the scientific research is Nature—and by this we mean, according to Table 9–1, matter, life or society—the outcome of it is Nature subject to the interrogation of men. In the particular case of the social sciences, it exhibits another form of uncertainty given by the observed fact that the society's answer to the interrogation of men is not invariant with respect to the amount of information and the theory applied to process this information (cf. Morgenstern's absorption theory).

By interrogating "nature" the researcher tries to infer or identify T. The signals transmitted by T take the form of prices, employment, output, etc. They belong to the empirical domain E, and jointly with the researcher's ideas constitute the starting point for the identification of the theoretical structure T, in a theoretical-empirical approach to scientific model building. It encompasses the following stages:

i)   specifying the frame of reference in everyday language: the aim of the model with background reference to earlier significant literature;

ii) observation of reality, i.e., watching the functioning of T, or observing its signals;

iii) statement of the primitive ideas, the main analytic categories, and the level of disaggregation and aspiration for the model to be built;

iv) grouping of the observations according to the categories of analysis and planned level of disaggregation;

v)   *ex-ante* analysis of the signals by means of diagrams, ratios, index numbers, correlation, regression, etc.;

vi) specification of a descriptive or explanatory model M_1, as the theoretical representation of T;

vii) estimation of the unknown parameters of M_1 which gives an *estimated* structure S_1 of the *unknown* economic structure T;

viii) *ex-post* analysis, i.e., the estimated structure S_1 is used to forecast new signals generated by the unknown economic structure T. If the forecast accepts the null hypothesis of an insignificant difference between the observed (new signals) and the forecast values, we retain S_1 as an appropriate representation of T. If the null hypothesis is rejected, then we return to the first stage, starting again the *ex-ante* and *ex-post* process of analysis, in the quest of a relevant modeling of T;

ix) the application of knowledge, i.e., the practical utility of a model and its estimated structure, to be used for the purposes of description, explanation, prediction, and decision.

This process of model building corresponds to the matching or dialectical process between E and T in Wold's models for knowledge. Besides, the *ex-post* analysis brings to the fore the predictor specification approach to scientific model-building introduced and developed by Wold (1959, 1963, 1984) and his school of statistics and econometrics.

In the process of model building, three sets enter as essential elements and at least one of them enters in an explicit form in the corresponding model specification. They are, the set of economic agents $\mathcal{A}$, the set of technologies $\mathcal{T}$, and the set of institutions I. They form the triplet $\{\mathcal{A},\mathcal{T},I\}$. Those sets that play an explicit role in the model specification belong to the matching process in Wold's models for knowledge; the others belong to the frame of reference, conditioning as a datum the model specification.

The level of disaggregation introduced in stage ii) above determines the relevant markets and subsets object of inquiry. In its simplest form, a market for a given product is modeled by means of three statements, i.e., a supply function, a demand function, and an equilibrium condition. Should these statements exhaust the object of inquiry, then we are dealing, in the Marshallian tradition, with a partial equilibrium model. The equilibrium approach as a meaningful mode of theorizing an aspect of reality is being contested by the supporters of the disequilibrium approach stemming from Keynes' (1936) general theory. Cournot (1838) anticipated this type of approach when discussing the equilibrating and disequilibrating forces operating in each market. For further elaboration and discussion on this issue, see Perroux (1975).

Assuming a market for a given commodity and imposing the equilibrium condition, the only set that explicitly enters the model specification is the set of economic agents A, which is partitioned into two subsets, the producers (A_1) and the consumers (A_2).

The disequilibrium approach leads to a dynamic model specification. In the case of a single market, its simplest form requires a partition of A into three subsets, the producers (A_1), the consumers (A_2), and the intermediaries (A_3). Wold (1959) specified a dynamic market model as a recursive model, without imposing the equilibrium condition. This model was also discussed in Dagum (1968, 1969) in the context of structural stability.

In a single market, each subset of economic agents performs a role, and to each role is associated an endogenous variable. Hence, each role commands a statement purporting to explain it by accounting for the levels and variations of its associated endogenous variables, including the qualitative statements on the parameters and the partial derivatives.

In a multimarket model, each member of the partition set can play more than one role, such as the Keynesian model with three markets (product, money and labor), and two subsets of economic units (households and firms). The households play the consumer role in the product market, and the suppliers of labor in the labor market. The firms play the investor role in the product market, demanders for money in the money market, and demanders for labor in the labor market. The technology of the economy is represented by a production function, and the institutional aspect of the money market by the supply of money. Thus, this simple multimarket Keynesian model is able to explicitly incorporate the triplet $\{A,T,I\}$, formed by the sets of economics units, technology and institution, and to retain multiple roles for the partitioned members of A. This forms the core of the explanatory part of the Keynesian model to which is added the set of conventional statements (equilibrium conditions and identities) and primitive ideas such as the principle of effective demand that encompasses all Keynesian models. Once the equilibrium conditions and the identities are worked out in the model, it is reduced to seven statements and seven endogenous variables. The latter are real (y) and money (Y) income, real (w) and money (W) wage rate, price level (P), interest rate (r) and employment (n). The qualitative statements on the partial derivatives ensure the independence and consistency of the set of statements; then the model is complete and coherent.

A model is the synthesis that results from the dominant application of the inductive method of inquiry. It represents a coherent whole which is considered to show the truth more completely than a mere collocation of parts, and for this reason, the whole possesses the superadditive property relative to the additive verisimilitude of its parts. Theoretical empiricism, as a philosophy of science, allows reason to perform the jump from the observations-ideas interaction to scientific model building, cutting the Gordian knot of infinite regression. Once a model is specified, it is subject to the analytical method of inquiry for the deduction of useful theorems or derived propositions. This is a natural follow-up to the search for a system, i.e., the search for wholeness, that we called theoretical structure. The analytic method then enters in its orthodox Cartesian interpretation, i.e., the splitting of reality into smaller units, and the recognition of individual causal relationships, that correspond to Descartes' second precept of his *Discours de la Methode*.

6.2.1. SYSTEM, MODEL, AND STRUCTURE

Since the Thirties, the concept of *model* in economics, as it was used by R. Frisch (1935–36) and J. Tinbergen (1939, 1956), has been recognized to be similar to the concept of *system* that in the Fifties made its formal entrance in system science. Both concepts incorporate the essential dimensions of *structure, function,* and *evolution*.

L. von Bertalanffy (1968, p. 38) defines a system as a "set of elements standing in interaction." For Mesarovic (1963, p. 7), "a general system is a relationship defined on a Cartesian product," which is formally equivalent to von Bertalanffy's definition. In mathematics, a space is defined as an ordered triplet {A, *, a}, where A is a set of elements, a is a generic member of A, and * is a set of operations in A obeying a set of axioms. Compared with Mesarovic's definition, this is more formal and specific. The modern system approach includes all the attributes entertained in the former definitions plus an explicit consideration of the functions or roles performed by its active units, as is apparent from von Bertalanffy's "elements in interaction."

According to Gini (1953), "a model is a simplified representation of the manner in which certain phenomena are related, or the manner in which they evolve." Here again we find the concepts of structure and function, to which Gini added the concept of evolution, placing it in a dynamic context.

A general definition of *model* or *system* is here proposed.

Definition of Model. A model is a set of interactive elements, functioning within a network of relations, and evolving in time according to the roles performed by its active units.

This definition includes the three main dimensions of a system (Le Moigne, 1977, p. 38). They are (Figure 9–4), the *functional* (what an active unit *does*), the *ontological* (that is, i.e., the structure of relationships), and the *morphogenetic* (what an active unit *becomes*, i.e., its evolution). It follows from the functional-ontological-morphogenetic interaction, as is the case in observed economic systems, that what the active units do induces a dialectical process between being (the observed structure) and becoming (the evolving structure). The active units' performance shapes a new structure, which corresponds to the praxis, and the new structure acts upon the active units, modifying their function, which characterizes the inversion of the praxis. Another dialectical process underlying the system dynamics can also be outlined; it is between the couple structure-function and the environment. The function (praxis) of a class of subsets of economic agents transforms the environment, which in turn induces a change of the function, and with it, the structure (inversion of the praxis), and this process of interaction evolves over time.

Taking into account the specific characteristics and proper ties of economics as a science and the process of model building, a definition of *model* in economics is proposed.

Definition of Economic Model. An *economic model* is an idealized and simplified formal representation by means of a theoretical empirical set of singular scientific statements concerning the observed characteristics of regularity and stability of a given field of research.

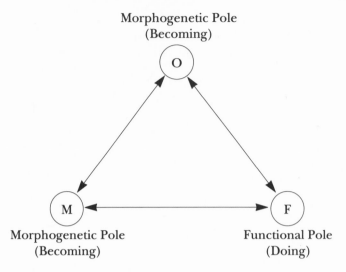

Figure 9-4. The Dynamics of the Active Units

The set of singular scientific statements deals with:

i)   the modes of action and interaction among the members of a relevant partition of a set of economic units encompassed by their retained roles (often called behavioral relations);

ii) the modes of production (often called technological relations);

iii) the social relations of production (often called institutional relations).

They are articulated within the framework of:

iv) a set of existential statements that introduces the basic or primary assumptions and primitive ideas.

These statements can be complemented by the following types of conventional statements:

iv) conditional statements (equilibrium relations); and

vi) universal statements (identities).

An economic model is always built from an implicit or explicit set of existential and conditional statements (types iv) and v) in our definition). They constitute the primitive and "unexplained" ideas and assumptions in the context of a field of inquiry, such as: the principle of effective demand, the supply-oriented economy, the law of supply and demand, the surplus value, the equilibrium or disequilibrium assumption, the class of subsets of economic units and perfect competitive markets. Their explanation can fall inside or outside the field of economics, or be interdisciplinary, but they are not the subject matter of inquiry within the specified field of research.

Statements of types i), ii) and iii) constitute the set of singular scientific statements, because they account for the functions or roles performed by a relevant partition of a set of economic units, the modes of production (i.e., the spectrum of technologies at work in a given field of inquiry), and the social relations of production or institutional structures. As singular scientific statements they can be submitted to statistical tests, i.e., they are testable.

Finally, the type vi) statements are always true by construction and are verified for all values of the specified variables. Therefore, they belong to the class of universal statements. They relate real and nominal variables such as real (y) and nominal (Y) income and the price level P, or are associated with a given partition of the set of economic units, such as the partition of the set A into households and firms, or into households, firms and government, which induce the identity Y=C+I, or Y=C+I+G, where the symbols Y, C, I and G stand for income, consumption, investment and government expenditures, respectively.

The historical and teleological properties of economics as a science determine the specification of unobservable variables such as planned, expected, and random variables. Each unobservable variable commands a new statement. The most important methodological approaches dealing with these types of unobservable variables are partial adjustment, adaptive expectation, Muth's rational expectation and Wold's soft models (path models with latent variables).

Table 9–2 presents a classification of the statements contained in our definition of an economic model.

Table 9–2

Classification of Statements

1)	Primitive ideas and primary assumptions (statements of type iv) and v)).	
2)	Singular scientific statements (types i), ii) and iii))	2.1) Modes of action and interaction of a relevant class of subsets of economic units.
		2.2) Modes of production.
3)	Universal statements (type vi)).	2.3) Social relations of production.

6.2.2. An Economic Interpretation of Lakatos' Methodology for a Scientific Research Program

Lakatos' (1978) contributions emphasize the growth of scientific knowledge. The structure of his methodology for a scientific research program represents a step towards Popper's and Kuhn's philosophies of science with respect to the assessment and validation of theories and models. To this end, Lakatos introduces important analytical categories such as the hard core, the protective belt, the positive heuristic, and progressive and regressive research programs. These analytical categories are put into correspondence with the class of statements introduced in our definition of economic model.

According to Lakatos, the *hard core* of a scientific research program comprises a basic set of assumptions which are protected from criticism and refutation. These assumptions are accepted by convention and considered irrefutable. This definition, however, is too dogmatic and has little applications in the social sciences, where ideology plays an important role in the coexistence of conflicting research programs. Why should the hard core be protected from criticism and refutation? Why should it be considered irrefutable? By whom? We should instead interpret the hard core as constituting the *cornerstone of a school of thought, paradigm* or *scientific research program*. In our definition of economic model, it corresponds to the primitive ideas and basic assumptions included under statements (iv) and (v), and to Wold's frame of reference in his models for knowledge.

In this sense, to the hard core belongs: (a) for the neoclassical school, the supply-side hypothesis, stemming from Say's law (supply creates its own demand), and the assumption of perfect competition in both the factor and the product markets; (b) for the Keynesian school, the principle of effective demand, the three fundamental Keynesian psychological factors, and the labor market disequilibrium assumption; (c) for the Marxian school, the class struggle, the assumptions supporting the labor theory of value and the appropriation of the surplus value; and (d) for the structural school of economics, the socio-economic infrastructure, which conditions the level of efficiency in the functioning of an economic system.

The acceptance of a hard core or set of primitive ideas and basic assumptions is of paramount importance for the design of an economic policy. Should the principle of effective demand be used in a case study, such as the U.S. and Canada's domestic demand for cars and textiles, where these domestic markets are competitioned from abroad (are not competitives), then an economic policy based on this principle will fail to materialize what the theory predicts. Therefore, the criticism of the hard core of an economic research program or economic school is essential prior to its application for decision purposes. That is, the acceptance of a hard core has unequivocal policy implications.

The criticism of a hard core takes the form of a conflict between school of thoughts. Indeed, the competing sets of primitive ideas or hard cores in Lakatos' terminology are the subject matter of discussion and controversy among schools of economic thought. Such is the case among the neoclassical, Keynesian, Marxian and structural schools.

The *protective belt* is defined as the set of auxiliary hypotheses that surrounds and protects the hard core, and is subject to confrontation with empirical observations. The protective belt in our definition of economic model is given by the set of singular scientific statements, i.e., those of types i), ii) and iii); in Wold's model for knowledge, it corresponds to the outcome of the dialectical process between E and T.

Practitioners of a scientific research program submit themselves to its hard core content. Their controversies take the form of a model specification dispute within a given school of thought, resulting in a sequence of models M_1, M_2,..., with different sets of auxiliary hypotheses and supported by the same primitive ideas. Such is the case in the sequence of Keynesian models and, more specifically, the sequence of Keynesian consumption function specifications (absolute, relative, permanent, and life cycle hypotheses).

According to Lakatos, the *positive heuristic* guides the scientist in the construction of a protective belt, which results in a series of theories T_1, T_2, T_3,..., in which "each subsequent theory results from adding auxiliary clauses to, or from the semantical reinterpretation of, the previous theory in order to accommodate some anomaly, where each theory in the series has as much empirical content as the unrefuted content of its predecessor" (Suppe, 1977 p. 662). It is "a powerful problem-solving machinery, which, with the help of sophisticated mathematical techniques, digests anomalies and even turns them into positive evidence." (Lakatos, 1978, p. 4).

In economics, the main body of positive heuristic is given by the content of econometric methods.

A research program is progressive if it is both theoretically and empirically progressive; otherwise it is degenerating. It is *theoretically progressive* if each new theory in the sequence, T_1, T_2, T_3, ..., has some empirical content over its predecessor, i.e., if it predicts some new facts. It is *empirically progressive* if some of the predicted new facts have been confirmed.

Lakatos (1978, p. 112) stated that "a research program is said to be *progressing* as long as its theoretical growth anticipates its empirical growth, that is, as long as it keeps predicting novel facts with some success (*progressive problem shift*); it is *stagnating* if its theoretical growth lags behind its empirical growth, that is, as long as it gives only *post hoc* explanations either of chance discoveries or of facts anticipated by, and discovered in, a rival program (*degenerating problem shift*)."

Observing the failure of the neoclassical monetarists and the Keynesians to cope with the problems of inflation, unemployment, government deficit, and interest rates we have to conclude that their programs are in a process of degeneration. The most we can say is that these programs are stagnating. Their practitioners are running behind empirical growth, adding auxiliary hypotheses, most of them *ad hoc* hypotheses, to preceding models in an effort to show some form of theoretical growth, and in this manner, trying to salvage the research program from degenerating.

6.2.3. PROPERTIES OF ECONOMIC MODELS AND THE APPROACHES TO SCIENTIFIC MODEL-BUILDING

Since economics is a factual science, the inductive and dialectical methods of inquiry come to the fore during the process of economic model-building (searching for systems). This process ends with the specification of an economic model by means of a set of singular scientific and conventional statements, which constitutes the axiomatic system within the framework of a hard core, i.e., a set of primitive ideas and basic assumptions. Thus, a model is the outcome of a process of observation-ideas-reason. Once the model is specified and accepted, the analytic and deductive method is applied, aiming at deducing the corresponding set of theorems or derived propositions. The axiomatic system and theorems form the theoretical empirical, axiomatic-deductive system or model belonging to an economic research program. Table 9–3 presents some of its properties.

Table 9–3

Properties of Economic Models

1) Logical	Axiomatic system	Consistency
		Independence
		Completeness
	Theorems: Logically true	
2) Empirical	Generality (theoretically progressive)	
	Validity (empirically progressive)	
3) Operative		

An axiomatic system is *consistent* if it does not allow for any contradictions; no axiom in the system should contradict any other axiom. It is *independent* if no axiom can be proved as a theorem by assuming the remaining axioms. It is *complete*, if it is consistent, independent, and contains one statement for each specified endogenous and unobservable variable.

The theorems or derived propositions have to be *logically true*, i.e., they have to be straightforward consequences of the analytical-deductive method applied to the axiomatic system.

A theoretical empirical axiomatic-deductive system satisfies the property of generality if it is a germane, coherent, and relevant representation of the aspect of reality which is the object of inquiry. It should be able to encompass and to account for all the relevant observed facts pertaining to that object of inquiry, and to predict some facts not predicted by its predecessors. This corresponds to a theoretically progressive research program. The system possesses the property of *validity* if its theorems are in close correspondence with the empirical domain of a given field of research, and some of the predicted new facts have been confirmed. This corresponds to an empirically progressive research program.

Finally, a model or system is *operative* if it is viable in terms of available techniques such as quantitative methods in econometrics, computer capability, and efficient technology.

A theoretical empirical axiomatic-deductive system possessing these logical, empirical, and operative properties is said to possess the attributes of *rigor, relevance,* and *realism. Rigor* is an attribute associated with the logical properties and resulting from the applied scientific methodology, starting with the research design and up to the model specification and its derived propositions, without ignoring the validation process of a model. *Relevance* is an attribute associated with the empirical properties and related to that aspect of reality which is the object of inquiry, the expectations of the scientific community, predictions, and the policy implications of the model. By *realism* is meant ontological, epistemological, and methodological realism.

For the factual sciences, the fulfillment of the logical properties is a necessary but not sufficient condition for a model to be a scientific part of knowledge; similarly for the empirical properties. The logical and empirical properties together are necessary and sufficient conditions. Figure 9–5 illustrates this statement, where L and E stand for logical and empirical property, respectively; the symbol $\wedge$ stands for the conjunction of two statements, and ~ for the negation of a statement.

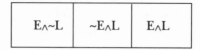

Figure 9–5. Models possessing logical (L) and/or empirical (E) properties.

The three cases illustrated in Figure 9–5 are related to the three approaches of the philosophy of science to the construction of a scientific model. $E_\wedge{\sim}L$ symbolizes empiricism; ${\sim}E_\wedge L$ idealism, and $E_\wedge L$ theoretical empiricism. To ${\sim}E_\wedge L$ applies Kierkegaard's assessment of Hegel's system quoted above, and also Bertrand Russell's (1919, p. 71) observation that "the method of postulating what we want has many advantages; they are the same as the advantages of theft over honest toil."

6.3. Estimation of the Theoretical Structure

Once the theoretical model of the observed structure is postulated as the explanatory model of a given field of inquiry, the next step requires its parameter estimation. For this we make use of the appropriate method. Wold discussed this issue in several seminal contributions. He made a comparative study of the properties of the maximum likelihood (ML) and the least squares (LS) methods of parameter estimation. Following Wold (1981, 1984), the former is parameter-oriented and the latter is prediction-oriented. In his analysis, Wold distinguished two categories of models, path models with manifest (directly observed) variables, and path models with latent (indirectly observed) variables. Wold (1984) observed that "prediction specification is of broad scope in three dimensions: data input, theoretical model, and operative purpose."

In econometrics, a model is defined as a family of structures. Hence, it can be parameterized, i.e., defined by means of a parameter space $\Theta = \{\theta \mid \cdot \}$, associated with the mathematical law of correspondence among the variables included in the model specification. Each $\theta \in \Theta$ defines a structure which is obtained by either a parameter-oriented or a predictor-oriented method of estimation. For a documented study of the properties, advantages and limitations of alternative predictor specifications, see Wold (1984) and the references in that paper.

6.4. Specification of a Target Structure

The model specification and its estimated structure correspond to the second and third steps, respectively, of our methodology of economic research program. They belong to the realm of *positive economics*, i.e., the ontological dimension of economics, more precisely an ontological realism, and purport to answer the question "what is."

Economics, as all factual sciences, is a science for action. Accordingly, the Spanish philosopher Juan Luis Vives (1492-1540) observed that knowledge is of value only when it is put to use, and Marschak (1953, p. 1) stated that "knowledge is useful if it helps to make the best decisions."

As a factual science, economics embodies the knowledge of an aspect of reality which takes the form of an economic structure. As a science for action, the knowledge it embodies helps the decisionmaker's specification of a target structure to be realized within a finite time horizon. Its specification belongs to the realm of *normative economics* and purports to answer the question "what should be."

The decisionmaker's specification of a target structure is a constituent part of his representation of the future of a society's national structures. In particular, the specification of a macro-economic target structure must be an attainable representation of the future in terms of the observed structure, and the decisionmaker's ideology and social philosophy.

6.5. Testing the Difference Between the Observed and the Target Structures

It follows from the last two (third and fourth) steps of the proposed methodology of economic research that we are confronted with two structures, the observed (S) and the decisionmaker's target (D) structures. Before the decisionmaker commits himself to carrying out a given course of action, he must decide first whether or not there is a significant difference between the observed and the target structures. There is here a parting of the ways between the classical ML methods of model evaluation, and the recent LS methods used in this volume for models estimated by fix-point and partial least squares methods, namely Stone-Geisser's (1974) test for predictive relevance and J. Tukey's jackknife assessment of standard errors. Stone-Geisser's test and the jackknife are set forth by Jan-Bernd Lohmöller in Chapter 1 of this volume, "The Basic Principles of Model Building."

In the ML methods of model evaluation, H_0: S=D is the null hypothesis, which means that there is no significant difference between S and D; hence S and D can be considered as two equivalent representations of the same theoretical structure T. The alternative is the composite hypothesis H_1: S≠D, which means that D represents a target structure significantly different from the observed structure represented by S.

For a test of a hypothesis based on a distance function between structures, we refer the reader to Dagum (1983).

6.6. Specification of a Decision Model

A decision model is a consistent set of statements specifying a course of action or strategy to achieve a given goal or target. Two essential concepts emerge from this definition: the course of action and the target. It is apparent that an explanatory model, with its associated set of endogenous, exogenous and lagged variables has a *cause-effect* base. Having the purpose of achieving a given target, a decision model should act on the causes to produce a desired effect. Hence it must act on the exogenous variables that are controllable by the decisionmaker. The selection of the controllable variables as steering variables defines the instrumental variables, and their corresponding tuning determines the course of action. The chosen targets correspond to the planned time path of the selected endogenous (effect) variables, called target variables.

The choice of the target variables and the intensity of their relative use in macroeconomic decision models clearly reveal the decisionmaker's ideology and social philosophy.

A decision model can pursue either a more efficient performance of the same structure, or a structural change. The former applies when we accept the null hypothesis of no significant difference between the estimated and the target structures; the latter applies when the null hypothesis is rejected. These two possible courses of action define, respectively,

  i) a conjunctural (business cycle) economic policy; and
  ii) a structural economic policy.

The former performs within the theoretical structure to accomplish its goals, whereas the latter aims at the change of a given structure as the more efficient, or only, course of action to accomplish the purported effect on the target variables.

In the developed industrialized countries, mainly Great Britain and the U.S., the failure to understand the *circumstance*[2] conditioning each type of economic policy is at the very base of the increasing frequency and intensity of recessions, the coexistence of inflation and unemployment, and the clear signs of the mainstream economic research program becoming a degenerating, or at least a stagnating, research program. Assuming theoretical growth, it lags behind the *fait accompli* (empirical growth), and most of the time the claimed theoretical growth is the result of an ingenious collection of *ad hoc* assumptions, or in Russell's incisive words, the result of postulating what they want.

7. THEORETICAL EMPIRICISM IN THE FACTUAL AND METHODOLOGICAL SCIENCES. SOME CLASSIC EXAMPLES FROM THE HISTORY OF SCIENCE.

The factual property underlying the construction of scientific models goes beyond the substantive science and is also observed in important fields of mathematics and statistics. Moreover, mathematics appears to have been the first scientific domain to formalize a highly sophisticated and consistent model as a theoretical counterpart to the empirical domain. This was done by Euclid about 23 centuries ago, and could be presented as an archetype of theoretical empiricism.

In a lively contribution, von Neumann (1947) discussed the empirical background of mathematics. He stated (p. 182) that "it is undeniable that some of the best inspirations in mathematics—in those parts of it which are as pure mathematics as one can imagine—have come from the natural sciences.... Geometry was the major part of ancient mathematics.... There can be no doubt that its origin in antiquity was empirical and that it began as a discipline not unlike theoretical physics today. Apart from all other evidence, the very name 'geometry' indicates this. Euclid's postulational treatment represents a great step away from empiricism, but it is not at all simple to defend the position that this was the decisive and final step, producing an absolute separation." Von Neumann's observation about Euclid's postulational treatment representing a great step away from empiricism is consistent with the theoretical empiricism philosophy of science, whereby reason introduces a point of discontinuity in the process of observations, ideas, and reason. Hence, it is a great step away from empiricism, leading to the abstract specification of a theoretical model, and keeping at the same time the observation-ideas interaction as a supporting base for the model specification and validation.

Another classic example of scientific model-building in the context of theoretical empiricism can also be drawn from mathematics. It is calculus, or rather all analysis stemming from it, which constitutes the first accomplishment of modern mathematics. There is undeniable evidence supporting the empirical origin of calculus, which evolved to become real analysis, which, by its degree of abstraction, represented a great step away from empiricism. Archimedes' and Kepler's attempts at integration of surfaces and volumes with curved surfaces, respectively, are cases in point. The main discoveries in the field by Newton and Leibnitz had an explicit physical motivation; they served as a mathematical method for the development of classical mechanics.

In astronomy, an outstanding example of scientific empiricism is found in the work of Tycho de Brahe, Kepler and Galileo. After realizing that astronomical tables based on the Ptolemaic model were much too inaccurate, Tycho compiled astronomical observations that led him to abandon the Ptolemaic model without accepting the Copernican one. These observations, carried over for more than twenty years and accomplished in pre-telescope times, were left with Kepler in Prague, where Tycho moved to and met Kepler in 1599. On the basis of Tycho's observations, Kepler formulated his theory. His main contributions were addressed to explaining the form or structure of the phenomena. The dynamic approach, i.e., how the phenomena evolve in time, is Galileo's concern. Thus Tycho, the observer, and Kepler and Galileo, the theorists, are at the very base of the theoretical empirical development of modern natural science.

In the social sciences and humanities, the use of observations to support scientific model building took place later in time and showed a less spectacular progress than in the natural sciences. Von Neumann and Morgenstern (1944, p. 4) observed that "the empirical background of economic science is definitely inadequate. Our knowledge of the relevant facts of economics is incomparably smaller than that commanded in physics at the time when the mathematization of that subject was achieved." *A fortiori*, we could say the same for all of the social sciences. Morgenstern (1950) rigorously developed this subject matter in his classic research on the accuracy of economic observations. Nevertheless, the social sciences also exhibit some important examples of theoretical empiricism such as that of Pierre Bayle, Voltaire and Montesquieu. Bayle is regarded as a founder of 18th century rationalism. His masterpiece *Dictionnaire historique et critique*, first published in 1697, was an extraordinary source of historical information and criticism. Bayle's observations and criticism of historical life allowed Voltaire to write his celebrated *Essai sur les moeurs et l'esprit des nations*, a masterpiece of historical analysis of the customs and the spirit of different peoples. His work does not consider outstanding features such as political conspiracies, revolutions, wars and battles, without intertwining them with the customs and spirit of societies. Montesquieu complemented Voltaire's contributions to both the structural and the dynamic approaches. For him, the ultimate reality and prime mover in the growth of nations are not made of fixed patterns but of acting impulses, and above all, the decisionmakers' acting impulses.

The French physician F. Quesnay appears to have been the first scholar to set down in some detail the rudiments of an economic model. His contributions were not the outcome of the theoretical empirical approach to model-building, but rather an analogic mode of inquiry, whereby his famous *Tableau économique* evolved from a biological analogy, i.e., the blood circulation in human beings. Almost half a century later, Adam Smith provided a coherent analysis of the nature and causes of the wealth of nations, without offering a formal model as we understand it today. His contributions recognized an empirical background, that of England's rising industrial and financial capitalism at the time of the first industrial revolution, and embodied a clear policy implication: economic liberalism.

Among other contributions, Ricardo advanced a theory of income distribution based on the marginal and surplus value principles. These methodological principles and his scientific contributions provided the bases for the development of both the neoclassical and the Marxian schools of economics. The former adopted exclusively the marginal, and the latter the surplus value, principle.

The observed population and food growth rates supported Malthus' specification of the geometric and arithmetic series for the time path of population and food outputs, respectively, and to the Malthusian model of population growth and existence minimum.

Cournot modeled the monopolistic market and advanced the first systematic thought on the theory of general economic equilibrium, which later on became Walras' most celebrated achievement. With Walras, mainstream economics started to depart from the theoretical empirical mode of scientific model-building and became dominated by an aprioristic, i.e., an idealist, philosophy of science.

8. CONCLUSION

As a philosophy of science approach to the construction of scientific models in the factual sciences, theoretical empiricism is considered to be the highroad leading to the explanation of an aspect of reality, be it based on either matter, life, or society. The implied scientific model is designed to be rigorous, relevant, and realist. Compared to former model specifications of the same aspect of reality, it has a greater generality and validity, and thus it belongs to a theoretically and empirically progressive research program. It has explanatory power, and under the assumption of some form of structural stability, it has the capability to predict expected and new events, whereby some of the new events predicted are afterwards confirmed. This approach is associated with the contributions of Aristotle and Saint Thomas Aquinas, and the resulting specified model is the outcome of an intertwined and dialectical process among observations, ideas, reason, and scientific model-building.

Two particular and extreme versions of theoretical empiricism are the empiricist (Democritus, Bacon, Locke and Condillac) and the idealist (Plato, Descartes, Kant and Hegel) philosophies of science. The former gives too much attention to observations and neglects the creative roles of ideas and reason, whereas the latter neglects the role of observations, overemphasizes the roles of ideas and reason, resulting in *a priori* constructions of science detached from reality. In synthesis, theoretical empiricism shares with empiricism the determination to learn primarily from experience, and with idealism the importance attached to ideas and reason. Wold's models for knowledge are a cogent synthetic representation of theoretical empiricism as a general system for scientific model-building.

A program for a methodology of economic research is proposed and discussed within the framework of theoretical empiricism. Economics as a science for action brings to the fore the policy implications of scientific model building, and the historical and teleological properties condition the general rationale to scientific model building. These properties motivate the active participation of the path (memory variables) and the decisionmaker's representation of the future (project variables and expectations) in the process of model building. The economic units, like the god Janus, look both backward and forward before making decisions. The first three steps in the proposed research program in economics correspond toWold's models for knowledge; of the remaining three steps, the null hypothesis is of a methodological character, and the specifications of a target structure, and of a decision model belong to the realm of normative economics.

Some classical examples drawn from the history of science substantiate the role of theoretical empiricism as a general approach to scientific model building in both factual and methodological sciences.

END NOTES

1 Should the stretching of the theory fail to fit unexplained phenomena, then the last three steps in Kuhn's approach would follow. If this is the case, we

move from the dialectical process between E and T leading to a sequence of model specifications within the same paradigm or research program, to a process of paradigm change.

2 To the term "circumstance" is attached the rich philosophical meaning that summarizes J. Ortega y Gasset's philosophical thought. Ortega y Gasset (T. VI, p. 347) wrote: "I am myself and my circumstance. My work is, in essence and presence, circumstantial. By this I mean that it is deliberate, because without deliberation, and moreover in spite of opposing purposes, it is clear that man never has done anything in the world that was not circumstantial."

3 I am indebted to Wold for this information.

4 W. Heisenberg (1958, p. 24) states that "the object of research is no longer nature itself, but man's interrogation of nature."

REFERENCES

Aquinas, T. 1964. *Summa Theologica.* New York: McGraw-Hill.

Borel, E. 1937. Sur l'imitation du Hasard. Compte-Rendus de l'Academie des Sciences, Paris, seance du 25 janvier.

Cournot, A. 1838. *Recherches sur les principes mathematiques de la theorie des richesses.* Paris: Hachette.

Dagum, C. 1968. On methods and purposes in econometric model building. *Zeitschrift fur Nationalokonomie,* 28:381–398.

Dagum, C. 1969. Structural permanence. *Zeitschrift fur die Gesamte Staatswissenschaft,* 125 Band/2 Heft: 211–235.

Dagum, C. 1977. Ideologie et methodologie de la recherche en science economique. *Economies et Societes,* Serie philosophie et sciences de l'homme, Cahiers de l'ISMEA, Tome XI (3):553–586.

Dagum, C. 1983. On structural stability and structural change in economics, *Proceedings of the American Statistical Association, Business and Economics Section,* 143rd Meeting: 654–659.

de Montesquieu, C. 1748. *L'esprit des lois.* Paris: Edition de la Pleiade.

Frisch, R. 1935. On the notion of equilibrium and disequilibrium. *Review of Economic Studies,* 3:100–106.

Gini, C. 1953. Intorno all'uso dei modelli nelle scienze, e in particolare pella scienza economica. *Rivista di Politica Economica,* 52–53: 3–21.

Heisenberg, W. 1958. *The physicist's conception of nature.* New York: Harcourt, Brace and Company.

Hood, W.C., and T.C. Koopmans, eds. 1953. *Studies in econometric method.* New York: Wiley.

Jöreskog, K., and H. Wold, eds. 1982. *Systems under indirect observation,* I and II. Amsterdam: North-Holland.

Kant, I. 1787. *The critique of pure reason.* Chicago: Encyclopedia Britannica.

Keynes, J. 1936. *The general theory of employment, interest and money.* London: Macmillan.

Kuhn, T. 1962. *The structure of scientific revolutions.* 2d. ed. 1964 Chicago: University of Chicago Press.

Lakatos, I. 1978. Posthumous paper in *The methodology of scientific research programmes,* eds. J. Worrall and G. Currie. Cambridge: Cambridge University Press.

Lange, O. 1964. Note on ideology and tendencies in economic research. *International Social Sciences Journal,* 16:524–528.

Le Moigne, J. 1977. *La theorie du systeme general.* Paris: Presses Universitaires de France.

Marschak, J. 1953. Economic measurements for policy and prediction. In *Studies in econometric method,* eds. W. C. Hood and T.C. Koopmans, 1–26.

Mesarovic, M. 1963. Foundations for a General Systems Theory. In *Views on general systems theory,* ed. M. Mesarvic, 1–24. New York: Wiley.

Morgenstern, O. 1950. *On the accuracy of economic observations.* 2d ed. 1963 Princeton: University Press.

Morgenstern, O. 1972. Descriptive, predictive and normative theory. *Kyklos,* 25:699–714.

Munz, P. 1982. Transformation in philosophy through the teaching methods of Wittgenstein and Popper. *Proceedings of The 10th International Conference on the Unity of the Sciences.* Vol. 2, 1235–1262. New York: International Cultural Foundation Press.

Muth, J. 1961. Rational expectations and the theory of price movements. *Econometrica* 29:315–335.

Ortega Y Gasset, J. 1946. Wilhelm Dilthey and the idea of life. In *Concord and Liberty,* ed. Ortega y Gasset, 129–182. New York: W.W. Norton.

Ortega Y Gasset, J. 1947. *Obras completas.* Madrid: Revista de Occidente.

Palomba, G. 1981. Introduzione. In *Opere di Antoine-Augustin Cournot,* 7–107. Torino: UTET.

Palomba, G. 1984. *La distribuzione sociale del reddito nazionale.* Napoli: De Simone Editore.

Perroux, F. 1975. *Unites actives et mathematiques nouvelles.* Revision de la theorie de l'equilibre economique generale. Paris: Dunod.

Popper, K. 1972. *Objective knowledge.* Oxford: Oxford University press.

Russell, B. 1919. *Introduction to mathematical philosophy.* London: George Allen and Unwin.

Schumpeter, J. 1954. *History of economic analysis.* Oxford: Oxford University Press.

Stone, M. 1974. Cross-validatory choice and assessment of statistical predictions. *Journal of the Royal Statistical Society* B 36:111–147.

Suppe, F., ed. 1974. *The structure of scientific theories.* 2d ed. 1977 Urbana: University of Illinois Press.

Thom, R. 1975. *Structural stability and morphogenesis.* Reading: W.A. Benjamin, Incorporated.

Tinbergen, J. 1939. *Statistical testing of business cycle theories.* Vol. 1. Geneva: League of Nations.

Tinbergen, J. 1956. *Economic policy: Principles and design.* Amsterdam: North Holland.

Tinbergen, N. 1974. Ethology and stress diseases. *Science* 185(4145): 20–27. Also in Les Prix Nobel, en 1973.

Vollmer, G. 1984. The unity of the sciences in an evolutionary perspective. *Proceedings of the 12th International Conference on the Unity of the Sciences.*

von Bertalanffy, L. 1968. *General system theory.* New York: George Braziller.

Von Neumann, J. 1947. The Mathematician. In *The works of the mind,* ed. R. Heywood, 180–196. Chicago: University Press.

Von Neumann, J., and O. Morgenstern. 1944. Theory of games and economic behavior. 3rd ed. 1953 Princeton: University Press.

Wold, H. 1958. End and means in econometric model building. Basic considerations reviewed. In *Probability and statistics. The Harald Cramér volume,* ed. U. Grenander, 355–434. Stockholm: Almqvist and Wiksells. 2nd ed. 1959, New York: Wiley.

Wold, H. 1963. On the consistency of the least squares regression. *Sankyā* A 25:211–215.

Wold, H. 1969. Merger of economics and philosophy of science. *Synthese* 20:427–482. Also in Dagum, C. ed., 1979, Chap. 9.

Wold, H., ed. 1981. *The fix-point approach to interdependent systems.* Amsterdam: North-Holland.

Wold, H. 1982. Models for knowledge. In *The making of statisticians,* ed. J. Gani, 189–212. New York: Springer-Verlag.

Wold, H. 1984. Predictor specification. *Encyclopedia of statistical sciences,* eds. S. Kotz and W. L. Johnson. New York: John Wiley and Sons.

10

Discussion of Dagum's Paper

FRANCISCO AZORIN POCH

FUZZY SETS AND PARTIAL LEAST SQUARES

The first paradigm of uncertainty was Probability, as introduced by the "founding fathers": Cardano, Pascal, Fermat, the Bernoulli's, etc. Many years passed until a satisfactory axiomatic system was established. After impressive advances in model specification, estimation and evaluation, in the second half of this century a drive began to delve into other aspects of uncertainty and vagueness, transcending assumptions which were considered too stringent, and extending the foundations of model conception.

New paradigms emerged: Bayesian inference, Soft modeling (H. Wold) and Fuzzy Sets (L.A. Zadeh).

In Bayesian statistics there is a vagueness about prior probability, as has been the case with other statistical notions.

Softness is also related to vagueness and weak features, as opposed to hard, or crisp, distributional assumptions.

Some references on relationships between fuzziness (vagueness) and softness are F. Azorin (1975), F. Azorin (1979), F. Azorin (1983). In the first and third books, it is noted that fuzziness may appear in manifest variables of soft models, and also in parameters and relations, for instance, when equations, identities or definitions, and restrictions may belong to the model with a certain intensity, between 0 and 1.

In the second book, soft modeling is mentioned among notions of uncertainty and vagueness, when some variables do not appear to be quantifiable, but nevertheless must be quantified.

Recently, N. Corral and M. A. Gil (1984) dealt with the extension of the maximum likelihood principle, when the available experience provides only vague information.

The potentials of PLS in various Fuzzy Sets problems should be explored, for instance, by using partial least squares instead of maximum likelihood methods in point estimation problems with fuzzy information.

The cross-breeding between fuzzy sets and soft modeling could open new avenues of research and applications. An ambitious target would be to develop a general theory encompassing different aspects of subjective probability, fuzziness, and softness.

REFERENCES

Azorin, F. 1976. Conjuntos nitidos y modelacion laxa en taxonomia matematica (Fuzzy sets and soft modeling in mathematical taxonomy). In *Coloquio Internacional de Estadistica e Investigación Operativa*, ed. S. Rios, 39–48. Madrid: Consejo Superior de Investigaciones Cinentificas.

Azorin, F. 1979. *Alqunas aplicaciones de los conjuntos borrosos a 1a estadistica (Some applications of fuzzy sets to statistics)*. Madrid: Instituto Nacional de Estadistica.

Azorin, F. 1983. Notas sobre conjuntos vagos, modelacion laxa y taxonomia matematica (Notes on fuzzy sets, soft modeling and mathematical taxonomy). In *Atas de 2ᵉ Simposio Nacional de Probabilidade e Estadistica*, ed. D. Dorigo, 39–48. Rio de Janeiro: Campinas.

Coral, N., and M. Gil, 1984. The minimum inaccuracy fuzzy estimation: an extension of the maximum likelihood principle. *Stochastica* 8:63–81.

Wold, H. 1983. Fix-point method. In *Encyclopedia of Statistical Sciences* (EES), vol. 3, eds. S. Katz and N.L. Johnson, 148–156. New York: Wiley.

Wold, H. 1985. Partial Least Squares. In *Encyclopedia of Statistical Sciences*, vol. 6., eds. S. Kotz and N.L. Johnson, 581–591. New York: Wiley.

Zadeh, L., et al. 1975. *Fuzzy sets and their applications to cognitive and decision processes*. New York: Academic Press.

11

The Blending of Theoretical and Empirical Knowledge in Structural Equations with Unobservables

CLAES FORNELL

SUMMARY

The purpose of this paper is to show how theoretical and empirical knowledge can be combined in recently developed statistical methods. It is suggested that these new methods allow methodology to become more consistent with the modern philosophy of science. In particular, structural equations models with unobservable variables make it possible for the practicing scientist to depart from operationalism—a philosophical position insisting that theoretical concepts be synonymous with observable measures and to reject an early, long abandoned, in the philosophy of science, tenet of positivism—that theory and data are independent.

The paper begins with a discussion of theory-data interaction and the difficulties involved in separating the abstract (having to do with theory) from the concrete (having to do with data). Abstract meaning is then discussed as evolving from (1) attributional or dispositional definitions of the concept in question, (2) the antecedents of the concept, and (3) the consequences of the concept. Empirical meaning is, on the other hand, determined via correspondence rules linking the abstract concept to the empirical world.

Recognizing that abstract and empirical meaning depend on each other, a schematic for combining the two is suggested. Within the context of this model the issues of directionality of the abstract-empirical linkage are addressed. This question is closely related to deductive vs. inductive modes of thinking. That is, if we model the relationship between the abstract and empirical such that our theoretical model implies certain observations, we follow a deductive approach. If we, in contrast, take the theoretical as dependent upon the observed, we follow an inductive approach.

The issue of directionality between observed and unobserved has important implications for the bearing of theory vs. data in the analysis. This is illustrated in a simple example where covariance structure analysis is applied to estimate the correlation between two unobserved theoretical variables. The resulting estimate is shown to be much larger than what the corresponding data on observed variables indicate. Thus, theory plays a "dominating" role in the analysis.

If the analyst is unwilling to discard the data to the same extent and has somewhat less confidence in the accuracy of the theory, it is possible to let data have a greater impact on the estimation. Using the same data example, it it shown that a variance structure model, implemented via Partial Least Squares (PLS), provides this result. Further, it is shown, via an example from economics/political science, that it can make a great deal of difference how the relationship between the abstract and concrete is specified. The point here is that the validity of measurements (with respect to some unobserved theoretical construct) can be strongly affected by the theoretical structure and whether a deductive or inductive mode of relating the measures to the theory is followed.

1. INTRODUCTION

Not until recently has the practicing researcher had access to tools of statistical analysis able to deal with multidimensional phenomena in systems of relationships incorporating both observable and nonobservable terms that allow for an effective interplay between theory and data. These techniques have been referred to as "a second generation of multivariate analysis." Earlier statistical techniques forced the analyst, willingly or not, to either (1) conform to the doctrine of operationalism—a philosophical position essentially abandoned many years ago in the philosophy of science, and/or (2) to follow an early positivistic dictation about the independence of theory and data. For example, traditional econometric modeling almost always requires operational definitions of its variables; the theoretical concepts must be synonymous with a corresponding set of measurement operations. Psychometric modeling, on the other hand, while emphasizing the theoretical desirability of specifying underlying unobservable variables that account for some observed phenomenon (usually a response to a stimulus), also typically requires that data are independent of the context in which they occur. This is the case in classical test theory and its implementation in factor analysis. It is assumed that (1) "true scores" do exist and (2) that they are invariant across different theoretical networks.

As noted by Suppe (1974), "it seems to be characteristic, but unfortunate, of science to continue holding philosophical positions long after they are discredited" (p. 19). The problem is not necessarily that practicing researchers may be unfamiliar with the developments in the philosophy of science, but that methodology has lagged in development relative to the logical and epistemological advances in the philosophy of science.

Recently, however, significant progress has been made in statistical methodology. A new generation of methods enables researchers to rid themselves of at least some of the untenable facets of operationalism and logical empiricism. Specifically, it is no longer necessary to insist that theoretical concepts be synonymous with measured variables or to assume that observation is independent of theory.

The comments on this paper by Ray Pawson and Thomas Brante make several interesting points with respect to this issue. Pawson criticizes the so–called "double-language" model and writes that "...as soon as one allows for the interdependence of theory and observation, it seems pointless to refer to them as independent realms..." In a similar vein, Brante concludes that my reasoning is inconsistent when I first claim that it is not possible to make a distinction between theory and observation and then make this distinction (in different ways) in my illustrations. But this is precisely the point! There is no *per se* distinction that holds in all contexts and for all purposes. Nevertheless, the dilemma for the practicing scientist is that the distinction must somehow be made. Otherwise, we are forced to return to operationalism. Herein lies the paradox in Brante and Pawson's reasoning. If the distinction between theory and observation is not only *per se* impossible but also futile in an *ad hoc* sense, it follows that the two must be synonymous—which is the position of operationalism (which neither Brante nor Pawson subscribes to).

It seems to me that the relevant question is how the distinction between theory and observation can be made in the absence of *per se* rules. The answer is not an issue at the level of language, of course (as the title of Pawson's comments might lead a reader to infer). Rather, it is dependent upon context and purpose (with respect to the analysis or study in question). The difficulty lies in the fact that intertwined with context and purpose, the scientist makes a host of assumptions about the object under study and its environment. One of these assumptions refers to the line of demarcation between theory and observation and this assumption is, in principle, similar to the usual assumptions of *ceteris paribus*, closed systems, no specification error, etc. That is, the validity of these assumptions is essentially impossible to evaluate (at least within the particular study in which they are made; otherwise they would not be assumptions).

Not surprisingly, as practicing researchers begin to apply the new statistical methods, they are confronted with issues that remain largely unanalyzed in the methods literature, and are faced with numerical results that challenge some firmly held convictions about theory evaluation. This paper, in the context of the methods of covariance structure analysis and Partial Least Squares, discusses the implementation of the theory–data interaction and its implications in terms of theory testing (Jöreskog, 1973; Wold, 1975, 1982). Let us begin by briefly reviewing the status of abstract variables and their interaction with empirical data in contemporary philosophy of science. Subsequently, we present a discussion of abstract and empirical meaning and how the two are combined in analysis.

2. THEORY AND DATA INTERACTION

Measurement in science can be viewed as an attempt to tie a concept to the empirical world. In doing this, two contradictory forces become immediately apparent: on the one hand, there is the desire to faithfully reproduce the "empirical world" as it is known by its actors; yet there is also the ambition to discover the underlying and, thus abstract, properties of "world order." Faithfulness is always forfeited when abstraction is achieved. Yet, without abstraction there is no theory.

Abstraction can be accomplished in various ways and through various stages. For example, distinctions are sometimes made between observational terms (which can be directly observed), indirect observables (which require some sort of inference) and constructs (which have no direct linkage to the empirical world). Thus, in linking the abstract to the empirical, observational terms imply operational definitions; that is, the concept is synonymous with some corresponding set of operations. While operationalism might have value in terms of "faithfulness to reality" (although this is debatable), it is not a satisfactory substitute for abstraction and for theoretical work. The reason is two-fold according to Suppe (1974): (1) theoretical terms are not explicitly definable if the theory is to be axiomatized in first-order predicate calculus with equality and (2) alternative experimental procedures for measuring the same theoretical property make it unreasonable to identify the theoretical property with any one experimental procedure or even any specified set of alternative procedures.

The recognition of the difficulties in equating the theoretical and the empirical has led to a variety of suggestions concerning the linkages (correspondence rules) between them. As a consequence, operationalism has long been abandoned in the philosophy of science literature. More recent interpretations of theoretical terms are found in the realist approach and in the instrumentalist approach to theory. The former lets theoretical terms refer to real but nonobservable phenomena. The latter considers theoretical terms to be more or less expendable; they are not explicitly defined and their sole purpose is to define the class of theoretical laws for the theory. Nevertheless, whatever the role of theoretical terms is supposed to be, there is basic agreement about their abstract or nonobservable status. This is true for theoretical empiricism as well.

Examples of observational terms might be such things as volume, cell nucleus, or market share. Among the theoretical terms would be things like atoms, genes, virus, attitude, and demand elasticity. However, as argued by Achinstein (1968) a *distinction* between the observational vs. the theoretical is not possible because "observation" involves attending to something, and how many aspects of that something and which aspects one must attend to before it can be said that observation has taken place, will depend upon prior concerns and knowledge. That is,

(1) Observation if it is to be relevant, must be interpreted.
(2) That in terms of which interpretation is made is always theory.
(3) The theory not only serves as a basis of interpretation, but also determines what is to be counted as an observation, problem, method, solution, and so forth.

In other words, all information collected by a researcher is conditioned by the context into which the research is placed.

2.1. Abstract Meaning

Figure 11–1 presents a diagram that can be used to illustrate the idea of abstract or theoretical meaning. Here, for simplicity, the discussion is restricted to the interpretation of a single focal concept, F. In general, the meaning of F is obtained through a specification of three criteria: (1) the definition of F, (2) the antecedents, determinants or causes of F, and (3) the consequences, implications or results of F. Though a complete meaning of F is achieved only when all three criteria are addressed, it is possible that any particular study, depending on its purposes, may emphasize a subset. Generally, a minimal interpretation of F at the conceptual level requires a definition of F plus either an antecedent, A, or a consequence, C, and its relationship to F.

The definition of a concept can take a number of forms. Perhaps the most common is one that specifies the attributes, characteristics, or properties of F (termed an attributional definition). A concept will have a set of descriptors which can nominally be considered as definitionally equivalent to the concept. Typically this set consists of attributes whose content and number evolve over time, conditioned on intersubjective agreement among scientists.

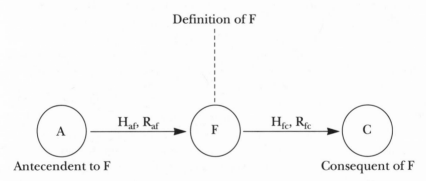

Figure 11–1. A Schematic for Ascertaining the Meaning of a Single Concept, F

We may further note two subtypes of attributional definitions: namely, the atomistic–analytical and the holistic–contextual. An atomistic–analytical attributional definition consists of a set of properties such that each property is a subdimension of the idea represented in the concept. For example, a definition of a market might include the following properties: two or more actors are involved; the actors are in communication with each other; each has something of value desired by the other; one is termed a buyer and the other a seller; the transaction is characterized by offers and counter offers, and so on. A holistic–contextual attributional definition, in contrast, comprises a number of elements and relationships among the elements. The definition of a concept requires specification of the entire network, and the elements and relations are exhaustive. This contrasts with the automatic–analytical attributional definition, where some properties are essential or necessary to a definition while others are non-essential to the essence of the concept but serve to elaborate a particular manifestation or subtype of idea implied by the concept. An example of a holistic-contextual attributional definition of a market might be: a meeting of minds where actors construct a shared reality concerning the allocation and distribution of goods and services.

Another basic form a definition might take is as a description of capacities, tendencies, or dispositions of a concept (termed a dispositional definition). Unlike the attributional definition, which is limited to a description of the properties of a concept (for example, the individual physical, psychological, or social characteristics implied by a concept, or a system of these characteristics), the dispositional definition refers to the intrinsic nature of a concept. Typically, this will encompass specification of the internal structure of a concept and its potential for either influencing another concept or being influenced by it in some way. For example, one might use a dispositional definition of an attitude to specify a structure of cognitions and evaluations having certain capabilities and linked in such a way that the introduction of a stimulus communication would lead to attitude change and this, in turn, would influence choice behavior. An attributional definition of attitude would be limited to a description of the elements of attitude (for example, a set of beliefs and evaluations) and perhaps a rule for combining the elements. A dispositional definition contains a representation of the ability or power of the concept to undergo change and to produce change in other concepts, in addition to specification of the elements of the concept and interrelations among elements. Although such capabilities might be implicit in the attributional definition, they are formally delineated in the dispositional definition.

The abstract meaning of a focal concept, F, is also determined by its antecedents (see Figure 11–1). Whereas a definition specifies what a concept is and perhaps what it is capable of being and doing, its antecedents supply information as to where it has been (that is, its history of development) and/or how it is formed or influenced. However, if one is to reveal the meaning provided by an antecedent, it is not sufficient to merely indicate what the antecedent is. Rather, as represented in Figure 11–1, one must also specify the content of the hypothesis, linking antecedent to the focal concept (that is, H_{af}) and the rationale for the hypothesis (that is, R_{af}). The content of a hypothesis consists of a statement of the nature of the relationship of antecedent to focal concept and is expressed in proposition form. This might entail a relatively nonspecific statement such as "the greater the magnitude or level of A, the less the magnitude or level of F," or it might entail a more specific statement as to the functional form of the relationship or even the amount of change expected in F as a function of A. The rationale for the hypothesis is needed to complete the meaning of F provided by A. In general, a rationale for a hypothesis can be obtained through specification of the mechanisms by which A influences F and/or the laws under which A and F are regularly conjoined.

In a parallel fashion, the meaning of F is also determined through its relations to consequences (see Figure 11–1). The implications of a focal concept, F, supply information as to where a phenomenon is going, what it can lead to, and/or what influence it has. Again, it is not sufficient to identify what the consequences are. Rather, one must also describe the nature of the hypothesis connecting focal concept to consequence (that is, H_{fc}) and the rationale for the hypothesis (that is, R_{fc}).

The depth of abstract meaning achieved through specification of antecedents and/or consequences depends on the extent of the description of the relationships and their rationale. Further, we may ascertain the adequacy of the meaning so provided through examination of the internal consistency of the propositions, analysis of alternative hypotheses, asking "what if" questions, performing thought experiments with regard to the system of propositions, and conceptually integrating and comparing the hypotheses to the existing body of knowledge related to the focal concept. Thus, it can be seen that, while much of the abstract meaning of concepts depends on logical (semantic and syntactic) criteria residing in definitions and in the relations of antecedents and consequences to a focal concept, empirical criteria also enter the picture. They do this through the normative of conventional standards imposed by a community of scientists as well as through the inductive generalizations of past research that guide the selection and formation of concepts and the hypothesized relations to other concepts in a theory. This infusion of empirical content has often been implicit and nonformal, however.

2.2 Empirical Meaning

The primary and formal route to the empirical meaning of concepts is through correspondence rules. As shown in Figure 11–2, a correspondence rule (cr) is a relational concept linking a nonobservational focal concept, F, to empirical measurements, $f_1, f_2, ..., f_n$.

With the exception of operationalism, perhaps the most common way that empirical meaning is achieved is shown in Figure 11–2 where the focal concept is specified as a unidimensional theoretical variable and each of n measurements represents either (1) alternative or redundant indicators of the concept or (2) conceptually independent subdimensions of the concept. In the first case, the n measures will covary as a consequence of their common content. We might think of the measures as correlates of the concept or as being caused or implied by the concept. In the second case, each measurement is an empirical manifestation of only an explicitly defined portion of the object or event implied by the focal concept. The n measures need not necessarily covary at a high or uniform level.

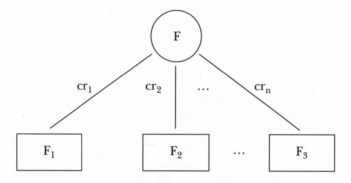

Figure 11–2. A Schematic for Ascertaining the Empirical Meaning of a Single Unidimensional Concept, F

The abstract-empirical relationships, as depicted in Figure 11–2, while more common in psychology than in economics, are a manifestation of the early logical positivist's assertion that data are neutral with respect to theory. In order to arrive at a more realistic representation, we can combine Figure 11–1 (depicting a process by which abstract meaning is formulated) and Figure 11–2 (depicting relationships between the abstract and the empirical) into a system that encompasses both abstract and empirical meaning. Figure 11–3 shows the result in this case. Here again we have the focal concept, F, determined by its antecedent, A, and determining its consequences, C. We also have linkages for each abstract concept to corresponding observations (i.e., a's, f's, c's). The empirical linkage need not be as simple and direct as suggested in Figure 11–3, but let us maintain this simplicity for now and focus on two important questions:

1. What is the directionality of the abstract-empirical linkage? That is, what comes first, theory or observation?

2. How can theoretical and empirical knowledge be balanced in the analysis? What type of knowledge should be given more weight and how can the weighting be implemented in analysis?

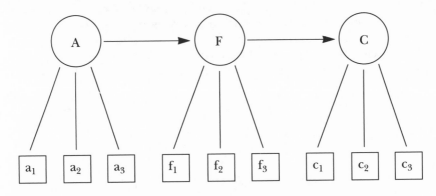

Figure 11–3. A Schematic for Both Abstract and Empirical Meaning

3. THE DIRECTIONALITY OF THE RELATIONSHIP BETWEEN THEORY AND DATA

While the discussion of observables-unobservables and the difficulty in making a general distinction between the two has a long history in the philosophy of science, it pales compared to the longevity of the debate regarding directionality: do our observations lead us to theory or do our theories lead to certain observations? In 1620, Francis Bacon wrote:

"There are and can only be two ways of searching into and discovering truth. The one flies from senses and particulars to the most general axiom, and from these principles, the truth of which it takes for settled and immovable, proceeds to judgment and to discovery of middle axioms. And this way is now in fashion. The other derives from the senses and particulars, rising by gradual and unbroken ascent, so that it arrives at the most general axiom last of all."

The first approach is deductive with its starting point in the abstract with propositions, that if true, imply specific observable events. The second approach is inductive and begins with observation and observational patterns that are formalized into theory. Our schematic for abstract and empirical meaning (Figure 11–3) can be augmented to include both inductive and deductive modes. Figure 11–4 illustrates a relationship between observables and unobservables as implied by a deductive approach.

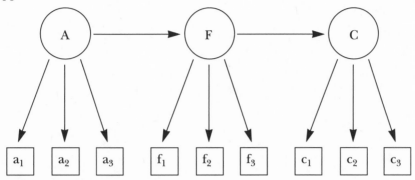

Figure 11–4. Deductive Modeling

In this model, the theoretical system represented by A, F, C and their relationships imply the observations a_1, b_1, c_1, $i = 1 \ldots 3$. In other words, the observations are reflective of the theoretical model.

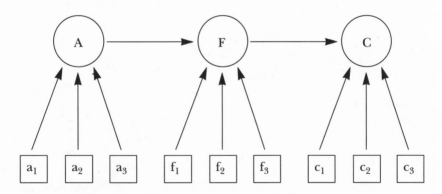

Figure 11–5. Inductive Modeling

In Figure 11–5, the observations a_1, b_1, c_1, $i = 1 \ldots 3$ "make-up" the theoretical variables A, F, C. Thus, the observations are formative (of the theoretical model).

Simply speaking, in the deductive case we take the observations as dependent upon the abstract theoretical model, whereas in induction the theoretical variables are taken as dependent upon the observed variables. As might have been surmised from our earlier discussion of the lack of a clear distinction between what is observable and what is not, it is equally problematic to make a distinction with respect to directionality. Certainly, knowledge is produced by a continuing dialogue between theory and data. The context of a specific situation must determine what should be regarded as unobserved or observed and what the linkage should look like. Similarly, the context determines the bearing of *a priori* theoretical knowledge in the analysis. And this is the question of how theoretical knowledge and empirical data should be balanced. Let us now turn to the implementation of these notions.

3.1. Implementation: Covariance Structure

The objective of covariance structure models is to construct a network of abstract theoretical variables that account for the *correlations* between observed variables. Thus, in this respect, it conforms to deductive reasoning as illustrated in Figure 11–4. For the sake of illustration, consider a very simple model.

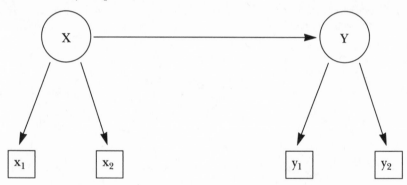

Figure 11–6. A Simple Model

In terms of product moment correlations, the above covariance structure model can be written:

$$\text{Cor}_{x^1 x^2} = (\text{Cor}_{Xx^2})\ (\text{Cor}_{Xx^1}) \tag{11-1}$$

$$\text{Cor}_{y^1 y^2} = (\text{Cor}_{Yy^2})\ (\text{Cor}_{Yy^1}) \tag{11-2}$$

$$\text{Cor}_{x^1 y^1} = (\text{Cor}_{Xx^1})\ (\text{Cor}_{XY})\ (\text{Cor}_{Yy^1}) \tag{11-3}$$

$$\text{Cor}_{x^1 y^2} = (\text{Cor}_{Xx^1})\ (\text{Cor}_{XY})\ (\text{Cor}_{Yy^2}) \tag{11-4}$$

$$\text{Cor}_{x^2 y^1} = (\text{Cor}_{Xx^2})\ (\text{Cor}_{XY})\ (\text{Cor}_{Yy^1}) \tag{11-5}$$

$$\text{Cor}_{x^2 y^2} = (\text{Cor}_{Xx^2}) \quad (\text{Cor}_{XY}) \quad (\text{Cor}_{Yy^2}) \qquad (11\text{-}6)$$

From estimating the correlations between the observed variables, we use equations 1–6 to solve for correlations involving the unobserved theoretical variables. For example, some simple algebraic manipulation gives:

$$\text{Cor}_{XY} = \pm \, [(\text{Cor}_{x^1 y^1}) \quad (\text{Cor}_{x^2 y^2})/(\text{Cor}_{x^1 x^2}) \quad (\text{Cor}_{x^1 y^2})]^{1/2} \quad (11\text{-}7)$$

and

$$\text{Cor}_{XY} = \pm \, [(\text{Cor}_{x^1 y^2}) \quad (\text{Cor}_{x^2 y^1})/(\text{Cor}_{x^1 x^2}) \quad (\text{Cor}_{x^1 y^2})]^{1/2} \quad (11\text{-}8)$$

In statistical estimation (using, say, Jöreskog's maximum likelihood program) a weighted average of the two algebraic solutions of Cor_{XY} is produced.

Consistent with the specification of reflective indicators, the abstract model specification plays a large role in determining the results; almost to the point that it "overrides" the data. For example, with noisy and unreliable data, we would expect low correlations between the indicators x_1 - x_2 and y_1 - y_2. Since the product of these correlations appears in the denominator, the lower the correlations between observed measures, the higher the resulting correlation between the abstract variables (relative to the x-y correlations). Thus, it is here that the researcher must make a decision about the relative weight that should be given to data vs. theory. If the indicator correlations are low, the only justification for this type of model is that much of the observed data can be "explained away" as random noise and that the theory is plausible enough to give it a dominating role in the analysis. As the indicator correlations increase, the observed data have greater impact. In the limit, with correlations at one, the theoretical variables become synonymous with the observed variables and we have a form of operationalism.

3.1.1. AN EXAMPLE.

Consider the following correlation matrix:

x_1	1			
x_2	.109	1		
y_1	.126	.114	1	
y_2	.190	.171	.260	1

All correlations in this matrix are fairly low. The correlations between x- and y-variables range from .114 to .190. If we construct theoretical variables as in Figure 11–6 using equations (11–7) and (11–8), what is the correlation between X and Y? Using the correlations in the matrix above, we find that equations (11–7) and (11–8) both give an estimate of .873. Clearly, this correlation is very different from the correlations between the observed x- and y-variables. Is this reasonable? That depends on how much the analyst is willing to discredit the observations (in terms of random noise) and stand by the theory.

Fortunately, alternatives to covariance structure analysis are available when the analyst is unwilling to depart too far from the data and wants to obtain a different balance between theory and observation. One such alternative is Partial Least Squares (PLS) developed by Herman Wold.

3.2. Implementation: Variance Structure

The objective of variance structure models, such as PLS, is to construct a network of abstract theoretical variables that account for the *variances* of theoretical and/or empirical variables. Note the critical difference between the covariance structure and the variance structure implementation. Covariance structure models always attempt to recover the full correlation matrix of observed variables; in variance structure models, the analyst specifies what variable variances he wants to account for. For example, in the model of Figure 11–4, it is implied that the model is designed to account for the variation of F, C, a_i, f_i, c_i, $i = 1 \ldots 3$. The model of Figure 11–5 is designed to account for the variation in F and C only.

In order to limit the distance from the data in analysis, the theoretical variables are required to be composed of nothing but a combination of the empirical variables. This assures that the analysis cannot go "beyond the data" as was the case in the covariance structure implementation. On the other hand, it is a restriction on theory in the sense that more weight is given to the data.

Several weighting schemes have been developed for the minimization of residual variances within the PLS algorithm (Lohmöller, 1983). Wold's (1966) original algorithm treats each residual separately by determining a set of local minimization criteria. For example, the minimization criteria of the model in Figure 11–6 apply to the residuals associated with Y, x_1, x_2, y_1 and y_2. Without going into the details of the algorithm used to accomplish a joint minimization of the local residuals, suffice it to say that a part of the minimization criteria is satisfied while some other part is considered to be known and, therefore, fixed. In the iterative estimation procedure, the local criteria treated as fixed in one cycle are relaxed in the next cycle, and vice versa, until convergence.

3.2.1. EXAMPLE 1

Let us again use the same data as before (the 4 x 4 correlation matrix) and the model in Figure 11–6. Recall that the observed x-y correlations were low (range .144–.190) but that the estimate of the theoretical correlations between X and Y were quite high (.873). What is the result from the PLS estimation? As expected, the coefficient turns out to be significantly lower at .292. While this is still higher than what the correlations between observed variables indicate, the data now play a larger role in determining the results.

Since variance structure models limit their focus to variances, the covariance of observed variables is not of primary interest. For the example here, where the covariance structure model recovers the correlation of observed variables perfectly, the PLS model does not.

The two models illustrated, covariance structure and variance structure with reflective indicators, represent very different types of combining the abstract with the empirical. Theory is given a much stronger voice in the covariance structure model. There are, however, other possible combinations of theory and data within similar types of models. If we change the specification from reflective to formative indicators, we obtain yet another data/theory mix.

Because the covariance structure model does not readily accept formative indicators, we limit our discussion to the PLS approach.

3.2.2. EXAMPLE 2

The illustration of the difference between formative (mode B in Wold's terminology) and reflective (mode A in Wold's terminology) indicators is taken from a theory developed by Albert O. Hirschman (1970)[2] The theory deals with consumer response to decline in quality. Basically, the dissatisfied consumer faces a choice between two options: exit or voice. The exiting consumer makes use of the market by switching brands, terminating usage, or by shifting patronage—all economic actions. Voice, on the other hand, is a political action: a verbal protest to the seller. The theory suggests that when the exit option is unavailable (as it might be in a monopoly), or when consumers are reluctant to change (as might be the case when cross-elasticities are low), voice will increase.

By this reasoning, exit should dominate in highly competitive markets, whereas the more a market resembles the monopoly situation, the more voice would be expected.

A much-discussed measure of monopoly power is industry concentration ratios. These ratios measure the market shares held by the largest four firms, eight firms, twenty firms, and fifty firms. If the ratios are high, the interpretation has been that this is an indication of monopoly power. More recently, however, it is generally recognized that concentration ratios are very fallible measures of monopoly power. Spence (1981), for example, shows that three or four firms may be sufficient for acceptable consumer welfare (if there is price competition). He warns against using measures of market share, such as concentration ratios, in public policy in order to enforce competition. A problem for public policy, however, is that there are not many comprehensive measures of competition or monopoly power within easy access. And, even though concentration ratios are fallible indicators of monopoly power, they probably contain *some* information about such power. The task is then to separate valid information (variance) from that which is not relevant.

Let us now consider how this could be done. If we create an unobserved variable from the four concentration ratios, should we use reflective or formative indicators? The answer to this question depends primarily on how one conceptualizes the theoretical variable and what the objective of the model is supposed to be. Let us present the results first and then return to these issues.

The theory predicts a negative relationship between monopoly power and exit and a positive relationship between monopoly power and voice. If we think of concentration ratios as *reflecting* the theoretical variable, monopoly power, two measures of consumer voice (aided and unaided respondent recall) as reflective of a theoretical consumer voice variable, and finally consider consumer exit to be synonymous with its measure, the following results are obtained:

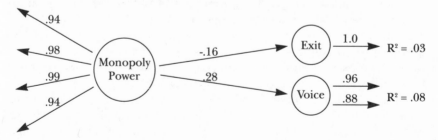

Figure 11–7. Exit-Voice with Reflective Indicators

Remodeling to formative indicators, we obtain these results:

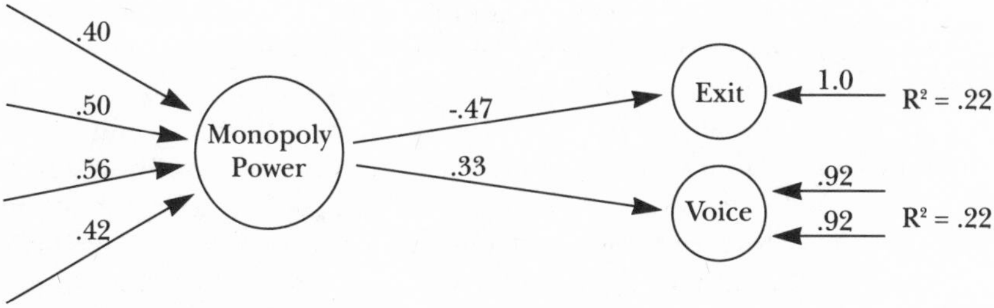

Figure 11–8. Exit-Voice with Formative Indicators

In both cases, the direction of the relationships is as predicted by Hirschman's theory, but the magnitude of some of the relationships vary markedly between the two models. First, consider the theoretical variable, monopoly power. If we consider monopoly power to be an underlying construct that is reflected in measures of industry concentration, we note that there is a close correspondence between the construct and its measures as indicated by loadings (here correlations of .94 to .99). Is this evidence in support of using concentration ratios as measures of monopoly power? In principle, the answer is yes, but only in the context of the particular exit-voice model. Thus, before one can draw any meaningful conclusions about the role of concentration ratios in the study of monopoly power, one has to examine the context in which the conclusions are supposed to hold. In this case, it is apparent that there is only very weak support for the theoretical model. The explanatory power as measured by R^2 is very low. Consequently, any practical use of this model to predict exit or voice from monopoly power (as measured here) is extremely limited.

The most striking difference between the results in Figure 11–7 (reflective indicators) and Figure 11–8 (formative indicators) is in the correspondence between concentration ratios and monopoly power and in the relationship between monopoly power and exit. On the average, only 22 percent of the variance in the concentration ratios [$(.40^2 + .50^2 + .58^2 + .42^2)/4 = .22$] is included in the monopoly power construct when indicators are formative. As a result, the theoretical variable is now very different and explanatory power for exit has increased over seven times ($R^2 = .22$).

Comparing the two models, the first shows strong "support" for concentration ratios as indicators of monopoly power but only in the context of very weak theoretical model results. Hence, given our earlier discussion about the interdependence between theory and data, one would be hard pressed to find any real support here for concentration ratios as measures of monopoly power. Only if we ignore the theoretical context, would it be possible to make a claim of support. Indeed, in our second model almost 78 percent of the variance in the concentration ratios is discarded (not extracted in forming the monopoly power construct). Given the (at least moderate) support for the substantive theory in this model, the implications about the quality of concentration ratios as indicators of monopoly power would be (1) that there is no close correspondence between indicators and construct but (2) there is a minor portion of information that is valid. Again, however, there is no justification for generalizing beyond the theoretical context in which the modeling was done.

Instead, we have now illustrated, via simple examples, the specification of meaning: that it has both a theoretical and an empirical aspect. This is nothing new to the "abstract methodologist" or to the philosopher of science, but this is certainly not the case for most practicing researchers, particularly in economics.

As Kaplan (1946) wrote on the definition and specification of meaning:

> The situation is like that of the delicately balanced constructions by Calder, in which the artist is free to add or remove weights whenever he pleases, but must make compensating changes to maintain the balance, and thus the specification at any stage is a provisional one, both as to the indicators included, and the weights associated with them. (Kaplan, 1946, p. 286).

Kaplan further notes:

> As the context of application grows, the specified meaning grows—and changes—with it. The stipulation of new indicators affects the weights of the old ones, while they in turn limit the range of choice in the stipulation. The adequacy of a particular indicator is not judged by its accordance with a pre-determined concept: the new and old indicators are appraised conjointly. (Kaplan, 1946, p. 287).

Had the quote above been of more recent vintage and read by someone interested in the statistical modeling of unobservables, Kaplan's statements might have been interpreted as directly concerned with some method of structural equations with unobservables. And, despite the fact that such methods were not developed until about 30 years after the publication of Kaplan's article, such an interpretation appears to be far from distorted. Whenever we add or delete indicators or change their status between formative and reflective, we also change their weights and the meaning of the unobservables.

3.3. Implications

The application of covariance or variance structure analysis implies fundamental changes in current research methodology, particularly in economics. What has been shown in the philosophy of science (e.g., Swinburne, 1971)—that empirical confirmation or verification is full of paradoxes and cannot serve as a meaningful criterion of science—becomes apparent in using these methods. Perhaps more critical, the popular alternative to verification—Popper's (1962) program of falsification—is equally elusive. The reason, of course, is found in the impossibility of obtaining "theory-free" data. In order to be able to falsify a theory empirically, it must be assumed that the interpretation of data is independent of the theory being tested and other theories as well. This assumption has more or less been declared obsolete in the philosophy of science, but is at least implicitly maintained in the traditional methodology of economics and other social sciences.

As was illustrated in the examples of this paper, the interaction between theory and data can have a substantial impact upon results. Research conclusions are highly dependent on how we specify the theoretical model as well as the relationships between model and data. Accordingly, it makes little sense to follow the common practice of assuring quality of measurement (via various reliability and validity tests) in *isolation* of the theory to which the measures relate and *before* they are used in a substantive context. The measurement model and the theoretical model should be analyzed simultaneously. Only after such an examination would it be possible to draw conclusions about the quality of measurements and theory, although one is always interpreted in the context of the other. If one is changed (e.g., theory), chances are that the way we interpret the other (e.g., data) changes too. For example, if the theory relations are changed in, say, a PLS or covariance structure analysis, the measurement relationships (i.e., the loadings) may change as well. Of course, this does not suggest that one's measurement model *always* changes as a result of a respecification of the theoretical model. It seems entirely possible that certain variables are indifferent to certain differences in theory. The point is that it would be better to test for the extent of data-theory dependence than to assume it away as would be necessary if one *first* subjects measurements to validity testing via, say, confirmatory factor analysis, and *subsequently* employs the measures found "valid" in a substantive context.

4. TOWARDS A UNIFICATION OF THE SCIENCES?

In view of the many substantial advances in natural science, it is perhaps understandable that many social scientists look to the methodology of natural science as a role model. Yet, much of the criticism leveled at logical empiricism charges that it is modeled on an early understanding of certain pieces of 19th century physics and that the natural sciences may not be an appropriate role model for the social sciences. The typical argument is that the subject matter of the natural sciences is so different from the subject matter of the social sciences that the methodology must also be different. Freedman (1987) speculates on what would have happened if Kepler had known multivariate statistics and suggests that the application of statistics would have led him to the best-fitting circular planetary orbits and the elliptical orbits would have been ignored.

While it is true that traditional multivariate statistics was almost never employed in physics and relatively seldom in chemistry, it appears that methods such as covariance and variance structure analysis may be relevant to all sciences. For example, modern physics (e.g., quantum theory) involves statistical relationships, unobservable variables, system behavior, and theory-laden observations. This is, of course, exactly the type of phenomena that these methods are designed to analyze. Thus, it may well be that the new statistical techniques that involve latent variables will not only have a profound impact upon methodology in the social sciences but will also perhaps unify some methodological aspects of the natural and social sciences.

NOTES

[1] This section draws heavily from Bagozzi and Fornell, 1982.

[2] The distinction of reflective vs. formative indicators was introduced by R. Hauser, 1966.

REFERENCES

Achinstein, P. 1968. *Concepts of science.* Baltimore, Md.: Johns Hopkins Press.

Bagozzi, R.P., and C. Fornell. 1982. Theoretical concepts, measurements, and meaning. In *A second generation of multivariate analysis*, Vol. 2, *Measurement and evaluation*, 29–38. New York: Praeger.

Freedman. D. 1985. Statistics in scientific methods. In *Cohort analysis in social research: Beyond identification problems*, eds. W. Mason and S. Fienberg, 345–390. New York: Springer.

Hauser, R. 1966. Family, school and neighborhood factors in educational performances in a metropolitan school system. Ph.D. diss., University of Michigan, Ann Arbor.

Hirschman, A.O. 1970. *Exit, voice, and loyalty-responses to decline in firms, organizations, and states*. Cambridge, Mass.: Harvard University Press.

Jöreskog, K.G. 1973. A general method for estimating a linear structural equation system. In *Structural equation models in the social sciences*, eds. A.S. Goldberger and O.D. Duncan, 85–112. New York: Seminar Press.

Kaplan, A. 1946. Definition and specification of meaning. *The Journal of Philosophy* 53:281–288.

Lohmöller, J.-B. 1989. *Path models with latent variables and partial least squares (PLS) estimation*. Würzburg: Physika Verlag.

Popper, K. 1962. *Conjectures and refutations*. New York: Harper and Row.

Spence, M.A. 1981. The leaning curve and competition. *Bell Journal of Economics* 12:49–70.

Suppe, F. 1974. *The structure of scientific theories*. Urbana, Illinois: University of Illinois Press.

Swinburne, R.G. 1971. The paradoxes of confirmation - A survey. *American Philosophical Quarterly* Vol. 8:318–330.

Wold, H. 1966. Estimation of principal components and related models by iterative least squares. In *Multivariate analysis*, ed. P.R. Krishnaiah, 391–420. New York: Academic Press.

Wold, H. 1975. Path models with latent variables: The NIPALS approach. In *Quantitative sociology: International perspectives on mathematical and statistical model building*, eds. H.M. Blalock et al., 307–357. New York: Academic Press.

Wold, H. 1982. Systems under indirect observations using PLS. In *A second generation of multivariate analysis*, Vol. 1, *Methods*, ed. C. Fornell, 325–347. New York: Praeger.

12

Comment on Fornell's Paper

RAY PAWSON

Let me begin with two central points of agreement with Fornell's paper. In his attempt to find methods which blend theoretical and empirical knowledge he puts his finger on what is undoubtedly the central dilemma in all social science research, namely, our need to come to a better understanding of the consequences of the interdependence of theory and observation. Furthermore, he is absolutely correct in charging that much of what passes for sound practice in social science data analysis is based on epistemological assumptions which obtained in the dark ages of the philosophy of science. In these respects what Fornell has to say needs to be shouted from the academic roof-tops—refinement in measurement and data analysis is redundant, indeed impossible in isolation from theoretical development.

THE DOUBLE-LANGUAGE MODEL

Where I disagree with Fornell is in terms of the manner of the impregnation of theory in data and some of the ramifications of their interdependence. In a nutshell my objection is that Fornell still uses what is referred to in the philosophical literature as a *double-language model* for theory and observation, a formulation which is most evident in his separate treatment of 'abstract' and 'empirical' meaning and the discussion of the 'directionality' of the relationship between theory and data. Now the double-language model represents a huge advance over empiricism in its recognition that careful observation of facts 'out there' is not the be all and end all of science and quite properly insists we acknowledge the role of theoretical discourse with its attendant use of abstractions, metaphors, models, mechanisms, and so forth. However, in the last decade or two, philosophical orthodoxy (if there be such a thing) has turned to the view that no useful distinction can be maintained between observational and theoretical terms and concluded that science does in fact speak with only one language.

The two-language model has been much criticized on the grounds that no satisfactory account of the status of correspondence rules has been formulated, the problem being that as soon as one allows for the interdependence of theory and observation, it seems pointless to refer to them as independent realms and as a consequence all accounts of the translation from theoretical to observational statements end up proclaiming the priority of one or the other. For instance, suppose one begins by trying to identify how the realm of observation is constituted. The obvious difficulty is that sensory experiences depend on the observer having certain general hypotheses about the nature of the thing observed. Recall Popper's famous invitation to his positivistically inclined students to make observations of their lecture room—the diversity of observational reports manifests their dependence on prior expectations of what is relevant. Recall also the plethora of illustrations from the psychology of perception (duck/rabbits, the dot and frame illusion, etc.) which show how even apparently direct sensory perceptions depend on or indeed *are* hypothetical judgements.

Starting from the opposite end and supposing we were attempting to decide between competing theoretical propositions on an issue, the double language model would have us adjudicate on the basis of the observational consequences that flow from the theoretical propositions via correspondence rules. But allowing for the interdependence of theory and observation obviously means that the selection of correspondence rules is itself made according to one's preferred theoretical postulates. Thus evidential assessment of theoretical propositions turns out to be no assessment at all. I cannot rehearse any further objections to the two-language model here (Papineau, 1979, Ch. 1); suffice it to say that the only way out of the circularity displayed in the logic above has been to resort to a position which asserts the ultimate priority of one or other of the two realms. Note in this respect, Fornell's (p. 156) remark that in structural equation models, '...the theoretical variables are required to be composed of nothing but a combination of empirical variables. This assures that the analysis cannot go "beyond the data"...'. This brings us to the central dilemma concerning statistical modeling in social science, that is, to what extent do they allow a genuine role for theory in their portrayal of the world?

POST-EMPIRICIST PHILOSOPHY

However, we are not yet in a position to answer the question until we know of some alternatives to the double-language model. Post-empiricist philosophy has in recent times produced some revised interpretations of the relationship between theory and evidence which can be briefly described under two or three headings as follows. First to go is the distinction between two languages for concepts and observables (Achinstein, 1968, ch. 5, Feyerabend, 1975, ch. 6,7); instead, all terms in science are said to take their meaning *discursively* or *wholistically* according to their place in relationships, definitions and laws, much in the manner that Fornell describes in his section on 'abstract meaning.' However, according to the newer philosophies, evidence, or what Fornell calls 'empirical meaning,' is constructed in exactly the same wholistic fashion, that is to say, evidence is constructed by understanding how a property is locked into a system of relationships rather than direct perception of the property or of its so-called indicators.

All this, of course, would come as no surprise in the natural sciences, where this more creative aspect of measurement is commonplace. To take the elementary example of the galvanometer: clearly in discussing its operation we are not dealing with direct and untainted observation since the very rationale behind the instrument is a theory of, and an ability to marshall, electromagnetic forces. We can report that the galvanometer needle moves but interpreting that movement needs an understanding of motion in electromagnetic fields. What is more, the actual construction of the instrument calls on a host of secondary theories—the galvanometer needle is set on jewelled bearing so as to minimize friction, it is as light as possible to deal with the effects of inertia, the instrument is encased to minimize the influence of extraneous magnetic forces and so forth. In short, the evidence drawn from such sources is empirical in the sense that it involves some manipulation, some intervention in the world but not in the sense that the evidence is directly experienced and thus can be considered to have epistemological priority.

Another recently emphasized feature of the meaning of scientific terms is their derivation from *generative mechanisms* which produce the relatively enduring regularities which structure the world (Harré and Madden, 1975; Bhaskar, 1975; cf. Fornell, p. 8). Hence, unlike much statistical modeling in social science, explanatory requirements are not satisfied simply by unearthing patterns and regularities in the occurrence of events, but by devising an understanding of the underlying mechanism that generates and constitutes the causal regularity. Again the idea is that scientific concepts should not be thought of as separate, singular objects or variables each answerable to its own element of reality. Rather we know the meaning of a concept (or synonymously, the parameters of a measure) by constructing models and analogies of the internal structures of physical (or social) systems, so as to show how a system passes from one state to another and it is this understanding which informs us of the relationship between the component properties of the system and thus provides knowledge of the numerical characteristics of those properties.

The time-honored example of this generative derivation of measurement properties is the establishment of the absolute temperature scale. The kinetic theory of gases depends upon the analogy of a swarm of microscopic particles moving in a confined space and uses the principles of classical mechanics to describe their motion and in so doing derives expressions for the temperature (average kinetic energy of the molecules) and other properties of a gas. The mode of reasoning tells us what temperature is, allows us to construe it as having a zero value and thus assign a metric scale, and finally to predict how it varies with other properties. Again the meaning is not derived from observation (since zero temperature has, of course, no empirical equivalent) and in fact the kinetic model supplies the parameters of temperature in advance of observation, the experimentalist being left to invent those instruments which best exemplify the idea.

One further feature of post-empiricist philosophy is worthy of our attention here. It draws on the idea that the basic units of scientific analysis are not concepts and observables but whole *networks* of theory and evidence (Hesse, 1974). That is to say, explanation deals with wholes or structures and it is these *research programs* in their entirety which are evaluated in the course of scientific debate (Lakatos, 1970). Pursuing the network metaphor further enables us to see the growth of science as the business of ever enlarging the numbers of threads converging on our existing stock of knowledge. The idea is that either experimentally or by deduction new concepts and new observations are grafted back into the network. The result is that some 'knot concepts' or 'systematic measures' come to have a key coordinating role in science; they are easily identified by many theories and many instruments (Kyburg, 1984).

Again one must draw a contrast between such programmatic thinking, and statistical modeling in social science which operates much more at the level of specific regularities and tends to draft in theory to explain such correlations on a rather *ad hoc* basis. The central question perhaps boils down to whether the notions of 'unobservables,' 'multiple indicators' and so forth represent an effort to move towards, or simply to disguise the lack of, these networks of coordinated reasoning which are so vital to measurement in science.

EXPLANATION AND STRUCTURAL EQUATION MODELING

I have argued for a revised understanding of the interdependence of theory and measurement which can be no better summarized than in Kuhn's words as follows:

> The laws of nature are so very seldom discovered simply by inspecting the results of measurements made without advance knowledge of these laws. Because most scientific laws have so few quantitative points of contact with nature, because investigations of those contact points usually demand such laborious instrumentation and approximation, and because nature itself needs to be forced to yield the appropriate results, the route from theory or law to measurement can almost never be travelled backwards. Numbers gathered without some knowledge of the regularity to be expected almost never speak for themselves. Almost certainly they remain just numbers. (Kuhn, 1961, p. 174)

This is the formulation which provides the authentic test of the aspirations of structural equation modeling with multiple indicators. To put the matter most starkly, measurement practice should be seen as a consequence of the formal networks of coordinated reason which constitute normal science explanation. Does such a situation apply in social science?

It is safe to say that social science in general in its empirical work has not operated in the manner described above. Rather we derive measurement parameters in ordinary language usage; that is, we utilize the counts, orderings and categories available in everyday descriptions of the topics in question (Cicourel, 1964). Examples of this will be familiar in every substantive area: sociologists use 'number of years of schooling' to indicate educational attainment, economists use 'market share held by x firms' to indicate monopoly power, psychologists use 'ratio of test items answered correctly' to indicate intelligence, and so forth. To adapt the idea to Fornell's terminology the problem is that we attempt empirical research in social science when abstract specification of meaning is terribly premature. We measure in the absence of the potential richness of meaning that he documents; definitional specification often goes no further than claiming the indicator is an 'aspect of' some broader theoretical construct and specification by antecedents and consequences seldom tells us more than to expect that there will be a (positive or negative) relationship between X and Y. In other words it is because our explanations are not holistic, generative, programmatic, network-like, and so on that allows or rather demands the creation of arbitrary, disconnected, first-order indicators to stand as our measures.

It is precisely this state of affairs which leads to the retention of the double language model in structural equation modeling. To utilize one of Fornell's own examples, one notes that in the absence of detailed knowledge of the mechanism whereby monopolistic power is achieved that we have no choice but to take our chance with an array of competing indicators. Similarly, if our understanding of the consequences of monopoly power allows us to venture no further than to 'predict a negative relationship between monopoly power and exit and a positive relationship between monopoly power and voice,' then, within certain limits of plausibility, anything goes in terms of selecting indicators to confirm such findings. In short, it is theoretical indecision which allows the observational level to live on in the form of common sense descriptions of the objects of investigation.

The first consequence of sticking with the double language model is the ultimate preference, mentioned above, for one or other of the theoretical and empirical domains in the production of results. I have argued elsewhere that, in general, in structural equation models with multiple indicators, the so-called theoretical constructs merely summarize observations made and the only important difference between the various estimation procedures is the method chosen to combine and summarize the information (Pawson, 1980). Thus, arithmetically speaking, no such models can go 'beyond the data'; the basic content of empirical generalizations is, after all, empirical information.

The important question that Fornell raises is the possibility that different estimation techniques (covariance analysis and partial least squares) can change the balance of observational and theoretical input. We need to be enormously careful in interpreting such a claim. What changes between the techniques as described by Fornell is not a reformulation of measurement practice; we fire off the same measurements and theory enters at a later stage to adjudge the veracity of the findings. So instead of theory informing us how to measure as in the network model, we measure anyway and the job of theory is to gauge how impressed we are by the results.

Hence the preference for formative or reflective indicators is not a choice which allows theory into the fabric of measurement decisions; it is a device which operates at the level of 'explanatory power' of a theory. And, typically, for the double language model, the concept of explanatory power of a theory turns out to favor a purely empirical connotation in terms of 'variance explained.' Thus the scope for theorizing in these models boils down to a choice between a decision to affirm an empirical generalization on the basis of what one acknowledges are low-quality indicators, or to maintain more qualified support for a generalization on the basis of what one assumes are high quality measures. Thus, one is asking theory to act as an extremely blunt instrument, which involves less the matter of explaining how a relationship comes about and more the matter of expressing faith in its significance. I fail to see that there can be any formulation of the general conditions for operating the proposed trade-off between indicator validity and explanatory power; the decision between them must rest, as Fornell admits, with knowledge of the contexts which pertain to each regularity studied. However, to repeat the whole point of my note, if one has detailed knowledge of the processes underlying a relationship, then this involves knowledge of the constituative properties in the first place. Knowledge of the mechanism brings knowledge of the measure. If, by contrast, one's understanding of a particular context is so flimsy that one is left with declarations of faith in a generalization or faith in a measure, then one has no business to be performing exact estimates of the said relationship in the first place.

CONCLUSION

Let me try to summarize my points of agreement and disagreement with Fornell. Starting from exactly the same premise that percepts without concepts are blind, and proceeding with exactly the same instinct that the processes of concept formation, theory construction, measurement and hypothesis testing are inseparable, we appear to disagree only on the potentialities of the various statistical estimation techniques. In so far as Fornell is saying that the discrepancies in the estimates under P.L.S and covariance models, reflective and formative indicators, and so forth demonstrate the plasticity of the relationship between theory and data, I can only shout "hear-hear"! If, however, he is claiming a solution and trying to champion one particular statistical estimation technique as somehow providing the authentic balance between the conceptual and the empirical, we totally disagree. Science, I would venture, progresses by delving into the mechanisms that constitute laws and regularities and not by opting out of the inner workings of relationships by settling for the safety of statistical estimates of them.

REFERENCES

Achinstein, P. 1968. *Concepts of science.* Baltimore: John Hopkins Press.

Bhaskar, R. 1975. *A realist theory of science.* Leeds: Leeds Books.

Cicourel, A. 1964. *Method and measurement in sociology.* New York: Free Press.

Feyerabend, P. 1975. *Against method.* London : New Left Books.

Harré, P., and E. Madden. 1975. *Causal powers.* Oxford: Blackwell.

Hesse, M. 1974. *The structure of scientific inference.* London: Macmillan.

Kuhn, T. 1961. The function of measurement in modern physical science. In *Quantification,* ed. H. Woolf, 31–65. Indianapolis: Bobbs-Merrill.

Kyburg, H. 1984. *Theory and measurement.* Cambridge: University Press.

Lakatos, I. 1970. Falsificationism and the methodology of scientific research programmes. In *Criticism and the growth of knowledge,* eds. I. Lakas and A. Musgrave, 91–196. Cambridge: University Press.

Papineau, D. 1979. *Theory and meaning.* Oxford: Clarendon Press.

Pawson, R. 1980. Empiricist measurement strategies. *Quality and Quantity* 14:651–678.

13

Pitfalls in Scientific Model Building: Unemployment, the Unemployed, and the Nazi Vote 1930-1933

JÜRGEN W. FALTER

1. INTRODUCTORY REMARKS

According to a 20-year-old statement by H. Wold (1964), each science may be regarded as a collection of models.[1,2] Scientific models are defined by the same author as the "systematic coordination of theoretical and empirical elements of knowledge into a joint construct"(Wold 1964: 4). The theoretical part of a model consists of hypothetical propositions and its empirical part of observational statements which are interpreted by means of the model. Furthermore, in his definition, Wold accepts not only highly formalized but also verbally stated models whose function can be either predictive or retrodictive, i.e., oriented towards the future or the past.

In essence, scientific model-building proceeds by a series of closely interrelated decisions which are part of a greater frame of reference where the problems to be solved by the model, as well as certain prescientific notions about the area under scrutiny and about criteria of relevance, are specified. Those decisions are directed towards the data used, the levels of measurement, the operationalization of theoretical concepts, statistical methods of analysis and their model implications, etc.

At each decision point pitfalls of scientific modeling may occur

(and, more often than not, remain undetected), such as overgeneraliza-
tion of findings, model misspecification, aggregation bias or other falla-
cies of the wrong level, etc. Cumulative research is only conceivable if
such pitfalls are detected and, in a continual process of methodological
criticism and replicatory efforts, eventually ruled out.

In the following I will attempt to unravel the various causes of some
strongly contradictory findings on the effects exerted by mass unemployment on the rise of National Socialism during the last years of the Weimar
Republic. The data set used as well as the analytic and computational
work done for the purpose of this paper are the result of a collaborative
effort by the author and his research associates which has been financed
by the Volkswagen Foundation during the last three years.

2. THE PROBLEM AND ITS IMPLICATIONS

There is widespread agreement among historians that mass unemployment was one of the major causes of the breakdown of the Weimar
Republic and the rise of National Socialism. And indeed, there is a striking parallel between the rise and fall of the unemployment rate and the
up and down of the National Socialist vote; see Figure 13–1.

It is not clear, however, whether the unemployed or the employed or
both became radicalized in the series of four Reichstag and two
Presidential elections between 1930 and 1933. The theories advanced
which postulate a causal relationship between the increase and duration
of mass unemployment on the one hand and the radicalization of the
German electorate on the other often lack adequate specification in this
respect, a fact which makes them all but irrefutable as we will see.

The first major empirical analysis using more or less adequate data
and statistical techniques was published in 1981 by two well-known Swiss
econometricians, B.S. Frey and H. Weck. As a result of their analysis they
propose a positive relationship between unemployment and the Nazi vote
while deliberately leaving open the question who was responsible for this
correlation, the employed or the unemployed.

Without the spectacular rise of mass unemployment between 1930
and 1932, the National Socialist share of the vote in the Reichstag election of July 1932, according to Frey and Weck (1981: 23), would have
amounted to only 22 instead of 37 percent; see Table 13–5 (a).

This finding is clearly at variance with the results of a series of similar studies conducted by myself and my collaborators. Using substantially
the same, i.e., similarly specified multiple regression equations as Frey

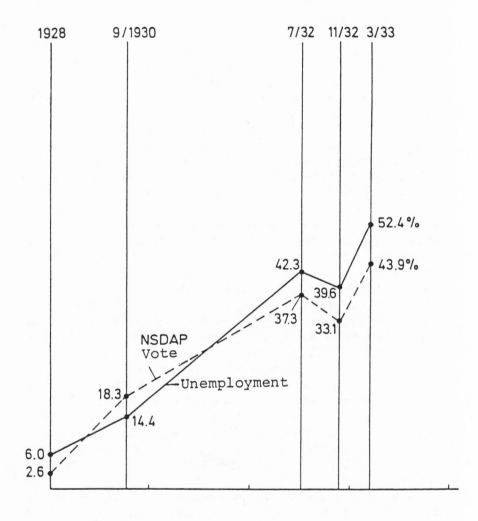

Figure 13–1. Unemployment and the NSDAP Vote, 1928–1933 (Unemployment Quota/Percentage of Valid Vote). Source: B.S. Frey and H. Weck (1981). NSDAP = Nationalsozialistische Deutsche Arbeiterpartei. KPD = Kommunistische Partei Deutschlands.

and Weck we discovered a consistently negative relationship between unemployment and the vote for Hitler. This holds true not only for the statistical association between percentage levels at each election but also for the increase of the National Socialist vote in dependence of the (level or change) unemployment rate; see Tables 13-1–13-3.

Furthermore, to rule out possible model effects, we analyzed our data by means of two different, quite elaborate PLS models with some 70 manifest and up to 23 latent variables. The findings discerned by these LVPLS models confirm and further differentiate our earlier results: unemployment displayed a negative influence on the Nazi vote (cf. Figure 13–3).

In our first PLS model developed in 1982 we concentrated on the two elections of July, 1932 and March, 1933 (see Figure 13–2). In both elections the NSDAP was able to increase considerably its share of the vote in comparison to the immediately preceding election. For the sake of clarity we left out the November 1932 election, where the NSDAP lost slightly. Instead, we introduced into our model the September 1930 election, which we did not treat as another dependent variable; in our PLS model it serves as an explanatory factor, a so-called lagged endogenous variable. The "real" background factors of the model, i.e., unemployment, occupation, urbanization and religious denomination, to name but a few, thus only explain the amount of change in the dependent variable, i.e., the NSDAP share of the vote between 1930 and 1932 and between 1932 and 1933. In other words, they only explain what has not already been accounted for by the results of the immediately preceding election (for further details see Falter et al. 1983).

Since we are here only interested in the effects of unemployment we will concentrate on this factor and leave out of consideration all other variables, however interesting they may be. Our analysis discerned a clear negative direct effect of the unemployment variable on the NSDAP vote. We were thus able to replicate by a far more complex statistical (and theoretical) model our bi- and multivariate analyses of the relationship between unemployment and the Nazi vote reported elsewhere (Falter et al. 1983; Falter 1985).

Briefly stated, in 1932 and 1933 both the NSDAP share of the vote and its increase tended to be lower where unemployment was high and vice versa (see Figure 13–2 and Table 13–4).

Table 13–1

The Correlation of Various Unemployment Variables with the 1930–1933 NSDAP and KPD Share of the Vote (Pearson's r)

	NSDAP				KPD			
	1930	1932J	1932N	1933	1930	1932J	1932N	1933
Unemployment Rate 1933	(-04)	-24	-23	-44	(75)	77	78	78
Unemployment Quota 1933	(-06)	-25	-24	-45	(76)	78	79	79
Unemployment								
December '31	(09)	-09	-09	-31	(63)	65	65	67
July 1932	(03)	-14	-14	-36	(69)	71	71	73
October 1932	(01)	-17	-17	-39	(69)	71	72	74
Welfare Unemployed 1930	06	-14	-14	-32	55	54	56	59
Welfare Unemployed 1932	(-02)	-20	-19	-41	(70)	72	72	73
Unemployed blue-collar	(-06)	-22	-21	-43	(77)	79	80	81
Unemployed white-collar	(02)	-20	-20	-36	(55)	53	57	58

Basis: 865 county units adjusted for boundary changes. Cases weighted with their population figures. Pearson's r x 100.

Variable definitions (for Tables 13-1–13-4 and Figure 13-4)

Unemployment rate 1933	: Unemployed x 100/Employed and Unemployed blue-collar and white-collar workers (Census 1933)
Unemployment quota	: Unemployed x 100/Employed blue-collar and white-collar workers (Census 1933)
Unemployed December 1931/July 1932/Oct. 32	: Unemployment rate (same definition as above)
Welfare Unemployed	: Unemployed living on welfare x 100/Total electorate
Unemployed blue-collar	: Unemployed blue-collar workers x 100/all blue-collar workers (Census 1933)
Unemployed white-collar	: Unemployed white-collar workers x 100/all white-collar workers (Census 1933)
NSDAP 1930–1933	: NSDAP vote x 100/total electorate
KPD 1930–1933	: KPD vote x 100/total electorate

Table 13–2

Regression Analysis of NSDAP and KPD vote on unemployment and other variables. Counties weighted by number of inhabitants. In brackets: Standardized regression coefficients x 100.

	1932A		1932B		1933	
	NSDAP	**KPD**	**NSDAP**	**KPD**	**NSDAP**	**KPD**
Constant	50.0	-6.65	43.4	-4.85	59.5	-5.17
% Catholic	-0.25	0.03	-0.22	0.08	-0.19	0.17
	(-78)	(01)	(-73)	(-04)	(-65)	(-09)
% Blue Collar	-0.10	0.24	-0.11	0.23	-0.12	0.19
	(-09)	(34)	(-11)	(32)	(-12)	(28)
% Urban	-0.04	-0.01	-0.05	-0.01	-0.05	-0.004
	(-14)	(-05)	(-20)	(-04)	(-19)	(-02)
% Unemployed	-0.31	0.61	-0.18	0.63	-0.45	0.60
	(-21)	(65)	(-13)	(66)	(-34)	(68)
Explained Variance	63.6%	68.8%	56.5%	70.4%	60.1%	70.9%
R^2-increase through Unemployed	1.4%	13.6%	0.6%	13.9%	3.6%	14.4%

Table 13–3

Unemployment and the percentage change of the NSDAP and KPD vote 1930-1933. Pooled multiple regression analysis: Standardized regression coefficients x 100.

	Unemployed	Catholic	Urbanization	Turnout	R2	Pearson's r with Unemployed
NSDAP	-17	-37	-18	-43	42%	0.12
KPD	60	-10	13	-09	50%	0.70

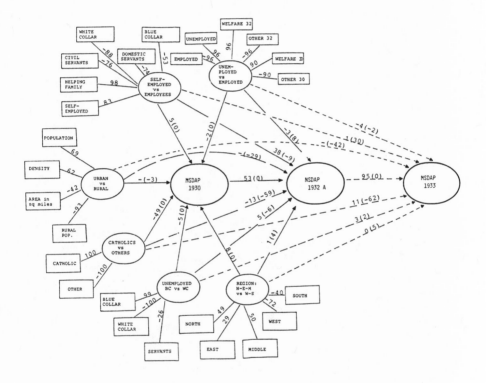

Figure 13–2. An Explanatory Model of the NS-vote 1932/33 Using Latent Variables Path Analysis with PLS Estimation. Numbers in brackets = indirect effects; numbers without brackets = direct effects.

Table 13–4

Factor loadings, factor weights, means and standard deviations of variables used in Latent Variables Path Analysis (LVPLS): Model I

Factor and Variables		Factor Loading	Factor Weight	Mean	SD
Urban vs. Rural					
Population	25	69	18	222.6	266.9
Population	33	69	18	232.9	278.9
Pop. Density	25	61	12	20.1	53.9
Pop. Density	33	62	12	19.2	49.8
Area in km²	25	-42	-9	56801.1	7658.7
Area in km²	33	-42	-9	56824.2	7663.9
% Urban	25	93	29	54.1	38.6
% Rural	25	-93	-29	45.9	38.6
Region					
North		49	43	11.6	32.1
East		29	20	26.4	44.1
Middle		50	41	16.2	36.9
West		-72	-56	23.8	42.6
South		-40	-33	21.9	41.4
Religion					
% Catholic	25	100	25	32.5	33.8
% Other	25	-100	-25	67.5	33.8
% Catholic	33	100	25	32.5	33.8
% Other	33	-100	-25	67.5	33.8
Occupation					
Self-Employed		83	21	19.5	4.1
Helping Family		98	28	18.2	13.6
Civil Servants		-76	-17	6.0	3.8
White Collar		-88	-24	12.9	8.2
Blue Collar		-53	-17	39.1	9.6
Domestic		-74	-16	4.2	2.1
Unemployed vs. Employed					
Employed/Retired		-96	-19	84.6	7.3
Unemployed	33	96	19	15.4	7.3
Welfare	30	90	15	1.2	1.1
Other	30	-90	-19	98.8	1.1
Welfare	32	96	19	5.8	4.2
Other	32	-96	-19	94.2	4.2
Unemployed BC vs. WC					
White Collar		-100	-52	83.6	7.4
Blue Collar		99	49	13.4	7.1
Domestic		-26	1	3.0	1.3
NS	30	100	100	14.8	5.9
NS	32A	100	100	30.9	11.0
NS	33	100	100	38.8	9.9

In still another, differently specified PLS model we were able to further corroborate the validity of our earlier findings. In this model which—in contradistinction to the PLS model reported above—contains not only structural but also performance-oriented economic indicators we chose to operationalize the dependent variables as follows: one LV which we may call the "constancy variable" indicates the average NSDAP share of the vote during the four Reichstag elections from 1930 to 1933; it indicates whether a county constantly displayed an above or a below average NSDAP vote. The other dependent LV which we may call the "increase variable" indicates the contrast between the 1930 and 1933 election with regard to an above or below average increase of the Nazi vote; counties which showed a smaller than average increase of the NSDAP vote between 1930 and 1933 have a negative value on this LV, and counties with an above average increase take positive values (for further details see Lohmöller *et al.* 1984).

Again, we are only interested in the effects exerted by unemployment on the NSDAP vote, and again we are able to show that in regions with a greater than average unemployment rate the NSDAP share constantly tends to be relatively low and that the increase of the Nazi electorate in those districts clearly lagged behind the national average. We thus face the problem of reconciling the Frey and Weck findings of a positive relationship between unemployment and the NSDAP vote with our own results, which constantly display a negative relationship between the two variables.

3. EXPLAINING THE REPLICATIVE DISCREPANCIES BY DIFFERENCES IN MODEL BUILDING AND MODEL SPECIFICATION

The contradictory results may be attributed to three separate causes: (a) differences in regional aggregation (the analysis by Frey and Weck is based on the 13 Labor Exchange Districts of the Reich; our own analyses, in contrast, are working with the 1100 to 1200 counties and townships of the Weimar Republic); (b) differences in the operationalization of the unemployment variable (the indicators used by Frey and Weck are calculated as quotas, i.e., unemployed over gainfully employed; if there are more unemployed than employed in a district the quota takes a value greater than one. Our analyses are based on the percentage of unemployed which, in turn, is calculated as the share of the unemployed on the basis of all employed and unemployed); (c) temporal aggregation; in order to increase the available number of observations, Frey and Weck pooled their 4 longitudinal and 13 cross-sectional observation points into one combined-data set. Our own analyses rely on separate cross-sectional and longitudinal estimations.

Table 13–5

Regression analysis of cross-sectional and longitudinal data, using as dependent variable % votes for National Socialists. All entries are multiplied by 100. For explanations, see Table 13–1.

| Data set | Predictor | | | | | | R² |
	Cath	Agri	Unempl	Work	Turnout	Constant	
(a)Frey and Weck data: Pooled cross-sectional and longitudinal data							
N=4x13, reported F/W	-16	58	59	-3	35	-29	89
N=4x13, replicated	-16	58	60	-3	30	-25	89
N=4x13, weight=#vot30	-15	55	57	-9	36	-26	91
(b)Pure cross-sectional data; weight = voters '30							
N=13, 1930	-7	15	14	-7	22	-6	67
N=13, 1932 July	-24	67	52	0	3	-1	96
N=13, 1932 Nov	-21	73	71	2	-8	-45	91
N=13, 1933	-14	48	28	2	-22	38	93
(c)Aggregated from county level: Pooled cross-section and longitudinal							
N=4x13, unweighted	-12	58	10	-42	164	-102	49
N=4x13, weight=#vot30	-12	46	5	-44	161	-94	49
(d)Aggregated from county level: Pure cross-sectional data							
N=13, 1930	-8	49	47	-39	41	-22	80
N=13, 1932 July	-22	64	31	-30	47	-8	88
N=13, 1932 Nov	-17	56	29	-30	35	-3	82
N=13, 1933	-16	70	31	-17	-5	34	83
(e)County level data: Pooled cross-sectional and longitudinal data							
N=4x865, unweighted	-23	6	-30	-28	88	-17	43
N=4x865, weighted	-18	14	-16	-26	88	-25	39
(f)County level data: Pure cross-sectional data, weight=#voters							
N=865, 1930	-12	3	-1	-9	-12	34	28
N=865, 1932 July	-28	15	-15	-21	29	29	65
N=865, 1932 Nov	-23	15	-15	-17	24	27	59
N=865, 1933	-21	23	-13	-16	-5	59	59

Table 13–6

The variables and data for Tables 13–5 and 13–7 and Figure 13–3. Frey/Weck: N=13 State Labor Exchange districts

voters	Eligible voters 1930
Cath	Catholics / religiously affiliated in total
Agri	in agriculture employed / Labor force
Unempl	Unemployed reported at Labor Exchange / employed members of health insurances (without disabled) : 1930 July, 1932 July, 1932 Oct, 1933 Jan
Work	Blue collar workers / Labor force
Turnout	Turnout / eligible voters : 1930 Sept, 1932 July, 1932 Nov, 1933 March
N	Observational units are N=13 Landesarbeitsamtsbezirke (State Labor exchange districts)
Source:	Statistisches Jahrbuch des Deutschen Reiches 1931 - 1933

County level data: N=865

voters	Eligible voters at each election
Cath	Catholics 1933 / Population 1933
Agri	In agriculture employed + working family members 1933 / Labor force 1933
Unempl	Unemployed as registered at Labor Exchange / Labor force 1933
Work	Blue collar workers 1933 / Labor force 1933
Turnout	Turnout / eligible voters
N	Observational units for elections and census data are "Stadt- und Landkreise" (counties), originally N=1200, aggregated on N=825 longitudinally stable counties. Observational units for seasonal unemployment figures are N=365 Labor Exchange districts, disaggregated into N=865 counties.
Sources:	Statistik des Deutschen Reiches

Distribution and intercorrelation of unemployment figures

Frey and Weck

	Mean	R			
1930 July	14%	100			
1932 July	42%	85	100		
1932 Oct	40%	83	98	100	
1933 Jan	52%	87	89	85	100

County level data

		Mean	R			
1931	Dec	17%	100			
1932	Jul	15%	97	100		
1932	Oct	14%	96	99	100	
1933	Jan	18%	98	98	98	100

In an extended replication of the Frey-Weck analysis we tried to find out step by step which effects account for the contradictory results mentioned above. Before discussing these results it might be advisable to describe the regional units used and to point out some peculiarities of the available data.

As a result of German history, the map of the Reich was characterized by a patchwork of kingdoms, dukedoms, counties, free cities and all sorts of enclaves and exclaves. This pattern, which survived the First World War, was gradually restructured by administrative reforms in the 1920s. At that time some 70,000 communities were grouped into some 1,200 counties which in turn were grouped into 72 major administrative districts (Regierungsbezirke) which in turn belonged to 18 federal states (Länder). To allow for longitudinal comparability in our data set, the counties have been slightly aggregated into 865 county units which remain nearly stable over the period 1925-1933. The election outcomes and the 1925 and 1933 census data are published in Statistik des Deutschen Reiches on the level of counties and larger communities.

The administration of labor and unemployment was performed by 352 Labor Exchange Agencies which were grouped into 13 State Labor Exchange Districts (Landesarbeitsamtsbezirke). Detailed unemployment statistics were collected and published in Germany on the level of the 352 Labor Exchange Agencies only from December 1931, when unemployment was close to its summit and showed little temporal variation. Earlier figures are available on the level of the 13 State Labor Exchanges.

Thus, two ways to construct a joint data set on employment and election data can be considered. First, all data can be aggregated on the level of the 13 State Labor Exchanges. This way was taken by Frey and Weck. Second, all data can be disaggregated on the level of the counties. This is the approach used in our research project on the NSDAP electorate. Since the 13 State Labor Exchanges do not perfectly fit the 35 Weimar election districts, there were some aggregation problems in constructing the Frey-Weck data set. Frey and Weck did not discover these problems. Since the effects were not too serious, however, there is no need for further discussion of this point (note, however, that in the Frey-Weck data set more than 1 million voters are regionally misclassified).

In the following I will show that the discrepancies between our findings and the Frey-Weck analysis are mainly to be attributed to regional aggregation. There is some additional influence of temporal aggregation as well, which will be discussed in Section V.

4. RESULTS OF OUR REPLICATION

In their statistically sophisticated and carefully argued investigation Frey and Weck (1981) introduced as additional predictors, besides unemployment, of the NSDAP vote the percentage of Catholics (at that time and even today by far the best predictor for election outcome in Germany), the percentage of agricultural workers, the percentage of blue-collar workers, and electoral turnout.

Observational units are, as pointed out, the 13 State Labor Exchange Districts at the four Reichstag elections 1930–1933. The data are arranged in a pooled cross-section/time-series data set with N=52 (=4x13) observational "units."

Table 13–5(a) presents, in row 1, the regression coefficients as reported by Frey and Weck, in row 2, our replication with the Frey/Weck data set (in our reconstruction), and in row 3, the same as in row 2, with covariances computed by using the numbers of eligible voters in 1930 as weights for the units (in order to account for differences in size of the regional units). In all three equations the regression coefficient of unemployment is positive (0.6) which indicates that unemployment displayed a positive influence on the rise of the Nazi party.

The same Table 13–5(b) shows four pure cross-sectional analyses, one for each election. With only 13 observations for each unit the results should not be expected to be sufficiently reliable and stable. All four regression coefficients for unemployment, however, are again positive, varying in size from 0.14 to 0.71, thus confirming the result of the pooled cross-sectional/longitudinal analysis.

Still in the same Table, (e) and (f) repeat the same analyses for N= 4x865 and N=865 county units. Now somewhat modified variables have to be used. The confessional and occupational data are taken from the 1933 census, and the unemployment figures are disaggregated from the 352 Labor Exchange Agencies. The 1930 election data are matched with the 1931 (December) unemployment data which are the indicators closest in time to the appropriate data.

The coefficients of the four separate cross-sectional regressions in Table 13–5(f) differ in several respects from the previous results: (*i*) The squared multiple correlation, previously between 0.7 and 0.9, now typically ranges between 0.3 and 0.7. (*ii*) The influence of the blue-collar variable, previously around zero, is now constantly negative, which means that the NSDAP fared below average in blue-collar districts. (*iii*) Most important for our problem here is the fact that the coefficients for the unemployment variable now switch from positive to negative, indicating that the NSDAP was less successful in counties with high unemployment figures.

In order to prove that this is not only an effect of different indicators, Tables 13–5(c) and (d) present the same analyses as before, but now the 865 county units are aggregated into the 13 State Labor Exchange Districts. Again, the influence of unemployment on the NSDAP result is positive, as reported by Frey and Weck.

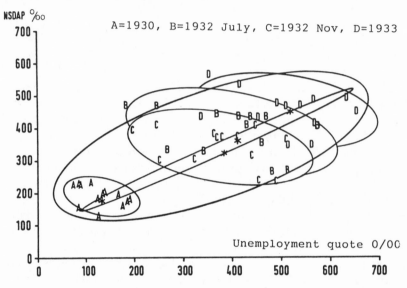

Figure 13–3. Scatterplot with separate cross-sectional and pooled longitudinal-cross sectional correlations (correlation ellipses) of unemployment and the NSDAP share of the vote.

See Figure 13–3 for a graphic illustration of the striking results in Table 13–5(a)–(e). The change from positive to negative coefficients when the regional level changes can also be shown in a longitudinal path model (Figure 13–4) where the lagged variables are introduced as predictors. The influence of unemployment on the Nazi share of the vote is positive when we use 13 regions, and negative or close to zero when we base our analysis on the 865 county units.

It should be clear by now that the results reported by Frey and Weck (1981) strongly depend on the regional level chosen by them. On a county level their findings cannot be replicated. Quite to the contrary, there can be no doubt that at least in 1932 and 1933 in counties with a below average percentage of unemployed the NSDAP received a higher share of

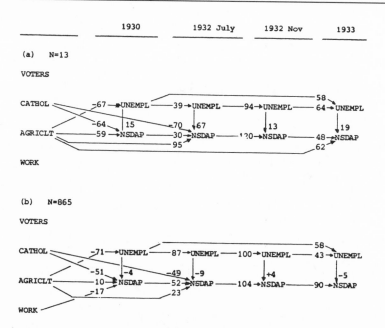

Figure 13–4. Longitudinal path model

the vote than in counties with an above average unemployment rate. This is not only true for the bivariate relationship between unemployment and the Hitler vote but also for a variety of multivariate models where we control for "intervening factors" such as religion, urbanization, turnout, etc. These findings, however, do not imply that no unemployed (or Catholics, blue-collar workers, etc.) had voted for Hitler in 1932 or 1933. Quite the contrary is true, as far as we know. Unfortunately, it is not possible to judge from the available data with the same certainty how many voters who were unemployed, Catholics or whatever, really did vote for or against Hitler. The findings of an extended series of ecological regression analyses as developed by Bernstein (1932) and Goodman (1953, 1959), however, all point in the same direction: The unemployed voted in disproportionately low numbers for the Hitler movement. This is especially true for unemployed blue-collar workers while unemployed white-collar workers (who were outnumbered by their blue-collar colleagues by 4 to 1), on the other hand, seem to have voted above average for the Nazi party. These results imply that against the conviction of many historians and against the tacit implications of the Frey and Weck findings a majority of the unemployed did not direct their hopes towards the NSDAP (cf. Table 13–7).

Table 13–7

**The Propensity of Unemployed Blue Collar and White Collar to
Vote for the NSDAP or KPD.**

Percent of total electorate. Values based on multiple ecological regression
analyses with religion and urbanization as moderator variables. For further details,
see Falter (1984a) and (1984b).

	NSDAP			KPD		
	1932J	1932N	1933	1932J	1932N	1933
Unemployed Blue Collar	13%	12%	10%	29%	34%	30%
Unemployed White Collar	28%	30%	43%	13%	16%	14%
All Voters	31%	27%	39%	12%	14%	11%

5. SUMMARY AND DISCUSSION

The answers to the question whether unemployment gave rise to the
electoral successes of the Nazis range from a correlation near unity (as
shown in Figure 13–1) to a regression coefficient of -0.30 (Table 13–5(e)).
Since the Frey and Weck findings are based on an extremely high level of
aggregation and since they do mix longitudinal and cross-sectional effects
in their pooled analysis as is shown in Falter *et al.* (1985), the validity of
their results has to be seriously questioned. They seem to mainly reflect
regional aggregation bias.

This is not to say that there was no influence of unemployment on
the Nazi vote. Quite the contrary is true, as illustrated in Figure 13–3,
where negative cross-sectional correlations form a positive longitudinal
correlation between unemployment and the NSDAP vote on the Reich
level. This influence, however, must have been an indirect one with
strongest effects in those counties where the unemployment rates were
low. Those were mainly counties with a farming or small-town population,
i.e., regions with (at least in the Protestant case) a conservative voting tra-

dition. In those counties the electorate became radicalized under the influence of the deepening economic crisis according to the prevailing local norms (which, in turn, favored the "right-wing" alternative). An analogous mechanism ended in a radicalization of the electorate towards the political left in those counties where unemployment was high, i.e., in the classical industrial areas of the Weimar Republic such as the urban centers of the Rhein and Ruhr area, parts of Saxony, the densely populated parts of Berlin or Hamburg, etc.

It is paradoxical that National Socialism could profit from mass unemployment mainly in those regions where unemployment was lowest. This paradox could not be detected by the analytic model used by Frey and Weck.

NOTES

[1] This paper appears upon special invitation of the editor. The author wants to emphasize that he chose not to attend the Washington conference of ICUS XIII.

[2] The findings presented here are the result of a collaborative effort of my research project on the voters of the NSDAP. The other members of the research group are (or were) A. Link, J. Lohmöller, H. de Rijke, D. Hänisch, and S. Schumann, as well as an ever-changing crew of research assistants.

REFERENCES

Bernstein, F. 1932. Über eine Methode, die soziologische und bevölkerungsstatistische Gliederung von Abstimmungen bei geheimen Wahlverfahren statistisch zu ermitteln. *Allgemeines statistisches Archiv* 22:253–256.

Falter, J.W. 1984. Politische Konsequenzen von Massenarbeitslosigkiet. *Politische Vierteljahresschrift* 25:275–295.

Falter, J.W. 1986. Unemployment and the radicalization of the German electorate, 1928–1933. An aggregate data analysis with special emphasis on the rise of national socialism. In *Unemployment and the radicalization of the great depression in Weimar, Germany*, ed. P.D. Stachur, 187–208. London: Macmillan.

Falter, J.W., and D. Hänisch. 1986. Die Anfälligkeit von Arbeitern gegenüber die NDSAP bei den Reichtagswahlen 1928–1935. *Sozialgeschichte* 26: 179–216.

Falter, J.W., A.Link, J-B. Lohmöller, J. de Rijke, and S. Schumann. 1983. Arbeitslosigkeit und Nationalsozialismus: Der Beitrag der Massenerwerbslosigkeit zu den Wahlerfolgen der NSDAP 1932 und 1933. *Kölner Zeitschrift für Soziologie und Sozialpsychologie* 35:525–554.

Falter, J.W., J-B. Lohmöller, A. Link, and J. de Rijke. 1985. Hat Arbeitslosigkeit tatsächlich den Aufstieg des Nationalsozialismus bewirkt? Eine Überprüfung der Analyse von Frey und Weck. *Jahrbücher für Nationalökonomie und Statistik* 200/2:121–136.

Frey, B.S., and H. Weck. 1981. Hat Arbeitslosigkeit den Aufstieg des Nationalsozialismus bewirkt? *Jahrbuch für Nationalökonomie und Statistik* 196:1–31.

Goodman, L.A. 1953. Ecological regression and behavior of individuals. *American Sociological Review* 43:557–572.

Goodman, L.A. 1959. Some alternatives to ecological regression. *American Journal of Sociology* 18:663–664.

Lohmöller, J-B., J.W. Falter, J. de Rijke, and A. Link. 1984. Der Einflub der Weltwirtschaftskrise auf den NSDAP-Aufsteig. In *Politische Willensbildung und Interessenvermittlung*, eds. J.W. Falter, C. Fenner and M.Th. Greven, 391–401. Opladen: Westdeutscher Verlag.

Lohmöller, J-B., J.W. Falter, A. Link, and J. de Rijke. 1985. Unemployment and the rise of national socialism: Contradicting results from different regional aggregations. In *Measuring the unmeasurable*, eds. P. Nijkamp *et al.*, 357–370. Doordrecht: Martinus Nijhoff.

Wold, H. 1964. The approach of model building crossroads of probability theory, statistics, and theory of knowledge. In *Model building in the human sciences*, ed. H. Wold, 1–38. Monaco: Entretiens de Monaco en Sciences Humaines.

14

Blood Flow in the Brain and Adulthood Aging of Cognitive Functions

JOHN HORN AND JARL RISBERG

INTRODUCTION

What necessary and sufficient neurological processes accompany thinking and individual differences in the ability to think? There has been much speculation about these relationships, and a little bit is known, but the broad domain these questions cover continues to be one of the largely uncharted areas of science—and one of the most important.

A new technology promises to give us revealing glimpses into this area—isotope-inhalation methods of measuring the flow of blood through the brain (Conn, 1955; Mallett and Veall, 1965; Obrist, Thompson, King and Wang, 1967; Obrist, Thompson, Wang and Wilkinson, 1975; Risberg, 1980; Risberg, Ali, Wilson, Wills and Halsey, 1975; Risberg, Uzzell and Obrist, 1977). These methods provide rather direct indications of neurological functioning in several different parts of the brain. Neurological functioning indicates psychological functioning. Different psychological processes thus can be shown to be linked to different neurological processes, and both can be shown to be associated with age, diagnoses and other indicants of the nomological networks of sound theory (Cronbach, 1975).

It is important, too, that isotope-inhalation methods for measuring blood flow in the brain produce no physical discomfort, are not harmful to a subject and are not terribly expensive. The technology thus opens many new possibilities for studying relations between neurological and psychological functioning.

New methods of analyzing data also promise to help us develop important insights about complex relationships such as those between neurological and psychological functioning. We refer particularly to multivariate modeling techniques. Recent work in several branches of science has produced notable advances in these methods (e.g., Blalock, 1971, 1984; Duncan, 1975; Fornell, 1982; Heise, 1975; Goldberger and Duncan, 1973; Horn and McArdle, 1980; Jöreskog, 1967, 1969; Jöreskog and Sörbom, 1977, 1984; Lohmöller, 1981; Lohmöller and Wold, 1982; McArdle, 1979, 1980, 1984, 1985; McArdle and McDonald, 1984; McDonald, 1978, 1979; Stone, 1974; Wold, 1966a, 1966b, 1975, 1979, 1982). It has become possible to specify and test very complex models of relationships between many precursor (independent or determinant) variables and many subsequent (dependent or outcome) variables. This is important because often the most interesting and difficult problems of understanding human functioning involve interactions among large numbers of influences, all of which must be considered in one analysis. Only by analyzing many variables is it possible to accurately represent the realities of multiple-influence systems.

This is a report of our use of these two new methods in a study of aging in adulthood. We used the "soft" modeling methods of Wold (programmed by Lohmöller, 1981) to analyze adulthood age differences in multiple measures of blood flow in the brain. Results from these studies point to distinct neural processes, each associated with separate intellectual capacities, and having a different developmental path over the course of human development.

Our guiding hypotheses in this work stemmed from a theory stipulating that events experienced by most people in the course of living can produce notable decreases in blood flow to the brain. These decreases can be greater in some areas of the brain than in others. Decreased blood flow can result in loss of neural tissue. In consequence of such loss, the demand for blood in affected areas will be decreased. This will be recorded in measures of the characteristic amount of flow in distinct areas of the brain. Thus, with increase in age there can be, on the average, a decrease in measures of blood flow to the brain, and this decrease can be more pronounced in some areas than in others.

Perhaps the most useful feature of this work is the illustration it provides of the kind of research that is needed in the future. If we are to make truly important advances in understanding human functioning, we need research that crosses the traditional but largely artificial boundaries of different intellectual disciplines, and we need research that is fundamentally multivariate. If a unity of knowledge is to be forged, it must be based on this kind of research.

MAPPING BLOOD FLOW THROUGH THE BRAIN

The flow of blood through bodily tissues is a direct indicator of the functional activity in those tissues, a principle adumbrated in the pioneering studies of Kety and Schmidt (1948). Oxygen and glucose are needed to generate the energy of the chemical reactions that define function. Each increase in activity demands an increase in these materials. This demand is met by an increase in blood flow to the tissues wherein activity is being increased. Some bodily tissues make greater demands for blood than do others. Although the brain weighs only about 1400 grams (less than 2% of body weight), it takes about 20% of cardiac output. Blood flow to the neurons of the brain—the gray matter—is approximately four times the flow to the white matter (Hoedt-Rasmussen and Skinhoj, 1966). These remarkable features of physiology have spurred the invention of several methods for assessing neural function by measuring the flow of blood to different regions of the brain.

One class of such methods involves putting a soluble radioisotope into the blood at an upstream site and recording, via scintillation detectors (similar to Geiger counters), changes in concentration of the isotope in particular tissues located at downstream sites. The rate of clearance of the isotope from these tissues indicates the rate of blood flow to those tissues and, thus, their level of functional activity.

In the early work with these isotope-tracing methods the solution containing the radioactive gas was injected into one of the main arteries feeding the brain. (See Lassen, Ingvar and Skinhoj, 1978, for a review of the findings based on these methods.) A requirement that the isotope be administered by injection very much restricted the use that could be made of these methods. Awareness of this restriction spurred attempts (the first by Conn, 1955) to develop ways to introduce a tracer isotope into the system without, as it were, spilling blood. Inhalation methods are results of these efforts (Mallett & Vealle, 1965; Obrist, et al, 1967, 1975; Risberg, 1980; Risberg, et al, 1975, 1977).

The radioactive tracer of the inhalation procedures used in this study is Xenon-133 (which emits .08 MeV gamma radiation). This is put into the bloodstream by having the subject breathe (for precisely one minute) a mixture of Xenon-133 and ordinary air (2.5 mCi/liter). There follows a 10-minute period in which the subject breathes ordinary air. The rate at which the isotope arrives and disappears at each of 32 detector sites in the brain is carefully recorded. The 32 detectors are positioned at right angles to the lateral surfaces of the head, 16 on the right side and 16 at homologous positions on the left side, as indicated in Figure 14–1.

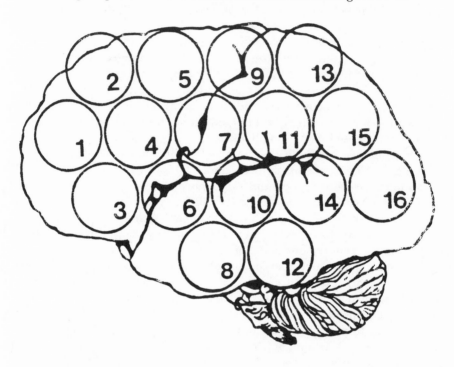

Figure 14–1. Location of 16 scintillation detectors on the left side of the head. Detectors on the right are located in the same (homologous) way.

Each scintillation detector is a lead tube (22 mm inside diameter, depth 20 mm) that restricts the area of sensitivity of the crystal [NaI(T1)] that reacts to the gamma rays emitted from nearby bodily tissues. A count of these reactions is the basic indicator of radiation.

A number of procedures are used to standardize the upstream entry of the isotope into the blood. The isotope is introduced through a mask that is tightly fitted over the subject's nose and mouth. A pretest period is used to enable the subject to become comfortable breathing through the mask and to learn that the procedures are not painful or harmful.

Measures of CO_2 in the expired air are used to detect and correct any undue anxiety reactions to the testing. There is careful control of the amount of the isotope that is allowed to enter the system: the time for breathing the isotope-air mixture is precisely standardized.

The downstream recording of radiation is also carefully standardized. The 16 detectors positioned on each side of the head are fastened together in a single unit, so each detector is always in the same location relative to other detectors. Using a procedure developed by Monrad-Krohn and Refsom (1964), the detectors numbered 6, 7 and 9 are placed over the Rolandic fissure. This positioning standardizes the location of the detectors. The standard location for the left side of the head is indicated in Figure 14–1.

The chemical properties of Xenon and the radioactive properties of Xenon-133 are well suited for measurement of the neuronal activity associated with blood flow. Xenon is absorbed into the gray and white matter of the brain at different rates. This difference, coupled with the different rates of blood flow to the gray and white matter, means that an increase in Xenon-133 radiation at a particular location in the brain is indicative mainly of an increase in neuronal (gray matter) activity.

Xenon is chemically inert and the isotope has a short half-life. When the tracer diffuses into brain tissue from arterial blood it does not generate chemical reactions. It is quickly cleared out by venous blood; thus it is rapidly removed from the physiological system. Well over 90 percent of the Xenon that enters the body via the procedures we have described is excreted within the first 10 minutes after entry. In practical terms this means that most of the isotope that is put into the bloodstream during a standard one minute inhalation period arrives "in a bunch," and only once, at a recording site. Over a 10 minute period at a given detector the curve of distribution for gamma radiation first rises rapidly to a peak about one minute after the start of inhalation and drops almost as rapidly in the following minute.

Several methods can be used to derive measures from the radiation curve of a detector. The analyses of our studies are based on measures of the initial slope index, or ISI (developed by Risberg, 1980). An ISI is mainly indicative of blood flow in rapidly perfused tissue (gray matter).

Each detector on which an ISI measure is based records in a section of the brain that forms a truncated cone about 2–3 cm in diameter that extends about 3 cm into the head directly under the detector. This means that ISI measures are mainly indicative of neural function in the surface sections of the cerebral cortex, not the innermost parts of the brain. It means, too, that a measure on one side of the brain involves little radiation from the other side of the brain—in particular, the homologous area of the other side of the brain.

There are several reasons why the inhalation isotope-tracing procedures are particularly appropriate for studying cerebral blood flow in humans. Perhaps most important, the methods are safe. Results from several studies (Bolmsjo, 1981 for review) indicate that when administered in the amounts and in the manner described above, Xenon-133 is not harmful to the subject or the administering technicians. The approximately 125 mrads of radiation produced in the subject's lungs is comparable to the radiation received when teeth are x-rayed in a standard dental checkup.

The evidence of many studies has established that ISI measures of regional cerebral blood flow (rCBF) are indicative of both traits and states of individuals (Risberg, 1980). Traits are stable characteristics that distinguish one person from another despite variations in the conditions and circumstances in which people can be found; states are characteristics that vary within a person and thus distinguish the conditions and circumstances which the person experiences (Horn, 1972).

There is evidence that the ISI measures indicate psychological functioning. For example, when one becomes engaged in a task that requires concerted attention, blood flow increases at some recording sites, decreases at other sites and does not change notably at still other locations (Prohovnik, 1980; Maximillian, 1980; Risberg, 1980; Risberg and Prohovnik, 1983). Different central nervous system diseases are associated with different patterns of relatively low blood flow for some of the regional indicators and relatively high flow for others (Gustafson, Risberg, Johanson and Brun, 1984; Risberg and Gustafson, 1983; Risberg, Gustafson and Prohovnik, 1981; Shaw, Mortel, Meyer, Rogers, Hardenberg and Cuaia, 1984). In general, losses in neural tissue, due to illness or injury or catabolic changes, will be accompanied by drop in blood flow to the affected tissue. This provides a basis for studying several kinds of behavioral consequences of changes and differences in blood-flow measures.

ADULTHOOD DEVELOPMENT: BRAIN AND ABILITIES.

The brain is constantly active as long as one is alive. Since we inevitably age, and change is a ubiquitous feature of aging, it is reasonable to suppose that the brain changes with age—and of course there is direct evidence to support this supposition. Can we discern the directions of such change? There is much belief about such matters, but it is surprising how little of this belief we can document with the evidence of empirical research. There are two main schools of thought: those who believe the change is for the better (except when a disease strikes), and those who believe the change is for the worse (except perhaps in a few rare cases). Probably both views are correct. As with so many things, the answer one gets depends on the question asked and where one looks for evidence.

Our reviews of evidence pertaining to the anatomy, histology, neurochemistry, and metabolism of the brain lead us to conclude that on the average over many adults, there surely are some debilitating effects associated with increasing age in adulthood (Brierly, 1976; Creasey and Rapaport, 1985; Horn, 1970, 1975, 1976, 1982; Horn and Donaldson, 1980; Nandy and Sherwin, 1977; Thompson, 1976). Most depressing, these effects seem to occur not only in a period of "very old age," but also through a period we refer to as the "vital years," from 20 to 65 years of age—"vital" because most of the most important work of a society is done by people in this age range. Different kinds of results (not always in agreement, of course, but generally) suggest that with increasing age the following kinds of outcomes in brain structure and function can be expected:

: atrophy of the brain. perhaps especially in the frontal lobe, the gyri, and cerebral gray matter
: concomitantly, enlargement of the "vacant" areas of the brain—increase in ventrical size, widening of cortical sulci
: increases in cerebral artherosclerotic lesions
: development of senile plaques and neurofibrillary tangles, granulovacuolar degeneration, accumulation of lipofuscin, and other such indicators, or concomitants, of neuronal decrement
: functional loss changes in the dopaminergic and cholinergic systems (and possibly other neurotransmitter systems)—i.e., changes associated with loss of such functions as memory and motor coordination
: decrease in cerebral blood flow, CBF, and related decline in brain metabolism of oxygen and glucose.

This list is not exhaustive, but it is sufficient to suggest that with advancing age in adulthood there is likely to be some loss of brain capacity. Why such losses occur, what behavioral functions are affected, the importance of the losses, their practical implications: these are questions for which we do not have complete answers.

While the changes we have just mentioned are correlated with advancing age, they may not be the inevitable consequences of aging. Studies of "very healthy men" give some credence to this position (Birren, Butler and Greenhouse, 1963; Duara, Margolen and Robertson-Tchabo, 1983). In these studies, considerable effort was devoted to ensuring that the men of the sample had no vascular or brain disease and in other respects were in excellent health. In the Duara, *et al.* (1983) study, for example, special controls in measurement were introduced to ensure that if a subject had any decrement in vision or hearing (possibly associated with aging), this would not affect the results. Under these conditions, and looking at glucose and oxygen metabolism, the Duara team found that the age-related decrements reported in other studies were not statistically significant in their sample of 40 men. Interestingly, however, when this team looked at loss of gray matter, increase in size of the ventricles, and decrease in CBF, they found significant differences between the healthy old and young men.

The evidence of age-related decrement in brain function should not be neglected, but neither should one assume that it tells the whole story. Researchers have looked for age decrements among many indicators of cerebral function, but have found such decrements for only relatively few indicators. Some of the age-related changes that have been observed may be improvements, not decrements. For example, Buell and Coleman (1981) found evidence of increase in dendritic branching with aging in adulthood.

The whole story must also indicate that aging change does not occur in all areas and systems of the brain, and different areas and systems are affected in different ways. Counts of the numbers of neurons in different sections of the brain suggest, for example, that age-related losses are large in some areas—superior frontal, superior temporal—and miniscule in other areas—the occipital. The hippocampus and areas near the hippocampus appear to be particularly susceptible to decrements associated with aging.

ABILITIES IN RELATION TO PATTERNS OF
BLOOD FLOW IN THE BRAIN

We know that the brain is a principal moderator of all psychological functions—motivation, temperament, emotion and ability. It is particularly central to expressions of intellectual abilities. Individual differences in such abilities are thought to relate most directly to individual differences in brain structure and function, although we know very little about specific links between what goes on in the brain and what we see in human performances.

What are the qualities of human abilities with which we expect changes in the brain to be most highly correlated? This is not the place to provide a full review of evidence pertaining to this question (see Cattell, 1971; Cronbach, 1970; Ekstrom, French and Harman, 1979; Horn, 1982, 1985a, 1985b). A bird's eye view of some of this evidence is needed, however, to put the present study into a proper perspective.

It has been well established that gross differences and changes in brains relate to gross differences and changes in a swath of abilities that collectively are referred to as indicating human intelligence. Beyond this, however, questions about "what is human intelligence and how does it relate to brain function" become very complex (Eccles, 1977). In analyzing this complexity one should recognize, first, that the human has a myriad of intellectual capabilities—too many for us to expect (at this stage of research) to be able to describe the links between separate capabilities and distinct neurological functions. There is a need to simplify the myriad. Needed is an empirically-based theory that enables us to accurately represent separate abilities in a manner that is manageable for research.

Theory about a single attribute, intelligence, is an outcome of efforts to specify such a system. A single-attribute theory is nicely parsimonious. Unfortunately, such a theory does not adequately represent what we have come to know about human abilities. Much evidence has accumulated to indicate that several separate capacities—several distinct "intelligences"—underlie the myriad of human intellectual abilities. The term "intelligence" turns out to be only a heading under which one can list distinct abilities. Following is a brief description of seven broad "intelligences" for which there is substantial evidence indicating that the abilities are distinct

Gc, Crystallized Intelligence. This form of intelligence is indicated by a very large number of performances indicating breadth of knowledge and experience, sophistication, comprehension of communications, judgment, understanding conventions, and reasonable thinking. The factor that provides evidence of Gc is defined by primary abilities such as verbal comprehension, concept formation, logical reasoning, and general reasoning. Tests used to measure the ability include vocabulary (what is a word near in meaning to temerity?), esoteric analogies (Socrates is to Aristotle as Sophocles is to_____?), remote associations (what word is associated with Bathtub, Prizefighting, and Wedding?), and judgment (determine why a foreman is not getting the best results from workers). As measured, the factor is a fallible representation of the extent to which an individual has incorporated, through the systematic influences of acculturation, the knowledge and sophistication that constitute the intelligence of a culture.

Gf, Fluid Intelligence. The broad set of abilities of this intelligence include those of seeing relationships among stimulus patterns, drawing inferences from relationships and comprehending implications. The primary abilities that best represent the factor, as identified in completed research, include induction, figural flexibility, integration, and cooperatively with Gc, logical reasoning and general reasoning. Tasks that measure the factor include letter series (what letter comes next in the following series d f i m r x e), matrices (discern the relationships among elements of 3-by-3 matrices), and topology (from among a set of figures in which circles, squares, and triangles overlap in different ways, select a figure that will enable one to put a dot within a circle and square but outside a triangle). The factor is a fallible representation of such fundamental features of mature human intelligence as reasoning, abstracting and problem solving. In Gf these features are not imparted through the systematic influences of acculturation but instead are obtained through learning that is unique to an individual or is in other ways not organized by the culture.

Gv, Visual Organization. This dimension is indicated by PMA's such as visualization, spatial orientation, speed of closure, and flexibility of closure, measured by tests such as Gestalt Closure (identify a figure in which parts have been omitted), Form Board (show how cut-out parts fit together to depict a particular figure), and Embedded Figures (find a geometric figure within a set of intersecting lines). To distinguish this factor from Gf, it is important that relationships among visual patterns be clearly manifest so performances reflect primarily fluency in perception of these patterns, not reasoning in inferring the patterns.

Ga, Auditory Organization. This factor has been identified on the basis of studies by Horn (1972b), Horn and Stankov (1981), Stankov (1978), and Stankov and Horn (1980) in which PMA abilities of temporal tracking, auditory cognition of relations, and speech perception under distraction-distortion were first defined among other primary abilities and then found to indicate a broad dimension at the second order. Tasks that measure Ga include repeated tones (identify the first occurrence of a tone when it occurs several times), tonal series (indicate which tone comes next in an orderly series of tones), and cafeteria noise (identify a word amid a din of surrounding noise). As in the case of GV, this ability is best indicated when the relationships among stimuli are not such that one needs to reason for understanding but instead are such that one can fluently perceive patterns among the stimuli.

SAR, Short-Terms Acquisition and Retrieval. This ability is comprised of processes of becoming aware and processes of retaining information long enough to do something with it. Almost all tasks that involve short-term memory have variance in the SAR factor. Span-memory, associative-memory, and meaningful-memory primary abilities define the factor, but measures of primary and secondary memory also can be used to indicate the dimension.

TSR, Long-Term Storage and Retrieval. Formerly this dimension was regarded as a broad factor among fluency tasks, such as those of the primary abilities labeled associational fluency, expressional fluency, and object flexibility. In recent work, however, these performances have been found to align with others indicating facility in storing information and retrieving information that was acquired in the distant past. It seems, therefore, that the dimension mainly represents processes for forming encoding associations for long-term storage and using these associations, or forming new ones, at the time of retrieval. These associations are not so much correct as they are possible and useful; to associate tea kettle with mother is not to arrive at a truth so much as it is to regard both concepts as sharing common attributes (e.g., warmth).

Other Possible Dimensions. Some additional factors have been found in more than one study but are not yet regarded as well established as independent dimensions. In regard to speediness, for example, several studies have suggested that there is a cohesiveness among speed of performance measures that is broader than the perceptual-speed primary ability (which, however, is at the core of the broader, Gs, dimension). This broad form of speediness emerges when tests become so easy that all people would get all items (problems) correct or have essentially the same score if the test were not highly speeded. It seems to be indicated also by tasks of speed of writing and printing. In two recent studies Gs was found to be largely independent of quickness in obtaining correct answers (CDS) and quickness in deciding to abandon a problem (QDS). These latter two forms of speediness may also represent broad independent processes (factors). However, the main point of results indicating speediness factors is that speediness (of one form or another) is separate from major dimensions of intelligence, memory, and perception. There is considerable evidence to indicate that speediness is important for understanding age differences in ability test performances (see Birren, 1965, 1974, for reviews).

Sensory detector functions are largely independent of major indicants of intelligence (Gf and Gc) and memory (SAR and TSR). Sda and Sdv represent findings that measures of immediate apprehension, as derived from dichotic listening tasks and an adaptation of Sperling's (1960) matrix-element recognition task, are reliably independent of the measures that define Gf, Gc, SAR, and TSR. The sensory detector measures seem to represent the human's capacities for becoming aware, but only for a very short time (a second or two), of a large number of the events that constantly compete for one's attention.

Several lines of evidence point to the distinctiveness of these intelligences (Horn, 1985a, 1985b). They are separate as we see them in human performances; they develop in different ways over the life span; they stem from different genetic determiners; they relate in different ways to a host of variables that make up what is called the "construct validity" of ability measures (Cronbach, 1970). They may have different relations to ISI measures of blood flow in the brain.

Two of the broad abilities above—Gf and SAR—decline with age in adulthood. This decline appears to reflect deleterious changes in the central nervous system (CNS). Two of the abilities—Gc and TSR—improve throughout much of adulthood (or at least do not decline). They seem to reflect aging enhancements of CNS function. We have very little direct evidence indicating which features of brain structure and function are most directly involved in expressions of these abilities and their decrements and enhancements.

Improvements in Gc and TSR stem from restructuring and consolidation of the person's knowledge system (Broadbent, 1966; Horn, 1982). In the CNS such changes might correspond to overdetermination of neural responses occasioned by dendrite proliferation and entanglement. There are suggestions, too, that improvements in these abilities are associated with developments in the white matter of the brain—the oligodentricites, myelin, supportive tissues and nutrient suppliers. We have not supposed that such changes will be closely related to rCBF measurements, although we have little empirical evidence to support this supposition.

The decline of Gf and SAR in adulthood is linked to losses in basic capacities for distributing attention, concentrating intensely, encoding spontaneously, and holding information in awareness (Craik, 1977; Horn, 1982; Horn, Donaldson and Engstrom, 1981; Reese, 1977). These capacities are notably affected by lesions and malfunctions in an area of the brain which we will refer to as Ht—representing the hippocampus, the upper parts of the temporal lobe, the fornix, the thalamus, mammillary bodies and other nearby structures (Butters and Cermak, 1975; Drachman and Arbit, 1966; Parsons, 1975, 1977; Sweet, Talland and Ervin, 1959; Turner, 1969). A principal function of this area—of the reticular formation in particular—is neural activation, i.e., "charging" the brain, keeping it alert, and monitoring the transmission of messages throughout the CNS.

Injuries to Ht that notably and permanently affect the capacities of

Gf and SAR can leave Gc and TSR relatively unaffected. Some of the mechanisms that produce malfunctions in the Ht may be implicated in processes that selectively bring about aging declines of Gf and SAR, but do not directly affect Gc and TSR.

What are these processes? One search for an answer leads to the notion that measures of blood flow in the brain might provide useful information.

DIFFERENCES IN BLOOD FLOW IN DIFFERENT REGIONS OF THE BRAIN

As mentioned before, the Ht area of the brain seems to be particularly vulnerable to fluctuations of blood flow (Hachinski, 1980). The arteries that supply this region are different from the arteries that supply many other regions of the brain. Instead of Y-branching with continuation, the arteries of this area branch at right angles from the main trunks and terminate in the area as end-arteries. This means that if there is a drop in blood pressure, there could be notable diminution in the blood supply in this area—that a blood pressure decline could become critical in the Ht region before it became critical—or when it never became critical in other regions of the brain. The Ht region is also a notable distance away from the main arteries of the brain, the carotid and vertebral. For this reason, too, the Ht region can be expected to be more affected by fluctuations in blood pressure than are other sections of the brain. Under any conditions of diminution of blood flow, the flow would cease earliest at the branches that are most distant from the primary suppliers.

If the delivery of blood to the Ht region is indeed notably decreased, this region would be more susceptible than other areas of the brain to damage that accompanies drop in blood pressure. Several consequences would follow. Infarcts, for example, would be more common (probabilistically) in this area than elsewhere in the brain. Corsellis (1976) found, indeed, that infarcts occur more frequently in the hippocampus than in other parts of the brain.

The conditions that seem to make the Ht region particularly susceptible to damage produced by alterations in blood flow exist elsewhere in the brain—in areas where rCBF measures are most sensitive. In particular, the peripheral sections of the brain receive blood from end-arteries that are relatively far from main arteries. Thus, in these regions, too, drops in blood flow can result in damage to the cerebral cortex and loss of function.

Several kinds of life events can produce decrease in blood supply to the head. Inebriation can do this, particularly if it is severe enough to produce loss of consciousness. Extreme use of alcohol appears to be associated with "early aging" and decline of intellectual abilities (Parsons, 1975, 1977; Tarter, 1975). Blows to the head, as can occur in several sports, loss of consciousness for any of several reasons, heart attacks, and several kinds of illnesses can bring about notable changes in the distribution of blood to the head. The consequence can be loss of neural tissue in areas of the brain that are particularly vulnerable to loss of blood supply. There is evidence suggesting that such factors are linked to aging decline of intellectual abilities (Heikkinen, 1975; Herzog, Schaie and Gribbon, 1978).

Almost anyone can experience the kinds of life events that produce diminution in blood supply to the head. These events occur as a function of time in living. They are more likely to have occurred in older than in younger people. Thus, over the course of what can be regarded as normal aging in adulthood, for any of several reasons, the blood supply to vulnerable areas of the brain can be expected (probabilistically) to drop below critical levels and result in loss of the neurological basis for some intellectual capacities. With the loss of neural tissue there would be a corresponding decline in the demand for oxygenated blood and a decrease in rCBF.

On this basis we can expect the following:

1) aging in adulthood will be associated with decreases in blood flow to the brain; 2) these decreases will be larger in some areas than in others —decreases will be relatively larger in the Ht region and the peripheral areas of the cerebral cortex than in other areas of the brain; and 3) ISI measures of rCBF can indicate some of these aging effects.

Let us now consider the modeling analyses that were used to examine these expectations.

MODELING METHODS

The logic of our application of partial least-squares (PLS) modeling methods (Lohmöller, 1981; Wold, 1980, 1982) rests on an assumption that is fundamental in much scientific work. This is an assumption that differently obtained measurements—often referred to as manifest variables—are only indirect indicators of variation in underlying processes of a system—latent variables. When we use a test to measure the size of a person's vocabulary, we recognize that our estimate is no more than an indicator of a process—something we might refer to as the person's true vocabulary. That process involves a host of factors that determine what is seen in the manifest variable—the obtained vocabulary score. Such a process is a part of a system of structural and developmental determinants. How does one infer the process? The trick of scientific investigation is to analyze observed relationships in ways that yield reliable clues about underlying processes that cannot be seen. The trick is to understand manifest variable relationships so well that one can infer a model indicating how latent variables bring about what is seen in manifest relationships.

PLS is particularly valuable for this purpose because it permits analyses of large numbers of variables in ways that reveal systematic influences operating among variables. These systematic influences can represent factors other than those anticipated in a particular theory, and may be sample specific, but at least in part, they stem from the structural and developmental determinants about which inferences are sought. The results from PLS analyses thus provide information about the underlying processes that operate in a system.

Other contributors to this volume have described the intricacies of PLS methods. They point out that any of several quite distinct models can be fitted with PLS. We have considered only a few of these possible models.

The basic model of our analysis can be summarized with the following matrix equation:

$$(14\text{--}1) \quad A = FDUD'F'$$

In this equation A is an (m+q)-by-(m+q) matrix of associations (correlations, covariances, cross-products) among obtained ISI measures and control variables. For our analyses all variables can be scaled, without loss of information, to standard-score form. Under such conditions A is a matrix of correlation coefficients. The D, U and F matrices will be defined in statements that follow.

The following kinds and numbers of variables are represented in the matrices of equation (14–1):

a total of m ISI (manifest) variables:
m = 32 in most of our analyses.
a total of q control variables (also manifest):
q = 10 in the main analyses reported here.
a total of n latent variables defined within the model.

A relationship between any two of these variables can be either (but not both) of the following:

> Directed: In this case one variable is a function of (is directed by) the other, as indicated in a (scalar) equation of the form
> (14–2) W = aV
> in which W is estimated to be an a-proportion of V.

> Undirected: In this case two variables are related, as in a covariance, correlation or variance (i.e., the covariance or correlation of a variable with itself), but neither variable is defined as a function of (is directed by) the other.

These possible relationships are illustrated in Figure 14–2, which is drawn in accordance with definitions suggested by McArdle (1980, 1985). Directed relations are represented by single-headed arrows. The extent of a directed relationship is represented by a d_jk symbol or number within an arrow. The d_jk symbol indicates that variable j is a function of the variable k. If there is a number in a directed arrow, the number is an explicit parameter estimate of d_jk; that number indicates the extent of the relationship in the same way that a b-weight in regression analysis indicates the extent of a relationship. Undirected relations are represented by two-headed arrows; the extent of these relationships is a numerical value symbolized by u_jk. To help make the figure fairly easy to decipher, only a few u_jk's have been entered.

The numbers from 1 to 16 within the squares and circles of the figure identify the scintillation detectors, represented in Figure 14–1, from which ISI measures were obtained. The squares containing these numbers represent the measures as actually obtained—i.e., are manifest variables. The several arrows directed at each of these squares indicate the statistical controls of our models. The part of an ISI manifest variable that could be estimated (linearly) from the information of the control variables was removed, leaving the residual ISI variable that is represented by a circle. These latent variables have been purged of effects associated with the control variables.

The matrix D of equation (14–1), square and of order (m+q+n), is the inverse of a difference between an identity matrix and a matrix in which the d_jk elements appear below the main diagonal and zeroes appear above the diagonal; D' is the transpose of D. The U matrix—square and symmetrical, of order (m+q+n)—contains the u_jk elements. F is a "filter" matrix of order (m+q)-by-(m+q+n), used merely to distinguish manifest variables from latent variables. F' is the transpose of F.

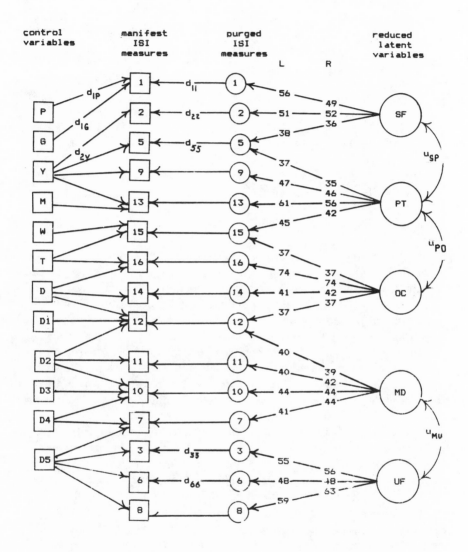

Figure 14–2. Illustration of a mathematical-statistical model for analysis of ISI measures of blood flow in the brain.

Abbreviations Used In Figure 14–2:

P =   Percent CO_2

G =   Age to nearest year

Y, M, W, and T = the year, month of the year, day of the week, and time of day respectively when the blood flow recordings were taken

D =   Whether or not a diagnosis was available for a person

D1, …,D9 = Dummy variables representing major different diagnostic categories available on members of the sample.

SF =   Superior frontal

PT =   Parietal

OC =   Occipital

MD =   Mid-diagonal

UF =   Underside frontal

L =   Left hemisphere

R =   Right hemisphere

The matrix equation of (14–1) asserts that the model relationships specified in D and U on the right in the equation are equal to the obtained relationships on the left. This assertion is never quite true: the "equals" sign of the equation represents only an approximation. This approximation can be reasonably close or it can be far from close. PLS is a set of algorithms for using the obtained relationships of the A-matrix of equation (14–1) to calculate "best" (in an average least-squares sense) estimates of the specified d_jk and u_jk elements. Under several assumptions of statistical theory, these estimates can be interpreted as parameters for a population model that could generate the observed a_jk relationships in accordance with the equality assertion of the equation.

Only a small subset of all possible d_jk and u_jk relationships can be estimated. These parameters are represented by the arrows that appear in Figure 14–2. Many arrows that do not appear in the figure could appear. These represent the many possible relationships that could exist between variables, but have not been specified and thus are not estimated parameters (in this particular model). The algorithms of PLS will do the best least-squares job they can to estimate the parameters of a model regardless of whether "correct" or "incorrect" relationships have been specified, but if correct relationships are not specified and/or incorrect ones are, the resulting model-side (right side) of equation (14–1) will not provide a good estimate of the obtained (left) side. This is indicated by descriptive and inferential model-evaluation statistics that are calculated within PLS. These statistics are based on accumulated differences (over all a_jk elements) between the obtained a_jk coefficients and the a_jk coefficients estimated using the model-side of equation (14–1). The smaller the number of parameters estimated (not set equal to zero), the more demanding is the model—i.e., the more unlikely it is that model-evaluation statistics will indicate that the model is an acceptable representation of reality.

PLS breaks away from the most common approach to model evaluation—in particular, the distinction between exploratory and confirmatory modeling. This distinction is regarded as redundant or not needed (as argued by Wold in the introduction and Lohmöller in Chapter 1 of this volume). This argument is based on the use of Stone-Geisser's cross-validation test in PLS. The answer provided with this test is not a simple "yes" or "no" to a question about whether or not a model fits data; rather, the test provides a statement of the degree to which a model predicts (accounts for) the data. Thus, PLS methods are not directed at confirming or disconfirming a hypothesis that a model fits—the question of confirmatory modeling—nor are the methods devoted only to exploring the data to determine what kind of model might fit. When Stone-Geisser tests are applied in PLS, the study can be regarded as neither confirmatory nor exploratory, but merely directed at determining how well a model accounts for the data. The logic of the Bentler-Bonett (1980) and Tucker-Lewis (1973) evaluation statistics can be interpreted in this way, too.

In Chapter 9 of this volume, Dagum points out that when scientific problems are viewed in terms of whether or not a model fits, the Idealist position in the philosophy of science is being assumed (perhaps implicitly), whereas when the modeling effort is evaluated with a test of model predictability the approach is consistent with the Empiricist position. Wold argues in the introduction to this volume that most scientists today probably operate most of the time on the basis of the Empiricist position. They assume, for example, that probably no model really fits reality (an assumption developed by Horn and McArdle, 1980, for example). It makes sense, therefore, to ask about model predictability, not about model fit. Wold has designed PLS to ensure that the methods provide answers in accordance with this epistemology, rather than in terms of the Idealist position.

Regardless of the characteristics of PLS, as such, the design and conduct of a study can be more or less aimed at either "checking" (on what one believes to be true prior to conducting the study) or "searching" (to find what might be true when one has only vague ideas about the structure of data). This checking-or-searching distinction has some of the connotations of the confirmatory-or-exploratory distinction. It represents an important difference in the basis for interpreting model-evaluation and/or model-fit statistics. The consumer of research results should know whether model-evaluation or model-fit statistics were obtained with a search or check application of modeling methods (Horn and McArdle, 1980). For the results can reflect capitalization on chance, particularly in small samples (although not only under these conditions; Horn and Knapp, 1973).

When modeling methods are used to check hypotheses, the model relationships are specified quite independently of "seeing what the data says." The decision to estimate particular d_jk and u_jk relationships is made on the basis of theory and empirical generalization from previous studies, without using the associations of the data-in-hand to "guide" the specification.

There are two general ways in which modeling methods can be used to search data to find a model that provides a close fit to a given set of data—(a) using a metatheory and (b) using an empirical search.

Metatheory-search methods require that one provide the modeling program with the general instructions of a theory that exists quite independently of any substantive theory about data. The theory of oblique simple structure (Thurstone, 1947; Horn, McArdle and Mason, 1983) is a metatheory. A metatheory does not derive from any particular substantive considerations, but instead is based on epistemological and mathematical conditions. A model specified in accordance with a metatheory might fit any of many different substantive interpretations, but it need not fit any such interpretation. In the metatheory of simple structure, for example, it is required that manifest variables have only very few nonzero relationships with latent variables, and that latent variables have only few nonzero relationships with manifest variables, but the theory says nothing about which particular manifest variables are expected to have nonzero relationships with which particular latent variables.

In metatheory-search analysis, as in a checking analysis, specification of the model rigidly precedes estimation of model parameters and examination of results. In empirical-search exploration, on the other hand, examination of results obtained with the data-in-hand precedes specification. In one version of this approach to data analysis, the association matrix, as such, is scanned to find clues about how to specify the relationships for latent variables. In another version of this approach, one estimates parameters for several different models and uses the results in further specification. Frequently, an investigator begins with a substantive theory that guides a first specification for a model. Up to this point, the methods would have been used in a checking manner. But after finding that the specified model does not reproduce the A-matrix of equation

(14–1) very well, the investigator uses the parameter estimates, model-evaluation and/or goodness-of-fit statistics to adjust the old model and thus make it into a new model. This adjustment defines the study as one of search. If the new model does not produce a good fit for the data, further adjustments might be made, the fit examined again, after which additional adjustments might be made. This process might be repeated several times until what is regarded as a good model for the data is found.

The algorithms of a PLS make the discrepancy (squared) between obtained a_{ij} and estimated a_{ij} as small (on the average) as is possible regardless of whether a checking or searching approach to data analysis has been used to specify the model. The algorithms also produce the same kinds of model-evaluation statistics under each of these conditions. But the results should not be regarded in the same way in each case. Application of an empirical search to develop a model erodes the basis for using model-evaluation or goodness-of-fit statistics to make inferences about a population model and the likelihood that results will replicate (Horn and McArdle, 1980). The empirical search approach capitalizes on chance and non-replicable aberrations in the particular set of data from which the model was derived (Horn and Engstrom, 1979; Horn and Knapp, 1973; Horn and McArdle, 1980; Horn, et al., 1983). The statistical theories of modeling are not Bayesian; they do not apply when models are constructed in a *post hoc* manner. On the other hand, these theories can be properly applied to models specified (exclusively) in accordance with substantive (empirical generalization) theory and/or metatheory, provided the sample size is reasonably large: assumptions of the theory are reasonable for the data, and the model is not modified by using modeling results to change specified relationships to make them more nearly agree with the investigator's ideas about "what makes sense" (Horn and Knapp, 1973).

In the research reported here, PLS was applied in an empirical search manner in three separate samples of approximately 100 adults. First, a simple structure metatheory was used to guide the search. Empirical search methods were tried out with the resulting solutions. The results from this exploratory work were used to design a large-sample checking study. This was based largely on the metatheory results from the pilot studies. The "hardiness" of this model was then examined by evaluating model predictability under several different conditions of drawing subsamples of subjects from the total sample. The results from these various analyses led to the conclusions we summarize in subsequent sections of this report.

MODELS OF BLOOD FLOW IN THE BRAIN

ISI measures taken at different places on the head could be indicative of merely one thing—blood flow throughout the brain. Another possibility is that the measures taken at one place are indicative not only of blood flow throughout the brain, but also of particular processes. It is possible, too, that the measures indicate only particular processes—i.e., are not at all indicative of flow throughout the brain. Such "particular processes" need not necessarily involve measures that are physically close together, although there are good reasons to suppose that they would. But if areas of the brain that are relatively far apart operated in unison in "demanding" blood, this could appear as a systematic relationship indicating a particular process. As was suggested in the last section, the methods of PLS are designed to indicate which of these kinds of models best represents observed relationships.

Results from our exploratory analyses suggested that all the ISI measures are indicative of blood flow throughout the brain. This is consistent with other findings (Hagstadius and Risberg, 1983). But a simple structure metatheory about the data also appeared to be appropriate. Five common-factor latent variables were indicated. The patterns of relationships indicated these variables were very similar on each side of the brain.

Figure 14–2, previously discussed, contains results that illustrate the conclusions we just stated. The explicit numbers within arrows in this figure are parameter estimates for directed relationships obtained with data from 841 subjects. Age, pC02, several conditions of measurement, and dummy variable representations of clinical diagnoses were controlled in the manner we described previously. (To minimize clutter, these relationships, and all relationships smaller than 0.3, have been excluded from the figure.) The parameter estimates were obtained under the constraints of the Equamax criterion (Crawford and Ferguson, 1970; Saunders, 1960). This is a simple structure metatheory that also requires that the variances of the latent variables be as nearly equal as is possible and that the intercorrelations be zero among these latent variables. These requirements were imposed on the latent variables on the far-right in the figure. We required in addition that if a directed relationship for these latent variables had been smaller than 0.15 in the exploratory analyses based on an Equamax metatheory, that relationship would not be estimated (would be modeled to be zero) in the analysis of Figure 14–2. The parameter estimates for both the left (L) and right (R) hemispheres were obtained in a single analysis, rather than separately.

Because the sample size is large, it is easy to reject (using a likelihood ratio or chi-square test) the notion that the model of the figure is precisely the model for these data. But the residuals for this solution are small (average .016), and the Bentler-Bonett (1980) and Tucker-Lewis (1973) indices of reliability are high, indicating that the model is probably a reasonably good approximation of a model that accounts for different gatherings of comparable data—i.e., is replicable.

It is almost an epistemological question, but one can ask if it is reasonable to suppose that any particular model should precisely represent all samples. A model of the form shown Figure in 14–2 might provide a reasonable approximation to the model for any sample, but models that fit particular samples should perhaps vary in nonrandom ways, reflecting different conditions operating in each sample (Horn and Engstrom, 1979; Meredith, 1964; Horn, et al., 1983; McArdle, 1984). Figure 14–3 has been drawn to give credence to this idea. It suggests how models that fit the data of particular samples vary from one sample to another.

The figure is a distillation of results from several different analyses on several different samples of the total sample of 841 subjects. Different kinds of latent variables, corresponding to different levels of abstraction, are represented in it. The "purged" ISI latent variables of Figure 14–2 are represented as circles, some large, some small. The enclosed groupings of these circles correspond to the latent variables represented with large circles in Figure 14–2, but here it is suggested that these be regarded as bracketed groupings, rather than as circles. This represents a finding that some ISI measures are more surely indicators of the large-circle latent variables of Figure 14–2 than are other ISI measures. In looking at the results from different analyses with different samples, one sees that the groupings are stable, but the ISI variables represented by large circles in Figure 14–3 are more consistently highly related to the latent variables of "their" groupings than are the ISI variables represented by small circles. It is as if the variables represented by large circles are near the center of gravity of the particular (neural) function of the grouping, while the variables represented by small circles are between such centers of gravity and thus can be drawn mainly to one or another of the center of gravity functions, depending on the perturbations produced in a particular sample of subjects and observational conditions.

This suggests that neurological organizations are located approximately in the regions of the separate latent variables on the right in Figure 14–2, but we should not expect to pinpoint the location of these organizations because the resolution of the measures is limited and many influences operate in many different ways from one sample of data to another. The bracketings of Figure 14–3 indicate, roughly, where the organizations are centered.

Age in our sample ranged from the early 20s to the late 70s; most of

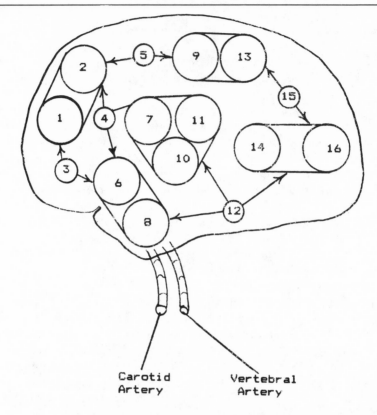

The areas that enclose the large circles represent the "cores" of latent variables that indicate separate functions. The small circles represent "blinker" detectors—i.e., they "blink" in two or three different directions and, depending on influences operating in particular samples of observations, may mainly align with one or another of the "core" organizations at which they "blink."

Figure 14-3. Stable organization among rCBF measures.

the subjects were between 30 and 60 years of age. All 32 of the ISI measures had significant correlations with age. These correlations ranged from -23 to -58; the negative sign of the coefficients indicates that the greater the age, the lower the blood flow.

The patterns of the ISI relationships with age varied systematically in accordance with the models presented in Figures 14–2 and 14–3. Most of the common covariability with age centered around the latent variables labeled SF and MD in Figure 14–2. This is shown in Figure 14–4 for a representation like that of Figure 14–3. The pCO_2 relationship is also shown in Figure 14–4.

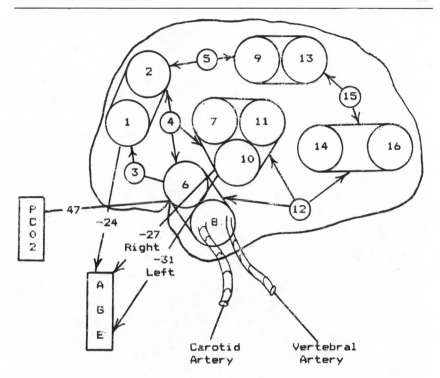

Figure 14-4. Relation of age and pCO₂ to blood-flow latent variables

Root mean squares:		Communality	= .921
Residuals: Theta	.016	Tucker-Lewis	= .83
Psi	.031	Bentler-Bonnet	= .85

What this figure means is that when all the relationships are considered in the model of Figure 14–2, SF and MD are found to be central to the common covariance between age and the blood flow measures. The relationships for the left and right hemispheres are essentially the same, so only one relationship is given for pCO_2 and the age relation to FS. But to suggest the order of difference between relations for the two hemispheres, the two estimates for MD have been included in the figure.

These findings are, for the most part, in agreement with the results obtained by Hagstadius and Risberg (1983, and more recent, unpublished work). In their 1983 study Hagstadius and Risberg found aging decreases for all ISI measures, as here, but no significant differences between the aging decreases of different ISI measures. The age range was narrower and the sample size smaller in that study than in the present investigation. (The sample size of the present study is larger than in any previous work; there is considerable power to detect differences.) In their recent studies Hagstadius and Risberg have increased the size and age range of their sample. Under these conditions they have found that aging declines are more extreme in the frontal and temporal regions than elsewhere in the brain. These findings thus agree with the results found in the present study using PLS techniques of data analysis.

PLS is well-suited to efficiently take account of all the covariability among all the measures of an analysis. Effects indicated with these procedures can be noteworthy when pair-comparisons for corresponding individual measures are not large and seemingly not noteworthy.

Different kinds of controls also contribute to the findings of the present study. There was statistical control for whether or not a subject had a diagnosis of illness, for differences in these diagnoses and for a number of other variables that could (if they were not controlled) produce different forms of variation. Although the effects achieved with any one of these controls were usually small (but notice the relation for pCO_2 in Figure 14–4), collectively such controls can substantially refine data—i.e., reduce "noise." We have found this to be true in a number of rather diverse studies (e.g., Horn, 1973; Horn and Cattell, 1982; Horn, Donaldson and Engstrom, 1981; Horn, Wanberg and Adams, 1974; Hundal and Horn, 1977; Rossman and Horn, 1972; Stankov and Horn, 1980).

SUMMARY

Correlational analyses of ISI measures obtained at 32 different locations in the brain indicate the cohesiveness of blood flow throughout the brain; PLS analyses of these measures indicate the following five distinct functions corresponding to separate sections of the brain: SF, superior frontal; PT, parietal; OC, occipital; UF, underside frontal; and MD, middiagonal. MD best represents the first principal component of covariance among all the ISI measures. There is aging decrease in blood flow throughout the brain, but there is a multivariate sense in which this decline is focused in functions represented by SF and MD. The neural processes associated with these latent variables appear to be particularly susceptible to damage resulting from decrease in blood flow to the brain.

Such decrease could come about for any one of many reasons. If only random processes produced decrease, then the longer one lived, the more chances there would be to experience a decrease. For this reason alone—if there were no necessary maturational decline—older persons, relative to younger ones, would be expected to show decrement in the neural functions that are most affected by decreased blood flow to the brain.

The effects indicated in this study need not be unique to aging. Effects associated with aging could be brought about by factors that are not intrinsic to aging, *per se*. Also, of course, a probabilistic association is not necessarily indicative of an inevitable relation.

The pattern of the evidence adumbrated in this study is compatible with a hypothesis that periodic decreases in blood flow to the brain reduce neurologic activation capabilities, probably in the Ht and peripheral sections of the brain more than in other regions, and this is responsible for at least some aging decline of Gf (reasoning) and SAR (short-term apprehension and retrieval) abilities. The aging of Gf abilities is associated with a decline in capacities for maintaining close concentration, holding attention on target, remaining spontaneously aware, educing relations, and encoding these relations for relatively long-term retention.

REFERENCES

Bentler, P., and D. Bonett. 1980. Significance tests and goodness of fit in the analysis of covariance structures. *Psychological Bulletin*, 588–606.

Birren, J. 1974. Psychophysiology and speed of response. *American Psychologist* 29:808–815.

Birren, J., R. Butler, S. Greenhouse, *et al.* 1963. Interdisciplinary relationships: Interrelations of physiological, psychological and psychiatric findings, in healthy elderly men. In publication 986 of *Human aging I, a biological and behavioral study*, eds. J. Birren, R. Butler, S. Greenhouse *et al.*, 283–305. Washington, D.C.: United States Government Printing Office, United States Department of Health Education and Welfare.

Blalock, H. 1971. *Causal models in the social sciences*. Chicago: Aldine-Atherton.

Bolmsjo, M. 1981. *The physical and physiological aspects of Xenon isotopes in nuclear medical applications*. Lund: Lund University.

Brierly, J. 1976. Cerebral hypoxia. In *Greenfield's neuropathology*, eds. W. Blackwood and J. Corsellis 331-342, London: Arnold.

Broadbent, D. 1966. The well ordered mind. *American Educational Research Journal* 3:281-295.

Buell, S., and P. Coleman. 1981. Quantitative evidence for selective dendritic growth in normal human aging but not in senile dementia. *Brain Research* 214:23–41.

Butters, N., and L. Cermak. 1975. Some analyses of amnesic syndromes in brain-damaged patients. *The Hippocampus* 2:377–409.

Cattell, R. 1971. *Abilities: Their structure, growth and action.* Boston: Houghton-Mifflin.

Conn, H. 1955. Measurement of organ blood flow without sampling. *Journal Clinical Investigation* 34:916.

Corsellis, J. 1976. Aging and the dementias. In *Greenfield's neuropathology*, eds. W. Blackwood and J. Corsellis, 652-684. London: Arnold.

Craik, F. 1977. Age differences in human memory. In *Handbook of the psychology of aging*, eds. J. Birren and K. Schaie, 384-420. New York: Van Nostrand Reinhold.

Crawford, C., and G. Ferguson. 1970. A general rotation criterion and its use in orthogonal rotation. *Psychometrika* 35:321–332.

Creasey, H., and S. Rapoport. 1985. The aging human brain. *Annals of Neurology* 17:2–10.

Cronbach, L. 1976. *Essentials of psychological testing.* 3d ed. 1970 New York: Harper and Row.

Drachman, D., and J. Arbit. 1966. Memory and the Hippocampal Complex II. Is memory a multiple process? *Archives of Neurology* 15:52–61.

Duara, R., R. Margolin, E. Robertson-Tchabo, *et al.* 1983. Cerebral glucose utilization as measured with positron emission tomography in 21 resting healthy men between the ages of 21 and 83 years. *Brain* 106:761–775.

Duncan, O. 1975. *Introduction to structural equation models.* New York: Academic Press.

Eccles, J. 1977. *The understanding of the brain.* New York: McGraw-Hill.

Ekstrom, R., J. French, and M. Harman. 1979. *Cognitive factors: Their identification and replication.* Multivariate Behavioral Research Monographs. Fort Worth: Texas Christian University Press.

Fornell, C., ed. 1982. *A second generation of multivariate analysis. Vol. 1, Methods.* New York: Praeger.

Goldberger, A., and O. Duncan. 1973. *Structural equation models in the social sciences.* New York: Seminar Press.

Gruzelier, J. 1984. Individual differences in the aging brain: Comments on studies of cerebral blood flow. *The Thirteenth International Conference on the Unity of the Sciences.* Washington, D.C.: Paragon House Publishers.

Gustafson, L., J. Risberg, M. Johanson, and A. Brun. 1984. Evaluation of organic dementia by regional cerebral blood flow measurements and clinical and psychometric methods. *Monographs in Neural Sciences* 11:11–117.

Hachinski, V. 1980. Relevance of cerebrovascular changes in mental functions. *Mechanisms of Aging and Development* 10:1–11.

Hagstadius, S., and J. Risberg. 1983. The effects of normal aging on rCBF during resting and functional activation. *rCBF Bulletin* 6:116–120.

Heise, D. 1975. *Causal Analysis*. New York: Wiley.

Herzog, C., W. Schaie and K. Gribbon. 1978. Cardiovascular disease and changes in intellectual functioning from middle to old age. *Journal of Clinical Psychology* 33:872–883.

Hoedt-Rasmussen, K., and E. Skinhoj. 1966. *In vivo* measurements of the relative weights of gray and white matter in the human brain. *Neurology* 16:515–520.

Horn, J. 1970. Organization of data on life-span development of human abilities. In *Life-span development psychology,* eds. L. Goulet and P. Baltes, 423–466. New York: Academic Press.

Horn, J. 1972. State, trait and change dimensions of intelligence. *British Journal of Educational Psychology* 42:159–185.

Horn, J. 1973. On extension analysis and its relation to correlations between variables and factor scores. *Multivariate Behavioral Research* 8:477–489.

Horn, J. 1975. Psychometric studies of aging and intelligence. In *Aging Vol. 2, Genesis and treatment of psychologic disorders in the elderly,* eds. S. Gershon and A. Raskin, 19–43. New York: Raven.

Horn, J. 1976. Human abilities: A review of research and theories in the early 1970s. *Annual Review of Psychology* 27:437–85.

Horn, J. 1982. The aging of human abilities. In *Handbook of developmental psychology,* ed. B. Wolman, 847–869. New York: Prentice Hall.

Horn, J. 1982. Whimsy and misunderstandings of GF-Gc theory. *Psychology Bulletin* 91:623–633.

Horn, J. 1985. Remodeling old models of intelligence: GF-Gc theory. In *Handbook of intelligence,* ed. B. Wolman, 264–300. New York: Wiley.

Horn, J. 1986. Intellectural ability concepts. In *Advances in the psychology of human intelligence,* Vol. 3, 35–77. Hillsdale: Erlbaum.

Horn, J., and J. McArdle. 1980. Perspectives on mathematical statistical model building (MASMOB) in research on aging. In *Aging in the 1980s,* ed. L. Poon, 503–541. Washington, D.C.:American Psychological Association.

Horn, J., and G. Donaldson. 1980. Cognitive development in adulthood. In *Constancy and change in human development,* eds. O. Brim and J. Kagan, 445–529. Cambridge: Harvard University Press.

Horn J., and R. Engstrom. 1979. Cattell's screen test in relation to Bartlett's chi-square test and other observations on the number of factors problem. *Multivariate Behavioral Research* 14:283–300.

Horn, J., and J. Knapp. 1973. On the subjective character of empirical base of Guildord's structure-of-intellect model. *Psychological Bulletin* 80:33–43.

Horn, J., G. Donaldson, and R. Engstrom. 1981. Apprehension, memory and fluid intelligence decline in adulthood. *Research on Aging* 3:33–84.

Horn, J., K. Wanberg, and G. Adams. 1974. Diagnosis of alcoholism. *Quarterly Journal of Studies on Alcohol,* 147–175.

Hundal, P., and J. Horn. 1977. On the relationships between short-term learning and fluid and crystallized intelligence. *Applied Psychological Measurement* 1:11–21.

Jöreskog, K. 1967. Some contributions to maximum likelihood factor analysis. *Psychometrika* 32:443–482.

Jöreskog, K. 1969. A general approach to confirmatory maximum likelihood factor analysis. *Psychometrika* 34:183–202.

Jöreskog, K., and D. Sörbom. 1977. Statistical models and methods for analysis of longitudinal data. In *Latent variables in socioeconomic-models,* eds. D. Aigner and A. Goldberger, 285–325. Amsterdam: North Holland.

Jöreskog, K., and D. Sörbom. 1978. *LISREL-IV: Analysis of linear structural relationships by the method of maximum likelihood.* Chicago: National Educational Resources, Incorporated.

Kety, S., and C. Schmidt. 1978. The nitrous oxide method for the quantitative determination of cerebral blood flow in man: theory, procedure and normal values. *Journal of Clinical Investigation* 27:476–483.

Lassen, N., D. Ingvar, and E. Skinhoj. 1978. Brain function and blood flow. *Scientific American* 239:62–71.

Lohmöller, J. 1981. *LVPLS 1.6 program manual: Latent variables path analysis with partial least squares estimation (Forschungsbericht 81.04 Fachbereich Padagogik).* München: Hochschule der Bundeswehr.

Lohmöller, J., and H. Wold. 1982. Introduction to PLS estimation of path models with latent variables, including developments on mixed scales variables. In *Cultural Indicators for the Comparative Study of Culture,* eds. G. Melischek, K. Rosengren and J. Stappers, 501–509. Vienna: Oesterreichische Academie der Wissenschaften.

Mallett, B., and N. Veall. 1965. The measurement of regional cerebral clearance rates in man using Xenon-133 inhalation and extracranial recording. *Clinical Scientist* 29:179–191.

Maximillian, V. 1980. *Functional changes in the cortex during mental activation.* Malmö, Sweden: CWK Gleerup.

McArdle, J. 1979. The development of general multivariate software. In *Proceedings of the Association for the Development of Computer-Based Instructional Systems, Annual Meeting,* 824–862. Akron: University of Akron Press.

McArdle, J. 1984. On the madness in his methods: Catell, R. Contributions to structural equation modeling. In *A Slim Volume: An evaluation of the evolu-*

tion of a psychological theory, ed. J. Horn, 245–267. Fort Worth: Multivariate Behavioral Research.

McArdle, J. 1985. The development of general equation modeling software. In *The second handbook of multivariate experimental psychology,* eds. J. Nesselroade and R. Catell, 561–614. New York: Plenum Press.

McArdle, J., and R. McDonald. 1984. Some algebraic properties of the reticular action model for moment structures. *British Journal of Mathematical and Statistical Psychology* 18:1–18.

McDonald, R. 1978. A simple comprehensive model for the analysis of covariance structures. *British Journal of Mathematical and Statistical Psychology* 31:59–72.

McDonald, R. 1979. The structural analysis of multivariate data: A sketch of a general theory. *Multivariate Behavioral Research* 14:21–28.

Meredith, W. 1964. Notes on factorial invariance. *Psychometrika* 29:187–185.

Monrad-Krohn, G., and S. Refsom. 1964. *The Clinical Examination of the Nervous System.* London: H.K. Lewis.

Nandy, K., and K. Sherwin, eds. 1977. *The Aging Brain and Senile Dementia.* New York: Plenum.

Obrist, W., H. Thompson, C. King, and H. Wang. 1967. Determination of regional cerebral blood flow by inhalation of 133-Xenon. *Circulation Research* 20:124–135.

Obrist, W., H. Thompson, H. Wang, and W. Wilkenson. 1975. Regional cerebral blood flow estimated by 133-Xenon inhalation. *Stroke* 6:245–256.

Parsons, O. 1975. Brain damage in alcoholics: Altered states of unconscious. In *Alcoholism: Clinical experimental research,* ed. M. Gross, 51–60.

Prohovnik, I. 1980. *Mapping brainwork.* Malmö, Sweden: CWK Gleerup.

Reese, H. 1977. Memory development through the lifespan. In *Brennpunkle der Entwicklungspsychologie,* ed. L. Montada, 167–185. Stuttgart: Kohlhammer.

Risberg, J., Z. Ali, E. Wilson, E. Wills, and J. Halsey. 1975. Regional cerebral blood flow by Xenon-133 inhalation: Preliminary evaluation of an initial slope index in patients with unstable flow compartments. *Stroke* 6:142–148.

Risberg, J., B. Uzzell, and W. Obrist. 1977. Spectrum subtraction technique for minimizing extracranial influence on cerebral blood flow measurements by Xenon-133 inhalation. *Stroke* 8:380–382.

Risberg, J. 1980. Regional cerebral blood flow measurements in 133-Xenon inhalation: Methodology and applications in neuropsychology and psychiatry. *Brain and Language* 9:9–34.

Risberg, J., and L. Gustafson. 1983. Xe cerebral blood flow in dementia and in neuropsychiatry research. In *Functional radionuclide imaging of the brain,* ed. P. Magistretti, 151–159. New York: Raven Press.

Risberg, J., and S. Hagstadius. 1983. Effects on the regional cerebral blood flow of long-term exposure to organic solvents. *Acta Psychiatrika Scandinavia* 67:92–99.

Risberg, J., and I. Prohovnik. 1983. Cortical processing of visual and tactile stimuli studied by non-invasive rCBF measurements. *Human Neurobiology* 2:5–10.

Risberg, J., L. Gustafson, and I. Prohovnik. 1981. rCBF measurements by 133-Xenon inhalation: Applications in neuropsychology and psychiatry. *Progress in Nuclear Medicine* 7:82–94.

Rossman, B., and J. Horn. 1972. Cognitive, motivational and temperamental indicants of creativity and intelligence. *Journal of Educational Measurement* 9:265–286.

Saunders, D. 1960. A computer program to find the best-fitting orthogonal factors for a given hypothesis. *Psychometrika* 25:199–205.

Shaw, T., K. Mortel, J. Meyer, R. Rogers, J. Hardenberg, and M. Cutaia. 1984. Cerebral blood flow changes in benign aging and cerebrovascular disease. *Neurology* 34:855–862.

Sperling, G. 1964. *The information available in a brief visual presentation.* Psychological Monographs 74. Washington, D.C.: The American Psychological Association.

Stankov, L. 1980. Ear differences and implied cerebral lateralization on some auditory factors. *Applied Psychological Measurement* 4:21–38.

Stankov, L., and J. Horn. 1980. Human abilities revealed through auditory tests. *Journal of Educational Psychology* 72:21–44.

Stone, M. 1974. Cross-validatory choice and assessment of statistical predictions. *Journal of the Royal Statistical Society* B 36:111–147.

Sweet, W., G. Talland, and F. Ervin. 1959. Loss of recent memory following section of fornix. *Transactions of the American Neurological Association* 84:76-79.

Tarter, R. 1975. Psychological deficit in chronic alcoholics: A review. *International Journal of the Addictions* 10:327–368.

Thompson, L. 1976. Cerebral blood flow, EEG and behavior in aging. In *Neurobiology of Aging,* eds. R. Terry and S. Gershon, 141–163. New York: Raven Press.

Thurstone, L. 1947. *Multiple factor analysis.* Chicago: University of Chicago Press.

Tucker, L., and C. Lewis. 1973. A reliability coefficient for maximum likelihood factor analysis. *Psychometrika* 38:1–10.

Turner, E. 1969. Hippocampus and memory. *Lancet* 2:1123–1126.

Wold, H. 1966. Nonlinear estimation by iterative least squares procedures. In *Festschrift for J. Neyman: Research Papers in Statistics,* ed. F. David, 411–444. London: Wiley.

Wold, H. 1966. Estimation of principal components and related models by iterative least squares. In *Multivariate Analysis,* 391–420. New York: Academic Press.

Wold, H. 1980. Model construction and evaluation when theoretical knowledge is scarce. In *Evaluation in economic models,* eds. B. Ramsey and J. Kmenta, 47–74. New York: Academic Press.

Wold, H. 1982. Soft modeling: The basic design and some extensions. In *System under Indirect Observation. Casualty, Structure and Prediction,* Vol. 2, eds. K. Jöreskog and H. Wold, 1–54. Amsterdam: North Holland.

15

Soft Modeling and the Measurement of Biological Shape

FRED L. BOOKSTEIN

SUMMARY

Morphometrics, the study of biological shape and shape change, is based on geometrical deformation as a model for the correspondence of parts that the biologist calls homology. Morphometrics represents forms as polygons of landmarks, points which have a biological characterization as well as a geometric location ("the bridge of the nose, *there* on the x-ray"). In this context, as foreseen by D'Arcy Thompson, the notion of a deformation becomes a latent variable (LV) whose indicators are the set of all size and shape measures, homologous distances and their ratios, that might have been measured.

The simplest possible morphometric data set is the triangle of landmarks. The analytic geometry of change in its shape may be represented using three particular indicators: one size measure together with two normalized Cartesian coordinates embodying all the shape information for the triangle. Once loadings have been estimated for these indicators, we can pass to the construction of a new shape indicator which makes manifest any LV pertaining to the triangle.

For soft modeling of biological shape change, every triangle of landmarks is represented by a first-order latent variable; its block of indicators will eventually be replaced by a single new tensor indicator without loss of information. Deformations of more than three points are second-order LVs estimated as linear combinations of the first-order blocks. The second-order LVs describe correlated changes in all size or shape measures anywhere in the interior of the landmark configuration. From second-order LVs we pass to new indicators by the graphic device of the biorthogonal grid, a coordinate system customized for the representation of deformation.

This essay exemplifies the soft modeling of sets of morphometric indicators, and the generation of new summary indicators, in four empirical contexts: descriptions of mean differences in form for a single triangle and for a set of four landmarks, and extractions of the most stable single dimension of shape for the triangle and for the quadrilateral.

From this application of soft modeling I draw a recommendation for its other applications. The relation between indicators and latent variables should not be a one-way passage; rather, one returns from the estimation of a soft model with notions about indicators more appropriately aligned with the LVs unearthed, indicators to be measured before the next data analysis. When a latent variable bears a puzzling pattern of signs, for instance, one should search for a new indicator which, by analogy with the role of shape variables in morphometrics, adumbrates the apparent contrast as precisely as possible by amplifying discrepancies. Over cycles of modeling and subsequent remeasurement, latent variables should become steadily more manifest, steadily more explanatory.

1. THE COMPARISON OF BIOLOGICAL FORMS AS A LATENT VARIABLE

In his classic *On Growth and Form* of 1917, the great British natural philosopher D'Arcy W. Thompson introduces the study of form-comparisons thus:

> ...The morphologist, when comparing one organism with another, describes the differences between them point by point, and "character" by "character." If he is from time to time constrained to admit the existence of "correlation" between characters..., yet all the while he recognizes this factor of correlation somewhat vaguely, as a phenomenon due to causes which, except in rare instances, he can hardly hope to trace; and he falls readily into the habit of thinking and talking of evolution as though it had proceeded on the lines of his own descriptions, point by point, and character by character.

...But when the morphologist compares one animal with another, point by point or character by character, these are too often the mere outcome of artificial dissection and analysis. Rather is the living body one integral and indivisible whole, in which we cannot find, when we come to look for it, any strict dividing line even between the head and the body, the muscle and the tendon, the sinew and the bone. Characters which we have differentiated insist on integrating themselves again; and aspects of the organism are seen to be conjoined which only our mental analysis had put asunder. The coordinate diagram throws into relief the integral solidarity of the organism, and enables us to see how simple a certain kind of correlation is which had been apt to seem a subtle and a complex thing.

But if, on the other hand, diverse and dissimilar fishes can be referred as a whole to identical functions of very different co-ordinate systems, this fact will of itself constitute a proof that variation has proceeded on definite and orderly lines, that a comprehensive "law of growth" has pervaded the whole structure in its integrity, and that some more or less simple and recognizable system of forces has been in control (Thompson, 1961 (1917), pp. 274–275).

In this manner Thompson explicitly identifies the object under discussion, namely the relationship between biological forms, with a latent variable (LV): an abstraction for the efficient explanation of diverse, covarying comparisons distributed over the organism. His identification of this LV with a "system of forces" reflects the biomechanical understanding typical of his era, obsolete now; what remains, the idea of a "simple and recognizable" geometrical pattern of explanation (Figure 15–1), has fascinated mathematical biologists and morphologists from Thompson's day to the present.

The endurance of Thompson's insight owes to its felicitous blending of two previously unrelated descriptive traditions. The latent variable of which he speaks had hitherto been studied in biology and in mathematics separately, where it went by two different names. The biologist knew it as *homology*, the rules by which parts of different organisms were understood to correspond, whereas the mathematician knew it as the pointwise *deformation*, "Cartesian transformation," acting to distort a picture plane or other specifically geometric representation of form. The identification of these two formal models in the study of a single empirical problem lies at the foundation of modern morphometrics (Bookstein, 1982a; Bookstein *et al.*, 1985).

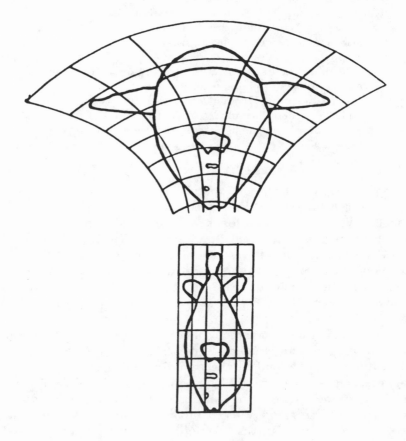

Figure 15–1. Cartesian transformation from Diodon to Mola, after Thompson (1961).

1.1. Landmarks.

To reliably quantify the forms of organisms varying in shape, the biologist needs to pass from a homology of *parts* to one of (mathematical) *points*. The observed form is thereby abstracted into a configuration of *landmarks* having both a geometric location and a biological identification: for instance, "the bridge of the nose, *there* on the x-ray." The two attributes correspond to the two sources of information combined in the LV model. Each landmark, located in all the forms of a series, is a systematic one-point sample of the homology function. For instance, the bridge of *this* nose is homologous to the bridge of *that* nose, by definition, and so the point-deformation which is the homology of these two x-rays must map this point to that one.

Such a representation of deformation, the mention of one point at a time along with its image, is mathematically clumsy. From configurations of landmarks the researcher usually passes directly to an explicit homology function by an interpolation that is smooth in between the landmarks at which it is observed (Bookstein, 1978). For empirical comparative studies of biological form, a LV may thus be operationalized as a geometrically smooth effect on shape: a systematic shape difference spatially distributed over the interior of a configuration of N homologous landmarks. Because a LV is an explicit deformation, we will be able to diagram it directly as an effect upon the typical form. In place of dry parameter vectors of inner and outer weights, we will be able to visualize the actual geometrical quantities explained by the LV, the spatial pattern of correlated changes in form.

1.2. Morphometric variables.

In practice, a LV is inseparable from its manifest indicators. What sort of indicators might be appropriate in the study of deformation? One might guess that the natural space of indicators is spanned by the $2N$ Cartesian coordinates of the N landmarks under study. However, it is not biological forms separately that we seek to measure, but relations *between* forms; these are not measured by vectors (two coordinates per point) but by symmetric *tensors* (three parameters per point), as will be explained in Section 2. Although landmark coordinates make up the raw archive of our data, their comparison requires a different, richer set of constructs: the *shape* and *size measures* that can be derived from the coordinate records by manipulations of greater or lesser complexity.

A *size measure* is a function of the landmark coordinates which is linear in geometric scale and which is computed homologously from form to form. Examples include the distances between landmarks in pairs, the distance from one landmark to a point 30 percent of the way from a second to a third, etc. By a *shape measure* we mean, in essence, the ratio of a pair of size measures. Such ratios will be of dimension zero in a geometric scale. The more familiar shape measures are functional transformations of such ratios; for instance, an angle is the arc-cosine of the ratio of distances given by the Law of Cosines. Particular comparisons of form can always be described by a systematic pattern of size measures representing geometrically parallel or perpendicular extents upon the organism—the *biorthogonal grid* to be sketched in Section 3. These patterns encapsulate the LV under study with optimal descriptive efficiency.

2. ANALYSIS OF A SINGLE TRIANGLE OF LANDMARKS

In landmark-based morphometrics, the universe of indicators of form has only a finite number of degrees of freedom. The coefficients of any LV are capable of carrying all the information needed to reconfigure the landmarks appropriately. It is convenient to introduce the study of these LVs and their indicators, the shape and size variables, using a measurement space of the simplest possible structure. When landmarks are taken three at a time, in triangles, there are only three degrees of freedom for form-description: two for shape and one for size. We therefore begin the study of deformation with shape changes of triangles. The LVs which result from conventional soft modeling in this context can be *made manifest* as new indicators, and remain manifest even when we restore size information (the third degree of freedom) to an analysis. The later examples of Section 3 deal with more extensive configurations of landmarks. In these models for LVs, the indicators corresponding to one triangle will make up one first-order LV; the set of these will make up a block of their own, each contributing to the representation of a deformation as a second-order LV.

2.1. Shape coordinates for a triangle.

Shape measures, by definition, are ratios of size measures. In the study of triangles, the most convenient size measures are the lengths of edges. Let us select one edge of the triangle $\triangle ABC$—say, the edge AB—and scale the triangle so that the length of that edge is constant at 1. After scaling so, we may register landmark A at the Cartesian point

(0,0) and landmark B at the point (1,0) (Figure 15–2). If landmark A were originally at (x_A, y_A), B at (x_B, y_B) and C at (x_C, y_C), then the normalization on edge AB assigns landmark C the Cartesian coordinates (v_1, v_2) where

$$v_1 = \frac{(x_B - x_A)(x_C - x_A) + (y_B - y_A)(y_C - y_A)}{(x_B - x_A)^2 + (y_B - y_A)^2},$$

$$v_2 = \frac{(x_B - x_A)(y_C - y_A) - (y_B - y_A)(x_C - x_A)}{(x_B - x_A)^2 + (y_B - y_A)^2}.$$

(15–1)

Because all triangles of the same Euclidean shape will yield the same point (v_1, v_2), all information about the shape of the triangle $\triangle ABC$ must be coded in this coordinate pair.

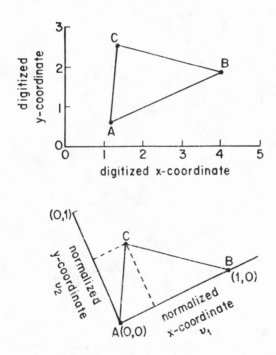

Figure 15–2. One set of shape coordinates of triangle $\triangle ABC$: the coordinates of point C in a Cartesian system with A at (0,0) and B at (1,0).

2.2. One degree of freedom for shape variables.

Consider any shape variable that can be computed from a triangle of landmarks. Figure 15–3a, for instance, illustrates the variable ∠ACB. Considering A and B to be fixed in position, any shape variable is constant on some curve through C; the angle∠ACB happens to be constant along the circle through A, C, and B. Neighboring curves, in this case other circles through A and B, correspond to neighboring, nearly equally spaced values of the shape measure.

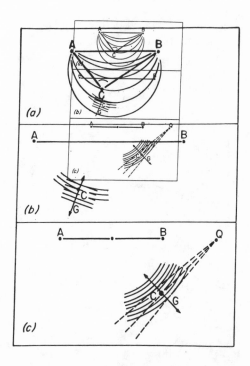

Figure 15–3. The geometry of shape variables in small regions of the shape coordinate plot. (a) Example: isopleths of the shape variable ∠ACB are circles through A and B. (b) Approximating a shape variable by a Cartesian coordinate. The variable is represented by G, the direction of its gradient. (c) All shape variables with the same gradient near a mean form are statistically equivalent. Dashed lines, isopleths of the angle ∠AQC; solid curves, isopleths of distance to the midpoint of AB. These variables are statistically equivalent only near the one point indicated.

In a small region of this plot, this set of curves can be approximated by a family of parallel, equally spaced straight lines, Figure 15–3b. The shape variable varies fastest perpendicular to these curves, in the direction of the axis G, the *gradient* of the shape variable. The smaller the variation in a population of triangles, the better a shape variable is characterized by the direction of its gradient.

There is thus one family of linearly equivalent shape variables for every direction through the point C. For instance, the direction G in Figure 15–3c is the gradient of the angle $\angle AQC$, where Q is the point at 1.5 on the x-axis (in the coordinate system with A at 0 and B at 1). Another measure with the same gradient is the ratio to AB of the distance to the midpoint of AB. These two unfamiliar shape measures are linearly equivalent at C, as are all others bearing the same gradient there.

Every useful shape variable has a gradient in some direction. Since there is a semicircle's worth of directions around any point C, there is only a semicircle's worth of linearly different shape variables in the vicinity of a typical shape $\triangle ABC$. For any two distinct shape gradients G_1, G_2 at C, every other shape variable G is linearly equivalent to (i.e., has the same gradient near C as) some linear combination $aG_1 + bG_2$ of G_1 and G_2.

The effect of changing the choice of baseline—for instance, from $\overline{AB}$ to $\overline{BC}$—is to rotate all three edges $\overline{AB}$, $\overline{BC}$, $\overline{CA}$ of the mean triangle by the same angle, and rescale them all inversely to the change in baseline length. For any triangle, the constructed (v_1,v_2) following this change will differ from the former (v_1,v_2) by that additional rotation together with the same rescaling. Therefore, under change of the choice of baseline, the entire (v_1,v_2) scatter corresponding to a sample of triangles mainly rotates and changes its scale (Bookstein, 1984b). To this order of approximation, any statistical analysis in the (v_1,v_2) plane which is invariant under rotations, translations, and rescaling will yield the same findings whatever baseline was chosen for the construction. Our soft models will all have this property, and hence will represent analysis of shape independent of the (arbitrary) choice of a size measure.

2.3. From gradient to shape variable: making a latent variable manifest.

The obverse of this reduction of shape variables to gradients is the realization of particular gradients by particularly useful shape variables. For triangles, the deformation modeling any statistical summary of change in the configuration may be taken as geometrically *uniform*. Such a deformation may be represented everywhere inside the triangle by the *principal axes* of its *strain tensor*: the directions which bear the greatest and least ratios of change of length between the poles of the comparison. These directions must remain at 90° over the course of the contrast or trend they describe, just as the axes of an ellipse, longest and shortest diameters, lie at 90°. Figure 15–4 summarizes this representation and indicates how the principal strains may be observed directly by reference to two measurable distances upon the form. The shape aspect of this change is best summarized by the change in proportion between these two measured distances; incorporation of information about size change further specifies the ratios of change for the distances separately.

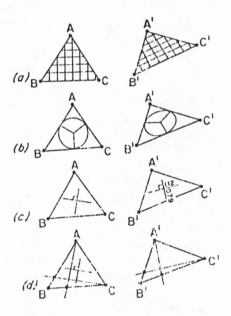

Figure 15–4. Homogeneous deformation as a symmetric tensor.
   (a) The uniform shear of triangles suggested by two sets of three landmarks. (b) Rates of change of length in various directions may be represented by the radii of the ellipse into which a circle is deformed. (c) The principal axes of deformation are the principal diameters of this ellipse, and the principal strains are proportional to their lengths. The corresponding diameters of the circle are perpendicular as well. (d) Because the principal axes have only direction, not location, they may be indicated by using transects through vertices each dividing the edge opposite in a computed ratio. Distances specified in this way are homologous from form to form according to the uniform deformation in (a) above. The ratio between them is the observable proportion most sensitive to this particular shape change.

The particular proportion optimally describing an observed mean shape difference in the (v_1, v_2) plane is constructed as in Figure 15–5. A small displacement Δv of the mean form (r,s) in this plane corresponds to a principal cross of length-change ratios differing by $|\Delta v|/|s|$ and oriented at $\pm 45°$ to the angle bisectors between Δv and the baseline (Bookstein, 1984a). Form by form, each of these lengths is measured as a transect from one vertex through a computed aliquot of the opposite edge; as these endpoints correspond according to the model of uniform deformation, the segments are homologous over a sample, and so their lengths are proper size variables. The shape variable which is the ratio of these measured lengths has a gradient precisely along Δv. Whatever the net size change, distances along one of these axes have the algebraically largest mean ratio between poles of the contrast, and those along the other have the algebraically smallest mean ratio, of all distances homologously measured over the set of triangular forms.

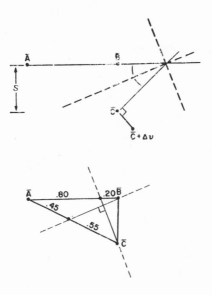

Figure 15–5. Constructing the proportion optimally describing a mean difference of position on the shape coordinate plot.
The example drawn corresponds to the gradient G at point C of Figure 15–3c. (a) From the vector between centroids to the principal cross. (b) From the principal cross to a simple proportion of finite measures. The same result would be obtained by applying the construction of the previous Figure to the deformation from $\triangle ABC$ to $\triangle AB(\overline{C}+\Delta v)$.

In matrix notation, this is the *polar decomposition* for an affine trans-formation (Bookstein, 1978, Chapter 8), its representation as a product $O(\theta')DO^{-1}(\theta)$ of three simple transformations. Each O is a rotation ("O" for "orthogonal") taking principal axes from horizontal and vertical to their orientations as observed in the starting form (θ) or the ending form (θ'), while D is a diagonal matrix of the differential extension ratios along the two perpendicular principal directions. If the analysis is to be drawn upon a single form, as when the second configuration is free to rotate, then the leftmost factor $O(\theta')$ may be omitted.

2.4. Indicators for a single triangle

A sample $\Delta A_iB_iC_i$ of triangular forms may be normalized upon their edges A_iB_i, form by form. Information about the size of $\Delta A_iB_iC_i$ is thereby lost; but the shape of each triangle, unaltered by this maneuver, must be embodied explicitly in the position of the movable vertex C_i. Shape variation of the population of triangles can therefore be studied in the scatter of the points C; after this construction, Figure 15–6a, and shape change may be studied in the scatter of pairs ($C_iC'_i$) at two times, Figure 15–6b.

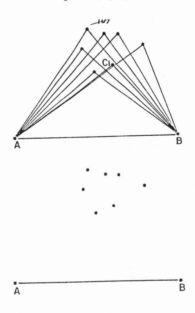

Figure 15–6a. Scatter plots for shape and shape change show in this diagram that a population of shapes may be represented by the scatter of locations of the third vertex after a registration (to various scales) upon the other two vertices.

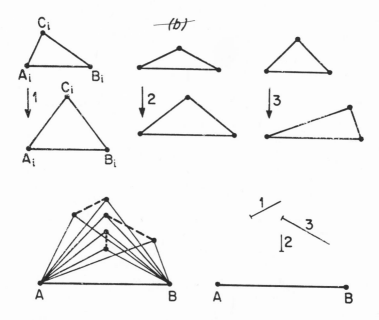

Figure 15–6b. The "pin plot" is depicted in this diagram of scatter plots for shape and change. A population of shape changes may be represented by vectors connecting the two registered locations of that third vertex. The directions of the vectors may be coded by a symbol (the "pinhead") at one end.

To adumbrate a true LV (the mean transformation) having the matrix $DO(\theta)$, a 2x2 matrix, we use as indicators the two vector components $(1,0)L_3O'DO$, $(0,1)L_3O'DO$, where L_3 is the column vector encoding the position of the third landmark using the other two landmarks as the baseline that the rotation O', chosen appropriately, sent to horizontal. From the observation of these two components we can reconstruct D and θ up to the change of scale of the baseline.

In all the soft models that follow, triangle by triangle the shape indicators will be such pairs of coordinates (v_1, v_2). Linear combinations of these will always be sums of simple regressions, Wold's "Mode A," because the gradient directions represented by the shape coordinates v_1, v_2 are always geometrically orthogonal vector components whatever their covariance in a sample; their covariance cannot be interpreted except as a consequence of their joint determination by the LV they embody. The first-order LVs corresponding to these little blocks of two will always be linear predictors of some other variable in the model, whether manifest (size, or age group, or sex) or latent (future shape or shape change). To the formula for the LV on such a block—the weighted combination of v_1 and v_2—corresponds a gradient in the shape space of its triangle. That gradient, playing the role of Δv in the preceding discussion, yields a particular shape measure, the ratio of two distances at 90°, which measures it *perfectly*. Therefore, *to each first-order LV corresponds a new manifest indicator identical with it as estimated case by case.*

Under a suitable null model (Bookstein, 1986), change in perimeter is nearly uncorrelated with the shape coordinates for a variety of triangular configurations. (It is exactly uncorrelated in the case of circular landmark location error for an equilateral triangle.) When size is measured in this way, change in mean size and change in mean shape may be interpreted as separate aspects of the net change observed in a triangle of landmarks, with all coefficients of the soft model to be estimated Mode A. Such an interpretive decomposition is valid even if this size measure is correlated with shape in the sample under study. Alternatively, size may be regressed on shape by using any pair of the (v_1, v_2) coordinates. The result is a canonical description of allometry, the covariance of shape with size, which may be used to predict size from shape or shape from size.

3. THE COMPUTATION OF DEFORMATIONS BY SOFT MODELING

The geometric and algebraic machinery is now entirely in place for describing systematic effects on shape and size in terms of latent variables of deformation. This section presents examples of the soft modeling of deformation for research designs at various levels of geometric or temporal complexity. The examples hint at a wider role for the generation of indicators after estimation, hints expanded on in Section 4.

3.1. Arrow diagrams including triangles

In the models to follow, each first-order LV stands for one triangle and represents a tensor, such as that of Figure 15–4, acting on that triangle. The position of these LVs in the model, together with the role of second-order LVs if any, will vary from example to example. The first-order LVs will be indicated by circles, after the usual semiotics of arrow diagrams; but inside each circle is sketched the triangle which the LV represents. Inside that triangle there will appear, after the model is estimated, a diagram of the manifest shape variable (ratio of a pair of distances at 90°) equivalent to the first-order LV identified.

3.2. A cephalometric data base

In craniofacial biology it is customary to produce x-rays of the bony cranium and jaws in a standardized fashion. The patient's head is placed some six feet from the x-ray tube and a few inches from a film cassette; the central beam of rays passes along the line joining his ear holes and intersects the film plane at 90°. X-ray images result on which edges of anatomical structures can be reliably traced in a conventional abstraction of normal anatomy. For instance, two kinds of curves are used—projections of true space curves, and edges of regression of bony surfaces; and landmark "points" may be true anatomical loci or intersections of shadows. Figure 15–7 shows a stereotyped tracing of the lateral cephalogram, with indications of five landmarks used in the course of the examples. Operational definitions of these points may be found in Riolo *et al.*, 1974.

The data for these four examples are landmark locations from cephalograms taken annually in the course of the University of Michigan University School Study. The sample is of Ann Arbor schoolchildren followed over various age ranges in the 1950s and 1960s.

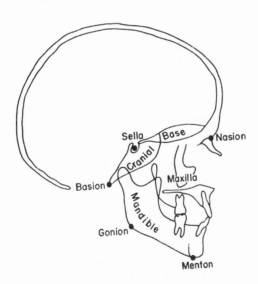

Figure 15–7. Conventional tracing of a lateral cephalogram, showing the structures and landmarks used in the examples. After Riolo et al. (1974).

3.3. Single latent variables

Example 1. Change in mean shape of a single triangle. Figure 15–8a shows the arrow diagram for the analysis of group differences in the shape of a single triangle. So simple a model needs nothing beyond the most elementary methods for its estimation. Application of the soft interpretation in this context, however, will aid in the transition to the second-order LVs which represent nonlinear deformations.

The data for this example represent the form of the triangle Basion-Nasion-Menton in Figure 15–7. This triangle is often used by orthodontists to summarize the so-called *splanchnocranium,* the whole head below the brain. From the University School Study archive we retrieved the coordinates of these three landmarks for a subsample of 36 males with cephalograms at both age 8 (plus or minus six months) and age 14.

The LV embodying the form of this triangle bears three indicators: the perimeter of the triangle and the coordinates of Menton in a system with Basion at $(0,0)$ and Nasion at $(1,0)$ (cf. Figure 15–8a). The scatter of these shape coordinates at the two ages is displayed in Figure 15–8b. For all these analyses, age is coded by a single dummy variable, "Age gp," that takes the value 0 for the 8-year-olds and 1 for the 14-year-olds.

We estimate our "soft model" using the covariance matrix between age and the indicators of the LV:

	Age gp	v_1	v_2	Size
Age gp	.25			
v_1	-.00004	.00382		
v_2	-.01633	-.00003	.00262	
Size	.03312	-.00073	-.00235	.00597

The outer weights for the LV embodying the change of form over time are estimated by mode-A regression of age upon the indicators of its block. They are just the quotients of the entries in the first column by .25: (-.0001, -.0653, .1325), equal, of course, to the differences in means of the indicators between the groups.

As indicated in Figure 15–8c, the proportion making the shape LV manifest is essentially the aspect ratio of the triangle under consideration, the ratio of its height (distance of Menton from the Basion-Nasion baseline) to its base (the distance Basion-Nasion). The dominance of this direction in facial growth has been known to craniofacial biologists for some time (Bookstein, 1983). Because size information is present as a third indicator for this first-order block, the net rates of growth observed

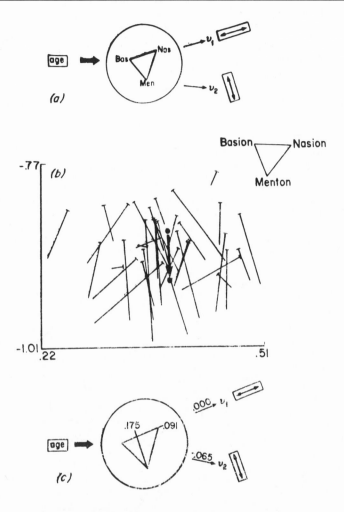

Figure 15–8. Change in mean shape of a single triangle. (a) Arrow diagram with one triangle. The indicators of the LV here, representing the mean shape change, are the two Cartesian coordinates of the landmark Menton in a coordinate system fixing Basion at (0,0) and Nasion at (1,0). (b) The complete data set: location of Menton in a Basion-Nasion coordinate system, for 36 males at ages 8 (heads of pins) and 14 (tails of pins). The solid vector connects the age-specific centroids; it is the LV we seek. (c) Arrow diagram after estimation Mode A. The vector of mean shape change given by the outer weights has been interpreted as a cross of perpendicular distances across the triangle according to the construction of Figure 15–5. Size change is restored to the mean ratios of change in distance along these directions.

in the two principal directions may be computed separately and indicated directly upon the diagram: .091 along the base, .175 along the "growth axis." The coefficient .132 of change in "size" (perimeter) is very nearly the average of these.

EXAMPLE 2. CHANGE IN MEAN SHAPE OF A POLYGON.

When there are more than three landmarks under study, the first-order LVs representing triangles one by one must be treated as indicators of a second-order LV representing "the transformation as a whole," the smooth deformation to which Thompson was referring. In this example we continue to analyze a mean change of shape over age, so as to ease the assimilation of the findings; but we consider a mosaic of triangles instead of just one.

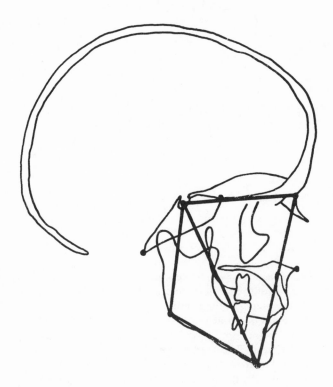

Figure 15–9a. Change in mean shape of a polygon shown through a quadrilateral and one triangulation.

Figure 15–9a shows a polygon from the *mandibular plane* to the *cranial* base, divided into two triangles Sella-Menton-Nasion, Sella-Menton-Gonion (see Figure 15–7) along a convenient diagonal which happens to be close to the growth direction unearthed in the previous analysis. The arrow diagram for this model is as in Figure 15–9b: the single exogenous variable, age, is presumed to drive a pattern of correlated shape changes throughout the form.

The covariance matrix relating the four shape indicators (two per triangle) and age is:

	Age gp	$v_{1,Nas}$	$v_{2,Nas}$	$v_{1,Gon}$	$v_{2,Gon}$
Age gp	.25				
$v_{1,Nas}$	-.00484	.00142			
$v_{2,Nas}$	-.01196	.00024	.00153		
$v_{1,Gon}$	.00144	.00005	-.00021	.00061	
$v_{2,Gon}$	-.00524	-.00018	.00037	-.00004	.00078

Again the outer weights are just the mean differences in shape coordinate between the groups: (-.01936,-.04783) for the first triangle, (.00573,-.02095) for the second.

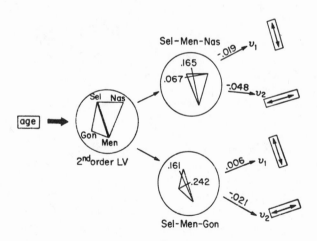

Figure 15–9b. Arrow diagram for the second-order LV that is the mean shape change of a polygon, with first-order LVs (the separate triangles), after estimation. Size change is restored to distances in the principal directions as in the previous example.

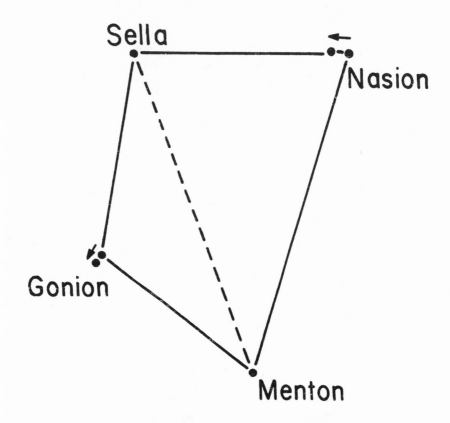

Figure 15–9c. The change in mean shape of a polygon is reflected in a reconfiguration specified by the outer weights (here, actual mean shifts). The baseline Sella-Menton is fixed by construction; the tensor analysis is independent of this choice of baseline.

The manifest shape measures corresponding to the LVs for the triangles separately do not appear to be equal. The second-order LV we have just estimated is therefore describing a *nonlinear* shape change. We visualize it by abandoning the finite triangles for the differential point of view (Bookstein, 1978). The estimated second-order LV explicitly specifies a reconfiguration of the landmark coordinates as drawn in Figure 15–9c. Reverting to the spirit of D'Arcy Thompson, we treat these points as a sample of the biological homology function throughout the interior, and interpolate their correspondence by a smooth computation, Figure 15–9d.

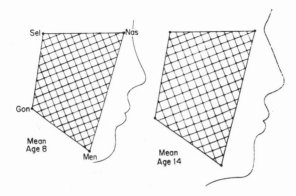

Figure 15–9d. The second-order LV, a smooth deformation corresponding to this reconfiguration in the change in mean shape of a polygon, here drawn as a Cartesian transformation (cf. Figure 15–1).

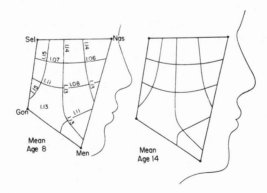

Figure 15–e. Biorthogonal grids for this deformation in the mean shape of a polygon: the coordinate system whose axes intersect at 90° both before and after the deformation. The decimal numbers are selected rates of growth, as the Cartesian transformation imputes them to its principal directions everywhere in the interior.

This picture of the LV is in fact the solution of a partial differential equation. If we write the mapping from left to right as $(x,y) \rightarrow (x',y')$, then the interpolated LV is in fact the solution of the vector partial differential equation

$$\nabla^2 x' = \nabla^2 y' = 0,$$

where ∇^2 is the Laplacian operator $\frac{\partial}{\partial x^2} + \frac{\partial}{\partial y^2}$. Informally, this equation states that there is no information about change of position supplied anywhere interior to the starting quadrilateral: each point there is mapped precisely to the centroid of the locations to which a square of its neighbors is mapped. The observed data, together with the requirement of linearity upon the outside edges of the quadrilateral of landmarks, become *boundary conditions* for the solution of this equation. Solving this system by the methods of linear algebra (Bookstein, 1978) is equivalent to computing loadings of this LV over a greatly enlarged space of indicators, namely, shifts of x- and y-coordinates for each of the mesh points in Figure 15–9d.

At every point of this correspondence there will be a pair of directions which, locally, serve the role of the axes of the ellipse in Figure 15–4: they are the principal axes of the affine derivative, directions of greatest and least local rate of change of length. The import of these crosses for understanding the deformation is considerably weakened by their location upon an arbitrary square mesh having nothing to do with the facts of the deformation under study. The deformation is better apprehended when we integrate the arms of these little crosses into a new coordinate system, the *biorthogonal grid*, which is everywhere parallel to one arm or the other in both forms, and thereby lies at 90° in both. Corresponding intersections of curves in the left and right grids are homologous according to the interpolation in Figure 15–9d. The pair of grids is thus an orthogonal coordinate system customized for representing this particular shape change.

The changes from left to right in the spacing between successive intersections of these grids represent a *symmetric tensor field* distributing the landmark shifts throughout the interior of the form. They depict the *affine derivative* of the map in Figure 15–9c, estimated as a weighted average of the affine derivatives $O(\theta')DO(\theta)$ representing the shifts at each boundary landmark with respect to its two neighbors.

This depiction of the LV in terms of a tensor field, Figure 15–9e, is much more amenable to biological interpretation. The biorthogonal grid indicates the principal features of the shape change independent of the original triangulation: that is, it draws out the second-order LV without further reference to the first-order indicators. The dilations indicated on the drawing are all relative to growth along the baseline Sella-Menton. We see that the overall shape change is highly directional in the maxilla, but less so in the lower face, and that the horizontal rate of growth is graded from top to bottom.

3.4. Several latent variables

Example 3. Forecasting the shape of a single triangle. Consider again the triangle Basion-Nasion-Menton of Example 1. The mean change of shape (Figure 15–8) is statistically significant (Bookstein, 1984a, 1984b), but does not appear to explain much of the data. The "pin plot" connecting corresponding shape coordinate pairs from the first age to the second indicates a considerable stability of relative position in this scatter. It is useful to know, then, exactly how the shape at the earlier age might abet prediction of the shape at the later. The soft model which allows an answer to this question is diagramed in Figure 15–10. The correlations among its indicators are as follows:

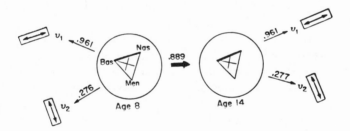

Figure 15–10. Forecasting the shape of a single triangle. Arrow diagram, after estimation, for one triangle at two ages. Note the stability of the estimated weights over six years.

	$v_{1,old}$	$v_{2,old}$	^{Size}old	$v_{1, yng}$	$v_{2,yng}$	^{Size}yng
$v_{1,old}$	1.0					
$v_{2,old}$	.0564	1.0				
^{Size}old	-.3175	-.1471	1.0			
$v_{1, yng}$	.8592	.0266	-.3643	1.0		
$v_{2, yng}$	.1305	.6443	-.0884	-.0532	1.0	
^{Size}yng	-.2909	.1350	.7891	-.2794	-.0309	1.0

Estimation of this model using only the two sets of two shape indicators results in the LVs shown, with weights (.96118,.27593) at the later age, (.96074,.27744) at the earlier. The correlation between these two LVs is 0.889.[1] (The second dimension of this data set yields a correlation much lower, some .62.) For males, one direction of shape variation is distinctly the most reliable, the direction approximately perpendicular to the growth axis. Approximately perpendicular to this gradient is the gradient direction of least shape reliability; here it is aligned closely with the vector from Basion to Menton.

Additional information about size makes the optimal forecasting of shape insignificantly more accurate, although size bears its own strong autocorrelation.

EXAMPLE 4. FORECASTING A MORE COMPLEX CONFIGURATION.

As Example 2 generalized the analysis of Example 1, so we can replace the first-order LVs of the preceding model by second-order LVs assembling diverse triangles. In this example, we use the same pair of triangles that was used in Example 2, and attempt to forecast between the ages as in Example 3. The model we are estimating is shown in Figure 15–11a with all the triangles filled in.

At convergence (Bookstein, 1982b), each LV is the sum of two partial predictors, each involving the indicators of one triangle with a net weight proportional to the strength of that partial prediction. Each partial predictor is the weighted sum of the two indicators for that triangle, with weights proportional to their correlations with the partial predictor. Thus both the combination of indicators into first-order LVs and the combination of the two first-order LVs into each second-order LV proceed without regard for sample correlations: both pairs are treated as conceptually orthogonal. Estimation of this same relationship by canonical correlations analysis—that is, by a single pair of first-order LVs tapping all four indicators equivalently—results in a correlation of .936 but with weight relations which have much less geometrical meaning.

The first-order LVs are approximately parallel between the ages, as shown in the diagram; the weights for the second-order LVs are nearly equal, indicating that predictability is fairly homogeneously distributed over the face. The correlation between the two second-order LVs is .9084.[2] Drawn out in Figure 15–11b, the second-order LVs appear to have a geometry of fair complexity.

The interpolation which distributes this LV throughout the interior of the landmark polygon is as in Figure 15–11c, and is summarized by the biorthogonal grid pair in Figure 15–11d. (Do not be perplexed by the six-sided singularity at the center; it surrounds an *isotropic point* at which the rate of growth is the same in all directions, and always appears when two adjacent sides of a quadrilateral increase in length faster than the diagonals [Bookstein, 1985].) The distance having the highest covariance with this LV is the distance Sella-Gonion; that having the lowest covariance is the segment Nasion-Menton. The shape measure most sensitive to this change, and thus most stable over normal male growth from age 8 to age 14, is not a ratio of perpendicular distances, as in the previous examples, but the ratio of nearly parallel distances Nasion-Sella:Gonion-Menton. The orthodontist knows this as the ratio of *anterior* to *posterior facial height* or, in another geometric guise, the *mandibular plane angle* between the segment Sella-Nasion and the segment Gonion-Menton.

These analytic strategies may all be generalized from data in two dimensions to data in three. The first-order LV representing the shape change of a tetrahedron is now a combination of five indicators, each one the result of premultiplying the true transformation matrix DO (now three-by-three) by an essentially arbitrary vector. Two of these indicators are those we have already been using: the components of the two-dimensional LV for shape change of one face of the tetrahedron. These are augmented by three additional indicators specifying the movement of the tetrahedron's fourth vertex when all three vertices of the face opposite are fixed in position. The visualization of such a LV is carried out by the generalization to three dimensions of the algorithms underlying Figures 15–9c–e or Figures 15–11b–d: conversion of outer weights to landmark shifts, interpolation of a continuous mapping consistent with those shifts and linear between landmarks, and interpretation of that mapping by its principal directions of greatest and least ratios of change in length.

4. TOWARD A CALCULUS OF INDICATORS

To further elaborate the role of soft modeling in morphometrics would render this essay arcane. Instead, in these closing paragraphs I wish to recapitulate one particular theme that speaks to a wider arena than the merely biometric: the role of soft modeling in generating schemes of new measurements.

The relation between indicators and latent variables is not a one-way passage. Through the patterns unearthed by covariance modeling and the interpretation of those patterns, soft modeling deals not only with the covariances of the indicators observed but also with the covariances of

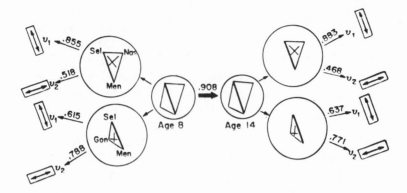

Figure 15–11a. Forecasting the shape of a quadrilateral: an arrow diagram with triangles, after estimation, for the relation of two second-order LVs representing the shape of the quadrilateral at the two ages.

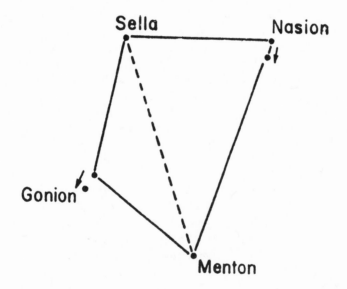

Figure 15–11b. Forecasting the shape of a quadrilateral: reconfiguration (to the baseline Sella-Menton) specified by the outer weights for a small multiple of the indicated latent dimension.

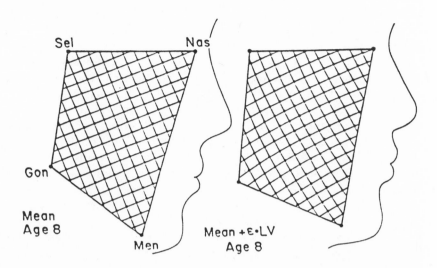

Figure 15–11c. Forecasting the shape of a quadrilateral: Cartesian deformation representing the second-order LV by the relation of the two configurations in the previous frame.

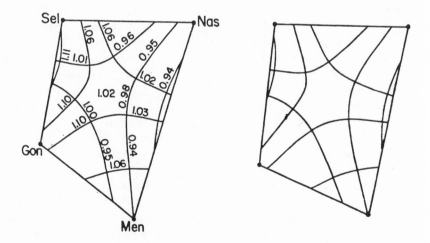

Figure 15–11d. Forecasting the shape of a quadrilateral: biorthogonal grid pair for the deformation of frame (c), with selected ratios. The most stable measure of shape is not a ratio of perpendiculars but a ratio of approximate parallels, Sella-Gonion:Nasion-Menton.

other indicators, indicators which might have been measured. One returns from a soft model with notions about better measurement, if not for this data set, then for the next.

In morphometric modeling there is an infinity of indicators, the size and shape measures, but one does not need them all. The crucial link between latent variables and indicators is the biorthogonal grid of principal strains at 90°. Representation of the LV by its grid, as in Figures 15–9 or 15–11, closes the loop of soft modeling by directing our attention to explicit new indicators which best adumbrate the LV out of all the indicators which could be assayed. The LV is a filter, in other words, which purifies our measurement scheme. In biometrics, the indicators specified in this way—latent variables made manifest—very often correspond to informal clinical knowledge hitherto untestable, and always seem to suggest new hypotheses and explanations.

Now, by virtue of the finite dimension of its subject matter, morphometrics is atypically rich in symmetries and analytic elegances. In other disciplines there are partial substitutes for the powerful analytic geometry of the plane that I have been wielding here: the endless idiosyncrasies of individual social indicators, the semantics of attitude probes, the biases of economic series, and so forth. When a LV bears a contrast between contributions with the same presumptive sense of regression (that is, when the modeling reverses the sign of a simple Pearsonian r), the investigator ought to imagine new variables that directly capture the discrepancies. This is an extension of the role played in biometrics by the preponderance of shape variables. Shape ratios, as explicit contrasts, tend to have far lower confounding correlations than size variables. Size need not appear more than once in an analysis once we have discovered that it is there; likewise, the general factor of a block of indicators, once discovered, needs to be augmented by the patterned contrasts contributing additional predictive power to the model. One must thereupon return to the real world in order to systematically oversample the indicators contributing to these contrasts.

Elsewhere in this volume there is considerable discussion of holistic "versus" reductionistic methods for the analysis of complex systems. I feel the use of the confrontational word "versus" is often based in a mere misunderstanding of the role played by measurement in the scientific activity of modeling. For the analysis of biological shape change, the methods I have proposed here explicitly bridge any gap there may be between the two approaches. If one begins in a reductionist spirit, collecting separate measures of shape change for various subsets of landmarks, the method of grids integrates their separate changes into a single construct, the shape change deformation distributed throughout the interior of the form. But if one begins instead, as Thompson did, with that deformation as the explicit object of study, a LV understood holistically, then, even so, any analysis of the variations of this LV over populations or over time must proceed by way of interpreting the (reduced) outer weights, which express the pattern of spatial covariances among shape coordinates of single triangles. We explain phenomena in terms of latent variables, but perform statistical analyses upon lists of their indicators; when we construe "holism" and "reductionism" in this cooperative spirit, there is no confrontation between them.

In either context, biometrics or the social sciences, the closure of the soft modeling loop is a passage from the covariances of the indicators back to their meaning and their own limitations. That reversal of emphasis serves as a *renewal*, augmenting the information available to the modeler. As such a cycle proceeds, the latent variables will be developed like latent images on a photographic plate: made steadily more manifest, steadily more explanatory. The lesson of biometrics for soft modeling is that one is never finished with measuring.

ACKNOWLEDGEMENT

Preparation of this paper was partially supported by USPHS grants DE–03610 to R.E. Moyers and DE–05410 to F.L. Bookstein. Prof. Herman Wold and the other members of Committee II responded to an earlier draft with many helpful suggestions.

NOTES

[1] As the correlations between the shape coordinates of a single block are mild, these weights do not differ materially from the canonical coefficients estimating the same model by Mode B.

[2] Analysis of the triangles separately, each treated as in Example 2 results in slightly lower correlations: .8966 for the triangle on Nasion, .9041 for that on Gonion.

REFERENCES

Bookstein, Fred L. 1978. *The measurement of biological shape and shape change.* Lecture Notes in Biomathematics, v. 24. New York: Springer.

Bookstein, Fred L. 1982a. Foundations of morphometrics. *Annual Reviews of Ecology and Systematics* 13:451–470.

Bookstein, Fred L. 1982b. The geometric meaning of soft modeling, with some generalizations. In *Systems under indirect observation: Causality, structure, prediction,* Vol. 2, eds. H. Wold and K. Jöreskog, 55–74. Amsterdam: North-Holland.

Bookstein, Fred L. 1983. The geometry of craniofacial growth invariants. *American Journal of Orthodontics* 83:221–234.

Bookstein, Fred L. 1984a. A statistical method for biological shape comparisons. *Journal of Theoretical Biology* 107:475–520.

Bookstein, Fred L. 1984b. Tensor biometrics for changes in cranial shape. *Annals of Human Biology* 11:413-437.

Bookstein, Fred L. 1985. Transformations of quadrilaterals, tensor fields and morphogenesis. In *Mathematical essays on growth and the emergence of form,* ed. P.L. Antonelli, 221–265. Alberta: University of Alberta Press.

Bookstein, Fred L. 1986. Size and shape spaces for landmark data in two dimensions. *Statistical science.* v. 1, 181-242.

Bookstein, Fred L., B. Chernoff, R. Elder, J. Humphries, G. Smith, and R. Strauss. 1985. *Morphometrics in evolutionary biology. The geometry of size and shape change, with examples from fishes.* Philadelphia: Academy of Natural Sciences of Philadelphia.

Riolo, M.L., R.E. Moyers, J.A. McNamara, and W.S. Hunter. 1974. *An atlas of craniofacial growth.* Monograph No. 2, Craniofacial Growth Series, Center for Human Growth and Development. Ann Arbor, Michigan: University of Michigan.

Thompson, D'A.W. *On growth and form* (1917, 1942). Ed. abr. J.T. Bonner. 1961. Cambridge: the University Press.

16

Categorical Data: Methodological Implications, and Analysis in the Field of Social and Cognitive Development

JEAN-LUC BERTHOLET

1. INTRODUCTION

In the last 15 years, many new methods for the analysis of qualitative data have been developed. Henning and Rudinger (1985), among others, have tried to classify these methods. These two authors propose a taxonomy which is composed of three main groups:

1. Latent attribute models (latent class, scalogram analysis...)
2. Prediction models (logit, LISREL, PLS...)
3. Multinomial response models (log-linear model, analysis of correspondence...)

We shall focus in our contribution on the PLS approach to categorical variables. According to Henning's and Rudinger's classification, PLS belongs to the second group of the taxonomy (Prediction models). We shall also emphasize the predictive feature of PLS. On the other hand, Section 2.4 mentions some connection to correspondence analysis which is classified in the third group. This will show that the border between these different groups is not definitely closed.

We shall refer to the conceptual frame of H. Wold (see his introduction in this book). His "E⇔T" scheme fits PLS perfectly, but not only because he is the author of the PLS algorithm. There is another, more elaborate, explanation related to the actual criterion used in qualitative analysis.

Many statistical methods used in the analysis of qualitative data are adapted from models for continuous variables (log-linear models from variance analysis correspondence and factors analysis from linear algebra, and likewise for LISREL and PLS). Thus many questions in the debate on qualitative analysis have been "imported" from the continuous world, for example the discussion about maximum likelihood and least squares. In addition to these well-known questions, one meets those specific to categorical variables, for example the difficulty most models have modeling empty cells in a contingency table.

The "E⇔T" scheme may then help to clarify the discussion in this very difficult context, because it has no direct link to particular methods (e.g., least squares versus maximum likelihood) nor to any particular kind of variable.

Before discussing PLS, let us mention a last problem which sometimes makes the understanding of categorical variable analysis unclear—that the definitions of *qualitative variable* and *categorical variable*. The meanings of these two kinds of data are not unique. For example, looking at the definition of *qualitative data* in the *International Encyclopedia of Statistics*, the reader is invited to refer to two articles: "counted data" and "interviewing in social sciences."

These two definitions show the ambiguity encountered when dealing with qualitative data. For some scientists, these data are nothing other than counted data, whereas for others they may be neither measured nor counted. We think that this confusion is due to simple situations where qualitative data are categories (e.g.: sex, success/failure). Most often qualitative data are only concepts (such as social status, school performance) or even raw material like interviews. These last two examples are clearly not countable, and therefore are far from being operational categories.

The basic problem is how to translate qualitative data into categorical data. More precisely, there are two questions to answer: How many categories are there to define (i.e., how many social levels, or how many themes to extract from an interview), and which criteria to apply for this categorization process. Guilford (1956) says:

> Classification is a basic psychological process which can be seen in rudimentary form even in the simplest conditioned response.[...] Useful classifications for counting purposes, however, depend upon a high type of logical analysis.

Nonetheless Guilford adds one page later that "there is no space here to give instructions on how to choose or construct useful categories."

Guilford's comments show that the discussion about classification pertains more to logic than to statistical methodology. Most statistical methods typically do not take this important question into account. We shall see in the next paragraph how PLS can partly, and, for the time being, incompletely, solve this problem.

A theory (T) more often involves qualitative data than categorical data. For example, a theory may state that the higher the social status of the parents, the more schooling their children will receive; it seldom expresses "a child from the fifth category of social status will often undertake university study."

This short discussion points out that a theory typically is expressed in terms of *qualitative* data whereas the matching, i.e., the statistical procedure, handles only *categorical* data.

Figure 16–1 serves to link our introductory section with the matching scheme E⇔T of Wold (1969).

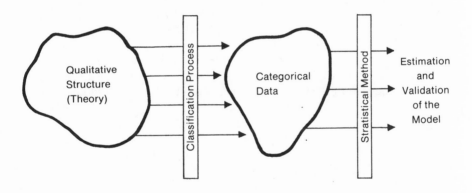

Figure 16–1. From Qualitative Structure to Categorical Data to Model building by way of Classification and Statistical Method.

Having outlined the general context of this paper, we are now in a position to undertake the discussion of some properties of PLS applied to categorical data analysis. Section 2 is a short exposition of PLS and its way of solving the classification problem. Section 3 is a practical example of a psychological model (Guttman scales).

2. PLS AND CATEGORIES

2.1. The matching

Before describing the basic assumptions of PLS, let us briefly recall an important difference between PLS and many other statistical methods: The E⇔T scheme involves the confrontation between theory and data, thereby the evaluation of the ensuing model. A general discussion is given in Chapter 1 of this volume (cf. Wold, 1982). To repeat, the PLS evaluation criterion is the prediction of the data, and not the construction of the covariance structure. The analysis of this proposition in the categorical data context needs further comment.

Many criteria of contingency tables analysis models are built on the ability of the model specification to reproduce the joint frequencies of the tables which are nothing other than the covariance structure. In PLS one does not aim exclusively at the reconstruction of the cells in the table, but also at prediction of the variables in a margin. Let us imagine an example of a two-way contingency table: social levels of parents versus types of apprenticeship of their children. In this case the PLS criterion is: does the knowledge of the social level help to predict the type of the apprenticeship in a better way than the marginal distribution of apprenticeship does? This criterion is very different from that used in other methods, where it is: how good is the estimate of the joint frequency of categories i and j made by means of a set of parameters for these two categories? (Note that PLS could specify such a model, but it would not bring more information than the predictive approach).

To illustrate these two criteria, we may use the scheme in Figure 16–2.

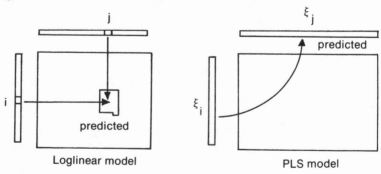

Figure 16–2. The Design of Log-linear and PLS Models Illustrated by Simple Models.

To give a practical numerical example, let us consider an independent contingency table ($f_{ij} = f_i.\ f._j$ where the dots denote the summation over all the indices i or j). Such a table is perfectly described by way of a simple (without interaction) log-linear model, and the resulting criterion coefficient will be optimistic in the sense it will convince the scientist that he has adequately described the data. In PLS, the evaluation coefficient of the same data will be pessimistic because no information on a margin helps to predict the other one. There is no PLS predictive power in that table.

2.2. Basic assumptions in PLS modeling of contingency tables

We are not going to give a general discussion about the technical aspects of PLS; this is to be found in other papers (Wold, 1982/1985). We shall now highlight some principles useful for the present developments (Bertholet and Wold, 1985).

PLS Mode A does not need any adaptation to cope with categorical data. PLS Mode B, because of the inversion of a non-full-rank matrix, needs some minor adaptations which do not at all interfere with the interpretation of the parameters.

The basic relations of PLS are the so-called inner and outer relations. Returning to our example of a two-way table of social level versus type of apprenticeship, we define two outer equations, one for each margin:

$$(16\text{--}1) \quad x_1 = \pi_{01} + \pi_{11}\,\xi_1 + \upsilon_1$$
$$(16\text{--}2) \quad x_2 = \pi_{02} + \pi_{12}\,\xi_2 + \upsilon_2$$

where x_i and π_{ik} are vectors. If there are, say, three categories of social levels, then the x_1 vector has three entries, one for each level. If an observation belongs to the second social category, the transposed vector reads: $x_1' = (0,1,0)$. The x_1 vectors are column vectors of the unity matrix showing to which category an observation belongs. x_2 has, then, as many entries as there are types of apprenticeship. These two vectors are the two blocks of manifest variables in our PLS model. Summing up the products $x_1 x_2'$ over the N observations gives the observed contingency table of the cross classification of social levels and types of apprenticeship. The other parameters, loadings and other unknowns, are those of the usual PLS modeling.

The only change from the scalar presentation of PLS lies in the particular form of the manifest variables which, as we have just seen, take the form of unity matrix vectors. The x_i are introduced in a way that makes them similar to multinomial distributed variables. Taking the expectation of x_i leads to

$$(16\text{–}3) \qquad E(x_i) = \pi_{oi} = \text{vec}(\text{prob }(x_{ik} = 1)) \quad k = 1 \ldots I$$

where I is the number of categories of the ith variable.

π_{oi} is then the vector of the marginal distribution of x_i. Similarly, we define:

$$(16\text{–}4) \qquad E(x_i|\xi_i) = \pi_{oi} + \pi_{1i}\xi_i = \text{vec}(\text{prob }(x_i| \xi_i) = 1))$$

This simple linear relation is the way PLS is extended to categorical data.

The second basic relation in PLS is the inner relation that links the latent variables according to the formal model sketched by the arrow scheme. This relation applies here without any further adaptation. In our two-block model, it reads:

$$(16\text{–}5) \qquad \xi_2 = \beta_{12}\xi_1 + \epsilon_2 \quad \text{with} \quad E[\xi_2| \xi_1] = \beta_{12}\xi_1$$

Hence the PLS arrow scheme is as shown in Figure 16–3.

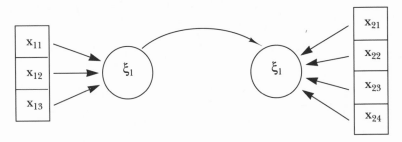

Figure 16–3. Arrow Scheme for Contingency Tables.

2.3. Interpretation of the conditional probability and of the latent variables

One of the most important and critical questions of applying PLS to categorical data is the interpretation of the latent variables. Muthen (1979) noted that latent variables are not new in the categorical data analysis. Some models (logit) take the form

(16–6) $(\text{prob } (x=1 \mid y_1...y_I) = \Phi\left(\sum_{i=1}^{I} \alpha_i\, y_i\right),$

where y_i are observables. Often the linear function of the y_i cannot be justified on formal theoretical grounds. It so happens that the y_i's are completely different in nature; one could relate the probability of success at an examination of school children to the income of their parents, the size of their family, and whatever else. In such a case, the linear form $\Sigma_i\, \alpha_i\, y_i$ may be considered an indirect estimation of a latent variable which measures the influence of parents' income, family size, etc., on the probability of success.

In the PLS framework of contingency tables we propose to interpret the latent variables as the operational representation of an inner model that links the various qualitative variables which are perceived through the contingency table. In PLS, the table is not considered to be a set of cells one tries to reproduce; it is the image of organized flows of information between *qualitative* variables one aims to catch by the use of latent variables.

The fundamental assumption of PLS is the existence of a *path model* that organizes the latent variables. This path model is formulated prior to the categorization. Categories enter at the stage of estimation.

2.4. Stability of the parameters

We said in the introduction that PLS partly meets the problem of categorization. There are many ways to discuss it; one of them is to undertake a discussion about the robustness of PLS for ill-conditioned contingency tables, for example, the mixture of two different populations. We do not have for the time being enough material to fully cover this important question. Some numerical experiments seem promising; they apply to a very simple situation called the Simpson paradox (cf. Wold and Bertholet, 1982).

Another way to proceed in the categorization problem is proposed by Benzecri (1973). His question is: how do the estimated parameters change when one has erroneously created two categories which should not theoretically be split? PLS, like correspondence analysis, will give accurate estimates. The theorem is as follows:

If two rows (or columns) in a contingency table are equal, then the PLS analysis will give the same estimates for this table as for another one in which these two rows (columns) have been aggregated; more precisely:

1. The estimated latent variables and path coefficients are the same in both tables.
2. The loadings of the two split categories are equal; in the new table, the corresponding loading is twice the previous one.

The demonstration is given in the Appendix. The particular shift of the loading in the second table is due to a general property of PLS Mode B: the sum of the loadings in a block is zero; as this property must hold for the new table, the value of the loading has to change.

2.5. Numerical example

Table 16–1 gives an illustrative numerical example based on real-world data, namely the cross classification of 321 apprentices, 14 to 16 years old. They are trained for different kinds of apprenticeship, numbered 1 to 6 (ironworker, engineering, drawer, motor mechanic, hairdresser, and house painter). They are distributed in the second margin of the table according to the social level of their parents in five groups indirectly measured by their income and their hierarchical position.

The table shows the observed frequencies (f_{ij}, i=1. . 6, j=1. . 5). The brackets contain the conditional frequencies for each row ($f_{ij}/f_{i.}$, where the dot is the summation over the five social categories).

Table 16–1

Numerical Example of a Cross Classification

		social levels					
		1	2	3	4	5	
types of	1	10	5	16	0	0	31
apprenticeship		(32)	(16)	(52)	(-)	(-)	
	2	24	10	11	13	9	67
		(36)	(15)	(16)	(19)	(13)	
	3	17	12	7	7	2	45
		(38)	(27)	(16)	(16)	(04)	
	4	44	10	28	6	1	89
		(49)	(11)	(31)	(07)	(01)	
	5	28	3	9	1	2	43
		(65)	(07)	(21)	(02)	(05)	
	6	30	4	10	0	2	46
		(65)	(09)	(22)	(-)	(04)	
		153	44	81	27	16	321

The two last rows of Table 16–1 are very similar according to their conditional frequencies. So we shall estimate two PLS models, one for the above table and one for a table in which the two last categories of apprenticeships have been summed.

Figure 16–4 shows the arrow scheme for the (first) PLS model, the data being given by table 16–1.

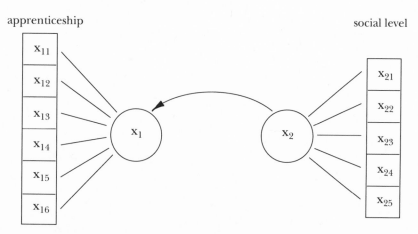

Figure 16–4. Arrow Scheme for the PLS Model Based on Table 16–1.

In the second model the first block reduces to five categories, the last one being the aggregation of the fifth and sixth of the original table.

The estimation of the two tables at issue are reported in Table 16–2.

The estimated loadings for the second margin are very close to each other, and so are the loadings for the first two categories in the type of apprenticeship margin. Note that the loadings of apprenticeships 5 and 6 are rather different in the first estimation, although they would be equal if the two corresponding rows of the contingency table were similar. The sum of these two loadings is close to the loading obtained in estimation for the aggregation of the two last categories (.0856 + .1136 = .1992). The difference is due either to sampling errors or to erroneous aggregation. It is surely unrealistic to aggregate two such different kinds of apprenticeship (house painter and hairdresser); nevertheless, with respect to social categorization, they seem similarly distributed. One explanation of this unexpected phenomenon is perhaps related to the length of study: these two apprenticeships are three years long, whereas the others are four years long. The decision to undertake extended study could be related to social position; such an interpretation should of course be verified by further investigation.

Table 16–2

Numerical Results of the Two PLS Models Based on Data from Table 16–1

Block 1 (kind of apprenticeship)

category	weight table 16–1	weight table 16–2	loading table 16–1	loading table 16–2
1	-1.1901	-1.1895	-.1149	-.1149
2	1.5492	1.5500	.3234	.3235
3	.9926	.9948	.1392	.1395
4	-.5354	-.5361	-.1484	-.1487
5	-.6387 }	-.7194	-.0856 }	-.1995
6	-.7926		-.1136	

Block 2 (social level)

category	weight table 16–1	weight table 16–2	loading table 16–1	loading table 16–2
1	.4119	-.4129	.1963	.1968
2	-.6840	-.6895	-.0938	-.0945
3	.8001	.8001	.2019	.2019
4	-2.3517	-2.3476	-.1978	-.1975
5	-2.1400	-2.1410	-.1067	-.1067

Path coefficient for Model 1: -.3660
Path coefficient for Model 2: -.3657

3. GUTTMAN SCALE

3.1. The model

In this section we shall use the E ⇔ T matching to explore the application of the Guttman scale in developmental psychology.

The Guttman scale is a theoretical hierarchical pattern of binary items. A simple example of a four-item pattern is given in Figure 16–5.

```
          items:
      1   2   3   4
    ┌─────────────────┐
    │ 0   0   0   0   │
    │ 1   0   0   0   │
    │ 1   1   0   0   │
    │ 1   1   1   0   │
    │ 1   1   1   1   │
    └─────────────────┘
```

Figure 16–5. Arrow Scheme Exhibiting the Guttman Scale.

When item 4 is one, then items 1, 2 and 3 are also supposed be one. When the answer to item 3 is one, then item 4 may or may not be one. The model assumes a unique pattern of psychological systems which is measured by the set of four items in Figure 16–5.

3.2. The PLS approach

For the PLS statistical treatment of Figure 16–5, we shall first note that it can be represented by a set of conditional probabilities, namely

$$\text{prob}(x_i = 1 \mid x_j = 1) = 1 \text{ if } j > i, \qquad (16\text{–}7)$$

where x_i is the value of the answer to the ith item ($x_i = 0$ or $x_i = 1$).

We have demonstrated in Bertholet and Wold (1985) that under such assumptions, the estimation of a particular model called the complete causal chain reduces to a more simple hierarchical model.

A complete causal chain is a model in which every PLS block is directly connected to all other blocks: one block, called the exogenous block, dominates all blocks, i.e., arrows go from it to all other ones. On the other hand, one block is fully dominated. An example of a complete causal chain is given in Figure 16–6.

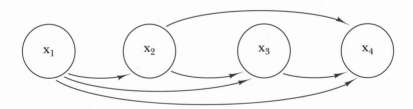

Figure 16–6. Arrow Scheme of a Complete Causal Chain with 4 Latent Variables.

Note that in Figure 16–6 each block receives or sends three arrows. Each block of this PLS model is built for one of the four items. x_1 denotes the latent variable for the first block; its manifest variables are the two categories of the first item (0 or 1).

The PLS estimation of the inner model (Figure 16–6) for the pattern of data (Figure 16–5) leads to a simplified model where every arrow links two consecutive items. All path parameters between x_i and x_j with $i-j \neq 1$ are zeros. The final model is now as shown in Figure 16–7.

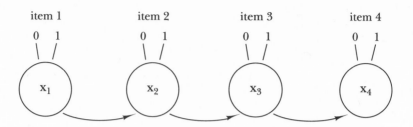

Figure 16–7. Arrow Scheme for the Simple Causal Chain of the Guttman Scale.

The manifest variables forming the four blocks are plotted on the scheme.

The theorem of Figures 16–6 and 16–7 allows us to test how the data do meet the theoretical model of the Guttman scale. Is this matching procedure adequate with respect to the basic psychological assumption which underlies the Guttman pattern? The next section will give a short discussion of the evaluation of the matching we have just proposed.

3.3. Evaluation of the matching

We have sketched on the one hand the psychological background of the Guttman scale, and on the other hand a technical testing device given by the current development of PLS. The problem which arises is evaluating the quality of the matching with respect to the theory (Guttman scale) and the theorem (PLS reduction to a simplified structure).

We have seen that the statistical treatment by PLS introduces as many latent variables as there are items in the scale. It may be objected that the PLS device at issue introduces complexity by means of numerous latent variables. This in some way contradicts the basic unitary structure the theory postulates, or, to put it in another way,

theory = simple ↔ theorem = complex.

Now a debate arises between the two approaches. We face here again our introductory discussion about qualitative, categorical and latent variables. The interpretation of the PLS latent variables in the context of a Guttman scale should now be established. There are two interpretations of latent variables and this is the reason for the present debate.

One side argues that a latent variable is a measure of the uniform

Guttman scale which, as we have seen, is a representation of unilineal progressions with stage skipping or regression processes going back to an earlier level of development (Henning and Rudinger, 1985). Following this definition, the present PLS solution does not incorporate a unique latent variable as an image of this uniform process. The multiplicity of the latent variables makes the PLS model inaccurate.

The other side argues that each latent variable is an image of a step in a Piagetian approach, and that each such step gives a latent variable, because of our incapacity to directly observe them. Let us quote Piaget (1969), speaking about the validation of psychological structure by means of experimental data: "We have now facts but no structure, that is no more a matter of theory but a matter of observations and experiments." Following Piaget, we may say that the latent variables which we have introduced are attempts to measure qualitative variables that we more or less successfully observe by means of items. To repeat, the theoretical model does not pertain to experimental data, but to qualitative elements of a psychological structure which we indirectly observe by a categorization procedure.

APPENDIX

The relations that enter the PLS Mode B algorithm are for a two-block model (estimated π_i are written p_i):[1]

$$(16\text{--}1) \qquad w_1' \, C_{12} = p_2' \qquad p_1 = C_{11} \, w_1$$
$$(16\text{--}2) \qquad w_2' \, C_{21} = p_1' \qquad p_2 = C_{22} \, w_2$$

The elements of the C_{12} matrix are the covariances between two categories which read $C_{12} = \| f_{ij} - f_{i.} \, f_{.j} \|$ where f_{ij} is the joint frequency of the ith row and jth column of the contingency table and $f_{i.}$, $f_{.j}$ are the marginal frequencies. C_{ii} is a diagonal matrix of the marginal frequencies.

If two rows of the contingency table, say the first and the second, are equal,

$$(16\text{--}3) \qquad f_{1j} = f_{2j} \quad j = 1...J,$$

it follows from (16–1) and (16–2) that the two first elements of the vectors w_1 and p_1 are equal.

If we now sum up the two first rows of the original contingency table, the new row will be twice the previous ones, namely

$$(16\text{--}4) \qquad f^*_{1j} = 2f_{1j} = 2f_{2j} \,,$$

where f^*_{1j} stands for the new aggregated frequency.
The new covariances for the first row read

$$(16\text{--}5) \qquad f^*_{1j} - f^*_{1.} \, f_{.j} = 2 \, (f_{1j} - f_{1.} \, f_{.j})$$

We see that the PLS algorithm relations (16–1 and 16–2) together with the general Mode B property[1] $\Sigma(f_{1.}w_{1i}) = \Sigma(f_{.j} w_{2j}) = 0$ lead to the same stationary point with $p^*_{1j} = 2p_{1j}$ and $w^*_{1j} = w_{1j}$. In contingency table analysis the estimated latent variables are nothing but the weights; hence the last equality shows that the estimated latent variables remain unchanged.

NOTE

[1]For a detailed description of the PLS Mode B algorithm applied to contingency tables, see Bertholet and Wold, 1985.

REFERENCES

Bentler, P.M. 1980. The study of cognitive development through modeling with qualitative data. In *Developmental models of thinking*, eds. R.H. Kluwe and H. Spada. New York: Academic Press.

Benzécri, J.-P. and F. Benzécri. 1973. *L'Analyse des donnés; I La taxinomie, II L'analyse des correspondances.* Ed. J.-P. Benzécri. Paris: Dunod.

Bertholet, J-L. and H. Wold. 1985. Recent developments on categorical data analysis by PLS. In *Measuring the unmeasurable*, eds. P. Nijkamp *et al.*, 253–286. Doordrecht: Martinus Nijhoff.

Goodman, L.A. 1978. *Analyzing qualitative/categorical data.* London: Addison-Wesley.

Guenther, P. 1983. Analysis of path model by partial least squares (PLS): A short story. In *Current Methodolgical issues in developmental psychology. A Reader. Bremer Beiträge zur Psychologie Nr. 22*, eds. P. Guenther and H.J. Henning. Bremen: University Press.

Guilford, J.P. 1956. *Fundamental statistics in psychology and education.* 1973 5th ed. B. Fruchter. New York: McGraw-Hill.

Guttman, L. 1950. The basis for scalogram analysis. In *Measurement and prediction,* eds. S.E. Szraffer et al., 60–90. Princeton: University Press.

Henning, H.J. and G. Rudinger. 1985. Analysis of qualitative data in developmental psychology. In *Measurement of individual and social change: Explanatory analysis,* eds. J.R. Nesselroade and A.V. Eye. New York: Academic Press.

Hildebrand, D.K., J.D. Laing, and H. Rosenthal. 1977. *Prediction analysis of cross classifications.* New York: Wiley.

Jöreskog, K.G. and D. Sörbom. 1981. *LISREL V; Analysis of structural relationships by maximum likelihood and least square methods.* Uppsala University: Dept. of Statistics, Report No. 81–8.

Muthen, B. 1979. A structural probit model with latent variables. *Journal of the American Statistical Association* 74:807–811.

Piaget, J. 1969. 11 articles in *Encyclopédie de la Pléiade: Logique et connaissance scientifique,* ed. J. Piaget. Dijon: Gallimard.

Rudinger, G., F. Chaselon, E.J. Zimmermann, and H.J. Henning. 1985. *Qualitative Daten - Neue Wege sozialwissenschaftlicher Methodik.* München: Urban & Schwarzenberg.

Wold, H. 1979. Model construction and the evaluation when theoretical knowledge is scarce. *University of Geneva: Cahier 79.06, Dept. of Econometrics.*

Wold, H. 1983. Fix-point method. In *Encyclopedia of Statistical Sciences* (ESS), Vol. 3, eds. S Kotz and N.L. Johnson, 148–156. New York: Wiley.

Wold, H. 1985. Partial least squares. In *ESS,* Vol. 6, eds. S Kotz and N.L. Johnson, 581–591. New York: Wiley.

Wold, H. and J-L.Bertholet. 1982. The PLS (partial least squares) approach to multidimensional contingency tables. *Metron* 41:105–126.

17

Discussion of Bertholet's Paper

BENGT MUTHEN

I have been invited to give some comments on the paper "Categorical Data: Methodological Implications and Analysis in the Field of Social and Cognitive Development" by Jean-Luc Bertholet (JLB from now on). I must say that I don't feel exceptionally qualified to do this since I haven't followed closely the development of the so-called PLS approach that JLB proposes. However, it may be useful to JLB to get an outsider's reaction to approaches which presently do not seem to be the most common ones applied to categorical data. Potential problems of communication can thus be diminished.

Let me limit my comments to two aspects of the JLB paper, the proposed taxonomy for qualitative data, and the example regarding apprenticeship's relation to social level. The taxonomy part of the JLB paper is a discourse on the recent taxonomy paper by G. Rudinger and H.J. Henning (1984).

The taxonomy distinguishes between three areas: latent attribute models, prediction models, and multinomial response models. I have some comments on both the choice of areas and the placing of topics within areas. In general, I don't find the suggested taxonomy to be as clear or as precise a structuring of this research field as would be desirable. I will start discussing topics within areas.

In the first group are, among other topics included, latent structure models, latent trait models, and factor analysis models. Firstly, the way

Lazarsfeld described latent structure analysis, continuous latent variables were included, hence not necessitating a separate Latent trait section 3. A more modern name for latent trait modeling is Item Response Theory (IRT), e.g., as described in the absent reference Lord (1980).

"Latent structure models" could hence be replaced by "Latent class models" for a start. "Factor analysis models" may be suitably kept separate from IRT (Latent trait), as is done here, since the latter traditionally works with a single factor. Here, however, many important references are missing, such as Bartholomew (1980), Bock (1972), Bock and Aitkin (1981), Muthen (1984), etc., also going beyond the dichotomous categorical case.

In the Prediction group (group 2) dichotomous response is very scarcely represented, for example, probit is not mentioned, nor are references given to the standard books by Cox and Finney. More importantly, the reference to LISREL structural equation models is misleading, since LISREL is not really aimed at categorical variables, nor is it prediction-oriented. A recent overview of structural equation modeling with categorical variables, including regression analysis and factor analysis is given by Muthen (1983), giving a large set of relevant references in biometrics, econometrics, and psychometrics. LISREL type modeling for categorical measurement was proposed in Muthen (1984), expanding work in Muthen (1979).

Regarding the choice of the three areas, I also find problems. For example LISREL type modeling (by which I mean the Muthén type) certainly involves latent attributes and hence would be more of a group 1 than group 2 research topic. The group 3 "Multinomial Response Models" does not define a distinct area at all, since reasonable models for categorical variables will all involve multinomial response formulations. Perhaps what JLB has in mind in group 2 versus group 3 is regression modeling (an asymmetric treatment of variables; dependent-independent) versus association modeling (a symmetric treatment of variables). Loglinear modeling would fall into the latter category, whereas logistic regression would fall into the former. Furthermore, a distinction not made clear is the choice of estimation procedure, i.e., minimizing prediction error versus maximizing fit to data—this would seem relevant to PLS. Another classification scheme was given in Fienberg (1977), but of a less ambitious nature.

The example regarding apprenticeship's relation to social level can serve as a basis for briefly discussing alternative analysis strategies for categorical data. In this example the two variables involved are viewed asymmetrically, such that apprenticeship is thought to be influenced by the family's social level. The independent variable social status (x) can be considered an ordinal variable, or an ordered categorical variable. The dependent variable apprenticeship (y) is observed on a nominal scale and its distribution conditional on x can be described by a multinomial distribution. A standard regression model for this situation would take into account that the y response is categorical, so that the conditional probabilities for each y category as predicted by the model should add up to one. To this aim multinomial logistic regression could be used, for example, as described in Bock (1975, chapter 8). Since we model y conditional on x, we need not be concerned with the nature of the x distribution; however, we could also model the joint y, x distribution, in which case the ordered nature of the x variable could be taken into account, for example by the methods of Goodman (1984). In any case, the aim of the analysis is to describe the relationship between x and y as well as possible.

The so called PLS approach seemingly differs starkly from the above analysis. The stated aim is not to fit a model to the full data at hand, but rather to minimize prediction errors. It is stated that the continuous variable PLS approach needs no adaptation to cope with categorical variables. This worries me since there would then seem to be no safeguard against predictions outside admissible y ranges (compare with the critique against ordinary OLS on 0/1 y variables possibly giving probabilities that are negative or greater than one, as opposed to the correct probit or logit approach).

Also, the model specification of one latent ksi variable underlying each of x and y is hard for me to grasp. If y had been an ordered categorical variable I could imagine that one could describe the relationship by a single dependent variable ksi, but with this unordered y, one needs a separate slope for each y category contrasted with all others. For a clear conceptual overview of such modeling concerns, see Amemiya (1981), covering biometric and econometric approaches.

Hence, I don't know how to interpret the "path coefficient" of -.3660 between the two ksi's. Perhaps this coefficient should not be interpreted but only used by the model for prediction purposes, as seems to be implied. The reason for this wish to obtain good prediction is not made clear enough to me, however. No guidance is given regarding how to evaluate the success of the analysis procedure. I would be interested in seeing a sampling experiment where prediction results are compared between PLS and the above-mentioned logistic regression approach.

In the above example, the PLS approach strikes me as closely related to some classical ones. Again, I am not well-versed in the background principles of PLS. However, how does the proposed JLB analysis differ from that of Lancaster and others in the area of canonical analysis, e.g., as discussed in Kendall and Stuart (1977, chapter 33) and more recently and expansively by de Leeuw (1983), connecting it with correspondence analysis ?

In conclusion I think that the proposed methods for categorical variables differ from ones more commonly used today in much the same way that PLS for continuous variables differs from ordinary regression models and LISREL analysis. Having a leaning towards "highly parametric" approaches with explicit distributional assumptions, as expressed in the discussion above and, for example Muthen (1984), it is difficult for me to readily embrace these more "soft" approaches. To "win over" researchers with my kind of "bias" JLB might try a more highly pedagogical approach in future expositions of their techniques. I want to emphasize that I am certainly not discarding their work despite my somewhat critical tone. Rather, I feel that a more convincing exposition is needed.

REFERENCES

Amemiya, T. 1981. Qualitative response models: A survey. *Journal of Economic Literature* 19:1483–1536.

Bartholomew, D. 1980. Factor analysis for categorical data. *Journal of the Royal Statistical Society* B 42:293–321.

Bock, R. 1972. Estimating item parameters and latent ability when responses are scored in two or more nominal categories. *Psychometrika* 37:29–51.

Bock, R. 1975. *Multivariate statistical methods in behavioral research.* New York: McGraw-Hill.

Bock, R. and M. Aitkin. 1981. Marginal maximum likelihood estimation of item parameters: Application of an EM algorithm. *Psychometrika* 46:443–459.

Cox, D. 1970. *The analysis of binary data.* London: Meuthuen.

de Leeuw, J. 1983. Models and methods for the analysis of correlation coefficients. *Journal of Econometrics* 22:113–137.

Fienberg, S. 1977. *The analysis of cross-classified categorical data.* Cambridge: The MIT Press.

Finney, D. 1971. *Probit Analysis.* Cambridge: Cambridge University Press.

Goodman, L. 1984. *The analysis of cross-classified data having ordered categories.* Cambridge: Harvard University Press.

Kendall, M. and A. Stuart. 1977. *The advanced theory of statistics.* Vol. 2. New York: Macmillan Publishing Company.

Lord, F. 1980. *Applications of item response theory to practical testing problems.* Hillsdale: Lawrence Erlbaum Associates.

Muthen, B. 1979. A structural probit model with latent variables. *Journal of the American Statistical Association* 74:807–811.

Muthen, B. 1983. Latent variable structural equation modeling with categorical data. *Journal of Econometrics* 22:43–65.

Muthen, B. 1984. A general structural equation model with dichotomous, ordered categorical and continuous latent variable indicators. *Psychometrika* 49:115-132.

18

Strategy for Science in the Modern University

WAYNE R. GRUNER

SUMMARY

Dr. Weinberg suggested that we talk about "Strategy of Science," denoting by that a discussion of research allocation. Dr. Wold notes that considerable interest might attach to a discussion of comparative "conditions in universities" worldwide. ICUS should constitute an admirable forum for either venture, but the international comparison is a project far too large for a single paper, or even for a single meeting of this committee. The present paper is devoted entirely to U.S. experience and focuses upon social and behavioral aspects of the science allocation process. Attention is invited to some major changes induced by 30 years' large-scale central government support of scientific research and comment offered relating these to the hopes and fears which attended initiation of the policy.

One major thesis offered is that—apart from general scale and intensity of effort—the most verifiable and probably most interesting effects of massive federal support are to be found, not in the directions taken by the *content* of research, but rather in the institutional and social posture of the research community.

U.S. science, before the war, obtained support from a great diversity of public and private sources, with no single source predominating. The public contribution was conveyed for the most part by or through the 48 individual states. In the years following WWII, however, U.S. scientific research rapidly came to depend *primarily* upon the federal government. For our nation, this marked a profound change.

Entry of the central government, though it offered the potential for greatly increased volume of support, raised fears among scientists that bureaucrats and politicians might try to dictate the content and method of research, or that quick and obvious application might take precedence over what was basic or fundamental.

As things turned out, the federal science agencies recruited many individuals who had sound scientific and research backgrounds. The incentive structure presented to these scientist-bureaucrats was such as to induce constructive behavior, and they tended instinctively to for use by the bureaucracy attitudes and practices traditional within the research community.

A diversity of competing arrangements for support of scientific research sprang up within the federal government, and instances of dangerous monopoly-of-decision have been quite uncommon. Over the first two decades something resembling a "market" in research proposals prevailed. The resulting overall system is characterized as one with very strong tactical capabilities and little capacity for making or enforcing grand strategy.

Alvin Weinberg's very influential paper (about strategy), "*Criteria for Scientific Choice*" is discussed from the point of view of the government administrator. A conclusion is offered that Weinberg's "timeliness" criterion is the one of greatest practical utility and the one most widely reflected in the behavior of the bureaucracy. Intellectually, greatest enlightenment is to be obtained from the "scientific merit" criterion as formulated by Weinberg. He himself pointed out its equivalence to a strong affirmation of the *unity of science.*

Ultimately, the science allocation process must be viewed in a space of many dimensions, some technical, some social, and some political.

Massive support by the federal government has greatly increased the speed and volume of scientific work. Questions are raised about the relationship of this greater speed to the "kinetics" and the desired rate of technological innovation.

Large scale and near universality of federal support have changed the relationship between scientist and sponsor, and even the conditions for a career in science. Resulting concerns over fairness and "due process" in the proposal evaluating system have resulted in its being formalized and "opened" to a degree that the writer believes is inconsistent with maximum creativity. Pressures for due process, total documentation, and "full disclosure" are manifestations of a fallacious belief that through a system of vigorous external monitoring and coercion the judgmental performance of individuals or agencies can be "perfected." Competition between rival individuals and agencies generally serves much better. Unfortunately, the "market" for research proposals has been much narrowed in the aftermath of the Mansfield amendment.

If one takes the von Humboldt/"modern German" model of university as the definition of "good academic practice," then it may be said that one cumulative effect of 30 years' federal research sponsorship has been to extend good academic practice to a much larger and wider group of U.S. universities than before.

Modification of the university system was surely not the original purpose of federal research sponsorship, and very few, if any, of the people involved knew anything about von Humboldt. But the outcome stands.

The main body of the paper is preceded by a brief comment on "unification" and "reduction," justified as maintaining continuity with previous years' discussions of this committee. A phrase "heuristic reduction" is introduced as mnemonic that: whether or not successful *as a program* the systematic attempt to interpret phenomena of one scientific realm in terms of concepts from another (e.g., chemical interpretation of biological phenomena) in fortunate cases provokes fruitful conjectures and leads to discovery of new phenomena in one or both of the fields involved.

In a concluding section attention is invited to the fact that a major social function of sciences resides in *rationalizing our expectations,* as advocated long ago by Epicurus. Speculation is offered as to where this interpretation of "social merit" might lead the science allocator.

1. FOREWORD

The focus of this paper is upon social and behavioral aspects of the science allocation process. This leads to discussion from that viewpoint of some major effects of 30 years' large scale government support of scientific research—and of how the changes relate to the hopes and fears with which people launched the enterprise.

The discussion is motivated by U.S. experience. Over the past three decades central governments in most of the "developed" nations have supported scientific research vigorously. The practice represented a bigger change in the U.S., perhaps, than in some other nations. Experience in different nations surely varied, as did the starting points. Nevertheless,

much of the discussion should be relevant in any national setting or context. In the following 1 shall maintain that—apart from general scale and
intensity of effort—the most systematic, most verifiable, and probably
most significant effects of massive science support have appeared, not in
the directions taken by the *content* of research, but rather in the institutional and social posture of the research community. (The latter, to be
sure, might easily engender future changes of content.)

In any given research situation several different versions of "strategy" may attract attention. Three of them are:

- Strategies *of* Scientists: The strategy, motivation, and behavior (they are
difficult to separate) of the scientists doing the research.
- Strategies *for* Science: The strategy and expectations of those who direct
or allocate funds and logistic resources (large equipment, etc.) in support
of research.
- Ideas *about* Strategy: The strategy that philosophers of science—possibly
long after the fact—will perceive the research to exemplify.

The last represents a point of continuity with previous ICUS discussions, so it is not inappropriate to devote a few words to it before plung-
ing into the main topic, which is Strategy *for* Science.

2. UNIFICATION

It is possible, and may be useful, to recognize differences between
the beliefs and intentions that people have about research while it is in
progress and the ultimate results of doing it. Last year's discussions in
Committee I dwelt at length upon abstract intellectual issues of reductionism and positivism. As a matter of natural history, however, the research
scientist or government administrator—at least in America—who is much
aware of these concepts as he goes about his daily work, or even as he
plans his next several years' work, is decidedly an exception. Many highly
competent U.S. scientists, in fact, don't have any definite idea as to what
meanings philosophers ascribe to these terms, or what may be their historical status. (The situation is said to be different in Europe.) One may
observe that the best researchers—and best science administrators—tend
to be ardent seekers of unification, some of them consciously, and some
perhaps not.

Whatever may have been the *a priori* beliefs of philosophers and of
the scientists involved, research carried out over the past 50 years appears
to have resulted in a great deal of "unification" and a not inconsiderable

degree of "reduction"—according to the most direct and literal meanings commonly attached to those terms.

Physics, chemical physics, physical chemistry, chemistry, biochemistry, molecular biology, etc., are rapidly being woven into a truly seamless fabric. Their connections with astronomy, geology, atmospheric science, oceanography, "material science," pharmacology, physiology, genetics, etc., have grown so intimate that no one can confidently say what natural boundaries partition science, or where. Crystallography and biochemistry have been mobilized to provide a molecular critique and interpretation of taxonomy. And the end is not in sight. Those changes have been witnessed by most ICUS participants. One might say that unification can scarcely be considered controversial.

As to whether or not all this represents an important degree of "reduction," the answer obviously depends upon one's interpretation of the word. "Reduction" to this writer signifies something considerably stronger than rejoicing in mere lack of evident contradiction—but less dramatic, perhaps, than disciplinary phagocytosis. Judging from the examples that all have witnessed, the issue is not whether physics can swallow biology, or biology can swallow physics; it is one of "reducing" physics and biology *together* to something both more compact and more powerful than the superficial union of the two. One is tempted to propose the phrase "*heuristic reduction*" to signify that in a favorable case, such as that of chemistry and biology, the program to interpret one set of phenomena in terms of the other leads to fruitful extensions of phenomenology or concept, or both.

What seems to be in progress is the condensation of science to a gratifyingly coherent whole whose parts not only are *believed* to be consistent but have been aggressively and constructively *demonstrated* to be so—or at least (with suitable apologies to professional philosophers) *not inconsistent.* The demonstration can never be exhaustive, but it can be conscientious and imaginative. Any observant science agency administrator is daily reminded of the tremendous instinct for "*intellectual triangulation*" typical of research scientists. If any two propositions can be brought to bear upon each other, or upon a third one, some scientist will propose putting matters to the test (even if it costs a million dollars).

As to the limits beyond which this trend cannot or will not go, perhaps one might best adopt a wait-and-see attitude.

2.1. Former Position in the United States

It is not likely that "scientific choice" or science allocation as a topic of discussion could have attracted much interest in the U.S. before WWII. There was no likely major *agent* of choice or allocation. Thus before the war, as is generally known, scientific research in the U.S. (with the exceptions of agriculture and aeronautical engineering) received little of its support from the federal (central) government. In this respect our situation differed from that of some other nations.

American research was supported by private donors or foundations and by the universities themselves out of their regular operating budgets which, in turn, were recruited from varied sources. Each research funding decision, therefore, depended idiosyncratically upon local circumstances, and those circumstances were extremely diverse.

Universities, for example, ranged from great liberal arts centers that more or less exemplified the *Humboldtian ideal* as it had developed and evolved in Europe[1] to some that were explicitly institutes of technology or of agriculture, and others that were simply "mills" for turning out school teachers and white collar workers. Many had started as "land grant" institutions explicitly charged, in unmistakably utilitarian spirit:

> "...without excluding other scientific and classical studies...to teach such branches of learning as are related to agriculture and the mechanic arts...in order to promote the liberal, and practical education of the industrial classes in the several pursuits and professions in life."[2]

Private foundations and philanthropists supported research projects reflecting motives that ranged from the entirely practical to the purely intellectual. They established precedents that very strongly influenced the post-WWII practices of the federal agencies. Some of their organizations and projects were:

- the Rockefeller Institute
- the Carnegie Institution of Washington
- the Mt. Wilson Observatory and 100-inch telescope
- the Mt. Palomar Observatory and 200-inch telescope
- the 184-inch Berkeley cyclotron
- the International Maize and Wheat Improvement Center
- the Gunnar Myrdal study of US. Negro sociology

Note that this list includes several precedents for the *scale* on which scientific research might be, or must be, conducted in order to be effective. "Big science" had been underwritten by private sponsors before the second world war.

Pure science for its own sake, however, was not very much in the public eye and not very popular. Astronomy, perhaps, was something of an exception and was occasionally treated as newsworthy. It was also the first of the "pure" sciences to become "big" (i.e., capital intensive), and its big science instrumentation was financed from private sources.

2.2. Lessons of the Second World War3

Transformations initiated at the end of WWII set U.S. science allocation processes on the path from more or less complete decentralization to what one might facetiously term "centralized decentralization."

Wartime successes of technology had the effect of greatly enhancing public appreciation of "basic science," and this was enormously gratifying to scientists. But it is prudent to acknowledge that, while the appreciation is justified, it may have been conferred as a result of misapprehension.

One thing demonstrated in the second world war, I think, was that clever people who are well trained in science, when highly motivated to turn their attention to applications, *can do applications* quite well. A second lesson was that both engineering and research (basic or applied) proceed much faster and better when they make full use of advanced technology and well-organized logistics. *Technology and investment enhance the productivity of science just as truly as science enlightens technology.* Much of the effort of "basic researchers," of course, is devoted to developing improved technology for use in research, and in that sense they *are* technologists.

To much of the public, however, science was allowed to appear as a kind of super engineering, and scientists as super engineers. (In the late 1960s some of these notions came back to haunt us.)

The impression also became widely disseminated that there is more or less unidirectional developmental flow of knowledge and ideas from "basic" science to "applied" science and thence to engineering and development—and that each stage in this process is dependent upon the preceding ones, but not vice versa. Many research scientists failed to oppose this idea, and worse, some appeared to believe it themselves.

2.3. A New System

In some ways, then, the political rhetoric of science may have displayed an unscientific lack of precision, but precision is not what politics is about. As a matter of practical politics wartime successes of applied science paved the way for initiation soon after the war's end of direct federal support of basic research—a policy that has taken hold beyond the most optimistic expectations of those who proposed it. After WWII Vannevar Bush[4], not a short-sighted person, visualized a half-decade of growth of federal science support leading to stabilization in the neighborhood of $100 million/year. Actual obligations for fiscal year 1984 have been reported as $6.4 *billion*. Thus since 1950 the level of support in nominal dollars has grown about fifty-fold from Bush's target level. Even when discounted for inflation the increase has been more than ten-fold.

Different people had different reasons for advocating federal support of science; there was considerable controversy at the outset about the exact form the arrangements should assume; and most scientists were at least a little apprehensive. In particular they were concerned about the possible impact of bureaucracy and centralized authority upon the *content* of research. Some feared:

> (1) that bureaucrats and politicians might try to dictate the specific research problems and methods to be pursued—or even, Lysenko like—to decree what results would be acceptable.
>
> (2) that quick and obvious application would take precedence over what was basic or fundamental.

Apparently less earnestly discussed, through it turned out to be vaguely premonitory of really significant social changes that would eventually emerge, was the fear:

> (3) that the role of universities would not be sufficiently appreciated and that government support would go primarily to industrial laboratories, or perhaps to big government–controlled research centers.

These fears, of course, derive plausibily from that potential for centralization and monopoly which is implicit in dependence upon central government. It finally turned out, as happens often in the U.S. government, that a *diversity of competing arrangements* for federal support of research came into existence. (Most of them still coexist today.) With the possible exception of high-energy physics, no dangerous monopoly of decision ever materialized, and the phrase "centralized decentralization" is only slightly facetious.

Favorable experience soon muted the scientists' fears, or at least shifted the level of aggregation at which they were felt to be relevant. Don Price[5] stated matters correctly when he wrote:

> Most scientists once feared that if they had to depend upon subsidies from federal agencies, they would be committed to work toward those agencies'

purposes, and thus lose their freedom. On the contrary, it is now clear that the university scientist of reasonably high status in his field...has more freedom by virtue of his ability to seek funds from a wide variety of federal and other sources than if he were entirely dependent upon the decisions of his university administration.[6]

2.3. The Scientist-Bureaucrat

Several other features of the new "system" also contributed to a highly favorable outcome. The science agencies mostly set up shop with *scientist*-bureaucrats—trained scientists, educated and socialized in the traditional research system. This practice differed significantly from what was customary in some other advanced nations.[7]

The scientist-bureaucrats, in turn, more or less instinctively adapted for use in research proposal selection the traditional refereeing practices of scientific journals. (They also had before them the model of the private foundations.) One might say that *government adapted to the folkways of scientists* rather than the reverse which had been feared.

The science bureaucracy gave the appearance of remarkable willingness to implement what might be termed a "passive linear amplifier model" of research support. The science agencies received suggestions (proposals) from the scientific community and amplified them without introducing any serious "distortion." The appearance was somewhat misleading; amplification was faithful, to be sure, but it was applied to very selectively chosen proposals.

What was extremely fortunate, the tradition became quite well established, so that:

> Research plans submitted in successful proposals need not, subsequently, be adhered to in detail. Even major deviations can be approved on the basis of mutual discussion between scientist and cognizant Bureaucrat.

Finally, it came about that the same scientist-bureaucrats who carry out the allocation of research funds to fields of science and to individual projects are in the position of first having to help *recruit* those funds. This they must do through a quasi-political process, competing in a "*policy market*" against the spokesmen for other fields of science and, to a degree, for other science agencies. Because their professional standing depends to a major degree on how well they succeed in this, they have a great incentive to recognize, encourage, and publicize promising or successful efforts within the scientific fields of their cognizance. The scientist-bureaucrat thus has every reason to seek out and publicize the best works of his constituency—which, of course, is at once an important aspect of leadership and a contribution to enlightenment of the polity.

These factors together had the effect of remarkably integrating strategy *for* science with strategy *of* science. It is not surprising that the system ran quite smoothly and that most scientists were pretty comfortable with it. Their comfort was enhanced by the fact that total appropriations for science grew very rapidly. But of course this fact entailed other dangers.

3. CRITERIA

3.1. Criteria for Scientific Choice

In 1963, therefore, Al Weinberg was writing, not about the project level allocations which had been the subject of scientists' original fears, but rather about the limits of ambition and about principles of allocation to *entire fields of science*, under conditions of mild shortage.[8]

In "Criteria for Scientific Choice," Weinberg pointed out that public funds for science could not continue to grow several times as fast as the overall economy indefinitely, and that this fact would sooner or later force the making of choices.

He looked beyond the generally agreed upon proposition that science is a "good thing" and a sound public investment and suggested, with specific examples, that some kinds of science may be *more* of a "good thing" or better public investments than others—both in the abstract and in terms of practical consequences.

He proposed several "criteria" in terms of which one might try to introduce more system and purpose into the process of allocation among fields of science. As "internal" criteria, representing judgments which might be made within a discipline, he proposed:

(1) timeliness, "Is the field ready for exploitation?"
(2) quality performers, "Are the scientists in the field really competent?"

As "external" criteria, representing judgments that must be made from outside the discipline, he proposed:

(1) technological merit,
(2) scientific merit,
(3) social merit.

Most interesting and most novel to the conventional public discourse of the time, though certainly not to the intuition of good scientists, was the criterion that Weinberg called simply "scientific merit." He said:

> That field has the most scientific merit which contributes most heavily to and illuminates most brightly its neighboring scientific disciplines.

To offer this judgment, Weinberg points out, *is to affirm the unity of science.* He emphasized the related point:

> When scientists praise a discovery or concept as "basic" or "fundamental" they are really asserting that it is *broadly applicable*—within science.

A corollary to this, one should hasten to add, is the near certainty that it will find broad application in technology as well. A truly basic result always has "technological merit." But note that the adjective "basic" is applied to the *result,* not to an activity! It's quite unavoidable that much of what is undertaken as "basic research" ends by yielding superficial or trivial results.

Without a doubt, the Weinberg "criterion" of greatest day to day practical utility, both for allocation among disciplines and for making decisions within disciplines down to the project level, is *timeliness.* Science appears to progress most rapidly (and most cost effectively) through episodes of opportunistic exploitation both of new ideas and—highly important—of new technologies. When a new piece of knowledge or a new research technique is set in place, it often opens a multitude of opportunities for positioning others. We then recognize the occasion as "timely" for that line of research.

In the actual allocative process continuity of effect must receive considerable deference; one cannot redirect a large fraction of ongoing research projects every year or two. The decisions that produce significant changes in allocative patterns usually assume the form of initiatives taken with a relatively thin margin of "new" or discretionary funds (often funds held in "reserve" at high levels within the agencies). There is no doubt that these crucial allocations are more often swayed by perception of "timeliness" than by any other factor.

"Criteria for Scientific Choice" in its own way was timely, as indicated by the rapid appearance of other articles that used it as starting point for further elaboration upon the problems of science allocation. And it still makes worthwhile reading today, because Weinberg clarified and made explicit several ideas that are strongly held by most good scientists but are usually pretty intuitive. Moreover he dealt forthrightly with some matters that must often be glossed over. At several points, for example, he brought up explicitly the importance of "*taste*" in the making of scientific judgments. Taste, one may be sure, plays nearly as important a role in the operations of public officials as it does for private foundations. It is not, however, an element that can be comfortably integrated into the formal recipes of the budget and legislative process. And it's not very miscible with the calculations of economists, political scientists, management specialists, etc.—not, one might add, with the dogmas of the new "relevance."

Weinberg's "Criteria...," then was forthright, enlightening, and influential. It pretty much established the vocabulary and defined the categories in terms of which these questions were argued in the U.S. for several years. Many of us in the government science agencies found his ideas useful in our internal discussions, and "Criteria..." was sometimes quoted back and forth in our negotiations with the Bureau of the Budget (known as the Office of Management and Budget).

3.2. Strong Tactics; Weak Strategy

It is paradoxical that while "Criteria..." influenced the way public officials spoke and thought about science allocation and pretty certainly, therefore, the allocations actually realized, the criteria *per se* probably exert little effect upon the practical situation. Mere use of the word "criteria" implies a degree of controlled order not easy to realize in practical affairs, and certainly unattainable in the case of arrangements as diverse as those by which U.S. federal support is conveyed to scientific research. The same diversity that guarantees reasonable autonomy of the individual scientist in his choice of research problems and methods also stands in the way of a deductive or rational science allocation process.

The real process is a complex juggling act, involving lots of lobbying and salesmanship—both scientific and political. Scientists, of course, differ individually in their salesmanship and lobbying skills, but the best are very skillful indeed. Professor Wigner, I remember, once remarked that "...(a certain well known high energy physicist)...is unreasonably persuasive in government committee meetings." Professor Wigner was right, as usual, but "persuasive" isn't necessarily the same thing as "bad." In government an ounce of politics can sometimes outweigh a great mass of rational scholarship. And certainly, a great deal of lobbying is required to "sell" an accelerator, a telescope, an ocean drilling program, or any similar effort which will cost several tens (sometimes hundreds) of millions of dollars. On the whole it's remarkable, and on balance fortunate for society, that scientists have gained acceptance for so many of these ventures.

"Criteria...," one might say, is an article about strategy for science. In practice the U.S. science agencies constitute a set of arrangements with *very strong tactical capabilities* and little provision for the making or enforcement of grand strategy. Their tactical doctrines, of course, are the traditional ones of the scientific community and its technical journals, carried over and transplanted into government in the heads of the scientist-bureaucrats whose role was discussed earlier.

3.3 Difficulties with the Practical Use of Criteria

No kind of "criteria" can be expected to circumvent the fact of unpredictability. We can't foretell the scientific future and frequently encounter big surprises. A good example is the use of synchrotron radiation for studies in chemistry, solid state physics, and biology. I am aware of an occasion at the Stanford University high energy lab (SLAC) when the solid state physicists wanted to operate the machine at higher energy than had been scheduled by the "high energy" physicists!

No rational wielder of criteria in, say, 1950 could have embarked upon the long, arduous, expensive development of accelerator technology because of an anticipation that it would someday be good for chemistry. Moreover, it is nearly unimaginable that chemists and solid state physicists, even after the technology was available, could have recruited the funds they now devote to constructing synchrotron radiation facilities were it not for the "big science" *funding precedents*—harking all the way back to pre-war telescopes and cyclotrons—that were established in other disciplines over a long period of time.

That's a spectacular example, and scarcely typical, but it did happen. In the matter of allocations between university "basic" and corporate "applied" research, one can quote various examples which may involve less money going in and perhaps more coming out. One is the discovery at the Bell Laboratories of magnetostatic-modes and spin-wave-degeneracy. It was made in the course of research on ferrimagnetic resonance with undeniably practical motivation, but the phenomena are extremely fundamental.

The MOHOLE project, which some of us regarded as frivolously extravagant at its inception, evolved ultimately into the Ocean Sediment Coring Program which gave impetus to a profound revision of geological ideas, and—although very expensive—is certain in the end to show a large net profit. And, quite apart from its intellectual and financial virtues, this coring program turns out to possess considerable "social merit" for the light it sheds on earthquake hazards, etc.

Sometimes we do not recognize the importance of a discovery for years or decades. The Nobel prize in biology was awarded a few years ago for work that even the prize recipient himself had not seen fit to pursue very vigorously for a rather lengthy period after his initial discovery.

Other, peculiar, difficulties confront the implementation of "external" criteria, especially that of "social merit." Public science policy does not change the facts of nature, but it does, presumably, influence the timetable on which we discover those facts. If speed of discovery is what public support of science is about, then *relative* speed of discovery must be what scientific choice is about, and criteria are useful to tell us not "whether" but rather "*how urgently*" particular classes of questions are to be answered.

Ideally, perhaps, it should be possible to attempt a crude quantitative estimate of the tangible benefits to society from learning, say, two years earlier, the essential parameters of the global atmospheric carbon dioxide problem. This could then be compared with the benefit estimated for early availability of some other socially valuable scientific knowledge.

Practical political difficulties are another matter. There are many, of course, who believe we already know enough about atmospheric carbon dioxide to fully vindicate the "social merit" and cost effectiveness of atmospheric research—and to justify some concrete action. Yet the practical policy consequences of atmospheric carbon dioxide research appear thus far to have been minimal. Imagine how much more difficult things might become in the case, for example, of criminal behavior or of pre-college school efficacy. Early warning is not of itself sufficient to produce social benefit, but it may represent the limit of science's capabilities and therefore of its responsibilities. There seems no plausible way to incorporate the stubbornness of public policy into estimates of research urgency based on "social merit." We can easily get into the position of searching urgently for knowledge that our best customers are going to ignore after we find it.

One might think it easier to obtain internal agreement among scientists about the relative urgencies of research, say, on turbulence and on phase transformations. But unresolvable doctrinal differences can arise for cases of this kind too.

Altogether, one is led to conclude that *the internal criterion of "timeliness" is easier to apply and furnishes more practical and reliable guidance than the external ones of "merit."* It is both easier to decide and easier to act upon the answer to the question: "What *can* we do most quickly?" than to the question: "What do we *need* to do most quickly?"

3.4. Dimensions of Allocation

Despite difficulties pointed out in the foregoing, the conscientious official cannot live without a compass; he must work toward a strategy as best he can. Weinberg's "Criteria" provide valuable tools for this purpose. But they address only one or two dimensions of allocation and by no means the entire "strategy" problem. After one has decided which fields of science are currently most promising according to (some) criteria, there remain a host of other strategy questions of a mixed political-technical flavor:

- What should be the overall size of a science budget? (Weinberg discussed this in the second of his "Criteria..." papers).
- Should we, in fact, attach support to "projects" at all or should we instead look for the most promising scientists and attach support to them as individuals? This approach has been used at one time or another, and to varying degrees, by most research sponsoring organizations. It is more feasible for private than for government sponsors, and it is quite irrelevant for "big science."
- To the extent that support is applied to individuals rather than projects, how should it be allocated as between mature proven scientists and young ones just starting out? This has been the topic of constant agitation and experimentation.
- Should we, perhaps, focus attention neither upon the individual nor upon the project but rather upon the *institution* within which the research is carried on? Also a vigorously debated topic.
- To what degree shall scientific research be (institutionally) concentrated?
- How shall funds be divided between salaries and equipment or facilities? This is an intricate problem that raises questions as to whether science agencies should be "in the employment business" at all and as to what degree of self-discipline it is possible to evoke from research scientists.
- What about "interdisciplinarity" or "problem orientation" as strategies? Each has been tried—in several forms. Few spectacular successes have been achieved, and even in these one may reasonably doubt that the "strategy" was the cause of the success. The writer tends to believe that interdisciplinary research is best pursued by *individuals* of interdisciplinary bent rather than by committees or groups self consciously assembled from diverse disciplines.

This much should suffice to illustrate that the real strategy problem exists in an "allocation space" of many dimensions, some of them technical, some social, and some political. In practice, public officials tend to become preoccupied at any one time with allocation in one or two of these dimensions. Quite often, new programs are minted in order to produce special allocative results in dimensions previously ignored. Whatever the conscious concerns of the moment, there generally occur some collateral allocative effects that were neither anticipated nor intended.

4. OUTCOMES

What can one see in retrospect to have been the important changes wrought by the deployment of vast increases in research funding guided by strong tactics, and weak strategy? Of what consequence were the actual "scientific choices?" How have they finally influenced the spectral distribution of scientific knowledge, research techniques, and scientists we have today?

The most important change, of course, has been an enormous increase in the total amount of scientific knowledge and a raising of the general tempo of scientific and technical activity to unprecedented levels. As to complexion, certainly the most verifiable and possibly the most important changes are to be found in the social and institutional posture of the scientific community rather than in the spectral distribution of scientific knowledge. "Scientific choice" (topical allocations within science) may have been less significant than other dimensions of "strategy of science."

Two caveats should be added promptly:

First, it is impossible ever to say what the *direct* negative consequences of scientific choice have been. Not even with the elegant statistical techniques that have been presented by the other speakers to this committee can one divine the nature—or the possibility—of discoveries that *might* have been made if things had been done differently. As the British novelist Josephine Tey points out, retrospective judgment (history) suffers from an inbuilt optimistic bias; those whose counsel was not followed are in an unfairly weakened position for demonstrating how creative it might have been.[9]

Second, "scientific choice" usually produces collateral effects in other allocative dimensions. For example, a decision to pour heavy support into high energy physics or radio astronomy usually has the effect of concentrating the funds used in a relatively few elite institutions. It can also generate constraints upon the teaching schedules of the participating scientists, and thus indirectly influence the organizational structure of their departments. Some of these unintended by-products have proven very controversial.

As to direct effects on the content of science, one may confidently judge that sharply reducing support allocated to them would have slowed or totally prevented development of certain projects or areas of "big science." And as Weinberg suggested, this would have extruded some talented people into other fields of science—or into endeavors wholly unrelated to science. We can say that our current stock of detailed knowledge of high energy physics phenomena would in that case have been less. *Not clear at all* is whether such a policy could have significantly speeded the advance of other branches of science or if so, which ones.

The writer is inclined to doubt that there could have been much beneficial effect; the whole enterprise was being run at a level close to saturation. (In this, as in many other areas of economic and social analysis, saturation effects tend not to receive the amount of attention due them.) The overall support of science continued to grow faster than might have seemed possible or plausible in 1963, and transgressions against any kind of criteria were more likely sins of commission than of omission. Reviewing the 30 years' activity, it is not easy to identify really promising or important projects that failed, ultimately, to find support. But again, remember Miss Tey!

As to other effects, the enormous increase of expenditure has underwritten:

(1) A great increase in the total number of scientists and of the number engaged in research.

(2) Very great enhancement of the equipment and facilities employed in research (i.e., improved research technology). Of particular importance here is a major shift away from dependence upon made-by-hand equipment to use of purchased instrumentation ordered out of catalogues.

(3) Considerable inflation in unity costs of research.

(4) Higher salaries and enhanced social status of scientists.

(5) A gradual shift from the early practice of awarding relatively frugal grants to a few outstanding scientists to the present situation in which, at least for most physical and biological sciences, a majority of reputable researchers receive substantial federal support—and, in fact, *must receive it if they are to survive professionally.*

4.1. Speed and Its Consequences

Changes (1) and (2), somewhat counteracted by (3), have resulted in a greatly increased speed of producing scientific knowledge and in generally accelerated research and development activity. Some intriguing questions can be raised about possible effects of greatly elevated research and development metabolism, the kinetics of innovation, and time lags of science application. (The following introduction may appear to be a digression, but is not.)

About 20 years ago the science and technology group in the offices of our Director of Defense organized a retrospective study (appropriately christened "HINDSIGHT") in which they attempted to identify and characterize the crucial antecedents of selected important technical (weapons systems) innovations.[10] Starting from (what then were) recently developed systems they looked backward at intellectual and technical genealogies which, of course, spread out laterally as one went to earlier times. To keep size manageable they terminated their retrospective exploration at a time horizon of about 20 years.

Conclusions of HINDSIGHT were not flattering to *recent* "basic" research. Those who carried out the study were quick to point out that this could be accounted for by the relatively short time horizon used (i.e., by assuming that it generally takes 20 years or more for "basic research" results to find their way into application.) Later, the National Science Foundation commissioned its "TRACES" study which had a much longer time horizon than HINDSIGHT. TRACES, of course, easily identified many valuable practical consequences of basic research.[11]

Neither TRACES nor HINDSIGHT dealt with a representative sample, each having started from events deliberately selected for unusual qualities, and having searched for antecedents of a special kind. Both studies, therefore, provide evidence that must be regarded mainly as "anecdotal." But they did agree on two points that are of interest in our discussion here and that appear to possess some generality.

A little-remarked-upon conclusion of HINDSIGHT was that in every case studied, major systems innovation or improvement became possible as a result of *confluence or simultaneous availability* of a number of contributory innovations or discoveries.

To a physical chemist this might suggest that the rate of innovation can exhibit *higher order kinetics* in the ambient overall level of scientific and technical activity. And in consequence society might reap both benefits and complexities in *more-than-linear* proportion to the enormous expansion of R&D activity. That is surely provocative.

And it leads to a second speculation. Both the architects and the critics of HINDSIGHT and TRACES agreed that, on average, considerable time (more, certainly, than 10 years) elapses before products of basic research become strong contributors to the stream of innovation. Thus the *present* rate of innovation which many people find portentous (and some find frightening) in some way reflects—or at least is adequately supported by—levels of basic research activity that existed 20 to 30 years ago. As we have seen, those levels were lower, perhaps by a factor of ten, than present ones. What might that imply for the future—especially if, as suggested above, the returns turn out to be more-than-linearly related to overall activity level? One must suppose that some kind of saturation effect prevents technological innovation from getting explosively out of hand. And indeed, both HINDSIGHT and TRACES reported that much more "*recent*" activity of an applied and developmental nature plays the dominant role in innovation.

4.2. Consequences of Changed Expectations

Widespread diffusion of federal research support and general *dependence* upon it, taken together with definitely improved social status, adds up to a fairly profound alteration in the relationship of scientists to society. A long time may be required for the effects of the change to become fully apparent. Little conscious thought seems to have been devoted to it. The traditional "socialization" of scientists has been rather special—as one is apt to remember when trying to reassure a congressman about the integrity of the peer review system. Being conveyed in large part through a close personal association of professors and students, this socialization may exhibit considerable inertia. But it does not remain completely unaltered in the face of such major changes of social climate.

Some appreciation of the possibilities may be gained by looking at this matter from the standpoint of government science agency officials:

When they are awarding frugal grants, in a spirit of special enablement, to a small number of elite scientists, they can and must invoke "criteria" and exercise (scientific) *taste*—if not autocratically, at least without apology. This was even more true, of course, for the private foundations before WWII. Those foundations' extraordinary record speaks well for this mode of operation, and for the quality of their officials.

Today's government officials, on the other hand, find themselves distributing public funds to a majority of the nation's active researchers, and each one's professional survival depends upon receiving such support. The agency officials come face to face with all sorts of questions of coverage, "due process," accountability, "fairness," etc. Eventually some fraction of their scientist clients get to viewing research grants as an "*entitlement program.*" And that profoundly changes the nature of the ball game.

As a result of such pressures, the National Science Foundation found it necessary in 1976 to set up a formal mechanism for "reconsideration" of declined research proposals and—in exceptional cases—for a second "reconsideration." Extremely few of the many scores of petitions submitted under these procedures have succeeded in overthrowing the original decisions. But the policy, together with the social pressures that necessitated its establishment, have required that every step in the review process be formally documented in minute detail and has "opened" that process far more than, in the writer's opinion, is consistent with maximum creativity.

Specifically, the new taste for documentation and accountability, combined with concern over "fairness," greatly reinforces whatever tendencies to *conformity and conservatism* are naturally present in the scientific community. The way for everyone concerned to avoid embarrassing challenges, criticism, or censure is for science agencies to seek the advice of comfortably established authorities and for these in turn to articulate conventional points of view.

A standard fallacy appears to me to be reflected in these recent developments. Essentially, they amount to attempts to "perfect" the allocation decisions of particular individuals or agencies through a system of vigorous monitoring and coercion. The more promising approach, and the one fortuitously realized in the U.S. for two decades following the war, is to rely upon diversity of sources and *competition* between them.

4.3. The Individual's Prospect

On the whole, a young American entering science before the war could look forward to a *very* quiet and relatively ill paid career. (To judge from what is set forth in an appendix to J.D. Bernal's "Social Function of Science" the same must have been true also for a young Briton.) Those who chose science generally did so for idealistic reasons, and because they enjoyed research. Now, on the other hand, one can regard a career in scientific research—like one in law, architecture, or medicine—as a comfortable, economically rewarding, and possibly glamorous proposition. At least a full generation of young scientists have entered the field with that prospect before them. Many are impressively bright and competent, and I think most of them enjoy their research. Still, the system holds out before them a different set of incentives; their expectations and their manner of participating in the scientific enterprise are sure to be different.

5. A VON HUMBOLDT PROGRAME?

It turns out that tendencies accentuated in American universities by large-scale federal research support over the past 30 years find parallels or origins in the transformation of Prussian universities of the 19th century.[12] Wilhelm von Humboldt (1767-1835) who was one of the intellectual leaders of this transformation insisted that universities must be something more than training schools for future teachers and bureaucrats; they should produce highly cultivated and truly exemplary individuals of good character (Geist; Bildung). He insisted that universities must carry on original research and explained that they:

> ...can achieve their purpose only if each confronts, insofar as possible, the pure idea of learning..." and that they must "...treat learning as a problem ever unsolved, and that they therefore are continually carrying on research.[13]

As chief of Prussia's Department of Educational Affairs, Humboldt initiated policies that resulted in really effective government control of academic appointments, and purposeful use of this control to make appointments and promotions reflect *research* achievement, even if at the expense of satisfactory lecturing. This policy in Prussia seems to have marked the inception of the "publish or perish" tradition, now fairly universal in the academic world. It is reported that this ("Vormarz") period:

> ...witnessed a gradual upswing in professional mobility and the rise of fervent struggles between universities to woo and win famous professors...(and)...the expansion of activities and institutions devoted to research into all academic fields.[14]

We noted in an earlier section that U.S. universities before WWII were of diverse types (as, indeed they still are). The most elite group reflected the German/von Humboldt model; they laid great stress on pure learning, cultural development (Geist und Bildung), original research, and research publication. Others hewed more closely to the explicitly utilitarian purposes specified in the Morrill Act which had established the land grant mechanism for colleges and universities. They were, of course, carrying on engineering, agricultural, and other research as had been contemplated by Morrill. (Morrill himself appears to have been aware more of the Agricultural Experiment Station movement in Saxony than of developments in German universities.) Finally, there was a great multitude of colleges and universities that were the scene of very little research if any.

Von Humboldt lived at a time, and occupied a position, such that he and a few others of like mind could remake the Prussian universities simply by autocratic exercise of the power of faculty appointment. In this way the postwar German universities were launched on the tradition of professorial research and "publish or perish." That tradition was long since well established in the best U.S. universities—both private and public—before WWII.

Post WWII U.S. policy might be said to have accomplished, as an inadvertent concomitant of the project research grant mechanism, a vast extension, in our country, of what von Humboldt initiated a century and a half earlier in Prussia. (Modification of the university system, one must emphasize, was not the original purpose, and very few, if any, of the people involved knew anything about von Humboldt.) Three decades of federal research support have served to so propagate and intensify that new-old tradition as to justify the metaphor:

> We have installed 20 universities in the top 10, 50 in the top 20, and 100 in the top 50.

Geist and Bildung, regrettably, seem not to have flourished in equal measure with research and publication. They have been victims, one may hope, more of the times and of popular "anti-elitist" rhetoric than of the research ethos.

5.1. Rationalizing Expectations—An Idealistic External Criterion

It may be allowed as appropriate to conclude with a few words on behalf of an especially interesting and important facet of "social merit."

Most of us take pride in the fact that science has been a major agent of cultural enlightenment—"the greatest of the humanities" according to Sir Watson Watt. For many, perhaps, that is what science is really all about and is what drew us into the profession.

Fritz Zwicky said: "The most important social contribution of science has been *to dispel the aberrations of the human mind.*" His phrase signifies something stronger than remediation of ignorance; it means substituting trustworthy knowledge for superstition and dogma. "It's not the ignorance that hurts so much as knowing all those things that aren't so!" said one 19th century American humorist, and a scattering of thinkers has always recognized this over at least the last 20 centuries.

In fact, a substantially equivalent view was advocated by Epicurus longer ago than that. As is well known, Epicurus was much interested in the question of *happiness.* He remarked that a principal cause of people's *un*happiness lay in what behavioral scientists today would call "dissonance of expectations and reality," or something equivalent. So Epicurus, who might otherwise not have been much concerned about science, advocated that people study nature so as to obtain a grip upon reality that could free them of superstition and spare them the sorrow of unnecessary disappointments:

> Epicurus' main concern was to teach an attitude toward life that would lead to personal happiness. ...Unsatisfied desires are painful, so the wise man learns to limit his desires to things that can easily be obtained... . Peace of mind, he thought, was threatened by ignorance about the natural world... 'If we were not troubled by doubts about the heavens, and about the possible meaning of death, and by *failure to understand the limits of pain and desire*, then we should have no need of natural philosophy'...[15]

Epicurus thus thought of the study of science as a means to *rationalize expectations*—an idea of eternal validity, more timely now than when he articulated it.

We can carry his wisdom over to the realm of "scientific choice," and when we are ranking fields of science as to their "social merit," remember to ask ourselves:

> Where, today, are the most pernicious "aberrations of the human mind?"

or

> Which of the current crop of popular expectations are based upon assumptions that we don't know to be true—or worse, that we suspect may be not true? i.e., which widely held expectations are likely to be *contradictory to nature?*

The answers, no doubt, will lead up repeatedly in the direction of the behavioral sciences. They involve riddles about the plasticity, and the limits, of behavior in areas such as aggressiveness, altruism, happiness, social cooperation, various forms of social deviance—and *both* the proximate *and* the long term evolutionary antecedents of these phenomena.[16]

The behavioral sciences have not, hitherto, matched the physical and biological sciences in speed of progress or reliability of results. But perhaps the time is not far off when that situation can begin to change for the better. Standards of criticism appear to be improving—as some of the work reported to this Committee illustrates. And if we see evolving a chemically-interpretable biology (as clearly is the case, though the feasibility of that would have been denied vehemently not long ago) why may we not look forward to the emergence of biologically-interpretable behavioral science?

NOTES

[1] Professor H. Wold has pointed out the relevance of our discussion of the ideas of W. von Humboldt who instigated major changes in the Prussian university system and strongly influenced the German conception of university.

[2] United States Congress; an Act Donating public lands to the several States and Territories which may provide colleges for the benefit of agriculture and the mechanic arts; Approved July 2, 1862.

[3] David J. Furley, "Epicurus" in *Dictionary of Scientific Biography* (Chas. Scribners Sons, 1971), 4:381.

[4] Vannevar Bush, *Science—the Endless Frontier: A Report to the President* (Washington, D.C., 1945), 33.

[5] Don K. Price, *The Scientific Estate* (Harvard Univ. Press, 1967), 181.

[6] Ibid. 61–62. Price discussed the significance of using scientists in the federal administrative apparatus and pointed out that it differed from the practice (of that time) in Great Britain.

[7] Bush, 33.

[8] Alvin M. Weinberg, "Criteria for Scientific Choice, I and II," *Minerva* 1:2 (Winter 1963) and 3:1 (Autumn 1964).

[9] Josephine Tey, *The Daughter of Time*. A "rehabilitation" of Richard III of England in the guise of a novel, it affords sharp commentary on the frailties of the historical record.

[10] Chalmers W. Sherwin and Raymond S. Isenson, "Project Hindsight," *Science* 156 (June 23, 1967), 1571–1577.

[11] *Technology in Retrospect—Critical Events in Science*, Illinois Inst. of Technology Report (1969). A more ambitious successor study is reported in *Science, Technology and Innovation* (Battelle, Columbus, Ohio, 1973).

[12] See note 1.

[13] R. Steven Turner, "The Growth of Professorial Research in Prussia, 1818 to 1848—Causes and Context," *Historical Studies in the Physical Sciences* 3 (1971), 151.

[14] Ibid, 145.

[15] Furley, 381.

[16] See, for example, Donald T. Campbell, On the Conflicts between Biological and Social Evolution and between Psychology and Moral Tradition, *American Psychologist* 30 (1975), 1103–1126.

19

Comment on Gruner's Paper

WERNER MEISSNER

The President's seal of one of the finest academic institutions in this country bears the motto: "Die Luft der Freiheit weht." Stanford has taken these words from Ulrich von Hutten, sixteenth century German poet and fighter for freedom. Two hundred years later it was the idea of "akademische Freiheit" (academic freedom) which for Wilhelm von Humboldt formed the basis for the foundation of the University of Berlin (1809) and for the reform of the German university system: The unity of research, teaching of learning, knowledge for purposes of technical and social evolution. Today universities almost everywhere hold to the view that teaching and research belong inseparably together. This view is in danger, however.

CHANGING ENROLLMENTS IN THE 1960S AND 1970S: PROBLEMS AND ANSWERS

During the 1960s and early 1970s there was a big expansion in higher education in most countries. All through, between 1960 and 1975, total enrollment in higher education was up by about 2.5 to 3.5 times in individual countries. Governments took steps to deal with this increase in demand for higher education by opening up new universities, and by reorganizing and expanding existing ones. Since the mid-1970s this expansion policy in the higher education sector has ended. In some countries this is due to a change in the demographic situation. In all countries a period of stagflation has created the need to curb public spending for higher education. University research was influenced by both measures: expansion and consolidation/contraction.

Because the major expenditures of universities are associated with salaries, student numbers are a principal determinant of the financing of universities. Income based on, or derived from, student enrollments is an important element in the finance of universities. The 1960s and early 1970s were a period of expansion not only in student numbers but in financial resources also. It was this expansion which started a process that sometimes led to the operational and institutional separation of teaching and research in universities.

Sweden is a case in point. The university budget was divided into two parts: one for undergraduate education, the other for postgraduate education and research. The rationale was to break the direct influence of varying student enrollments on university research, and give research a stable and independent existence. At the same time, however, there was the creation of two career paths within the university: one for teaching, one for research. The "university lecturer," a new level in the career, is a full-time, tenured undergraduate teacher. He was expected to follow developments in the field but was not required to carry out research himself. This innovation has been criticized by outstanding Swedish scientists from the beginning and, as a result, Sweden is now trying to restore a close connection between teaching and research.

The stagnation period had its problems, too. In the late 1970s there was a concern in a number of countries that the governments' policy of reorienting funds towards "relevant" and "applied" areas, and the end of the university boom, were joint factors leading to a decline in the propensity of funding basic research at the universities. A recent OECD report (1984) found that by the late 1970s the percentage of Gross Domestic Expenditure on Research and Development in the higher education sector was declining in most member countries. In general, support for university research has shifted to research project grants with a lower share of research being financed via general university budgets. This is not without problems for university research.

FUNDING AND DIRECTION OF UNIVERSITY RESEARCH: AUTONOMY AND THE DEMAND FOR "RELEVANCE."

In a system of research involving a deliberately pluralistic organization, government-sponsored research systems may and must determine the content of activities only to a limited extent. In industry, research and development are foremost within the responsibilities of enterprises. As far as basic research is concerned—and the main performer of basic research remains the university—the selection of subject matters and methods of research is a function to be carried out independently by scientific institutions.

The autonomy in the selection of problems and methods is not unlimited. It has to be seen in relation to changing patterns of funding. University research is funded through a variety of sources: funds from the university budget, from research councils, from private foundations, from government ministries, and from private industry.

With a growing proportion of outside funding, universities are much more open to science policy priorities. To paraphrase: more open to external influence upon the kind of research performed.

Obviously, when funds are derived from mission-oriented government departments and agencies (e.g., defense or energy), considerations of relevance for some practical objective are a major criterion for assessment. But things have changed with research councils as well. During the days of plenty, a policy was adopted according to which government would support practically every research project submitted by qualified researchers on the recommendation of recognized scientists in the field (Ben-David, 1977). Now the criteria on which government funds are allocated by research councils have changed. In place of the traditional responsive mode of operation, research councils have become more interventionist (OECD, 1981).

Of course, universities should pay attention to the question of what contributions they make to social welfare. This contribution is not easy to define. It could be stated as follows:

1. extending and deepening the level of scientific knowledge;
2. maintaining and increasing the efficiency and competitiveness of the economy;
3. conserving the resources and preserving the natural requirements of life;
4. improving man's working conditions and the well-being of civilization;
5. recognizing the implications and correlations of technological developments, discussing and balancing their opportunities against risks, and substantiating decisions of the use of technologies.

Universities have always made contributions to these ends directly and indirectly, through the beneficial effects of the diffusion of scientific knowledge. It is another matter, however, if university research is oriented to specific research topics, identified as being of national economic or social importance. One has to strike a balance. I want to give an example of such an effort: the funding mode of the Deutsche Forschungsgemeinschaft (West-German Research Foundation).

The DFG is an autonomous body of the (West-)German scientific community that formulates its own statutes, and itself selects the scientific and academic members of its agencies. It has for years made use of three quite different modes of research funding. *First,* there is the *normal procedure,* a responsive mode of funding. Any fully qualified research scientist may apply through the normal procedure to obtain financial support for a research project. The initiative therefore rests with the researcher himself, and as a matter of principle the DFG does not influence the contents of the project put forward for support. The normal procedure provides an important method for supporting young scientists. It gives the DFG an opportunity to identify at an early stage that the first tentative steps in a new research direction are taking place. These can then be given special attention when arrangements are being made for support under the terms of other funding procedures.

Second, there are the *priority programs* (*Schwerpunktprogramme*). The promotion of priority programs is a particularly important instrument of research policy. Research workers from a number of universities combine their efforts for a limited period of time in a focal-point program concentrating on an agreed aspect while working in their own research establishments. The theme of a priority program is—in contrast to normal procedure projects—established in advance. Through such support the DFG Senate seeks to further a particular line of research (directed support). The reasons for supporting priority programs vary. The first programs were introduced in 1972 chiefly for the training of the younger generation, and as a determined effort to catch up with developments in, for instance, geochemistry or crystal-structure research. Since then, support for priority programs has gained greater prominence, with the German Federal Government resuming participation in major joint international undertakings. Meanwhile, too, the priority programs support for particular subject matters is now principally used as an instrument for initiating work in unexplored scientific fields.

Third, there are the *Special Collaborative Programes* (*Sonderforschungsbereiche*). Here groups of scientists join together with the approval of their university for joint research, in which the university recognizes that their research has common ground, deserving support for a longer period of time. The university, rather than individual researchers, applies, and it must demonstrate its own financial commitment to the field in which it is applying.

It should be stressed that the DFG has not sought to develop these more interventionist modes of research support at the expense of the traditional response mode. The share of the normal funding procedure has remained more or less constant (about 40 percent) throughout the years. It is the policy to preserve this proportion. The normal funding mechanism is seen by the DFG as having the crucial advantage of flexibility, of permitting rapid response to a new research opportunity.

WHAT REMAINS OF THE HUMBOLDTIAN UNIVERSITY IDEAL TODAY?

The success of German research in the 19th century was attributed to the German university: to its principle of unity of research and teaching, but also to its self-government; Bernal, 1939 (Ben-David, 1977). Until the 1880s German universities were virtually the only institutions in the world in which a student could obtain training in how to do scientific or scholarly research. The impact of this system on the organization of universities in other countries was strong (less so in France, but very much so in the Northern countries since 1850). Such was the dominance of the German universities in the 19th century that it would have been difficult to imagine any country neglecting this model.

And today? Gruner's remark that large-scale federal research support over the past 30 years in the U.S. finds parallels or origins in the Humboldt model is important. Though important it is only one aspect. More can be said:

1. The most visible function of the university will be an educational one. It can be argued that it is more important today than ever before to learn how to learn. How could this be achieved better than by participating in research?

2. The Humboldtian concept of teaching and research for the purposes of technical and social evolution can still give guidance for the kind of research which should be carried out. It seems that industry has become increasingly unwilling to invest in research and development directed towards the development of fundamentally new technologies (cf. development in biotechnology). Radical innovations, however, are needed if low productivity growth, unemployment and inflation are to be tackled successfully. There should be substantial investment in strategic research so that the universities can make a significant contribution to the economy. This implies that universities should be part of a broadly determined national science policy. It will not suffice either to allow universities to

devote all their resources to research of purely scientific interest, or to drive them too far toward the performance of research of immediate industrial, i.e., technical, interest (cf. Meissner and Zinn, 1984).

3. The purpose of social evolution: research commissioned in furtherance of social policy has too often been constrained by a preoccupation with the quantification of well-recognized problems (OECD, 1978). But in this field, too, there should be strategic research. Social science research in the universities is increasingly squeezed between a growing dependence upon government funding for projects of immediate relevance, and a traditional disciplinary commitment to pure theory. Research involving several disciplines, however, is essential. Problems of the environment, of occupational health, etc., do not correspond to the approach of a single discipline. This opens up important possibilities for new methods and principles of model building which allow for the integration of different disciplines. The method which is so prominent in the present volume is an excellent example!

4. The principle of unity of teaching and research does not mean that today all university teachers have to be continuously engaged in research. The growing student population of the 1960s and early 1970s has fostered a tendency for teaching and research to grow apart. This should not lead to the conclusion that higher education can largely be provided by individuals who have no involvement in research. If the principle of unity of teaching and research cannot be realized in every single teacher, it is all the more important that the university should be a place where this principle is recognized and valid.

The purpose of technical and social evolution means that a balance between support for independent research of purely scientific interest and support for strategic research is needed. To paraphrase: a delicate balance between responsive and interventionist modes of funding university research is necessary. In this sense the Humboldtian ideal is still alive today, and its relevance for today's universities is obvious.

REFERENCES

Ben-David, J. 1977. *Centers for learning. Britain, France, Germany, United States.* New York: McGraw-Hill.

Bernal, J.D. 1939. *The social function of science.* London: Routledge.

Deutsche Forschungsgemeinschaft. 1984. Organization and functions. Bonn: DFG.

Federal Minister for Research and Technology. Sixth report of the Federal
    Government on research. Bonn: Bundesministerium für Forschung und
    Technologie.

Meissner, W. and K.G. Zinn. 1984. *Der neue Wohlstand. Qualitatives Wachstum und
    Vollbeschäftigung.* München: Bertelsmann.

OECD. 1984. Science and technology indicators, resources devoted to R&D. Paris:
    OECD.

OECD. 1981. The future of university research. Paris: OECD.

OECD. 1978. Social science and policy making. Paris: OECD.

20

Response to Werner Meissner

WAYNE R. GRUNER

Professor Wold has remarked that worldwide comparison of "conditions in universities" is a topic worthy of serious study. Professor Meissner's comments on a "Strategy for Science" serve nicely to illustrate and emphasize that view. The concerns and general principles Meissner has set forth are:

- that research and teaching should be intimately associated,
- that both the autonomy of basic research and the more utilitarian concerns of society ("relevance") must be respected and the two carefully balanced,
- that necessary to this end is some diversity both of institutional structures and of modes of financing.

These principles are internationally recognized (except, possibly, in the "socialist" countries) and more or less beyond controversy.

Specific manifestation of the problems and implementation of the principles varies from place to place and from time to time, and their comparison should generate lively interest.

Most nations experienced a "baby boom" at some point in the decade following WWII. But there were slight differences of *timing*. (In the U.S. there was a subsequent decline in the birth rate amounting, almost, to a "baby trough".) Over the following 25 years most nations also

experienced a great rise in the popular desire for university-level education. Here, too, there were probably differences in timing. The *relative*
timing of the two trends is very important for the economic demography
of higher education in any one nation.

In the U.S., moreover, these trends were *confluent* with the flourish-
ing of strong rhetoric for "upward mobility" and intense pressure for
greater participation of females and "minorities" in the upper echelons of
the work force. This writer is unable to comment about the presence or
absence of these latter factors in other nations.

Education can be regarded both as a "factor of production" (investment in "human capital") and as a "consumer good." Post-war developments in the U.S. have tended to increase popular and student emphasis
upon the first of these two interpretations. That is probably true in other
nations as well. Insofar as the character and outlook of its students determines the character of the university, those of us who care deeply about
universities should study this phenomenon thoughtfully.

That the growth of education and the growth of research can get
out of step and that this can generate centrifugal forces tending to
divorce the two has been demonstrated in several nations. But judging
from Meissner's comment, the details differ significantly between the U.S.
and some countries of Europe.

In the U.S. the number of PhDs increased very rapidly over the two
decades before 1970. There was also a great increase in (government
funded) research opportunities at the universities. Throughout the
forced draft expansion of our universities, the principle was consistently
maintained that tenured faculty should be qualified to do research and
should actually do it. Still, the supply of young PhDs outgrew the available
teaching positions in good universities. One effect was a significant
upgrading of the faculties at 2nd and 3rd rank universities. Another was
the emergence of proposals to set up "universities" that would confine
their activity to research and graduate education; this scheme proved to
be not viable politically.

The author feels it is his duty to caution gently concerning
Meissner's remark that "Obviously, when funds are derived from mission-
oriented government departments and agencies (e.g., defense or energy)
considerations of relevance for some practical objective are a major criterion of assessment." The statement is plausible and may well be true in
most national contexts. It is a fact, however, that from the war's end to
about 1970 three different agencies of the U.S. Defense Department, as
well as the Atomic Energy Commission, supported substantial programs
of basic university research with *essentially no insistence upon "relevance" cri-*

teria. Very likely this could happen only in the U.S. where we have what one political scientist has characterized as "a government of mixed and muddled powers." In any case we know it is possible because it happened.

One final point seems worthy of the greatest emphasis: Research and education are *not* "different" activities that we associate or link together for reasons of philosophical conviction or aesthetic preference. Research *is* education! It is the self-education of those members of society who manifest the greatest disposition to learn.

21

Discussion of Gruner's and Meissner's Paper

ENDERS A. ROBINSON

Strategy for science in the modern university is a large and important topic, and the expositions by Dr. Gruner and Professor Meissner give excellent treatments of this subject area. In these comments we want to enlarge upon the following two aspects of the development;

(1) the government and university as compared to industrial firms as sponsors of scientific projects and as sources of research directions.

(2) the great expansion of universities following 1945 to the present time.

In regard to point (1), private firms are usually directly involved in technology and industrial development rather than pure science. In this role they identify and subsidize promising technologies that have immediate commercial applications. Government agencies are attracted by the successes of these firms in creating jobs, boosting productivity, and increasing exports. As a result, government is willing to provide funds to universities to promote science and technology. In its enthusiasm to help scientific development, however, government sometimes gets directly involved in specific research directions. Such attempts by government to specify and promote specialized scientific endeavors are generally doomed to failure. Bureaucrats are not the right people to distinguish between scientific opportunities and dead ends. Even the foremost universities expect only one or two real successes out of every ten research projects.

Instead of targeting specific technologies or narrow scientific objectives, the proper role of government is to target the process by which new developments are made, that is, the process of innovation. In other words, government should focus on creating an environment in which new ideas and scientific innovation are likely to thrive. Ensuring that such an environment exists is the best way for government to help the development of new scientific results.

An innovative scientific environment should include a strong commitment to basic research in order to improve understanding of the fundamental processes that will form the bases of future industries and projects. Basic research is essential to build the foundation for future scientific enterprises and new technological products. However, because basic research is long-term, expensive, and unlikely to lead immediately to useful products, individual companies as well as universities cannot afford it, except in special cases. The government must therefore increase, not decrease, the funding of basic research in universities. However, product development and other applications based on this research should be privately, not publicly supported.

Another necessary factor for an innovative scientific environment is a strong educational capability, particularly in the sciences, to assure an ample quantity of scientific and technical personnel, as well as technically literate citizens. At present, the future demand for scientists and engineers is predicted to far outstrip the supply. The cost of educating technical people is very high. Universities struggle to attract enough qualified professors because industrial salaries are so attractive. As a result, the government should help universities to raise their pay scales and to modernize and improve their teaching and laboratory facilities.

With regard to point (2), the great expansion of universities during the past forty years calls for wholesale rethinking concerning the entire curriculum of subjects being taught. Part of the problem has arisen with the "information explosion." As more and more areas of study are uncovered, more courses, departments, and major study areas are established to deal with ever more specialized issues. There are now about 1100 different major programs available to students at American universities, whereas previously there were only about 200. Part of the problem also arises from the redefinition of education in recent decades—from an exercise for the elite to a necessity for the many. No longer havens for the pursuit of liberal education, universities have become training grounds for specialized skills. Of those 1100 major programs, about one-half are in occupational fields.

In order to promote a climate for an innovative environment within universities, the teaching of a body of common knowledge is called for. In order that innovation be fostered, and not suppressed, there must be a turning away from strictly occupational training to the teaching of a core of ideas, experiences, and stances, which all students ought to understand whatever their goal. At present education is too fragmented and too diffuse, and the students are given too little guidance before their specialization into occupational areas. The solution is to cut out the peripheral and to get down to what really matters, especially in scientific and technical education. In order for students to participate in an innovational environment, they need, above all, the capacity to distinguish the important from the merely interesting. In the face of the "information explosion," they need to know how to get to the point, and to resist distractions. In their own ways, universities have been more a part of the problem than a part of the solution, as universities have produced an ever-expanding number of study areas and the faculty sets the students loose to choose among them with little guidance. Although the intention is to be expansive, most of this is simply distracting.

Needed now are colleges and universities willing to teach a few things extremely well and to give the clarity of focus and the inspired simplification that is essential for new scientific innovation. In this way a student can obtain an awareness of technical distinctions and a familiarity with promising scientific approaches necessary for good research. It is time now to correct the present situation in which a university education is made up of the acquisition of specialized knowledge in fragmented and diffuse occupation fields.

Successful research and development efforts do not just happen. They are brought about in an innovative environment and by the effective management of programs tailored to a university's strong points. What works for one university is not necessarily useful for another. However, there appear to be certain general principles that can assist in finding research programs most appropriate to a particular university.

The first principle is to build on strength. A university improves its chances for success by formulating its program to emphasize areas in which it already has a competitive advantage. A university close to the ocean could develop oceanography, whereas one in the continental interior might specialize in geology. If a university is located in an area where certain types of industry prevail, then it should develop an expertise in these areas. For example, many of the great statistical centers were developed at universities in England and Sweden where the insurance industry is particularly strong.

The second principle is to focus. There are many forces that tend to diffuse and misdirect resources: the desire to address a broad range of problems, the diverse interests of the staffs, and the pet project of a senior professor, to name a few. In some departments there are more research projects than researchers. But experience has shown that the best results are achieved when the elements of the research program are carefully chosen and well coordinated, and here the research professors must carefully balance resources with aspirations. Sometimes an aspiration level that is too high results in no results at all. It is important to realize that such a focus does not have to come at the expense of the variety and creativity which are required for innovation. Instead, the proper focus means that the limited resources can be more effectively used.

The last principle is to "stick with the game plan." The entry of a new scientific fad should not mean that all resources should now be turned toward it and away from existing programs. Also, a project should not be abandoned because of a few initial failures. A research project may be on the right track even if major breakthroughs are not occurring every month. Good results are usually obtained by those who persist and do not give up easily.

It is a prevalent notion that if enough money is invested in research, it will magically produce winning results. However, the real problem is one of the allocation of resources. It may mean cutting back research in traditional areas and gambling on untried fields. An innovative and creative environment with freedom to try new ideas is more important than just money for the success of a research program.

There are many reasons why the whole structure of university education and research needs to be examined in view of the challenges that face society as we approach the end of the twentieth century. One could cite, for example, the alleged obsession with short-term goals, or, closely related, the lack of vision regarding the long term potential of science. One reason often cited is scientific illiteracy. Chastising administrators and managers for frequent lack of scientific sophistication is a universal pastime.

Scientists and engineers do research and development. They conduct experiments, design models, build prototypes, and devise processes. They constitute the foundations of all scientific enterprises both in universities and in industry. It must be realized that the individual scientist, wherever he is found employed, is basically the same person. This fact can be verified at a scientific meeting where all the scientists present form an integrated group, regardless of their individual employment histories. But these scientists often become overspecialized; with the exception of a small minority, they are uninterested in technical work beyond their own immediate fields. They tend to take little notice of contributions by other professionals, and do not want to venture far from their own speciality.

A good example of this specialized behavior can be found in the field of statistics. Most theoretical statisticians have received in their education a solid knowledge of the theory of maximum likelihood methods, and this training has served them well in their professional careers. However, as the work of Professor Wold demonstrates, there are many areas of application where a break with the maximum likelihood mainstream is called for. Even though the FP (Fix-Point) and PLS (Partial Least Squares) methods are clearly superior in such cases, the professional statisticians hesitate to take up these new approaches. This attitude is understandable since the FP and PLS methods are of recent date. This is in particular so as regards model evaluation—as reviewed by Dr. Lohmöller in this volume. FP and PLS modeling use Tukey's jackknife (1958) and Stone-Geisser's crossvalidation test for predictive relevance, evaluation methods which recently were shown to be distribution- and independence-free.

This insularity begins with the training that scientists receive. If one examines the curricula of science and engineering departments, one sees them dominated by specialized titles. This is all to the good. But where does one find scientists learning about broader issues? Scientists must also be inculcated with courses that teach ethical standards and ultimate values. Now universities turn out highly specialized technologists who delight in burrowing deep into their limited areas. They are content to leave to others the task of connecting the burrows into organized networks. Well-defined technical problems, such as the application of maximum likelihood, are easier to address than to try a different approach. Established methods require little compromise and little ability to deal with conflicting priorities and constraints. In contrast, the development of new methodology means tackling problems that can often barely be defined, much less easily solved.

The real world often has little use for elegant solutions to restricted problems. Yet the technical journals are crowded with such contributions. University scientists operate under the dictum of "publish or perish." The result is a flood of papers without applications, and which are so theoretical and involve so much arcane mathematics that they cannot be read by the very people who desire to use the results. Because the sheer number of papers published seems to be the desired criteria, and because there is little effective follow-up on the usefulness of published papers, the result is a proliferation of journals and handbooks that virtually no one reads. It is fair to say that the philosophy of "publish or perish" has reached its limit, and a more effective way of communicating research results is required. Research journals now serve more as depositories of fragmented results, than as an effective medium to organize and communicate new research.

The overemphasis on specialization is becoming obsolete. The advantages of robust and versatile educational systems that can meet unanticipated demands are rapidly becoming more apparent. The key to successful research is flexibility. The rapid expansion of the university system in the past years has made it difficult for universities to develop a broad and integrated outlook, but now is the time to establish centers which develop quality and perspective. University training must recognize that many incentives come from applications, and that the resources of science should come not just from the government sector but from education and industry as well. Universities have various ways of supporting research projects, and these should all be used whenever possible. Cooperative research centers offer exciting prospects for stimulating innovation. These centers are located at universities and are jointly funded by government and industry, under the criteria that the research must be good and that there must be a demand for it.

The present is a time of rapid change. It is also a time of opportunity, for it is now possible to create the better educational and research facilities that are necessary in order to meet the challenges mankind faces as the new century approaches.

REFERENCES

Geisser, S. 1974. *Journal of the Royal Statistical Society* B 36:141f, contribution to M. Stone 1974.

Stone, M. 1974. *Journal of the Royal Statistical Society* B 36:111–147, with written discussion.

Tukey, J. 1958. Abstract. *Annuals of Mathematical Statistics* 29:614.

Wold, H. 1985. Partial least squares. In *Encyclopedia of statistical sciences,* vol. 6, eds. S. Kotz and N.L. Johnson, 581–591. New York: Wiley.

Wold, H. 1983. Fix-Point Method. In *Encyclopedia of statistical sciences,* vol. 3, 148–149. New York: Wiley.

22

Comment on Robinson's Paper

WAYNE R. GRUNER

Professor Robinson asserts a need to reverse some tendencies visible in contemporary science and higher education. A number of his concerns, quite certainly, are shared by most of those who care deeply about education and about science. The problems he mentions include:

- fractionation and overspecialization of curricula,
- (possibly concomitant) failure to convey to students some appreciation of inter-relationships within knowledge or within culture (*unity of science!*),
- failure to inculcate in students some modicum of *scientific taste,*
- a great exfoliation of highly specialized papers which command little readership—and which reflect no regard whatever for *applications,*
- a tendency toward publication for its own sake, in reflection of the "publish or perish" dogma.

These problems are real enough and find their genesis, I believe, mainly in two historical developments:

- industrialization of research,
- democratization of higher education.

The first seems quite beyond human control; the second grows automatically from prevailing social philosophies.

The phrase "industrialization of research" is not used here to remark that science has become an important factor of production or that it has found favor with big business. Rather, it signifies that research is now a *user* of high technology and industrial-style logistics. Much scientific research now is capital intensive, highly organized, and conducted on a large scale in which quantity of results and *speed of their production* assume considerable importance. I don't think this can be avoided; it seems, rather, a fact of nature to which we shall have to adjust.

One aspect of the adjustment might be to recognize that the external garb of "good scientific taste" may assume unfamiliar forms. More important, there will be some *additional actors* expressing scientific taste. When you want to build a cyclotron, or an oceanographic ship, or to pre-empt use of a CRAY class computer, you need to recruit the acquiescence and support of many other people. Certain of them will have to be convinced on *aesthetic* grounds; their intellectual *taste* will be involved.

Quite inevitably, then, government *will* "get involved in specific research directions" and politicians, as well as bureaucrats, will play a role in "distinguishing between scientific opportunities and deadends." This must not be regarded as a defect in the system, nor should one seek an institutional "cure" for it.

We cannot but applaud the wisdom of Robinson's advice that government should "focus on creating an *environment* in which new ideas and scientific innovation are likely to thrive." My original paper was intended to indicate how—with very good luck—the U.S. science agencies in fact realized an approximation to that goal in the first three decades after WWII. One should emphasize again that this was an *unplanned* result of their diversity and of a (usually friendly) competition among them—factors which resulted in a market-like environment for research proposals.

It's extremely doubtful, in my view, that so felicitous a state of affairs could be created, or successfully imitated, by premeditation and "rational planning"—even if the planner were armed with Prof. Robinson's array of guiding principles. Those principles, one may note, are plagued by some mutual incompatibilities. Prof. Robinson, obviously, expects us to exercise good judgment in respect to the unavoidable trade-offs.

Problems linked to democratization of higher education require lengthier discussion than is appropriate here. Prof. Robinson has provided an elegant phrase: transformation "from an exercise for the elite to a necessity for the many." In this age of dramatic engineering achievement and massive social interventions we tend to be so preoccupied with how schools influence and transform the young that we overlook the decisive influence that students and their *attitudes* exert upon the schools. A strong case can be made that the single most important factor determining "quality" of a school is the kind of students it enrolls, and the most important thing about them, probably, is their attitude.

When university education is a *consumer good*, an aspect of personal adornment, and a path to *social* accreditation, one attitude will prevail. When it becomes a *factor of production*, an economic necessity for both student and society, and the sole path to *occupational* accreditation, a very different attitude will prevail. The difference is that between what is voluntary and what is compulsory, and we all know about that!

The changes in question influence everything from curricula to standards for graduation and the composition of the academic senate. We should eschew any fallacy that imagines government, universities, or faculty responsible for changes stemming from ideology and social philosophy—except insofar as they are themselves exponents of the philosophies in question. To expect that universities can enlighten reluctant students in the same manner as they do eager ones is unrealistically utopian.

Contributors

The ten first authors present my FP (Fix-Point) and PLS (Partial Least Squares) methods for systems analysis. Two authors give the theory, and seven authors give pioneering applications in different disciplines. It is rightly said there is a long distance, and, on the other hand, statistical method. FP and PLS are LS (Least Squares) approaches, which drastically reduce the distance, especially if we compare with ML (Maximum Likelihood) approaches. Well, the authors had heard my FP/PLS lectures, and then started using these methods. Hence the authors found me, and, in consequence, I found the authors.

The above-mentioned ten authors work at the research frontier, where novel knowledge is produced. The eleventh author sees the frontier at a distance, from the level of fund-disposing bureaucrats. The exposition shows a lacuna in the scientific library; there exists no universal overview of the widely varying conditions of the universities.

Herman Wold. Born 1908 at Skien, Norway. The family moved in 1912 to Sweden, and his education is entirely Swedish. Graduate studies in Stockholm at Stockholm University gave the Fil. Doctorate in 1938. Professor of Statistics at Uppsala University at 1942, at Göteborg University 1970, and Emeritus at Uppsala 1975. FP and PLS came at two levels. FP emerged 1958, an approach with manifest variables (LVs), but the approach was incomplete; the full treatment is joint work with Reinhold Bergström, 1983. The FP uses the classical standard error SE; in PLS the SE is often an underestimate, in an explicit case by 10.3%.

Jan-Bernd Lohmöller. Born 1943 near Oldenburg, Germany. Since 1970 assistant in Psychology in the Hochschule der Bundeswehr, Munich. In 1978 he produced the FP/PLS algorithm. In 1983 he received a Doctorate in Psychology. Since 1983 he has been consultant at the Free University, Berlin, the Center for Social Sciences, consulting in statistical applications in many branches, including psychology, educational science, and sociology.

Richard Noonan. Born 1942 in Bryan, Ohio. Ed.D. Columbia University, 1975; Ph.D. Stockholm University, 1976. Active in IEA cross-national educational survey research since 1969. Associate Professor of Education, Stockholm University. Consultant in educational measurement, survey research methodology.

Bernd Schips. Born 1939 in Stuttgart, Germany. Graduate student at Tübingen University; F.Dr. of Econometrics 1967 at Bochum University. Professor of Econometrics 1972 at Bochum University, and since 1974 at the Hochschule St. Gallen, Switzerland.

Camilo Dagum. Born 1925 in Salata, Argentina. Graduate studies at the National University of Cordoba; F.Dr. of Economic Sciences 1959. Teaching career 1949; Professor of mathematical statistics and mathematical economics 1956. C.D. left Argentina 1966; Visiting Senior research Economist 1966-68 at Princeton University, USA. 1968-70 Professor of Economics at the National University of Mexico; 1968-70 Professor at the University of Paris; 1970-72 Visiting Professor at the University of Iowa. Since 1972 Professor of Economics at the University of Ottawa, Canada.

Claes Fornell. Born 1947 in Stockholm, Sweden. Graduate studies at Berkeley, California 1972-74; Dr. of Economics at Lund University, Sweden 1976. Assistant Professor of Management Science at Duke University 1977. Associate Professor of Marketing at Northwestern University, Evanston, Chicago 1978, and since 1980 Professor of Marketing at the University of Michigan. Published "A Second Generation of Multivariate Analysis, I-II," 1982. New York: Praeger.

W. Juergen Falter. Born 1944 in Heppenheim, Germany. Graduate studies at Heidelberg 1963-64 and Berlin 1964-68; Dr. of Sociology 1973 at Saarbrüken, Germany. Professor of Sociology 1973-83 at Hochschule der Bundeswehr, Munich, since 1983 at The Free University, Berlin and now in Munich. In the correlation between the Nazi voters and the unemployed in the Weimar Republic 1930-33, first shown in a Swiss study on the 5 districts of Germany, a contrary result was shown by W.J.F. in 1980, using detailed scores of the voters in some 1500 voting districts.

John Horn. Born 1928 in St. Joseph, Missouri. Graduate studies in Melbourne, Australia; Dr. in Psychology at University of Illinois. Professor of Psychology 1961 at University of Denver and now in the Southern University of Los Angeles. Joint paper with Jarl Risberg, using a novel isotope measurement of blood flow in the brain.

Jarl Risberg. Born 1941 in Tidaholm, Sweden. Graduate studies for M.Dr. at Lund University 1973; since 1973 Docent in Neuropsychology at Lund University.

Fred L. Bookstein. Born 1947 in Detroit, Michigan. Graduate studies for Masters degree at Harvard; Ph.D. in Statistics at University of Michigan. Research scientist 1977 at the Center for Human Growth and Development, University of Michigan; Associate Professor 1982-84 in Radiology, since 1986 in Geology.

Jean-Luc Bertholet. Born 1954 in Geneva, Switzerland. Studies since 1974 in Econometrics and Statistics in the University of Geneva. Assistant since 1982 in the Departement de l'institut publique; 50% in sociological research service, 50% in statistical service.

Wayne R. Gruner. Born 1921 in Minneapolis, Minnesota. Studies at Minnesota and Berkeley, California, and Princeton. Writing on government supply of resources, and on the economic design of the learned profession. Consultant on physics and computers. Emphasis on the need for a universal overview of the widely varying conditions of universities.

* * *

The argument of theoretical empiricism is at two levels: statistical techniques, and the evolutions from logical empiricism to theoretical empiricism.

SOURCES

The primary sources of this volume were derived from papers presented in Committee II ("Theoretical Empiricism: A General Rationale for Scientific Model Building") at ICUS XIII ("Absolute Values and the New Cultural Revolution"). The symposium, one of seven sponsored by ICUS, of the International Cultural Foundation, Inc. was held at the J.W. Marriott Hotel in Washington D.C., September 2-5, 1984, and had as its organizing chairman, Herman Wold. The honorary chairman was Enders A. Robinson.

Index

Note: Italicized page numbers indicate illustrations